Lecture Notes in Artificial Intelligence   8113

Subseries of Lecture Notes in Computer Science

T0235636

Miloš Železný   Ivan Habernal
Andrey Ronzhin (Eds.)

Speech and Computer

15th International Conference, SPECOM 2013
September 1-5, 2013, Pilsen, Czech Republic
Proceedings

 Springer

Volume Editors

Miloš Železný
University of West Bohemia
Faculty of Applied Sciences
Department of Cybernetics
306 14 Plzeň, Czech Republic
E-mail: zelezny@kky.zcu.cz

Ivan Habernal
University of West Bohemia
Faculty of Applied Sciences
Department of Computer Science and Engineering
306 14 Plzeň, Czech Republic
E-mail: habernal@kiv.zcu.cz

Andrey Ronzhin
St. Petersburg Institute for Informatics
and Automation of the Russian Academy of Sciences
Speech and Multimodal Interfaces Laboratory
199178, St. Petersburg, Russia
E-mail: ronzhin@iias.spb.su

ISSN 0302-9743   e-ISSN 1611-3349
ISBN 978-3-319-01930-7   e-ISBN 978-3-319-01931-4
DOI 10.1007/978-3-319-01931-4
Springer Cham Heidelberg New York Dordrecht London

Library of Congress Control Number: 2013946024

CR Subject Classification (1998): I.2, I.4, H.3, I.5, H.4, F.1

LNCS Sublibrary: SL 7 – Artificial Intelligence

Typesetting: Camera-ready by author, data conversion by Scientific Publishing Services, Chennai, India

Printed on acid-free paper

Springer is part of Springer Science+Business Media (www.springer.com)

Preface

The Speech and Computer International Conference (SPECOM) is a regular event organized annually or bi-annually since the first SPECOM in 1996 that was held in St. Petersburg, Russian Federation. It is a conference with long tradition that attracts researchers in the area of computer speech processing (recognition, synthesis, understanding etc.) and related domains (including signal processing, language and text processing, multi-modal speech processing or human-computer interaction for instance). The SPECOM international conference is an ideal platform for know-how exchange especially for experts working on the Slavic and other highly inflectional languages and also know-how exchange between these, usually less-resourced languages and standard, well-resourced languages.

The SPECOM conference was organized alternately by the St. Petersburg Institute of Informatics and Automation of the Russian Academy of Sciences (SPIIRAS) and the Moscow State Linguistic University (MSLU) in their home cities. But there were cases when SPECOM was organized in different locations to stimulate the international nature of the conference. Thus, it was organized in 1997 by the Cluj-Napoca Subsidiary of Research Institute for Computer Technique (Romania), in 2005 by the University of Patras (Greece), and in 2011 by the Kazan (Privolzhsky) Federal University (Russian Federation, Republic of Tatarstan). This year (2013) the decision was made to move SPECOM close to the western border of the community of Slavic languages, the place where speech processing research has long tradition and good results, a bridge between two formerly separated political regions, and the place that can be seen as a bridge between different group of languages.

SPECOM 2013 was the 15th event in the series. It was our great pleasure to host the SPECOM 2013 conference in Plzeň (Pilsen), Czech Republic, organized this time by the University of West Bohemia (UWB), Faculty of Applied Sciences, Department of Cybernetics in cooperation with the St. Petersburg Institute of Informatics and Automation of the Russian Academy of Sciences (SPIIRAS). The conference was held in the Conference Center of the Angelo Hotel Pilsen (member of the Vienna International Hotel Chain) during September 1–5, 2013. Moreover, the SPECOM 2013 conference was organized in parallel with the TSD 2013 conference, an annual event traditionally organized (in odd years) by the Department of Computer Science of the same faculty. Organization of two separate conferences allowed the continuity of their traditions and their independence, while hosting them at the same venue and at the same time allowed participants to attend sessions of both conferences according to their interests. Experienced researchers and professionals in speech processing and related domains as well as newcomers found in the SPECOM 2013 conference a forum to communicate with people sharing similar interests.

Instead of competing between the two conferences for invited plenary talks, the decision was made to share them. Thus, the participants of both conferences could enjoy very interesting invited talks by Hynek Hermansky (Johns Hopkins University, Baltimore), Torbjörn Lager (University of Gothenburg, Sweden), Ron Cole (President of Boulder Language Technologies), Ralf Steinberger (Language Technology Project Manager at the European Commission's Joint Research Centre in Ispra), and Victor Zakharov (Saint-Petersburg State University) on the newest achievements in the relatively broad and still unexplored area of highly inflected languages and their processing. Invited papers are published in the TSD 2013 proceedings.

This volume contains a collection of submitted papers presented at the conference, which were thoroughly reviewed by members of the conference reviewing team consisting of around 60 top specialists in the conference topic areas. A total of 48 accepted papers out of 90 submitted, altogether contributed by 135 authors and co-authors, were selected by the Program Committee for presentation at the conference and for inclusion in this book. Theoretical and more general contributions were presented in common (plenary) sessions. Problem-oriented sessions as well as panel discussions then brought together specialists in limited problem areas with the aim of exchanging knowledge and skills resulting from research projects of all kinds.

Last but not least, we would like to express our gratitude to the authors for providing their papers on time, to the members of the conference reviewing team and Program Committee for their careful reviews and paper selection, and to the editors for their hard work preparing this volume. Special thanks are due to the members of the local Organizing Committee for their tireless effort and enthusiasm during the conference organization.

June 2013   Miloš Železný

Organization

SPECOM 2013 was organized by the Faculty of Applied Sciences, University of West Bohemia in Plzeň (Pilsen), Czech Republic, in cooperation with the St. Petersburg Institute of Informatics and Automation of the Russian Academy of Sciences (SPIIRAS), Russian Federation. The conference website is located at: http://specom.zcu.cz/.

Program Committee

Laurent Besacier, France
Denis Burnham, Australia
Jean Caelen, France
Vlado Delić, Serbia
Christoph Draxler, Germany
Thierry Dutoit, Belgium
Peter French, UK
Hiroya Fujisaki, Japan
Sadaoki Furui, Japan
Jean-Paul Haton, France
Rüdiger Hoffmann, Germany
Pavel Ircing, Czech Republic
Dimitri Kanevsky, USA
Alexey Karpov, Russian Federation
Walter Kellerman, Germany
Michael Khitrov, Russian Federation
Steven Krauwer, The Netherlands
Lin-shan Lee, Taiwan
Boris Lobanov, Belarus
Benoit Macq, Belgium

Heinrich Niemann, Germany
Dimitar Popov, Bulgaria
Rodmonga Potapova, Russian Federation
Josef Psutka, Czech Republic
Aleš Pražák, Czech Republic
Gerhard Rigoll, Germany
Andrey Ronzhin, Russian Federation
John Rubin, UK
Murat Saraclar, Turkey
Jesus Savage, Mexico
Tanja Schultz, Germany
Milan Sečujski, Serbia
Pavel Skrelin, Russian Federation
Yannis Stylianou, Greece
Luboš Šmídl, Czech Republic
Daniel Tihelka, Czech Republic
Jan Vaněk, Czech Republic
Christian Wellekens, France
Miloš Železný, Czech Republic

Local Organizing Committee

Miloš Železný *(Chair)*
Kamil Ekštein
Ivan Habernal
Alexey Karpov
Miloslav Konopík

Václav Matoušek
Roman Mouček
Irina Podnozova
Andrey Ronzhin

Acknowledgments

Special thanks to the reviewers who devoted their valuable time to review the papers and thus helped to keep the high quality of the conference review process.

Sponsoring Institutions

International Speech Communication Association, ISCA
Czech Society for Cybernetics and Informatics, CSKI

About Plzeň (Pilsen)

The new town of Pilsen was founded at the confluence of four rivers – Radbuza, Mže, Úhlava and Úslava – following a decree issued by the Czech king, Wenceslas II. He did so in 1295. From the very beginning, the town was a busy trade center located at the crossroads of two important trade routes. These linked the Czech lands with the German cities of Nuremberg and Regensburg.

In the fourteenth century, Pilsen was the third largest town after Prague and Kutna Hora. It comprised 290 houses on an area of 20 ha. Its population was 3,000 inhabitants. In the sixteenth century, after several fires that damaged the inner center of the town, Italian architects and builders contributed significantly to the changing character of the city. The most renowned among them was Giovanni de Statia. The Holy Roman Emperor, the Czech king Rudolf II, resided in Pilsen twice between 1599 and 1600. It was at the time of the Estates Revolt. He fell in love with the city and even bought two houses neighboring the town hall and had them reconstructed according to his taste.

Later, in 1618, Pilsen was besieged and captured by Count Mansfeld's army. Many Baroque-style buildings dating to the end of the seventeenth century were designed by Jakub Auguston. Sculptures were made by Kristian Widman. The historical heart of the city – almost identical to the original Gothic layout – was declared a protected historic city reserve in 1989.

Pilsen experienced a tremendous growth in the first half of the nineteenth century. The City Brewery was founded in 1842 and the Skoda Works in 1859. With a population of 175,038 inhabitants, Pilsen prides itself on being the seat of the University of West Bohemia and Bishopric.

The historical core of the city of Pilsen is limited by the line of the former town fortification walls. These gave way, in the middle of the nineteenth century, to a green belt of town parks. Entering the grounds of the historical center, you walk through streets that still respect the original Gothic urban layout, i.e., the unique developed chess ground plan.

You will certainly admire the architectonic dominant features of the city. These are mainly the Church of St. Bartholomew, the loftiness of which is accentuated by its slim church spire. The spire was reconstructed into its modern shape after a fire in 1835, when it was hit by a lightning bolt during a night storm.

The placement of the church within the grounds of the city square was also rather unique for its time. The church stands to the right of the city hall. The latter is a Renaissance building decorated with graffiti in 1908–1912. You will certainly also notice the Baroque spire of the Franciscan monastery.

All architecture lovers can also find more hidden jewels, objects appreciated for their artistic and historic value. These are burgher houses built by our ancestors in the styles of the Gothic, Renaissance, or Baroque periods. The architecture of these sights was successfully modeled by the construction whirl of the end of the nineteenth century and the beginning of the twentieth century.

Thanks to the generosity of the Gothic builders, the town of Pilsen was predestined for free architectonic development since its very coming into existence. The town has therefore become an example of a harmonious coexistence of architecture both historical and historicizing.

Table of Contents

Conference Papers

Automatic Detection of the Prosodic Structures of Speech Utterances

Katarina Bartkova[1] and Denis Jouvet[2]

[1] ATILF - Analyse et Traitement Informatique de la Langue Franaise
44 Av De La Libration, BP 30687, 54063 Nancy Cedex, France
katarina.bartkova@atilf.fr
[2] Speech Group, LORIA
Inria, Villers-lès-Nancy, F-54600, France
Université de Lorraine, LORIA, UMR 7503, Villers-lès-Nancy, F-54600, France
CNRS, LORIA, UMR 7503, Villers-lès-Nancy, F-54600, France
denis.jouvet@loria.fr

Abstract. This paper presents an automatic approach for the detection of the prosodic structures of speech utterances. The algorithm relies on a hierarchical representation of the prosodic organization of the speech utterances. The approach is applied on a corpus of radio French broadcast news and also on radio and TV shows which are more spontaneous speech data. The algorithm detects prosodic boundaries whether they are followed or not by pause. The detection of the prosodic boundaries and of the prosodic structures is based on an approach that integrates little linguistic knowledge and mainly uses the amplitude of the F0 slopes and the inversion of the slopes as described in [1], as well as phone durations. The automatic prosodic segmentation results are then compared to a manual prosodic segmentation made by an expert phonetician. Finally, the results obtained by this automatic approach provide an insight into the most frequently used prosodic structures in the broadcasting speech style as well as in a more spontaneous speech style.

Keywords: prosodic groups, automatic boundary detection, prosodic trees.

1 Introduction

The prosodic component of speech conveys the information used for structuring the speech message, such as emphasis on words and structure of the utterance into prosodic groups. However such information is usually neglected in the manual transcription of speech corpora, as well as in automatic speech recognition. Hence, it is important to investigate automatic approaches for recovering such information from speech material. The first application is of course the detection of the prosodic structures for speech data in manually transcribed corpora, in view of making possible large scale analysis of prosodic behaviors and phonostyles whether specific to a type of discourse, a type of radio channel [2], or specific to a speaker, instead of just studying the variations of the prosodic parameters in a global manner [3]. Automatic detection of the prosodic structuring will also help for adding punctuation in the output of speech transcription

M. Železný et al. (Eds.): SPECOM 2013, LNAI 8113, pp. 1–8, 2013.

systems which currently consists in mere sequences of words. Automatic detection of prosodic structure will also provide the basis for investigating further the links between prosodic structures and syntactic structures, as well as investigated approaches for the usage of prosodic structures in automatic processing of speech.

Even if not perfect, the use of an automatic approach for prosodic segmentation is interested especially as the agreement on manually annotated prosodic events (boundary levels, disfluences and hesitation, perceptual prominences) between expert annotators is quite low (68%) and even after training sessions the agreement does not exceed 86% [4]. Moreover, it is difficult for human annotators not to be influenced by the meaning of the speech, annotators can be tempted to associate a prosodic boundary at the end of a syntactic boundary or at the end of a semantic group instead of focusing solely onto the prosodic events. A further advantage of an automatic processing is that, once the values of the parameters are normalized, they are always compared to the same threshold values, which is a behavior extremely difficult to follow when human (hence subjective) annotation is concerned.

This paper deals with the automatic processing of prosody using an approach based on a theoretical linguistic framework. The automatic detection of the prosodic structure is based on a theoretical description of prosodic trees; the framework was first developed for prepared speech [1] and later adapted for the semi-spontaneous speech in [5]. The approach is revisited in this paper and applied on various types of speech material, including spontaneous speech.

The paper is organized as follows. Section 2 describes the approach used. Section 3 presents the speech corpora used as well as the computation and normalization of the prosodic parameters. Section 4 presents and discusses the results obtained on the speech corpora. A conclusion ends the paper.

2   Prosodic Segmentation and Prosodic Structure

The approach is based on the assumption that there is a prosodic structure that organizes hierarchically the prosodic groups (accented groups). The prosodic structure results from contrasts of melodic slopes observed on stressed syllables. The prosodic structure is a priori independent of, but yet associated with, the syntactic structure although each structure has its own set of constraints.

There is a general agreement to focus on or around stressed syllables for the description of prosodic phenomena. Minimal prosodic units contain possibly a final lexical accent and optionally an initial (didactic or secondary) stress. A minimal prosodic unit contains a lexical unit (a word of an open grammatical category), and optionally grammatical units (words of closed categories), and usually, its length does not exceed 8 syllables.

To detect prosodic boundaries, our approach uses prosodic parameters measured on word final syllables (vowel duration and F0 movement), as well as rhythmic constraints in order to prevent as much as possible too long prosodic groups. The approach uses phoneme and word boundaries obtained by forced alignment and takes into account some lexical constraints for the determination of the minimal prosodic units.

The identified prosodic groups are then organized in a prosodic tree structure which is not limited in the number of levels. The prosodic parameters and the melodic movements of the prosodic groups have to respect the constraints imposed by the prosodic structure, which are defined by the two main following rules:

- Inversion of the melodic slope (IPM)
- Amplitude of melodic Variation (AVM)

2.1 Prosodic Parameters

We choose to consider the values of the prosodic parameters only on vowels, thus ignoring consonants as they introduce mostly micro melodic disturbances of the parameters studied. In addition, taking into account only the vowel durations avoids problems resulting from the various structures of the syllables (closed vs. open syllable, syllable with complex attack or coda, etc.). In fact, vowel durations can be considered as more homogeneous than syllable durations, because they are less constrained by the internal structure of the syllables than consonants.

The duration of the vowels are computed from the phonetic segmentation that results from the forced alignment. The energy of each vowel corresponds to its mean value calculated on all the frames of the vowel segment. The vowel energy and the vowel duration are then normalized with respect to local mean values computed on non-stressed vowels of the current breath group. In practice we used the vowels that are not in a a word final position. In order to make the local estimation of the mean values more reliable, if necessary, we extend the search of non-stressed vowels on the left (or on the right) of the current breath group, up to collecting data from at least 5 non-stressed vowels. This extension of the search is usually required for short breath groups.

For each vowel the F0 slope is calculated by linear regression on the speech frames corresponding to the vowel. This approach allows to smooth inappropriate F0 values, as, for example, the first values of F0 after an unvoiced plosive consonant. In addition to the slope, we calculate also, for each vowel, the delta of F0 movement with respect to the preceding vowel.

2.2 Methodology for Segmenting and Structuring

The segmentation of the speech signal by prosodic parameters is preceded by an initial segmentation of the text into potentially stressed prosodic units. This is achieved by grouping grammatical words with lexical words. Prosodic parameters are then considered only on last syllables (vowels) of the potentially stressed groups in order to determine if each prosodic group is accented or not.

Two main parameters, the F0 slope and the normalized duration of the vowels (other than the schwa vowel in final position when the word is plurisyllabic) are used to detect prosodic boundaries. The duration threshold that separates stressed vowels from unstressed vowels was determined from the analysis of the distribution of the duration of vowels in unstressed positions (syllables other than last syllables of the lexical units) and in stressed positions (syllables followed by a pause): a vowel whose normalized duration exceeds 150% is considered as stressed. The same approach was applied for determining the threshold that separates the values of the slopes of F0 on prosodic and non-prosodic boundaries (more precisely, because of the glissando definition, the actual parameter considered is the F0 slope times the square of the vowel duration). The analysis of the distribution of the values of the slopes between unstressed vowels (in internal syllables of plurisyllabic words) and stressed vowels (in syllables followed by a pause) confirmed the threshold value of 0.32, that is the threshold of glissando ($0.32/T^2$) obtained on speech by [6]. A third parameter, the delta F0 value (obtained as the difference in F0 between the current vowel and the previous one not separated from the current vowel by a pause) is also calculated over the vowel of the last word in the prosodic groups. If the delta F0 value is higher than 5 semi-tones then a prosodic boundary is set on this syllable.

The algorithm also evaluates the depth of the prosodic boundaries. A prosodic boundary which is marked by a steep F0 slope (higher than the glissando threshold for speech) and a long vowel duration (longer than 150% of the locally calculated mean vowel duration), or a very long vowel duration (200%) and a more moderate F0 slope (higher than the glissando threshold for vowels) receives the symbolic annotation of C1. If the prosodic boundary is marked only by a steep F0 slope or a long duration, it is considered as being closer to the leaves in the prosodic tree and is annotated by C2. And if the prosodic boundary is marked only by a vowel lengthening or a moderate F0 slope or a relevant delta F0 value, then its depth is annotate as C3 (close to the leaves of the prosodic tree).

To avoid a too fine-grained prosodic segmentation, prosodic boundaries whose symbolic annotation is C3 and whose length is less than 2 syllables, are neutralized and attached to the following prosodic group. Also, when the prosodic group exceeds 10 syllables, an intermediate prosodic boundary is searched around the middle part of the group using this time lower threshold values for vowel duration and F0 slope detection. When an appropriate split is found, the prosodic group is cut into 2 groups, otherwise the group regardless of its length is maintained as one single prosodic group.

The symbolic annotations (C1, C2, ...) are used to construct prosodic trees for each breath group (speech signal preceded and followed by a pause). In the prosodic tree construction, a prosodic group is attached to the next prosodic group if the next group has a lower symbolic mark (i.e. if the next group is closer to the root of the prosodic tree).

3   Experimental Set Up

The approach was applied on speech from radio broadcasts and TV shows: the ESTER2 [7] and the ETAPE [8] speech corpus. The ESTER2 data corresponds to French broadcast news collected from various radio channels, it contains prepared speech, plus some interviews. The ETAPE data corresponds to debates collected from radio and TV channels, and is mainly spontaneous speech.

The values of F0 in semitones and the energy values are calculated every 10 ms from the speech signal using the ETSI/AURORA [9] acoustic analysis. The phonetic transcription of the text, necessary for the forced alignment processing, is obtained from the BDLEX [10] lexicon, and an automatic grapheme-to-phoneme transcription [11] is applied for words absent from the lexicon.

The speech signal is segmented into phonemes and words using forced alignment provided by the Sphinx tools [12]. This alignment was used to compute sound durations, as well as the location and duration of pauses. As the speech signal quality is rather good, it can be assumed that the segmentation is carried out without major problems. However a gap between the signal and its phonetic transcription can occur when the orthographic transcription does not reflect the exact content of the speech signal, or when pronunciation variants are missing in the pronunciation lexicon.

4 Experiments and Discussions

Experiments were conducted on ESTER and ETAPE speech data. Whole training and development sets have been processed: computation of frame features, forced alignment, computation of prosodic features (absolute and normalized values), and finally automatic segmentation into prosodic groups and determination of the prosodic structures.

4.1 Evaluation of Prosodic Segmentation

A small part of the corpus has been segmented manually into prosodic groups. It is important to note that this manual prosodic segmentation was done fully manually (i.e. this was not a checking of an a priori automatic segmentation), consequently there is no bias in the evaluation of the prosodic segmentation. The reference (manually annotated) material amounts to about 1400 prosodic groups (and about 4500 words) on the ESTER data, and about 1200 prosodic groups (and about 3300 words) on the ETAPE data.

Table 1. Analysis of automatic prosodic boundary detection

Speech data	Number of boundaries in reference data	Percentage		
		Found	Deleted	Inserted
Ester subset	1405	83.4%	16.6%	20.4%
Etape subset	1167	77.0%	23.0%	12.9%

The prosodic boundaries (end of prosodic groups) obtained automatically have been aligned (matched) with the manual reference prosodic boundaries. About 80% (slightly more on ESTER data, slightly less on ETAPE data) of the boundaries matches between the automatic and the manual prosodic segmentations. The insertion and deletion rates are of the order or lower to 20%. Detailed results are reported in Table 1.

A refined analysis was conducted on matched boundaries. Fig. 1 shows the precision on those boundaries, by reporting the percentage of matched boundaries for which the distance between the automatic and the corresponding manual boundary is smaller than a given value (from 10ms up to 1sec). The results show that 74% to 84% of the matching boundaries are situated within less than 100 ms of their manually set (correct!) position.

4.2 Analysis of Prosodic Segmentation and Structures

The length of the prosodic groups have been analyzed on the ESTER and ETAPE data. The results are reported in Fig. 2 which display the percentage of prosodic groups of a

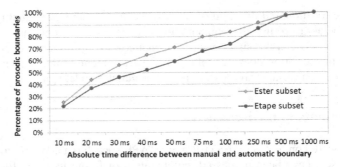

Fig. 1. Precision of the automatically prosodic boundaries: percentage of prosodic boundaries that are within a given distance of the corresponding manual boundary

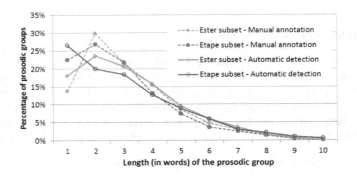

Fig. 2. Frequency analysis of the length (in words) of the prosodic groups on the Ester and Etape development data for manual and automatic prosodic segmentation

given length (from 1 to 10 words). The curves show rather similar behavior between the distributions observed on prosodic groups resulting from manual annotation and from automatic detection.

The most frequent prosodic trees are those containing two branches (two prosodic groups) having mainly rising movements of the slope on their two components. Rising F0 slopes are slightly more frequent on the prosodic borders (38%) that downward slopes (26%). In 12% of the cases the border is neutralized and in 24% of case it is the vowel duration parameter which determined the prosodic border.

For speech sequences up of three prosodic words, the prosodic structure the most frequently found is that of the enumeration with rising slopes having roughly the same amplitude. These data corroborate those observed in the study [5], where prosodic structures with primarily rising slopes are found, with few oppositions based on the inversion of the slopes. However, the broadcasting style can be regarded as prepared or in any case semi-spontaneous, consequently it is also connected with the prepared style. Indeed, the prosodic structuring is expressed here also by the inversion of the F0 slopes as well as by the variation of F0 slope amplitudes. Apart from the enumeration, the preferred prosodic trees used to organize 3 prosodic components in a hierarchy are those

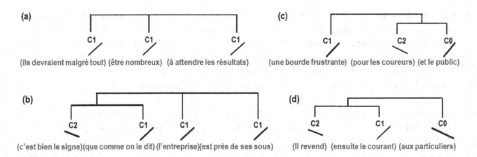

Fig. 3. Example of prosodic trees corresponding to an enumeration (a), an inversion followed by a repetition of F0 rising slopes (b), a connection on the left (c) and on on the right (d)

using the inversion and the amplitude variation of the F0 slopes in a dependence on the right (between C2 and C0) or on the left (between C2 and C1) (cf. Fig. 3, (c) & (d)). When the breath group contains 4 prosodic groups, the prosodic structure the most frequently observed is the one with an inversion of slopes at the beginning and containing a structure of enumeration on the remaining components while privileging rising F0 slopes (cf. Fig. 3, (b)).

5 Conclusion

This paper has presented an automatic approach for segmenting speech material into prosodic groups and for structuring the prosodic groups into a hierarchical structure. The prosodic hierarchical organization constituting the basis of the approach was initially described for prepared read speech, and was more recently adapted for semi-spontaneous speech. Although the initial approach for prepared speech was using only the F0 criteria for structuring the speech data, the revisited approach presented here uses also the duration criteria. The approach relies on a very limited set of prosodic-based features, for which their normalized values are compared to thresholds in order to decide on the prosodic group boundaries.

The approach has been applied on broadcasts radio data which contain more or less prepared speech, and on radio and TV shows that are mainly spontaneous speech. Results of the automatic prosodic segmentation have been compared to manual prosodic segmentation. Results are promising, although further detailed analysis is required to investigate deeper the differences between manual and automatic prosodic segmentations.

References

1. Martin, P.: Prosodic and rhythmic structures in French. Linguistics 25, 925–949 (1987)
2. Hupin, B., Simon, A.C.: Analyse phonostylistique du discours radiophonique. Expériences sur la mise en fonction professionnelle du phonostyle et sur le lien entre mélodicité et proximité du discours radiophonique. Recherches en communication 28, 103–121 (2009)
3. Goldman, J.-P., Auchlin, A., Simon, A.C., Avanzi, M.: Phonostylographe: un outil de description prosodique. Comparaison du style radiophonique et lu. Nouveaux Cahiers de Linguistique Franaise 28, 219–237 (2008)

4. Lacheret-Dujour, A., Obin, N., Avanzi, M.: Design and Evaluation of Shared Prosodic Annotation for French Spontaneous Speech: From Experts Knowledges to Non-Experts Annotations. In: Proceedings of the 4th Linguistic Annotation Workshop, Uppsala, Sweden (2010)
5. Segal, N., Bartkova, K.: Prosodic structure representation for boundary detection in spontaneous French. In: Proceedings of ICPhS 2007, Saarbrcken, pp. 1197–1200 (2007)
6. 't Hart, J., Collier, R., Cohen, A.: A Perceptual Study of Intonation. Cambridge U.P., London (1990)
7. Galliano, S., Gravier, G., Chaubard, L.: The Ester 2 evaluation campaign for rich transcription of French broadcasts. In: Proc. INTERSPEECH 2009, Brighton, UK, pp. 2583–2586 (2009)
8. Gravier, G., Adda, G., Paulsson, N., Carr, M., Giraudel, A., Galibert, O.: The ETAPE corpus for the evaluation of speech-based TV content processing in the French language. In: Proc. LREC 2012, Istanbul, Turkey (2012)
9. Speech Processing, Transmission and Quality Aspects (STQ); Distributed speech recognition; extended advanced front-end feature extraction algorithm; compression Algorithms, ETSI ES 202 212 (2005)
10. de Calmès, M., Pérennou, G.: BDLEX: a Lexicon for Spoken and Written French. In: Proc. LREC 1998, Grenade, pp. 1129–1136 (1998)
11. Jouvet, D., Fohr, D., Illina, I.: Evaluating grapheme-to-phoneme converters in automatic speech recognition context. In: Proc. ICASSP 2012, Kyoto, Japan, pp. 4821–4824 (2012)
12. Sphinx (2011), http://cmusphinx.sourceforge.net/

A Method for Auditory Evaluation of Synthesized Speech Intonation

Anna Solomennik[1] and Anna Cherentsova[2]

[1] Speech Technology Ltd., Minsk, Belarus
`solomennik-a@speechpro.com`
[2] Speech Technology Center Ltd., St. Petersburg, Russia
`cherentsova@speechpro.com`

Abstract. The paper proposes an approach to diagnostic testing for suprasegmental quality of Russian TTS-generated speech. We describe a two-step evaluation strategy to measure the perception of prosodic features on the basis of an arbitrary selection of synthesized sentences from an existing representative inventory. As a result of a series of auditory tests, an integral intonation intelligibility coefficient is calculated, enabling us to compare intelligibility and expressiveness, i. e. the functional aspect of the TTS prosodic component. The method is demonstrated on several Russian TTS voices. A psycholinguistic test requiring a linguistic decision on the type of perceived utterance (statement/question/exclamation/non-terminal phrase) was offered to native Russian speakers, along with a quality test of the naturalness of the phase melody (0-2 scale). Subsequently, several observations are proposed for further enhancement of the formal aspect of prosody, to facilitate finding solutions to the problems detected in course of the evaluation procedure.

Keywords: speech synthesis, intonation, TTS evaluation, Russian.

1 Introduction

In the domain of high quality speech synthesis development, clear and natural intonation of the synthetic speech is gaining more and more importance. There are various approaches to modeling intonation, rule-based and corpus-based, they usually include pitch resynthesis, various stylization methods, concatenation of pitch syllable contours, production-oriented model and linguistic models based on overlaid and tone sequence theories [1].

The problem of TTS quality evaluation includes several aspects [2]. Evaluation can be either subjective, on the basis of mean opinion score (MOS) tests, or objective, by comparing pitch, energy and duration of synthesized and natural utterances (different measures of distance can be used). The task of prosody generation for synthetic speech consists of two stages. Firstly, intonation should be predicted from text and, secondly, specific tone, duration and energy features should be assigned to speech sounds. Errors may occur at both stages. Let us consider synthetic speech intonation intelligible if it is possible to reconstruct the punctuation of the original text from the auditory impression just as well as it can be done when listening to a natural voice.

M. Železný et al. (Eds.): SPECOM 2013, LNAI 8113, pp. 9–16, 2013.

An expanded two-step approach to measuring the adequacy of prosodic features of synthesized speech with respect to its perception by native Russian speakers is proposed below, combining both Prosody Intelligibility index (estimating how clear the distinction is between different intonation types) and General Appropriateness index (estimating how natural utterances of different prosodic structure sound for the human ear). Following the strategy unveiled in [3], both measures refer to the functional component of prosody, while further research can be carried out on the formal component, to find out how to adjust and enhance prosodic parameters implemented in a speech synthesis system for more natural performance. The auditory method described in the paper mostly deals with the functional aspect of prosody, and only a few observations are given as to the formal component, due to the fact that humans are much more precise and consistent in distinguishing prominence and boundaries in an utterance, correlating them with a certain suprasegmental meaning, rather than the precise tonal configuration associated with these parameters, which are not regularly perceived by a human, as argued by Wightman [4]. Thus the paper deals with the perceptively detectable mistakes, failures or incoherencies of synthesized speech in the broad sense, enabling the enhancement of a speech synthesis system by taking into account the weak points in the intonation structure of the generated utterances for more subtle prosodic refinement of its algorithms.

The method has been developed as highly language specific and will probably remain as such, being strongly dependent on the text material, which has been selected using the existing knowledge of various intonation patterns of multiple syntactic structures based on annotated speech databases, as well as on general tests of Russian TTS systems.

2   Intelligibility Estimation

The criterion of basic intelligibility as the main function of intonation takes as a reference point the rough opposition between terminal (falling '\'), non-terminal (slightly rising '/-') and interrogative (significantly rising '/') intonation, described for English and Russian by Sukhareva [5]: falling F0 at a low rate, not followed by rising – terminal phrase; F0 rising at an average rate – non-terminal phrase; F0 rising higher than average – interrogative phrase.

Level tone (-) is specific for parenthetical constructions, for example, remarks or appellations in postposition (as in 'Ty prava, mama' – 'You are right, mummy').

A few more intonation markers are used to identify exclamations and commands, such as emphatic stress (**) and glottal stop (|). In accordance to these features, an inventory of phrases with various intonation patterns (typical of Russian natural speech) was created (see section 4), the textual form of which was used for the selection of sentences to synthesize and offer as stimuli for the auditory test. A sufficient criterion of adequate prosody of the synthesized phrases is generalized to their correct auditory perception, estimated with the help of a linguistic decision test [6].

3   General Appropriateness Estimation

Even intelligible intonation may sound uneven and disturbing and thus interfere with smooth and comfortable perception of synthetic speech. Correct understanding of the message may be affected due to obvious deviation of what is heard from the listener's expectations. For example, a neutral tone of an emotional exclamation or an aggressive imperative (pronounced evenly or with a glottal stop, as in Russian 'Kakaya priyatnaya neojidannost'!' – 'What a nice surprise!') may be treated as ironic; a friendly unaccentuated manner to pronounce a threat or a warning (such as 'Opasnaya zona! Nemedlenno pokin'te territoriyu!' – 'Danger! Leave urgently!') may result in a cognitive conflict. Auditory assessment of the appropriateness of a prosodic form of a synthesized phrase to transmit a certain message was included in the method to verify the way this sort of interference affects intelligibility.

4 Sentence Inventory

For the representative data on Russian intonation an annotated speech corpus was used, consisting of recordings of stylistically varied texts read by 8 professional speakers, 4 male and 4 female, about 10 hours of sound data per speaker. 13 intonation types [7] were retrieved in the process of corpus annotation, corresponding to the extended set of 7 intonation constructions (IC) generally used to describe the intonation paradigm of Russian [8].

Apart from the database, a representative inventory of prosodically balanced sentences in Russian was collected, each sentence illustrating a single intonation pattern, totaling over 230 simple text units. The sentences were divided into 6 groups according to their prosodic function determined on the basis of punctuation marks along with lexical-grammatical identifiers, such as frequent adjectives and adverbs characteristic of exclamations, or imperative verbs indicating commands.

The groups were further divided into subgroups according to the number of intonation centers (nuclei), as well as to the presence of specific connotations or syntactic markers affecting intonation. Thus each subgroup combined sentences having a unique, or slightly varying, intonation pattern: 1) basic single-accent phrases, 2) extended phrases with the same syntactic structure and communicative goal as the corresponding basic phrases and 3) possible specific patterns within a group. To illustrate the patterns, similar samples of natural voice from the corpus were assigned to each subgroup, processed with a sound editor. As it will be seen from the examples below, extended phrases, due to their length, tend to add another nucleus and thus acquire a ⌐/\₋-style shape, the main nucleus retaining the basic pattern. Specific variants of each pattern were found to be slightly different from the basic pattern, or patterns (they bear more stress, begin or end up with an extra unit of level tone or slightly deviate in F0 movement). Several instances of all 13 intonation types defined as a result of corpus annotation were present among the selected natural voice samples, so the sentence inventory was representative.

The text units were selected as most unspecific, with no connotation and minimal amount of lexical or syntactic markers of communicative strategy, potentially acquiring various meanings (at least two) if presented out of context and with no punctuation marks. This fact allowed us to rely on intonation performing a crucial role in transferring the speaker's communicative intention. A few markers, however, were present, mainly conjunctions and interrogative words marking wh-questions ('Gde vy rodilis'?') and exclamations ('Kakoy den' chudesnyy!'), as well as imperative verbs and characteristic adverbs indicating imperatives ('Sidi doma!'). In spite of a less significant contribution of intonation to the correct understanding of these phrases, they were added to the inventory to distinguish between independent phrases pronounced separately and nonterminal phrases of the same structure that were fragments extracted from a coherent text. For example, a wh-question in spoken or read direct speech would bear intensive stress on the interrogative word and have dynamical basic frequency, while the same text encountered as indirect speech would be pronounced with an inexpressive tone, or even smoothed to neutral, and have a displaced accent pattern. The examples of groups and subgroups of sentences are given below. Accented words are indicated with an asterisk (*), emphatic stress with a double asterisk (**).

Group 1. Simple statements
Basic pattern: **Rising-level [Falling nucleus] Level-falling** ('Pojezd sledujet do konechnoj *sta(\)ncii.')
Extended pattern (binuclear): **[Rising nucleus] + basic / Basic + [falling nucleus]** ('Po *vechera(/)m on predpochitajet hodit po gorodu *peshko(\)m.')

Group 2. Wh-questions
Basic pattern: **Level [Falling nucleus] Level-falling** (('Kto *govori(\)t?'; ('Gde vy *rodili(\)s?')
Extended pattern: **Rising nucleus + basic / Basic + [Falling nucleus]** ('*Kto(/) mozhet otvetit na moj *vopro(\)s?')
Specific pattern: **Basic + [Level nucleus]** ('Otkuda on *zna(\)jet, chto etogo slova v slovare net(-)?')

Group 3. Interrogative intonation
The speech corpus intonation analysis made it possible to extract, apart from the simple yes-no question (bearing an accent on the last word of the phrase) and the extended yes-no question (with an accent shift on the predicate) two specific groups of questions: the alternative question with the conjunction "ILI" ("OR"), which were grouped together with the extended yes-no question due to the similar basic pattern, and the contrastive question with the conjunction "A" ("AND", "BUT").
Basic pattern: **Level [Rising nucleus] Falling** ('Eto *apte(/)ka?'; ('Rech idet o *serje(/)znoj summe?')
Extended pattern (binuclear): **[Rising nucleus] + basic / Basic + [Falling nucleus]** ('U vas *je(/)st zagranichny *pa(\)sport?'; 'Vy predpochitajete *gosti(/)nicu ili chastnuju *kvarti(\)ru?')
Specific patterns: **[Level-falling nucleus] + Basic** ('[Kogda on vernetsa,] vy *vstre(/)tites s nim?'); Falling-rising nucleus ('A *za(\/)vtra vy rabotajete?')

Group 4. Imperative sentences
Based on the types of imperatives classified in the database of imperative sentences of Russian dialog [9], imperative and prohibitive commands were put in a separate group distinct from statements and exclamations as intonationally marked models. A specific intonation pattern was assigned to brusque or emotional commands, frequently marked with such adverbs as 'nemedlenno' ('immediately'), 'seychas je' ('right now'), 'ni v koem sluchae' ('by no means') etc.:

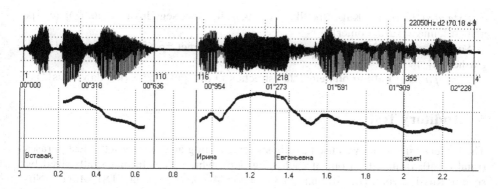

Fig. 1. F0 and waveform for the phrase ('Vstavay! Irina Evgen'evna jdet!'- ('Get up! Irina Yev-genievna is waiting! Both nuclei are marked with intensive accents; the characteristic curve of strong emphasis is obvious on the F0 contour

Basic pattern: **[Falling nucleus] + emphasis** ('**Ostoro(\)zhno!'; ('Ne pridavajte etomu **nikakogo *znache(\)nija!')

Specific pattern: **Basic + more emphasis** ('Opasnaja **zo(\)na! Nemedlenno pokinte *territo(\)riju!')

Group 5. *Exclamations*

As major linguistic means of expressing emotions, exclamations provide most intonationally varied speech examples. When dealing with read speech data generally used for TTS systems, exclamations may appear prosodically unmarked, but the relevant use of exclamations requires that the phrase nucleus bear an emphasis.

For Russian, Yanko [10] observes that the common binuclear intonational contour characteristic for exclamations (IC-5), may be considered a variant of the emphatic accent extended between two syllables, or, vice versa, the emphasis of a short single nuclear exclamation is a compression of IC-5 extended accent. This point of view makes it possible to classify IC-5 exclamations as a specific subtype of the basic pattern.

Basic pattern: **Emphasis (or glottal stop)** ('Vot **vidite!'; ('Kako(|)j-to zahudalyj *zavodishko!')

Specific pattern: **Two-syllabic emphasis** ('*Kaka(/)ja *ra(\)dost!'; ('Chut *sve(/)t u vashih *no(\)g!')

Group 6. *Non-terminal phrases*

Three types of rising intonation, marking strong coherence between the syntagms of the phrase, are described for Russian by Yanko [10]: rise-fall (IC-3), rise-level (IC-6), rise with a curved characteristic of emphasis (IC-4). Rising intonation of any of the types regularly occurs in constructions with subjective modality (expressed by conjunctive words 'konechno' ('certainly'), 'uvy' ('alas'), 'k sojaleniyu' ('unfortunately') or parenthetical modal clauses expressing attitude, mental activity or sense perception) [11], in multiple topic constructions (in enumerations), in clauses followed by a dash etc. Samples of slightly falling tone are also classified and annotated with linguistic identifiers.

Basic pattern: **Rise-fall / rise-level / emphatic rise** ('K *sozhale(/)niju, [vse bilety prodany].'; '*Vyno(/)slivost [cennoje kachestvo].')

Extended pattern ('Kak *to(/)lko vy *skazali, chto segodnya *uleta(/\)jete, [ja nemed-lenno zakazal nomer].')

Specific pattern: **Multiple nuclei** ('Neobhodimo imet *pa(/)sport, *vi(/)zu [i pri-glashenije].')

Basic pattern: **Falling nucleus** ('Ja vstrechus s nim *po(\)zzhe, [kogda vernus].')

5   Auditory Test

The sentence inventory was used as a basis for selecting an arbitrary set of test phrases (total of 40, from 1 to 3 out of each subgroup), which were further synthesized by several Russian voices of different TTS systems: Alyona (Acapela TTS), Milena (Nuance TTS), Olga (Loquendo TTS), Julia and Vladimir (VitalVoice TTS) [12–15]. The same set of phrases, pronounced by a native Russian female speaker (28 years old), was recorded to provide a reference point.

In course of the listening test, participants were prompted to mark the text with punctuation marks. Along with making a linguistic decision on the type of each utterance, the subjects were to estimate naturalness of its intonation. A 0-2 scale was used for test results processing: 2 was assigned if punctuation was recognized correctly and intonation estimated as natural, 1 in case of correct recognition but intonation estimated as unnatural, 0 for the phrases where punctuation marks were not recognized correctly.

10 subjects, aged from 23 to 50, all native Russian speakers, 4 male and 6 female, participated in the evaluation test procedure. All were selected as trained in phonetics and with analytic listening experience (according to reliability measurements based choice of subjects for test procedures on synthesized speech evaluation [16]).

6   Results Estimation and Discussion

Two indices were calculated to estimate prosodic quality: General Appropriateness index (the percentage of phrases with correctly recognized prosody, with intonation marked as appropriate, 2 on the scale) and Intelligibility index (the percentage of phrases with correctly recognized prosody, intonation marked as inappropriate, 1 and 2 on the scale). A mean weighted value was used to calculate the indices, the corpus-based distribution values for each intonation pattern (subgroup of the inventory) taken as weights.

The results of the auditory test are presented in the tables below.

The estimated General Appropriateness of intonation of the TTS voices participating in diagnostic testing (normalized on natural voice) varies from 49 % (Olga) to 72 % (Vladimir).

The Intelligibility index showed less inter-voice dispersion, approaching to 70 % for all the evaluated TTS voices. The auditory perception of the voice of Olga (Loquendo) may have been slightly interfered with background music present in the voice demo.

The indices calculated separately for various intonation types allow to assess the weak points of each TTS system in particular with respect to the implementation of certain intonation patterns. The lowest Intelligibility index throughout all intonation types was obtained for wh-questions and exclamations.

Table 1. General Appropriateness (G. A. I) and Intelligibility (I. I.) indices for TTS voices (standard deviation is given in parenthesis). Minimal values are marked with bold.

		Terminal	Wh-quest.	Yes-no quest.	Exclamat.	Non-terminal	Total
Alyona	G.A.I.	0.72 (0.24)	**0.14 (0.12)**	0.24 (0.17)	0.19 (0.16)	0.49 (0.17)	0.54 (0.13)
	I.I.	0.74 (0.10)	0.45 (0.10)	0.31 (0.09)	**0.21 (0.14)**	0.77 (0.08)	0.67 (0.07)
Milena	G.A.I.	0.83 (0.14)	0.10 (0.09)	**0.08 (0.13)**	0.19 (0.14)	0.54 (0.08)	0.60 (0.07)
	I.I.	0.84 (0.15)	0.26 (0.27)	**0.21 (0.24)**	0.26 (0.13)	0.62 (0.38)	0.66 (0.08)
Olga	G.A.I.	0.51 (0.25)	0.30 (0.19)	**0.11 (0.11)**	0.19 (0.19)	0.50 (0.16)	0.45 (0.16)
	I.I.	0.66 (0.24)	0.45 (0.12)	**0.21 (0.24)**	0.24 (0.17)	0.75 (0.17)	0.65 (0.16)
Julia	G.A.I.	0.88 (0.11)	**0.25 (0.12)**	0.25 (0.22)	0.34 (0.18)	0.50 (0.16)	0.64 (0.07)
	I.I.	0.88 (0.11)	**0.33 (0.11)**	0.59 (0.15)	0.41 (0.19)	0.70 (0.17)	0.72 (0.08)
Vladimir	G.A.I.	0.86 (0.13)	**0.24 (0.17)**	0.38 (0.30)	0.25 (0.15)	0.61 (0.22)	0.66 (0.15)
	I.I.	0.87 (0.10)	0.39 (0.19)	0.57 (0.25)	**0.25 (0.15)**	0.74 (0.19)	0.72 (0.09)
Nat. speech	G.A.I.	0.97 (0.02)	1.00 (0.00)	**0.78 (0.16)**	0.89 (0.10)	0.94 (0.08)	0.92 (0.03)
	I.I.	0.99 (0.00)	1.00 (0.00)	**0.78 (0.16)**	0.90 (0.09)	0.94 (0.08)	0.93 (0.02)

Table 2. General Appropriateness (G. A. I) and Intelligibility (I. I.) indices for TTS voices normalized on those of the natural voice. Minimal values are marked with bold.

		Terminal	Wh-questions	Yes-no questions	Exclamations	Non-terminal	Total
Alyona	G.A.I.	0.74	**0.14**	0.31	0.21	0.52	0.59
	I.I.	0.75	0.45	0.40	**0.23**	0.82	0.72
Milena	G.A.I.	0.85	**0.10**	0.10	0.21	0.58	0.65
	I.I.	0.85	**0.26**	0.27	0.29	0.66	0.71
Olga	G.A.I.	0.52	0.30	**0.14**	0.21	0.53	0.49
	I.I.	0.67	0.45	**0.27**	0.27	0.80	0.70
Julia	G.A.I.	0.90	**0.25**	0.32	0.38	0.53	0.70
	I.I.	0.89	**0.33**	0.75	0.45	0.74	0.77
Vladimir	G.A.I.	0.88	**0.24**	0.49	0.28	0.65	0.72
	I.I.	0.88	0.39	0.73	**0.28**	0.79	0.77

No focus was placed on separate estimation of phrase accent location and syntagm boundaries, although both of the parameters have undoubtedly affected the General Appropriateness measures. To focus more profoundly on these problematic aspects of prosodic functionality, the diagnostic method may be further elaborated.

Let us also note that the results obtained from the auditory testing procedure only provide a rough estimation of the naturalness of the phrases. The present method provides a source of finding instrumental solutions to the problems we unveiled. Linguistic analysis of the sentence inventory used in the method is potentially a way of improving intonation modeling in TTS.

References

1. Krivnova, O.F.: Generation of Phrase Tone Contour in Speech Synthesis Systems. In: Computational Linguistics and Intellectual Technologies: Proc. of Int. Conf. "Dialog 2000", Protvino, vol. 2, pp. 211–220 (2000) (in Russian)
2. Solomennik, A.I., Talanov, A.O., Solomennik, M.V., Khomitsevich, O.G., Chistikov, P.G.: Synthesized Speech Quality Evaluation: Problems and Solutions. Instrumentation 56, 38–41 (2013) (in Russian)
3. Vainio, M., Hirst, D., Suni, A., De Looze, C.: Using Functional Prosodic Annotation for High Quality Multilingual, Multidialectal and Multistyle Speech Synthesis. In: SPECOM 2009 Proceedings, St. Petersburg, pp. 164–169 (2009)
4. Wightman, C.: ToBI or not ToBI? In: Proceedings of the First International Conference on Speech Prosody, Aix-en-Provence, pp. 25–29 (2002)
5. Sukhareva, E.: Distinctive Features of Terminal and Interrogative English Intonation. Bulletin of Voronezh State University. Linguistics and Intercultural Communication 2, 101–104 (2009) (in Russian)
6. Van Heuven, V.J., Van Bezooijen, R.: Quality Evaluation of Synthesized Speech. In: Speech Coding and Synthesis, New York, pp. 723–725 (1995)
7. Volskaya, N.B., Skrelin, P.A.: Intonation Modeling for TTS, Ufa (1998) (in Russian)
8. Russian Grammar, Moscow (1982) (in Russian)
9. Kodzasov, S.V., Arhipov, A.V., Bonch-Osmolovskaya, A.A., Zakharov, L.M., Krivnova, O.F.: The Database on Intonation of Russian Dialogue: Commanding Propositions. In: Proc. of Int. Conf. "Dialog 2006", Moscow, pp. 236–242 (2006) (in Russian)
10. Yanko, T.E.: Intonation Strategies of Russian Speech in Comparative Aspect, Moscow (2008) (in Russian)
11. Soldatenkova, T., Vergauwen, R.: Notes to the Problem of Linguistic Means Classification and Subjective Modality Meanings. Bulletin of Voronezh State University. Linguistics and Intercultural Communication 2, 165–167 (2009) (in Russian)
12. Online Demo: http://www.acapela-group.com/text-to-speech-interactive-demo.html
13. Online Demo: http://enterprisecontent.nuance.com/vocalizer5-network-demo/index.htm
14. Online Demo: http://www.loquendo.com/en/demo-center/interactive-tts-demo/
15. Online Demo: http://cards.voicefabric.ru/
16. Grice, M., Vagges, K., Hirst, D.: Assessment of Intonation in Text-to-Speech Synthesis Systems - A pilot Test in English and Italian. In: Proc. Eurospeech 1991, Genova, vol. 2, pp. 879–882 (1991)

Acoustic Modeling with Deep Belief Networks for Russian Speech Recognition

Mikhail Zulkarneev, Ruben Grigoryan, and Nikolay Shamraev

FSSI Research Institute "Spezvuzautomatika", Rostov-on-Don, Russia
zulkarneev@mail.ru,
r.grigoryan@niisva.org,
ncam1977@yahoo.com

Abstract. This paper presents continuous Russian speech recognition with deep belief networks in conjunction with HMM. Recognition is performed in two stages. In the first phase deep belief networks are used to calculate the phoneme state probability for feature vectors describing speech. In the second stage, these probabilities are used by Viterbi decoder for generating resulting sequence of words. Two-stage training procedure of deep belief networks is used based on restricted Boltzmann machines. In the first stage neural network is represented as a stack of restricted Boltzmann machines and sequential training is performed, when the previous machine output is the input to the next. After a rough adjustment of the weights second stage is performed using a back-propagation training procedure. The advantage of this method is that it allows usage of unlabeled data for training. It makes the training more robust and effective.

Keywords: Speech Recognition, Hidden Markov Models, Deep Neural Networks, Restricted Boltzmann machines.

1 Introduction

Nowadays speech recognition systems widely employ Hidden Markov models (HMM) for acoustic modeling and Gaussian mixtures (GM) for state modeling [1]. Popularity of the models results from their simplicity as well as from effective theoretically-based training and decoding algorithms. Along with the simplicity of the models they show high recognition accuracy when they are tested on different speech recognition tasks[1].

Nevertheless these models have some shortcomings. First, they quite roughly model context relation - the connection between states is determined by the a single parameter - state transition probability. Second, GMs are ineffective for modeling data located in non-linear set or near it. For example modeling points located close to the sphere surface requires just a few parameters, if you use the appropriate class of models, however, it requires a great number of parameters, if you use Gaussian mixture with diagonal covariance matrix (this model is often used in speech recognition systems).

Paper [2] suggests using recurrent neural networks for context modeling. The hidden layer of this networks has recurrent transitions, and it enables keeping information on

---

[1] The work was financially supported by the state contract GK 07.524.11.4023 (Minobrnauka RF).

M. Železný et al. (Eds.): SPECOM 2013, LNAI 8113, pp. 17–24, 2013.

the past. But information on the future is also essential in speech recognition, therefore paper [2] offers a bidirectional recurrent neural networks model. Per se these are two recurrent neural networks - in forward and back directions. The networks have the same output layer receiving output signal from both networks. In addition the authors suggest applying a technology named long short-term memory for enlarging the length of the context being used [3].

Involvement of neural networks allows overcoming the second disadvantage of HMM+GM, as they proved to be universal approximates for non-linear functions. New efficient training algorithms and computing machinery came up and they allow training of neural networks with more hidden layers and larger output layer. As a result many research groups obtained positive results using neural networks for speech recognition [4].

The present paper suggests using DBN combined with HMM for continuous Russian speech recognition. Recognition is performed in two stages. At the first stage we use DBN to calculate phoneme states for feature vectors from sequence $O = o_1, ..., o_T$, representing speech message (melcepstral coefficients or their cosine transformation are used as features). The second stage involves Viterbi decoder for obtaining resulting word sequence.

2   Method Description

The paper investigates a possibility to implement hybrid system DBN+HMM for continuous Russian speech recognition. DBN are used for calculation of probabilities of phoneme states $p(s_i|o_t)$ for feature vectors for sequence $O = o_1, ..., o_T$, representing speech message. These probabilities are further applied for speech recognition by token passing algorithm [6] - the regular procedure for HMM and Gaussian mixture based speech recognition systems. The token passing algorithm uses likelihood $p(o_t|s_i)$, and DBN produces a posteriori probabilities of states $p(s_i|o_t)$, therefore Bayes formula is used to recalculate these values:

$$p(o_t|s_i) = \frac{p(s_i|o_t)p(o_t)}{p(s_i)} \tag{1}$$

where $p(s_i)$ - prior probability of state s_i. $p(o_t)$ doesn't change for fixed o_t when calculating $p(o_t|s_i)$, therefore it can be omitted and we can use $p(s_i|o_t)/p(s_i)$ as likelihood.

For speech recognition decoding we used HMM and HDecode from HTK tool set [7], and thus we face a problem of transmitting the obtained probabilities into the utility. To solve this problem $p_i^{(t)} = p(s_i|o_t)/p(s_i)$ is transformed by $x_i^{(t)} = f(p_i^{(t)})$ and presented as a file of parameters compatible with HDecode. Furthermore HMM phonemes are prepared for parameter files processing: a tree-states HMM is generated for each phoneme, each state being described by normal distribution with zero means vector and dispersion vector whose elements have huge absolute value ($\approx 10^{30}$), apart from element i, where i - number of the given state with dispersion equal 1. When we choose these normal distribution parameters and transformation $f(p_i^{(t)})$ in the form $x_i^{(t)} = \sqrt{log(p_{i\,max}^{(t)}/p_i^{(t)})}$

normal distribution value for vector $x^{(t)} = \{x_i\}$ will be proportional to value $p_i^{(t)}$, but at the same time it will not go beyond 1 ($p_{i\,\max}^{(t)}$ - maximum value of $p_i^{(t)} = p(s_i|o_t)/p(s_i)$, considering that $p_{\max}(s_i|o_t) = 1$, this value equals to $p_{i\,\max}^{(t)} = 1/p_{\min}(s_i)$).

2.1   Neural Networks Used for Acoustic Modeling

The DBN with the layer number not greater than 7 are investigated in the paper. However this limit isn't fundamental and is due to the limit of time required for training. The output for an element is value $y_j = \sigma(x_j)$, where $\sigma(x) = 1/(1 + e^{-x})$ is a sigmoid function, $x_j = b_j + \sum_i y_i w_{ij}$ is activation of neuron, b_j - bias of element j, i - index of element of lower layer, w_{ij} - weight of connection between element j and element i. Apart from the elements with a logistic function there is an output layer softmax which serves as a transfer function, and produces probabilities each state in each HMM:

$$p_j = \frac{e^{x_j}}{\sum_k e^{x_k}} \tag{2}$$

where k = index of output layer elements. Activation is counted by this formula:

$$x_k = b_k + \sum_i y_i w_{ik} \tag{3}$$

2.2   DBN Training

Back-propagation Procedure

We used procedure of object function derivative back-propagation. It is assumed that we set a training sample $\{x_i, t_i\}$. Object function represents disparity between the network output value and the object value (correct neuron output value). In case we use function softmax as an output function, it's naturally to choose cross entropy between target probabilities d and output probabilities p as object function:

$$C = -\sum_j d_j \log p_j \tag{4}$$

We used negative object function gradient in parameter space as increment of DBN parameters because we are interested in minimum value of object function:

$$\Delta w_{ij} = -\epsilon \frac{\partial C}{\partial w_{ij}} \tag{5}$$

where ϵ is learning rate.

In the training set D we exchanged object function C for as mean value by the whole sample

$$\langle C \rangle = \frac{1}{|D|} \sum_{e \in D} \sum_j d_j^{(e)} \log p_j^{(e)} \tag{6}$$

However in case of large training samples such as speech training databases it is more efficient to calculate gradient not by the whole training sample but by it's small random batch. For gradient smoothing we introduced "moment" $0 < \alpha < 1$ which suppresses fluctuation of gradient in minimum object function area and thus encourages convergence:

$$\Delta w_{ij}(t) = \alpha \Delta w_{ij}(t-1) - \epsilon \frac{\partial \langle C \rangle}{\partial w_{ij}(t)} \tag{7}$$

For the purpose of training of displacement b_j they are interpreted as weights of pseudo elements with outputs equal to one.

Two-Staged DBN Training

Training of DBN with a large number of layers using back-propagation procedure is quite embarrassing due to vanishing/exploding effect resulting from linearity of expressions for loss function gradient recalculation. This fact hindered training of DBN with a large number of layers. However the situation changed after work [5] had been published. The paper suggested two-staged training for DBN using restricted Boltzmann machines (RBM). The backbone idea is that we should perform rough front end adjusting of models weights by back-propagation procedure. It enables more efficient training as it removes vanishing/exploding effects and decreases impact of the retraining.

On the first stage Deep Belief network (DBN) is created as an RBM stack. To perform it we train RBM whose output is used for next RBM training and we keep on this procedure until we gain the required number of DBN layers. (Fig. 1 shows an example of three-layered DBN training). As a result we design a multi-layered generative model (Fig. 1c).

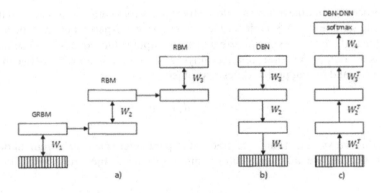

Fig. 1. DBN-DNN training

At the second stage we added softmax layer to the obtained model and built the so-called DBN-DNN model, trained by the error back-propagation method. During the training process model parameters undergo only a slight change (with the exception of W_4) and model parameters are adjusted.

RBM Training

RBM is a bilateral graph (see Fig. 2) where visible elements represent input vector v while h represent feature vector generated on the basis of input vector and weigh matrix W. RBM elements are binary and stochastic as their states are determined by the joint probability $p(v, h|\theta)$.

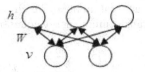

Fig. 2. Restricted Boltzmann machine

In RBM joint probability of vectors v and h is determined by energy:

$$p(v, h|\theta) = \frac{e^{E(v,h|\theta)}}{Z} \tag{8}$$

$$E(v, h|\theta) = -\sum_{i=1}^{V}\sum_{j=1}^{H} w_{ij}v_i h_j - \sum_{i=1}^{V} b_i v_i - \sum_{j=1}^{H} a_j h_j \tag{9}$$

where $\theta = (W, b, a)$, b and a - bias vectors for visible and hidden layers, V and H - number of visible and hidden elements, Z - normalization factor which is called static sum:

$$Z = \sum_{v}\sum_{h} e^{-E(v,h|\theta)} \tag{10}$$

As there are no transitions between hidden states, probability $p(h|v, \theta)$ can be represented as product of factors, each factor being dependent on one element of vector h. Due to this fact probability $p(h_j = 1|v, \theta)$ can be represented as:

$$p(h_j = 1|v, \theta) = \sigma(a_j + \sum_{i=1}^{V} w_{ij}v_i) \tag{11}$$

The same is true for probability $p(v_i = 1|h, \theta)$:

$$p(v_i = 1|h, \theta) = \sigma(b_i + \sum_{j=1}^{H} w_{ij}h_i) \tag{12}$$

Maximum likelihood training can not be implemented for large RBM because the problem of calculation of log probability derivative for training data D is exponential. However paper [8] offers an efficient training procedure implying increment of parameters as the following:

$$\Delta w_{ij} \propto \langle v_i h_j \rangle_{data} - \langle v_i h_j \rangle_{reconstruction} \tag{13}$$

The first right summand is occurrence frequency, when $v_i = 1$ and $h_j = 1$ simultaneously, when input receives vector v from the training sample and h is calculated by means of random-number generator in correspondence with probability distribution (11). The second summand is frequency of the same occurrence when vector v is reconstruction of input data corresponding to probability (12). It's essential that reconstruction should not depend on input vector v, hence procedure of generation h and further reconstruction of v is repeated several times.

When input vector elements are real numbers we eliminate an unlimited growth of elements for vector v through transforming energy equation as the following:

$$E(v, h|\theta) = \sum_{i=1}^{V} \frac{(v_i - b_i)^2}{2} - \sum_{i=1}^{V}\sum_{j=1}^{H} w_{ij}v_ih_j - \sum_{j=1}^{H} a_jh_j \tag{14}$$

And equation $p(v_i|h, \theta)$ like this:

$$p(v_i|h, \theta) = N(b_i + \sum_{j=1}^{H} w_{ij}h_j, 1) \tag{15}$$

where $N(\mu, \Sigma)$ - normal distribution with mean vector μ and covariance matrix Σ. The present paper uses normalized input data therefore covariance matrix is identity matrix. RBM with real input vectors is called Gaussian-Bernoulli RBM (GRMB).

2.3   Experiment Description and Results

The paper takes up an experimental research into hybrid DBN-HMM systems for continuous Russian speech recognition. Experiments were carried out on a telephone database collected by speech processing lab of FSSI "Research Institute "Spezvuzau- tomatika", Transcribed part of the database was divided into three parts: 25 hours were used for training, 1 hour was used for validation and 1 hour for test. In addition 17 hours of unlabeled speech were used for pretraining of DBN.

We used Theano [9] library for neural networks, this library is implemented in Python with C extensions. We used HTK library for speech recognition and evaluation of testing results.

26 melcepstral coefficients normalized by global dispersion were used as feature vectors. 15 feature vectors widow was used to take the account of context. Therefore the resulting feature vectors came to 390.

Our research investigated DBN with 2, 3 and 5 layers with 1000 elements for one layer. We used the above-mentioned procedure for DBN training.

Continuous speech recognition involved 650 000 words vocabulary. 2-gram and 3-gram language models trained on the database collected by speech processing lab of FSSI "Research Institute "Spezvuzautomatika" (200 million words), were applied for recognition. Recognition was performed on the basis of probabilities, obtained by DBN.

The process involved 2 stages:

 – recognition with 2-gram language model and lattice building
 – lattice rescoring with 3-gram language model

Table 1. Results of test

Model	Accuracy
triphones	41%
DBN: 2 layers x 1000 el.	28%
DBN: 3 layers x 1000 el.	33%
DBN: 5 layers x 1000 el.	45%

As base system we used a context dependent HMM (phones) based system. The results are presented in table 1.

2.4 Conclusion

HMMs possess a number of drawbacks which impose a limitation on the further increase of accuracy of speech recognition. Multilayered neural networks are promising substitution for HMMs. The progress of computer technology and appearance of new algorithms of training of multilayered neural networks made it more actual. The research efforts of multilayered neural networks in the field of speech recognition have intensified recently and significant progress is already achieved in this area. In this article deep neural networks were applied for modelling phonemes of Russian with the subsequent recognition of speech. The window of the big size (15 windows in the size 0.01 sec.) was used to include the context, which captured a feature vectors, belonging to adjacent phonemes. Deep neural networks calculated a posteriori probabilities of phonemes states which then were used for recognition of speech. The experiments on recognition of speech from the telephone channel have shown, that deep neural networks can demonstrate better quality of acoustic modelling in comparison with HMMs. The further progress of the described approach is connected with an increase of an amount of data for the pretraining stage of deep neural networks training and investigation of possible applications of deep neural networks with other configurations.

References

1. Rabiner, L.R.: A tutorial on hidden Markov models and selected applications in speech recognition. Proceedings of the IEEE 77(2), 257–285 (1989)
2. Graves, A., Fernández, S., Schmidhuber, J.: Bidirectional LSTM Networks for Improved Phoneme Classification and Recognition. In: Duch, W., Kacprzyk, J., Oja, E., Zadrożny, S. (eds.) ICANN 2005. LNCS, vol. 3697, pp. 799–804. Springer, Heidelberg (2005)
3. Hochreiter, S., Schmidhuber, J.: Long Short-Term Memory. Neural Computation 9(8), 1735–1780 (1997)
4. Hinton, G., Deng, L., Yu, D., Dahl, G., Mohamed, A.-R., Jaitly, N., Senior, A.W., Vanhoucke, V., Nguyen, P., Sainath, T., Kingsbury, B.: Deep Neural Networks for Acoustic Modeling in Speech Recognition. Signal Processing Magazine (2012)
5. Hinton, G.E., Osindero, S., Teh, Y.: A fast learning algorithm for deep belief nets. Neural Computation 18, 1527–1554 (2006)

6. Young, S.J., Russel, N.H., Thornton, J.H.S.: Token Passing: A Simple Conceptual Model for Connected Speech Recognition Systems, Cambridge University, technical report (1989)
7. Young, S.J.: The HTK Book. Version 3.4 (2006)
8. Hinton, G.E.: Training products of experts by minimizing contrastive divergence. Neural Computation 14(8), 1711–1800 (2002)
9. Bergstra, J., Breuleux, O., Bastien, F., Lamblin, P., Pascanu, R., Desjardins, G., Turian, J., Warde-Farley, D., Bengio, Y.: Theano: A CPU and GPU Math Expression Compiler. In: Proceedings of the Python for Scientific Computing Conference (SciPy), Austin, June 30-July 3 (2010)

An Analysis of Speech Signals of the Choapam Variant Zapotec Language

Gabriela Oliva-Juarez, Fabiola Martínez-Licona, Alma Martínez-Licona,
and John Goddard-Close

Universidad Autonoma Metropolitana, Electrical Engineering Depto., Mexico City, Mexico
{fmml,aaml,jgc}@xanum.uam.mx, gaby7884@gmail.com

Abstract. The Zapotec language, as well as many other prehispanic languages in Mexico, is endangered for many reasons including a lack of use by the younger population who prefer to speak Spanish instead, and by the dying out of older native speakers. In this paper an analysis of the Choapam variant of Zapotec is presented; a list of words in this Zapotec was recorded, and a time and formant analysis was carried out in order to obtain basic information used to describe the language. The formant analysis focused on the vowels in the language, due complications which arise with them, and gives a first classification of them. Some of the difficulties experienced in the study, which are similar to those encountered with many other endangered languages, are detailed. Although this is a first approach to these languages analysis, it is hoped that the use of this information will contribute to further efforts aimed at helping preserve the language.

Keywords: Speech analysis, Zapotec vowels, Prehispanic languages.

1 Introduction

In communication, languages present the most dynamic behavior; languages are continuously evolving, and as a consequence, some of them prevail and others disappear. The use of a particular language, and the conservation of its primary characteristics, is a critical issue towards providing a sense of identification among the communities speaking it. When the language begins to fall into disuse, there is a risk of its extinction as native speakers die off and the new generations prefer to speak in modern languages such as English or Spanish. Migration also contributes to this phenomenon. In Mexico languages like Wiyot, Mascouten, Pochuteco or Mangue have become extinct and many others are about to if there are no concerted efforts to keep them alive [1]; the Zapotec language is an example of the latter, since it is spoken by only 425,123 inhabitants [2].

Within a language there may be variants, which are variations around the standard language that identify groups of people, like families or neighbors, or even communities. Some variations are so small that are hardly noticed, and the speakers can understand one other, whilst others are extremely noticeable and can prevent an adequate communication between speakers. The Zapotec language falls into the latter category. The Zapotec language comes from the Southeast part of Mexico and it is spoken in the states of Oaxaca, Veracruz, partly in Chiapas and in a few places in Mexico City.

M. Železný et al. (Eds.): SPECOM 2013, LNAI 8113, pp. 25–32, 2013.

Table 1. ISO 639.3 coding for some Zapotec variants

Zapotec variant	ISO639.3 Code
Asuncin Mixtepec	zpm
Choapam	zpc
Istmo	zai
Mitla	zaw
Ocotlán	zac
Rincón	zar
Zoogocho	zpq

In order to identify the language and its 57 variations the ISO639.3 standard assigned a three-letter code for each one [3], and some examples are shown in Table 1.

The Zapotec language belongs to the Oto-Mangue linguistic family, which is the biggest and most diverse in Mexico. It also belongs to the linguistic group of Zapote-cano that contains the macrolanguages chantino and zapoteca [1,4]. The significant characteristic of this linguistic family is that it is tonal, meaning that it is possible to distinguish words by focusing in the frequency shifts of the vocal folds. The fact that it contains so many variants means that the Zapotec language presents an interesting and challenging problem from a speech technologies point of view. Also, the fact that the language is spoken by fewer people each year, represents an important problem for the preservation of the cultural heritage of these prehispanic communities.

In this paper an analysis of the Choapam variant of Zapotec is carried out. The speech data was collected by recording utterances of a list of words by a native speaker. The duration of the sounds involved was obtained, using the SAMPA phonetic alphabet as a reference. Due to the tonal characteristic of the language, a spectral analysis of the vowels was conducted in order to classify them. The paper is organized as follows: section 2 describes the Choapam variant of Zapotec, section 3 presents details of the development of the database as well as the words selected, section 4 reports the results of the duration of the sounds and the formant vowel analysis and classification, section 5 presents a discussion of the results and issues found during the recording process and the experimentation, and section 6 gives some conclusions and mentions further work that will be undertaken.

2   Variant of Zapotec from Choapam

The Zapotec variant of Choapam is also known as the San Juan Comaltepec Zapotec and is spoken in the municipality of Choapam, which is part of the state of Oaxaca and, according to the Summer Institute of Linguistics, also in the state of Veracruz. The data was obtained from a speaker who lives in Arenal Santa Ana, a community of 1551 inhabitants located in Veracruz [5]; although differences have been reported between the Zapotec spoken in Choapam and Arenal Santa Ana, it should be noted that due to their geographically closeness, they are highly similar. This particular variant is classified as a moribund language by the Expanded Graded Intergenerational Disruption Scale (EGIDS) [6]. This means that the only fluent users, if any, are old and it is too late to restore the natural intergenerational transmission; it is estimated that the number of native speakers of this variant according to EGIDS is up to 10,000, as shown in Figure 1 [7]. The Choapam Zapotec alphabet consists of vowels and consonants [8], which are described in the following subsections.

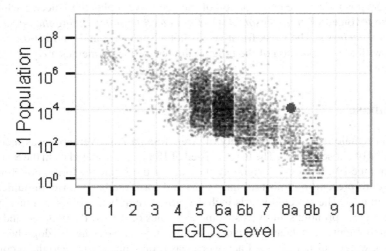

Fig. 1. Location of the Choapam Zapotec within the cloud of all living languages. (Source: http://www.ethnologue.com/cloud/zpc).

2.1 Vowels in Choapam Zapotec

The number of vowels used in the alphabet of this variant of Zapotec is six, five of them are the same as in Spanish plus a sixth vowel, and they are spoken with three different kinds of pronunciation: simple, short and long, as shown in Table 2. The most important characteristic of the pronunciations is the vowel duration. Simple vowels have a duration that is between the short and the long vowels. These latter two pronunciations use larynx modifications to produce an abrupt closure of the vocal cords in the case of the short vowels, and to produce a brief pause between the vowel sounds in the case of long vowels.

2.2 Consonants in Choapam Zapotec

In Choapam Zapotec there are 23 consonants, most of them are similar to Spanish. The consonants are weak occlusive (*b, d, g*), strong occlusive (*p, t, c, qu, k*), weak affricative (*dz, dy*), strong affricative (*tz, ch*), weak fricatives (*z, ż*), strong fricatives (*s, x, j*), nasals (*m, n*), liquids (*l, r*) and semivowels (*hu, y*). The affricative sounds are not familiar

Table 2. Vowels of Choapam Zapotec

Pronunciations	A	E	Ë	I	O	U
Simple	a	e	ë	i	o	u
Short	a'	e'	ë'	i'	o'	u'
Long	a'a	e'e	ë'ë	i'i	o'o	u'u

sounds in Spanish, dz is the combination of the occlusive d plus the voiced *z* while *dy* sounds like a voiced *ch; the consonant* tz *is produced by pronouncing the occlusive* t *and then a voiceless* s. The weak fricative *ž* is not a Spanish sound, and is pronounced as a *z* but with a back position of the tongue; the rest of the phonemes are pronounced as in Spanish.

3   Database

A Mexican female from the community of Arenal Santa Ana, Veracruz was recorded uttering a list of chosen words. The list consisted of 188 words selected from the Swadesh list for Zapotec [9]. Swadesh, originally devised by the linguist Morris, contains the words that are present in almost all languages and form the basis for communication between humans. The selected words included nouns (numbers, colors, animals, parts of the body, etc.), pronouns and verbs; some examples of the words recorded and their translation to Zapotec are: heart - lužtau' (officially: my heart), I - në'di', dog - bécu', to drink - ra'a, water - nisa, red - na. Each word was pronounced twice and the recording process took two sessions. The words were recorded on a desktop PC using Speech Filing System Version 4.8 [10], and a sampling frequency of 16 KHz was used. The speaker controlled the amplitude of the signals and the recording sessions were performed in a quite room. The speaker used headphones with an integrated microphone and repeated the word to be recorded if necessary; previously she checked the pronunciation of the words by asking the elder members of her family about the non-Spanish sounds.

4   Results

The recorded words were automatically segmented using the HTK segmentation model [11]. The consonants and vowels were separated and the duration of each phoneme was extracted. Figure 2 shows the distribution of the duration, in seconds, of consonants (left) and the vowels (right). It can be seen how long vowels duration media tend to have higher values compared to the simple and short pronunciations. It also should be mentioned that the vowels short o (o') and long u (u'u) did not appear in any word of the list, which is why there are only 16 vowels instead of 18. Also the liquid consonant r presented two variations: weak r and strong r, the latter was represented as rr.

   The vowel analysis began with the location of their first and second formant frequencies, in order to identify their properties and similarities to Spanish. Figure 3 shows the vowel location of the six vowel groups and, as expected, the formant configuration is much like those of the corresponding Spanish phonemes. In the analysis, the first five

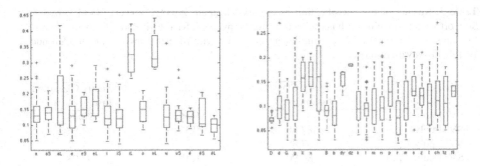

Fig. 2. Duration times of vowels (left, S:short, L:long) and consonants (right)

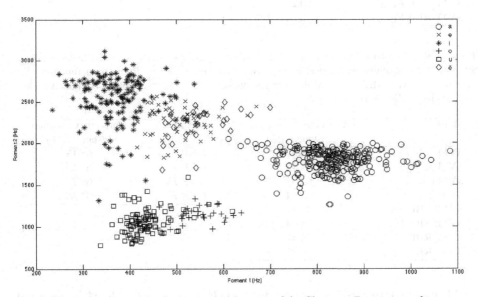

Fig. 3. Location of the first vs second formant of the Choapam Zapotec vowels

formants were extracted and two supervised learning methods were applied to the data for classification purposes. The methods used were support vector machines (SVM), using polynomial and radio basis kernels, and multilayer perceptrons (MLP), with one hidden layer and a number of hidden nodes equaling the number of classes; the results are given for a 10-fold cross validation. Table 3 shows the classification results obtained for the six vowels, and Table 4 shows the classification results of the vowels with their simple, short and long pronunciations Weka3-7-8 was used for all the experiments [12].

In the first case with six vowels, for all the methods tested, the principal conflict in the classification was between e and ë. Since the best results on the classification were obtained with MLP, the duration time was augmented to the format frequencies and the results were slightly inferior: 91.81% correct classification for MLP using formants 1 to 4 plus duration ($F_{1-4+duration}$) with 23% of corrected ë assigned, and 90.99%

Table 3. Results of the classification of the six Choapam Zapotec vowels. SVM kernel Fi-j: Support vector Machine with kernel and formants involved, RBF Fi-j: Radio basis function with formants involved, MLP F_{i-j}: Multilayer perceptron with formants involved (6 hidden nodes, 10-fold cross validation).

Method	Correctly Classified Instances (%)	Method	Correctly Classified Instances (%)
SVM poly F_{1-5}	86.90	MLP F_{1-5}	90.34
SVM poly F_{1-4}	87.88	MLP F_{1-4}	91.98
SVM poly F_{1-3}	87.88	MLP F_{1-3}	91.32
SVM poly F_{1-2}	86.90	MLP F_{1-2}	91.98
SVM: RBF F_{1-5}	60.22		
SVM: RBF F_{1-4}	60.06		
SVM: RBF F_{1-3}	60.22		
SVM: RBF F_{1-2}	50.24		

Table 4. Results of the classification of the six Choapam Zapotec vowels. SVM kernel Fi-j: Support vector Machine with kernel and formants involved, RBF Fi-j: Radio basis function with formants involved, MLP F_{i-j}: Multilayer perceptron with formants involved (6 hidden nodes, 10-fold cross validation).

Method	Correctly Classified Instances (%)	Method	Correctly Classified Instances (%)
SVM poly F_{1-5}	62.52	MLP F_{1-5}	65.13
SVM poly F_{1-4}	63.33	MLP F_{1-4}	66.12
SVM poly F_{1-3}	63.33	MLP F_{1-3}	66.77
SVM poly F_{1-2}	62.84	MLP F_{1-2}	67.26
SVM: RBF F_{1-5}	28.47		
SVM: RBF F_{1-4}	28.64		
SVM: RBF F_{1-3}	28.47		
SVM: RBF F_{1-2}	28.31		

for MLP using formants 1 and 2 plus duration ($F_{1-2+duration}$) with 3% of corrected ë assigned. For the case of sixteen vowels, the best configuration was augmented with the duration time and it was obtained a 67.59% of correct classification on the MLP $F_{1-2+duration}$ configuration; it was not possible to improve the simple, short or long correct classification percentages since all of them appeared disperse along the time and frequency domains.

5 Discussion

The analysis of an endangered language may be difficult because of a number of different aspects that have to be taken into consideration. For example, the grammar,as well as the orthographic rules, must be known in order to form the reference frame of the study; if only a few people speak the language, some of the sounds may change or evolve as a result of the influence of foreign languages and others may disappear. The

Zapotec language, having 57 variants with varying degrees of intelligibility between them, presents a challenge to the characterization and modeling of its sounds. Some facets to consider in the development of a database, and the analysis of the speech signals, have to do with the number of examples, the type of features extracted and the realization of the Zapotec phonemes.

The words selected in the present study, belong to a generic list that was not phonetically balanced. This means that some of the phonemes have few examples, whilst others do not have any. The low classification results might improve with a larger number of examples for each phoneme; this leads to search the words that contain the phoneme required and record them. In a deeper study of the Choapam version of the Zapotec grammar there are few words that contain sounds like the short *o* vowel or the consonant *ž*, a careful analysis of the words, sentences and texts is advisable.

In the Choapam variant of Zapotec the problem of pronunciation is evident. The speaker had doubts about the correct spelling of certain words of the list; although a consultation with a native speaker was made, a portion of the list had to be transcribed using other variants of Zapotec like Zogocho. During the analysis of some of the voiced phonemes, in particular the case of the vowels *e* and *ë*, a mimic phenomenon could be observed: the speaker tended to pronounce the sound much like the Spanish, not allowing the differentiation of the simple, short and long pronunciations of both vowels. The classification methods employed in the paper used the formant frequencies and time durations as their inputs, however, there are other acoustic features that could also be considered, such as intensity, pitch and Mel scale cepstral coefficients. These, together with a larger dataset, could improve the classification rate obtained.

6   Conclusions

A database of Choapam variant of Zapotec was recorded, and an analysis of time and formant frequencies was applied to the vowels. The vowel sounds of this Zapotec variant are similar to the Spanish sounds and a supervised classification method of a multilayer perceptron, with one hidden layer, achieved a high correct class assignation using these features. The problems that were encountered during the speech recording dealt with the confusion on the pronunciation of some words by the speaker and members of her community, which is a consequence of the language's high risk of disappearing. Work is continuing on the recording of more speech samples in this Zapotec, the incorporation of more acoustic and spectral features such as pitch, intensity or MFCCs, and the evaluation of other classification methods. This paper presents a novel approach to the analysis of prehispanic languages using acoustic features of the speech signals. It aims to provide useful information that help to model synthetic voices in order to preserve the language's legacy.

Acknowledgement. The first author would like to thank the Consejo Nacional de Ciencia y Tecnologa (Conacyt), Mexico, for a grant given to her by them.

References

1. Catalogue of the National Indigenous Languages of Mexico, National Institute of Indigenous Languages INALI (2009), `http://www.inali.gob.mx/clin-inali/`
2. National populations statistics, National Institute of Statistics and Geography INEGI, `http://www.inegi.org.mx`
3. ISO639.3 standard, Summer Institute of Linguistics, `http://www.sil.org`
4. Ethnologue Languages of the World, `http://www.ethnologue.com`
5. Social Development Secretary, Community information modules (2010), `http://www.microrregiones.gob.mx/zap/datGenerales.aspx?entra=pdzp&ent=30&mun=130`
6. Lewis, M.P., Simons, G.F.: Assessing Endangerment: Expanding Fishman's GIDS. Romanian Review of Linguistics 55(2), 103–120 (2010)
7. Zapotec, Choapam in the language cloud, `http://www.ethnologue.com/cloud/zpc`
8. Lyman-Boulden, H.: Gramtica Popular del Zapoteco de Comaltepec, Choapan, Oaxaca, 2a. Edicin, Summer Institute of Linguistic (2010)
9. Swadesh lists for Oto-Manguean languages, `http://en.wiktionary.org/wiki/Appendix:Swadesh_lists_for_Oto-Manguean_languages`
10. Speech Filing System, University College London, `http://www.phon.ucl.ac.uk/resource/sfs/`
11. Hidden Markov Model Toolkit, `http://htk.eng.cam.ac.uk/`
12. WEKA, University of Waikato, `http://www.cs.waikato.ac.nz/ml/weka/index.html`

Analysis of Expert Manual Annotation
of the Russian Spontaneous Monologue:
Evidence from Sentence Boundary Detection

Anton Stepikhov

Department of Russian, St. Petersburg State University,
11 Universitetskaya emb., 199034 St. Petersburg, Russia
a.stepikhov@spbu.ru

Abstract. The paper describes the corpus of Russian spontaneous monologues and the results of its expert manual annotation. The corpus is balanced with respect to speakers' social characteristics and a text genre. The analysis of manual labelling of transcriptions reveals experts' disagreement in sentence boundary detection. The paper demonstrates that labelled boundaries may have different status. We also show that speakers' social characteristics (gender and speech usage) and a text genre influence inter-labeller agreement.

Keywords: sentence boundary detection, spontaneous speech, oral text, monologue, manual annotation, Russian language resources.

1 Introduction

After more than fifty years of studying Russian spontaneous speech, the problem of its segmentation into sentences remains one of the key issues for both linguistics and computer science [1,2,3]. The problem is that the oral speech, unlike a written text, does not specifically mark sentence boundaries and therefore cannot be segmented into sentences unambiguously [2,4]. This characteristic is determined by both the very nature of unscripted speech replete with disfluencies of different kinds and language-specific features, e.g. widespread use of asyndetic connection between clauses.

To define units for further analysis, linguists have to tackle the task of oral text segmentation. Though sometimes preference might be given to non-sentence units (e.g. *elementary discourse units* in [5]), a sentence remains the basic syntactic unit for both description and analysis of spontaneous speech. Acquiring information on sentence boundaries is also crucial for natural language processing and automatic speech recognition as it improves language processing techniques and enhances human readability of recognised speech [6,7].

Information about sentence boundaries in unscripted speech may be obtained automatically or manually. This paper describes the results of expert manual annotation of the corpus of Russian spontaneous monologues. They may be of a special interest for both oral speech researchers and ASR algorithms developers because the automatic sentence boundary detection in Russian spontaneous speech is still far from satisfactory [3]. Analysis of experimental data may also attract attention of psycho- and sociolinguists.

M. Železný et al. (Eds.): SPECOM 2013, LNAI 8113, pp. 33–40, 2013.
© Springer International Publishing Switzerland 2013

2   Data and Method Description

2.1   Corpus

The study is based on the corpus of spontaneous monologues. It consists of 160 texts (~55,000 words) recorded from 32 speakers (5 texts from each). The corpus data are balanced with respect to speakers' social characteristics and text types. The speakers were split into several groups based on their gender, age, educational level, and use of speech in everyday life. For the latter criterion we had 3 speakers' categories:

- users: those for whom speech is a means of communication only;
- specialists: those for whom speech is either a subject for study (e.g. linguists) or an "instrument" for teaching (teachers, lecturers non-linguists/philologists);
- professionals: those for whom speech is both subject for study and an instrument for teaching (lecturers linguists/philologists).

There were 8 speakers' groups consisting of 2 males and 2 females. The groups are shown in Tab. 1.

Table 1. Distribution of the speakers between groups according to their social characteristics. Each group marked with a + consisted of two male and two female speakers.

Educational level	Use of speech	Age		
		17–24	25–44	45–65
Upper secondary	Users	+		
	Specialists	+		
Higher/Middle level professional	Users		+	+
	Specialists		+	+
	Professionals		+	+

Spontaneous speech was elicited using five different tasks. In the first task, the speakers read a story (Ivan Bunin's *Bast Shoes*) and subsequently retold it from memory. In the second, they read a descriptive text and subsequently retold it from memory (an extract from Bunin's *Antonov Apples*). In the third task, they examined a cartoon strip *The Hat* by H. Bidstrup and simultaneously described it. The fourth was a description of a landscape painting *The Cottages* by Van Gogh. In the final exercise, speakers commented on one of two themes: "My leisure time" or "My way of life".[1]

The speakers were well acquainted with the person making the recording, which made their speech natural in maximum extent. The recordings were made either in the soundproof room at the Department of Phonetics of St. Petersburg University or in a quiet space in field conditions. Overall duration of the recorded texts is about 9 hours.

---

[1] The obtained texts are characterised by different levels of spontaneity and, hence, speaker's improvisation in the process of text production. Spontaneity and improvisation range from the minimum in text retelling determined by input text features to the maximum in a topic based story which gives the speaker maximum freedom.

2.2 Method

Recordings of unscripted speech were transcribed orthographically by the author. The transcription did not contain any punctuation. For the annotators to concentrate on textual rather than prosodic information, graphic symbols of hesitation (such as *eh, uhm*) and other comments (e.g. *[sigh], [laughter]*) were also excluded. Thus, we tried to focus on semantic and syntactic factors in boundary detection. This is because these factors have been shown to greater affect segmentation than prosodic ones (see [1]). Moreover, as [3] shows, prosodic clues alone do not allow automatic detecting boundaries with reasonable extent of precision in Russian spontaneous speech. It is suggested, however, that the absence of explicit information about a speaker's prosody be to some extent compensated by annotator's prosodic competence, which makes segmentation possible in inner speech.

The transcriptions were manually segmented into sentences by a group of experts consisting of 20 professors and students of the Philological Faculty of St. Petersburg University (Russia) and of Faculty of Philosophy of the University of Tartu (Estonia). Experts were mostly women, and all were Russian native speakers. They were asked to mark sentence boundaries with full stops or any other symbol of their choice (e.g. a slash). Information about the speaker's social characteristics was not provided. According to our approach to segmentation described above, the experts did not have access to the actual recordings. As a result, for each of 160 corpus texts 20 versions of their segmentation into sentences were obtained (3,200 marked texts in total).

3 Data Analysis

3.1 Inter-labeller Agreement

For each position in the text we computed the number of experts who had marked the boundary at this position. This number can be interpreted as a "boundary confidence score" (BCS) which ranges from 0 (no boundary marked by any of the experts) to 20 (boundary marked by all experts = 100% confidence). A reasonable approach would be to accept the place with the BCS not less than 12 (60% of the experts) as the sentence end.

The total amount of positions with BCS > 0 in the analysed texts is 9968. Figure 1 shows that, within the proposed approach, only 27% (2686) of marked positions may be considered as sentence boundaries. Another 73% do not achieve the established threshold.

It should also be mentioned that the number of positions with low expert agreement (BCS < 6) constitutes 52% of all labelled positions, with 22% of the latter positions marked by only one expert. This fact reveals the high extent of ambiguity in sentence boundary detection in unscripted speech.

Sentence boundaries which were defined within the described approach indicate the different extent of, firstly, expert agreement and, secondly, precision in boundary detection. Consequently, we computed two measures: expert agreement and precision.

Expert agreement is computed as $(N_{relevant}/N_{total})*100$ where $N_{relevant}$ is the number of positions with BCS above the threshold (confirmed boundaries), N_{total} is

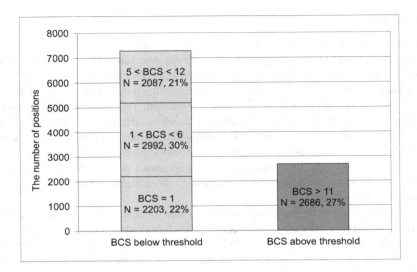

Fig. 1. The number of positions (N) with a certain BCS in the corpus with respect to their relevance for sentence boundary detection

the number of positions with the BCS > 0 (both unconfirmed and confirmed boundaries). Thus, agreement indicates the amount of confirmed boundaries in a text. Lower agreement reveals greater difficulty in sentence boundary detection.

Sentence boundary precision indicates the number of boundaries defined with high extent of accuracy (BCS > 18, 95–100% agreement). Precision is calculated as $(N_{high}/N_{relevant})*100$ where N_{high} is the number of positions with BCS > 18. The higher precision rate the larger the number of sentence boundaries of high status, i.e. boundaries with high agreement rate.

Figure 1 demonstrates that the average agreement in the corpus is 27%. As only 730 positions of 2686 with BCS not less than 12 have BCS > 18, average precision rate in the corpus is 27.2%. In fact, the discrepancies between these two measures may be more significant as it will be shown below.

3.2 Dependence of Annotation and Speakers' Social Characteristics

Gender. The analysis reveals significant dependence between the gender of a speaker and the amount of confirmed boundaries in texts, produced by that speaker (agreement). The experts show higher agreement on speech obtained from female speakers (31.6%) than male (24.4%) (χ^2 (1, $N = 9968$) = 60.2, $p < 0.001$).[2]

There is also significant dependence between gender and the amount of sentence boundary precision. The precision rate is higher in female texts than in male – 30.9% vs 24.6% (χ^2 (1, $N = 2686$) =13.0, $p < 0.001$). The correlation between these measures and speaker's gender is illustrated in Fig. 2.

---

[2] In all cases Chi-squared statistics was computed based on raw counts in corresponding contingency tables. We report percentages for ease of comparison.

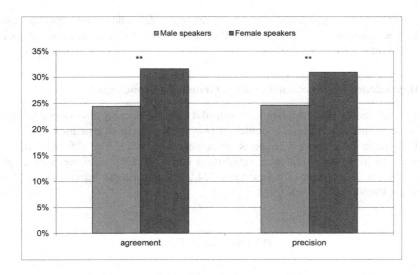

Fig. 2. Inter-labeller agreement and speaker's gender

Age. The data shows no statistically relevant influence of speakers' age on expert agreement (χ^2 (2, N = 9968) = 2.71, p = 0.257) and precision (χ^2 (2, N = 2686) = 1.73, p = 0.421) (Tab. 2).

Table 2. Expert agreement (%) and precision (%) and speakers' age

Age	Agreement	Precision
17–24	25.7	26.4
25–44	27.1	26.3
45–65	27.7	28.7

Educational Level. The results indicate (Tab. 3) no correlation between speakers' educational level and expert agreement (χ^2 (1, N = 9968) = 2.38, p = 0.123) and precision (χ^2 (1, N = 2686) = 0.226, p = 0.634).[3]

Table 3. Expert agreement (%) and precision (%) and speakers' educational level

Educational level	Agreement	Precision
Upper secondary	25.7	26.4
Higher / Middle level professional	27.3	27.4

Speech Usage. There is no significant difference in expert agreement between 3 speakers' categories formed according to speech usage (see 2.1). The results are 27.1% (users), 28.1% (specialists), and 25.8% (professionals) (χ^2 (2, N = 9968) = 4.77,

---

[3] Note that one of the age groups (17–24) overlaps completely with one of the educational levels.

$p = 0.092$). The precision rate is, however, dependent on speech usage (χ^2 (2, $N = 2686$) = 7.28, $p = 0.026$). Precision is lowest in professionals' speech (24.0%). In other categories the results are 29.0% (users) and 28.7% (specialists).

3.3   Dependence of Annotation and the Genre of a Monologue

The analysis shows that the extent of inter-labeller agreement also depends on the genre of a monologue (Fig. 3). Sentence boundary detection appears to be easiest in a description of a cartoon (experts agreement = 34.5%). The difficulty then increases in the following sequence: retelling a story (32.5%), retelling a descriptive text (29.0%), a description of a landscape (24.9%), and a topic based story (22.0%) (χ^2 (4, $N = 9969$) = 122, $p < 0.001$).

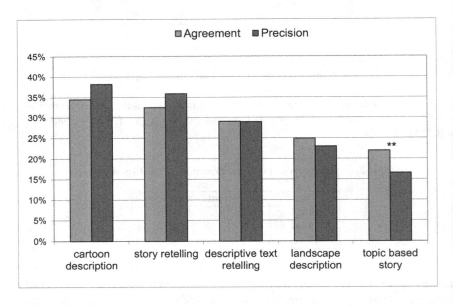

Fig. 3. Inter-labeller agreement and the genre of a monologue

There is also significant dependence between a text genre and the degree of precision in boundary detection. The precision rate discrepancies follow the same sequence: a cartoon description (38.2%), story retelling (35.9%), descriptive text retelling (28.9%), a description of a landscape (23.0%), and a topic based story (16.5%) (χ^2 (4, $N = 3416$) = 59.8, $p < 0.001$).

Note that the precision rate in a topic based story is more than half of that in a cartoon. Furthermore, the difference between agreement and precision in a topic based story is statistically relevant (χ^2 (1, $N = 4572$) = 12.2, $p < 0.001$).

4 Discussion and Conclusions

We have studied inter-labeller agreement in sentence boundary detection. The results are based on the analysis of expert manual labelling of a corpus of Russian spontaneous monologue. We have computed the 'boundary confidence score' (BCS) for each position which was interpreted as a sentence boundary by at least one expert. This step allowed considering the results of manual annotation in terms of expert agreement and precision in boundary detection. We suggest that a wide range of agreement (BCS 12–20) indicates different status of sentence boundaries: the higher agreement, the higher boundary status. Precision shows the number of boundaries of high status (BCS 19–20). Information about the unequal status of labelled boundaries may be valuable data for those involved in ASR development. We have also found that inter-labeller agreement is influenced by speaker's social characteristics and the genre of the text.

The high extent of disagreement in sentence boundary detection manifests itself in, firstly, an unequal number of boundaries marked by different experts in the same text. This may be connected with the labellers' divergent semantic sensibilities about the meaning of the text as a whole.

The other reason for expert disagreement is a different interpretation of the sentence boundary position. This is affected by the fact that, in the process of segmentation, a text segment may be associated with both the previous and following context[4]:

<...> *барыня не могла настаивать и уговаривала Нефеда не ехать 5 не надеясь на успех такой поездки (15). Он тем не менее принял решение и отправился соответственно одевшись в эти Новоселки (20).*

'<...> *the lady couldn't insist and begged Nefyod not to go 5 without any hope for the success of such a trip (15). He nevertheless made a decision and went accordingly dressed to this Novosyolki (20).*'

In this fragment, the adverbial modifier can be attributed to different subjects – the lady and her servant Nefyod, though the second option is inferior to the first one in semantic terms. This ambiguity determines the syntactic function of the segment: an adverbial modifier of reason or concession.

The data analysis indicates that the extent of experts' agreement is significantly influenced by, firstly, speakers' gender and, secondly, the genre of a monologue. The labellers show higher agreement on speech obtained from female speakers than male. This difference between genders was highly significant and can be potentially used as another parameter in automatic gender identification. In the future we plan to explore further the relations between the gender of the speaker and the gender of the expert.

As for the genre of a monologue, sentence boundaries are easier to detect in the description of a plot-based picture, which may be explained by the more transparent semantic and syntactic structure of this text. The finite number of cartoon images (12) influences the choice of lexical and, partly, syntactic items. The main syntactic constituents and cause-effects relations are determined by a limited chain of events in the series. This leads to minimising the extent of the speaker's improvisation and simplicity

---

[4] The numbers show BCS for each case. Round brackets indicate BCS above the threshold considered as a sentence boundary.

of these texts.[5] The second easiest genre for segmentation is story retelling. Consequently, we argue that presence of a plot in a text causes higher inter-labeller agreement and precision.

On the contrary, the agreement is lowest in a topic based story. It is a case of a speaker's maximum creative latitude, which influences and complicates the text structure. As a result, labelling becomes more difficult, which is also proved by the significant difference between agreement and precision.

Thus, such measures as agreement and precision not only indicate the level of inter-labeller agreement and amount of accurately detected boundaries. They also reflect semantic and syntactic complexity of an unscripted speech.

Acknowledgments. The paper has benefited greatly from the valuable comments and questions of Dr. Anastassia Loukina and Dr. Walker Trimble. The author also thanks all the speakers and experts who took part in the experiment.

References

1. Vannikov, Y., Abdalyan, I.: Eksperimental'noe issledovanie chleneniya razgovornoj rechi na diskretnye intonacionno-smyslovye edinicy (frazy). In: Sirotinina, O.B., Barannikova, L.I., Serdobintsev, L.Y. (eds.) Russkaya Razgovornaya Rech, Saratov, pp. 40–46 (1973) (in Russian)
2. Kibrik, A.A.: Est' li predlozhenie v russkoj rechi? In: Arkhipov, A.V., Zakharov, L.M., Kibrik, A.A., et al. (eds.) Phonetics and Non-phonetics: For the 70th Birthday of Sandro V. Kodzasov, pp. 104–115. Jazyki slavjanskih kul'tur, Moscow (2008) (in Russian)
3. Chistikov, P., Khomitsevich, O.: Online Automatic Sentence Boundary Detection in a Russian ASR System. In: Potapova, R.K. (ed.) SPECOM 2011. The 14th International Conference "Speech and Computer", Kazan, Russia, September 27-30, pp. 112–117 (2011)
4. Skrebnev, Y.M.: Vvedenie v kollokvialistiku. Izdatel'stvo Saratovskogo universiteta, Saratov (1985) (in Russian)
5. Kibrik, A.A., Podlesskaya, V.I. (eds.): Night Dream Stories: A Corpus Study of Spoken Russian Discourse. Jazyki slavjanskih kul'tur, Moscow (2009) (in Russian)
6. Nasukawa, T., Punjani, D., Roy, S., Subramaniam, L.V., Takeuchi, H.: Adding Sentence Boundaries to Conversational Speech Transcriptions using Noisily Labelled Examples. In: AND 2007, pp. 71–78 (2007)
7. Gotoh, Y., Renals, S.: Sentence Boundary Detection in Broadcast Speech Transcripts. In: Proceedings of the International Speech Communication Association (ISCA) Workshop: Automatic Speech Recognition: Challenges for the New Millenium (ASR 2000), Paris, France, September 18-20, pp. 228–235 (2000)

---

[5] Only cartoon description provoked the following reaction from a regular expert: "I so hate that Bidstrup!"

Application of l_1 Estimation of Gaussian Mixture Model Parameters for Language Identification

Danila Doroshin, Maxim Tkachenko, Nikolay Lubimov, and Mikhail Kotov

STEL Computer Systems Ltd.,
Bolshaya Pochtovaya. 55/59, 105082 Moscow, Russia
{doroshin, tkachenko, lyubimov, kotov}@stel.ru
www.speech.stel.ru

Abstract. In this paper we explore the using of l_1 optimization for a parameter estimation of Gaussian mixture models (GMM) applied to the language identification. To train the Universal background model (UBM) at each step of Expectation maximization (EM) algorithm the problem of the GMM means estimation is stated as l_1 optimization. The approach is Iteratively reweighted least squares (IRLS). Also here is represented the corresponding solution of the Maximum a posteriori probability (MAP) adaptation. The results of the above UBM-MAP system combined with Support vector machine (SVM) are reported on the LDC and GlobalPhone datasets.

Keywords: language identification, irls, map, robust gmm estimation.

1 Introduction

This article discusses the use of robust estimation of Gaussian mixture model (GMM) parameters for the problem of Language identification (LID). Most modern systems use the Expectation-maximization (EM) algorithm and algorithms based on it for solving this problem [1], [2].

Despite its popularity EM algorithm has strong instability of the initial parameters and of the inconsistent data [3]. Review of the methods based on modeling the inconsistent data is presented in [4]. There are some methods of l_1 robust estimation with application to the related clustering problem that could be found in [5], [6], [7]. In this paper we apply l_1 optimization to get the robust estimates of Gaussians means. The approach to solve the l_1 optimization problem is Iteratively Reweighted Least Squares (IRLS) [8].

The organization of our paper is as follows. In Section 2. we describe the l_1 modification of EM algorithm for GMM training. In Section 3. Maximum a posteriori probability (MAP) adaptation based on l_1 is presented. Section 4.1 describes our feature set and gives a review of our LID system. Finally, section 4.2 discusses experiments and results.

2 Robust l_1 Modification of EM Algorithm

Consider the problem of GMM training with the EM-algorithm from the data $X = [x_0, x_1, \ldots, x_{T-1}]$. Consider the set of unknown parameters of GMM $\Theta = \{c_k, \mu_k, \Sigma_k\}$,

M. Železný et al. (Eds.): SPECOM 2013, LNAI 8113, pp. 41–45, 2013.

where c_k, μ_k, Σ_k are Gaussian weight, mean and covariance matrix respectively. EM-algorithm is iterative, and it is assumed that we have the values of $\Theta_m = \{c_{k,m}, \mu_{k,m}, \Sigma_{k,m}\}$ on the m-th iteration. The problem is stated as an optimization of function $U(\Theta, \Theta_m)$ on each iteration:

$$\Theta_{m+1} = \arg \max_\Theta U(\Theta, \Theta_m). \tag{1}$$

The objective function has the following form:

$$U(\Theta, \Theta_m) = \sum_S P_S\{S|X, \Theta_m\} \log(f_{X,S}(X, S|\Theta)), \tag{2}$$

where $S = [s_0, s_1, \ldots, s_{T-1}]$ is the set of unknown hidden states of the GMM and the sum is taken for all possible S. As it was shown in [9] iteration process (1) converges to a local maximum of likelihood function $\log(f_X(X|\Theta))$. Computing posterior probabilities $\gamma_{k,m}(t) = P_S(s_t = k|\Theta_m)$ at the E-step, the optimization problem (1) reduced to the following:

$$\max_{c_k, \mu_k, \Sigma_k} \sum_{t=0}^{T-1} \gamma_{k,m}(t) \left(\log |\Sigma_k^{-1}| - (x_t - \mu_k)^T \Sigma_k^{-1}(x_t - \mu_k) + 2\log c_k\right). \tag{3}$$

The form of weight $c_{k,m+1}$ and covariance $\Sigma_{k,m+1}$ re-estimate is the same as in ordinary EM [10]. To get the robust means estimate we replace the l_2 part of (3) to the l_1 part:

$$\mu_{k,m+1} = \arg \min_{\mu_k} \sum_{t=0}^{T-1} \gamma_{k,m}(t) \|x_t - \mu_k\|_{l_1}. \tag{4}$$

To solve this problem, we use an approach based on IRLS. Let $\mu_{k,m,n}$ are estimates obtained from n-th IRLS iteration. The approach is to replace the l_1 part of (4) by a weighted l_2 one for each IRLS iteration:

$$\mu_{k,m,n+1} = \arg \min_{\mu_k} \sum_{t=0}^{T-1} \sum_{i=1}^{d} \gamma_{k,m}(t) w_{k,m,n}(t,i)(x_t(i) - \mu_k(i))^2,$$

where d is feature dimension and i is an index of component. Weights are computed using parameters $\mu_{k,m,n}$ taken from the n-th IRLS iteration [8]:

$$w_{k,m,n}(t,i) = \left(|x_t(i) - \mu_{k,m,n}(i)|^2 + \epsilon\right)^{-1/2},$$

where ϵ is a small value that solves the case of undefined weights.

Let $\gamma_{k,m,n}(t,i) = \gamma_{k,m}(t) w_{k,m,n}(t,i)$. The expressions for the $n+1$-th IRLS re-estimate can be represented as follows:

$$\mu_{k,m,n+1}(i) = \frac{\sum_{t=0}^{T-1} \gamma_{k,m,n}(t,i) x_t(i)}{\sum_{t=0}^{T-1} \gamma_{k,m,n}(t,i)}. \tag{5}$$

After the iterations of IRLS stopped on the $\bar{n}$-th, assign values of M-step re-estimation: $\mu_{k,m+1} = \mu_{k,m,\bar{n}}$.

3   MAP Adaptation Based on l_1

Below we consider the problem of constructing MAP model from the UBM using l_1 optimization method described above. Suppose we have a parameters of UBM, specifically the set of Gaussian means μ_k^{ubm}. Initially one iteration of EM is performed, using the only expressions (5). Gaussian weights and covariances are not evaluated. Denote the result of μ_k^{irls}. The MAP estimates μ_k^{map} are obtained in analogy with the usual MAP adaptation method [11]:

$$\mu_k^{map} = \mu_k^{ubm} + \nu_k \left(\mu_k^{irls} - \mu_k^{ubm} \right), \tag{6}$$

where $\nu_k = \frac{\sum_{t=0}^{T-1} \gamma_{k,1}(t)}{\sum_{t=0}^{T-1} \gamma_{k,1}(t) + \tau}$ and τ is a parameter controlling the rate of MAP update.

4   Experiments

4.1   Work of the System

Firstly, it should be trained the UBM. A part of data from each language is taken for training. The initial model is constructed by K-means, and then the EM algorithm is applied. Further there is a re-estimation of the model parameters using the l_1 modification of EM algorithm described above. GMM model of the each language is constructed using the MAP adaptation (6). The third part of our system is SVM. For each language the two-class SVM with the Gaussian radial basis function is trained. Features for SVM

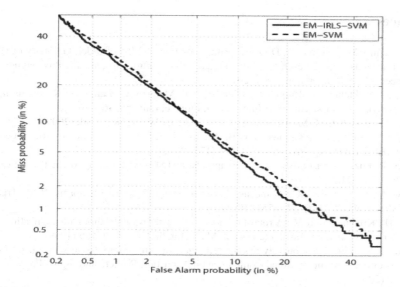

Fig. 1. Language identification results. EM-IRLS-SVM is the robust system (EER = 6.84%), EM-IRLS-SVM is the ordinary EM-based system (EER = 7.16%).

are the z-normalized differences of language GMM and UBM likelihoods for the each data set file. The final result of the identification corresponds to the maximum of all SVM distances.

4.2 Experiments

Experiments were performed using the CallHome, TIMIT, CallFriend, GlobalPhone and LDC Arabic Fisher data sets. Voice activity detector was applied to all the training data. We used PLP-RASTA with SDC (d = 1, p = 3, k = 7) [12] as the features for GMM training. There are 13 coefficients Hamming window and the step is equal 10 ms. To train the UBM we chose 10% data from the each language and mixed it. Below are the results for UBM contained of 256 Gaussian mixtures. To get the robust l_1 estimates 10 EM iterations with 30 IRLS iteration on the each M-step were performed. The each MAP adaptation was with 1 EM and 30 IRLS iterations on M-step. The tests have shown that for your dataset $\tau = 320$ is the optimal. Comparison of the system with and without the use of robust estimation shown in Figure 1. EER of ordinary EM-based system is 7.16%. Robust system gave ERR equal to 6.84%.

5   Conclusion

We have presented a new language identification system based upon robust l_1 GMM parameter estimation. Comparison with purely acoustic approach based upon the EM training showed advantages of new approach.

References

1. Penagarikano, M., Varona, A., Diez, M., Rodriguez Fuentes, L.J., Bordel, G.: Study of Different Backends in a State-Of-the-Art Language Recognition System. In: Proceedings of Interspeech, Portland, Oregon, USA (2012)
2. Martinez, D., Plchot, O., Burget, L., Glembek, O., Matejka, P.: Language Recognition in iVectors Space. In: Proceedings of Interspeech, Firenze, Italy, pp. 861–864 (2011)
3. Huber, P.J., Ronchetti, E.M.: Robust Statistics, 2nd edn. Wiley, New York (2009)
4. Forero, P.A., Kekatos, V., Giannakis, G.B.: Robust clustering using outlier-sparsity regularization. IEEE Trans. Sig. Proc. 60(8), 4163–4177 (2012)
5. Kersten, P.: Fuzzy order statistics and their application to fuzzy clustering. IEEE Trans. Fuzzy Syst. 7(6), 708–712 (1999)
6. Bobrowski, L., Bezdek, J.C.: C-means clustering with the l_1 and l_∞ norms. IEEE Trans. Syst., Man, Cybern. 21(3), 545–554 (1991)
7. Frigui, H., Krishnapuram, R.: A robust competitive clustering algorithm with applications in computer vision. IEEE Trans. Pattern Anal. Mach. Intell. 21(5), 450–465 (1999)
8. Chartrand, R., Yin, W.: Iteratively reweighted algorithms for compressive sensing. In: Proceedings of the 33rd International Conference on Acoustics, Speech, and Signal Processing, ICASSP (2008)

9. Dempster, A.P., Laird, N.M., Rubin, D.B.: Maximum likelihood from incomplete data via the EM algorithm. J. Royal Stat. Soc. B 39(1), 1–38 (1977)
10. Young, S.J., Evermann, G., Gales, M.J.F., Hain, T., Kershaw, D., Moore, G., Odell, J., Ollason, D., Povey, D., Valtchev, V., Woodland, P.C.: The HTK Book, version 3.4, Cambridge University Engineering Department, Cambridge, UK (2006)
11. Gauvain, J.L., Lee, C.H.: Maximum a posteriori estimation for multivariate Gaussian mixture observations of Markov chains. IEEE Trans. Speech Audio Process. 2, 291–298 (1994)
12. Campbell, W.M., Singer, E., Torres-Carrasquillo, P.A., Reynolds, D.A.: Language recognition with support vector machines. In: Proc. ODYS, pp. 41–44 (2004)

Application of Automatic Fragmentation for the Semantic Comparison of Texts

Varvara Krayvanova and Elena Kryuchkova

Altai State Technical University, Lenina st., 46, 656038, Barnaul, Russia
krayvanova@yandex.ru,
kruchkova_elena@mail.ru
www.altstu.ru

Abstract. The article considers the algorithm of extraction of elementary semantic information from texts. Processed texts present articles from natural-science area and have large size and quite arbitrary structure. It is shown that the condensed syntactic graph has enough semantic information for the primary cluster analysis. A two-level model of the semantic cluster analysis is proposed. It's first phase is based on the syntactic graph of the text fragments. We can identify not only keywords, but also non-uniform structural relationships between objects due to the qualitative and quantitative analysis of the lexical items and syntactic relations between them. A simple and efficient method for preprocessing comparison of scientific publications is presented. This method is based on the calculation of clusters of text fragments.

Keywords: semantic analysis, condensed syntactic graph, cluster analysis, text fragmentation.

1 Introduction

A number of researches on the construction of information systems designed to meet the needs of advanced users [1] has strongly increased in recent years. Scientific publications in any area are not subject to strict standardization neither writing procedure and writing style, nor mainly used limited lexicon. This fact naturally complicates the automatic text processing problem of scientific publications for bibliographic and patent search, forming a collection, comparisons and analogies, etc. Most of these problems can be reduced to the automatic cluster analysis problem or to the problem of splitting the set of texts of scientific papers (objects for clustering) into subsets. Objects in each subset would be similar in some parameters, and objects of different subsets should differ in the same parameters as much as possible. The processing of publications in mathematics, physics and other natural-sciences is particularly difficult [2]. The scientific publications research problem which solution is based on preprocessing by comparing information from text fragments is considered in this article.

Real knowledge derived from natural language text can be presented in artificial intelligent systems in the form of semantic graphs, where individual concepts (words or firm word-combinations) are linked by edges [3–5]. But syntactic constructions are no less interesting than it, because syntax carries out semantic information too. Syntactic

M. Železný et al. (Eds.): SPECOM 2013, LNAI 8113, pp. 46–53, 2013.

graph can be considered from multiple positions [6, 7]. From our point of view, syntactic relations are primitive semantic relations between objects they associate. Thus, they can be the primary basis for the deeper semantic analysis.

We propose to use two levels of text processing in this article:

- An elementary semantic level, which corresponding to the syntactic graph. This level is a largely dependent on natural language.
- A fundamental semantic level. This level defines a language-neutral relationships between different objects. Moreover, this level is determined solely by the semantics of objects, by their attributes and operations on them.

Problems, which at first sight depend solely on the semantics of the text, can be effectively solved not only with suitable basic semantic data, but also on the basis of preprocessing of text at the elementary level.

2 Mathematical Text Model

2.1 The Fragmentation Problem

Any scientific publication has uniform structure. In such text we can select some text fragments of different types:

- A description of the problem in general, i. e. information that contains data, which is related to the topic of publication, but it is not main content of the text.
- Meaningful description of the problem and its solution. It is the main goal of scientific publication. This part can be represented as a semantic content in a single fragment or as a set of such fragments.
- Not very informative text. For example it is a link to the source (possibly with a detailed discussion), gratitudes, information on the financing of research, etc.

It is necessary to select text fragments with different semantic specification for a correct semantic analysis of article as a whole text with complex structure. So we need to process a scientific publication by the analysis of fragments.

Scientific texts are already divided into sections and subsections by captions, but these boundaries do not coincide with the required ones. For example, we can find the description of the objects interaction and definitions in one section, and on the contrary, the description of the objects interaction can be separated into several non-contiguous sections.

We will consider natural-science texts of the middle and big size (number of words – from 5000) in Russian.

2.2 Syntax Graph of the Text

Syntax networks [8] between words in text can be represented as syntactic graph. Vertices of the graph correspond to the words of the text, and the edges are labeled by types of syntax relations in the sentence. One sentence is the smallest unit of information that allows us to construct a syntax network. Syntax graph of sentence is, in general, a forest, where each tree corresponds to a syntactic construction.

We will assume that such a tree represents an elementary sentence, which has some semantics. In fact, we can assume that each node, that has N children, corresponds to N-place predicate. Then one elementally sentence corresponds to the superposition of the elementary predicates, and, therefore, is a logically related text fragment. It is obviously, that if the word met repeatedly in the elementary sentence, then the graph of this sentence has multiple vertices with the same label to correctly display the tree.

Let's introduce the following designations: $W(T)$ is the list of all (not just unique) words in the text T; $W_{Noun}(T)$, $W_{Adj}(T)$ and $W_{Verb}(T)$ are lists of all the nouns, verbs and adjectives, respectively; $C_{Noun}(T) = |WNoun(T)|/|W(T)|$, $C_{Adj}(T) = |W_{Adj}(T)|/|W(T)|$, $C_{Verb}(T) = |W_{Verb}(T)|/|W(T)|$ – proportions of nouns, verbs and adjectives in the text.

The syntax graph of the sentence $G_{Synt}(p) = \langle W^U(p), E(p) \rangle$ is the parsing result of the sentence p, where $W^U(p)$ – the set of unique words in the sentence p, and $E(p) = \{\langle w_i, w_j, t \rangle\}$, where $w_i, w_j \in W^U(p)$, t – the type of syntax relation between words w_i and w_j. We use Dialing[9] parser to obtain syntax graph.

The two operations are performed during statistical analysis of text: the dictionary condensation of text graph, and the calculation of the weights for the vertices and edges, that correspond to their frequency characteristics. Way to set the weights of vertices and edges depends on goals of fragmentation [8]. For our problem, the weight of vertex w is the number of occurrences of the word w in the text, and the weight of the edge $\langle w_i, w_j, t \rangle$ is the number of occurrences of this edge in uncondensed text graph.

Let's introduce similar designations for the sets of unique words: $C_{Noun}^U(T) = |W_{Noun}^U(T)|/|W^U(T)|$ for nouns, $C_{Adj}^U(T) = |W_{Adj}^U(T)|/|W^U(T)|$ for adjectives, $C_{Verb}^U(T) = |W_{Verb}^U(T)|/|W^U(T)|$ for verbs. Concentration of these parts of speech is various in different parts of the text and depends on specifics of a text fragment. For example, the quantity of unique verbs increases considerably at the description of a research method or process of objects interaction in comparison with the section of definitions.

As a result, built syntax graph has the following properties:

- words are represented as vertices, and each word is assigned to one of four sets: W_{Noun}^U – nouns, W_{Verb}^U – verbs, W_{Adj}^U – adjectives, others;
- each word corresponds to at most one vertex;
- edges between vertices of the graph are labeled by types of syntax relations between words in the sentence;
- all vertices and edges have weight.

Text is an ordered sequence of sentences $T = \langle p_1, p_2, ..., p_n \rangle$. Syntax graph of the text is an ordered pair $G_{Synt}(T) = \langle W^U(T), E(T) \rangle$, where $W^U(T) = \bigcup_{i=1}^n W^U(p_i)$ – the set of unique words in the text, $E(T) = \bigcup_{i=1}^n E(p_i)$.

Syntax graph $G_{Synt}(T)$ for the long article is a complex structure with a large number of relations. However, a human does not perceive whole text as an indivisible entity while reading, and divides it into definite logical parts, such as the definition of the objects and their properties, the description of object interaction, etc.

Graph $G_{Synt}(T)$ has a number of characteristics [6], that allows to describe the specifics of the text. Let's distinguish some key metrics to be used for fragmentation:

- $C_{Noun}(T) - C^U_{Noun}(T)$;
- $C_{Adj}(T)$;
- $C^U_{Adj}(T)$;
- $C_{Verb}(T)$;
- $C^U_{Verb}(T)$;

The proportion of nouns in scientific texts is much more than the proportion of verbs and adjectives. This fact, in particular, is the high level noise cause in the metrics of $C_{Noun}(T)$ and $C^U_{Noun}(T)$ shear windows on one sentence.

Automatic text decomposition will locate logical and stylistic related text fragments and apply further processing algorithms depending on their features.

2.3   The Text Windows and the Text Fragments

The text window $T_{i,j} = \langle p_i, ..., p_j \rangle$ is a continuous sequence of sentences of text T, where i is the first sentence number, j is the last sentence number, $L = j - i$ is the window size. Sentences from scientific text are not always natural language phrases. The text can contain artificial language expressions, for example, mathematical or chemical formulas. In addition, sentences have different lengths and play different roles in the text. The window size L should be chosen due to these factors and be large enough to smooth out perturbations in syntax characteristics of the graph.

The text fragment is the window $T_{a,b}$, where all subwindows $\langle T_{a,a+L}, ..., T_{b-L,b} \rangle$ belong to one cluster, and windows $T_{a-1,a+L-1}$ $T_{b-L+1,b+1} \rangle$ belong to the other clusters. Strictly speaking, the boundaries of clusters and fragments are fuzzy.

2.4   The Condensation of Syntax Graph

In fact, the structure of syntax network is determined by the problems to be solved on this basis. In this paper, we construct a syntax network for text preprocessing from the position of the cluster analysis. So, this graph should, first, contain statistics of the processed text fragment, and, second, keep the basic structure relations.

Graph $G^C_{sp,L}(T) = \langle W^U_{sp}(T), E_{sp}(T,L) \rangle$ is a condensation of syntax graph $G_{Synt}(T)$ by the part of speech sp. Here $W^U_{sp}(T)$ is a list of unique words, referring to part of speech sp, $E_{sp}(T,L) = \{\langle w_i, w_j \rangle\}$, where $w_i, w_j \in W^U_{sp}(T)$ and there is route in graph $G_{Synt}(T)$ between w_i w_j with length no longer than L, and this route does not contain words from $W^U_{sp}(T)$.

Example of a condensation graph $G^C_{Noun,L}(T)$ of relationship between nouns is shown at Figure 1.

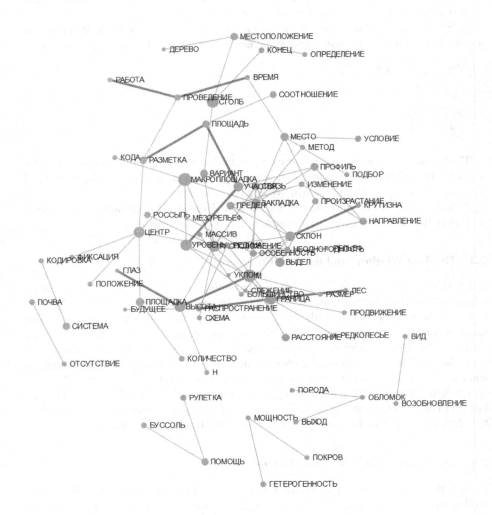

Fig. 1. The condensation graph

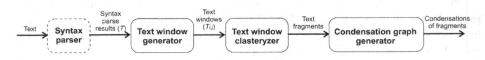

Fig. 2. The general scheme of the fragmentation algorithm

3   The Fragmentation Algorithm

The general scheme of the fragmentation algorithm is shown in Figure 2.

Natural language text is parsed by external syntax parser. A set of consecutive windows $T_{i,j}$ is formed from results of parsing T. Windows generator calculates characteristics for each window, that will be clustering by k-means method. The influence of window size L on the clusterization results is demonstrated by Kohonen map in Figure 3.

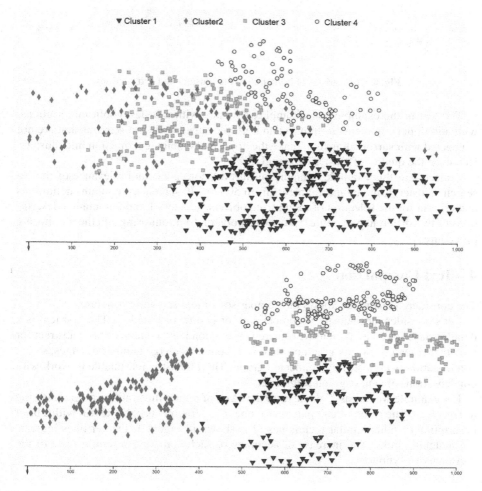

Fig. 3. The influence of window size on the clusterization results. The count of sentence in text is 797. The window size for upper diagram is 40, for lower diagram is 80.

The result of clusterizator's work is a set of fragments. These fragments are clearly divided into a description of methods, the description of concepts and description of the general approaches within a single text. The Figure 4 represents distribution of clusters from the Figure 3 along the text length.

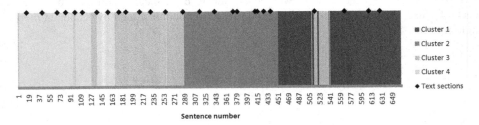

Fig. 4. Comparison of borders for four clusters and text sections

The text in the example has a complex structure with four-level split into sections, with additional comments in frames and multiple cuts. Small text sections that are not connected with surrounding text, make the noise in the main text division into clusters. However, the quality of clustering is high.

Cluster 4 in this example contains an introduction, goals and relevance of the research. Cluster 3 (including fragments from 505 to 540 sentences) contains definitions and criteria for the selection of monitoring objects. Clusters 1 and 2 contain a descriptions of two different procedures: preparing polygon for monitoring and the monitoring procedure.

4   Text Comparison

The considered technique allows the comparison of text semantic structure.

Let's consider mechanism of comparison for two texts T and Q. The first text is a detailed description of a scientific research. The second text contains a brief abstract for the other research. Syntax graph of the text T contains a large number of edges, so it's condensation is almost fully connected graph. Therefore it is reasonable to work with condensations of syntax graph fragments.

For example we use as T the text on the basis of which illustrations for a clustering are received. The result of comparison for one of the fragments of the text T with a brief description of other similar techniques Q is shown in Figure 1. Darker lines indicate the matching links. The increase of accuracy of such comparison requires use of the dictionary of synonyms.

5   Conclusion

This algorithm was tested on texts of various subjects and authorship, including translated texts. Experimental verification of the text pre-processing method showed completely satisfactory results for the initial semantic analysis. In future we will be able to consider syntactic networks in a semantic environment [8], that will significantly reduce processing time and improve the quality of analysis.

Illustrations for this article were obtained using the library D3.js [10].

References

1. Shokin, U., Fedotov, A., Barahnin, V.: Information search problems. Science, Novosibirsk (2010)
2. Solovyev, V., Zhiltsov, N.: Logical structure analysis of scientific publications in mathematics. In: WIMS 2011. ASM (2011)
3. Danushka, B., Yutaka, M., Mitsuru, I.: A relational model of semantic similarity between words using automatically extracted lexical pattern clusters from the web. In: Conference on Empirical Methods in Natural Language Processing, Morristown, NJ, USA, pp. 803–812 (2009)
4. Chenghua, D., Xinjun, L., Haibin, Z.: Wordnet-based summarization of unstructured document. W. Trans. on Comp. 7(9), 1467–1472 (2008)
5. Li, J., Zhao, Y., Liu, B.: Fully automatic text categorization by exploiting wordNet. In: Lee, G.G., Song, D., Lin, C.-Y., Aizawa, A., Kuriyama, K., Yoshioka, M., Sakai, T. (eds.) AIRS 2009. LNCS, vol. 5839, pp. 1–12. Springer, Heidelberg (2009)
6. Lvov, A.: Linguistic analysis of the text and author recognition (2008), http://fantlab.ru/article374
7. Ermakov, A.: Automatization of an onthological engineering for systems of knowledge mining in text. In: The International Conference on Computational Linguistics: Dialogue 2008 (2008)
8. Krayvanova, V., Krotova, A., Kryuchkova, E.: Construction of a weighted lexicon based on linguistic dictionaries. In: IIIrd AllRussian Conference "Knowledge - Ontology - Theory" (KONT 2011) with International Participation, Novosibirsk, vol. 2, pp. 32–38 (2011)
9. Automatic text processing, http://www.aot.ru
10. Data-Driven Documents, http://d3js.org/

Auditory and Spectrographic Analysis of the Words of 2-8 Years-Old Russian Children

Elena Lyakso, Evgenia Bednaya, and Aleksei Grigorev

St. Petersburg State University, St. Petersburg, Russia
lyakso@gmail.com

Abstract. The purpose of this investigation was to examine the peculiarities of recognition by native speakers of a lexical word meaning of Russian 2-8 years old children. Significant improvement of recognition by adult native speakers of words meaning of 8 years old children in comparison with 2-7 years old childrens is established. It was shown that by 7 years stressed vowels in words are significant longer than unstressed vowels; pitch values do not differ in stressed and unstressed vowels, that relevant for Russian. By 7 years accuracy of articulation of vowels, by 8 years most correct articulation of the majority of consonants is formed. The relation between child's age articulation skills and the word meaning recognition by native speakers are discussed.

Keywords: Children, Adult, Meaning of words, Auditory analysis, Spectral characteristics, Vowels.

1 Introduction

As tools for the investigation of speech development, acoustic studies are one of the directions of speech acquisition [1,2]. The most of them are related to analyzing early vocalizations of infants (for example [3,4]).

In Russian it is shown that knowledge of situational context is an important condition for meaning recognition of words and phrases of 2 years old children by adults. Adult native Russian speakers clearly defined the number of syllables and vowels from childs words. Meaning of 3 years old children's words are recognized by adults without situational context. Was revealed that the word stress is formed by the age of 4 years, and a stressed vowel could be distinguished on a base of duration and pitch values [5]. Articulation model of vowels by 5 years is still not formed [6]. The unfamiliar adults recognized the meaning 60-100% of words from the speech of normally developing children [7]. Significant differences in pitch values of stressed vowels from words of 6 and 7 years old are not revealed. Co-articulation effects are defined at 6 and 7 years [8].

The purpose of this investigation was to examine the peculiarities of recognition by native speakers of a lexical word meaning of Russian children of 2-8 years old. The tasks of the study: 1) to reveal the capacity of adult native speakers to lexical meaning 2-8 years old children's words recognition 2) to describe the characteristics of vowels in 2-8 years old children's words.

M. Železný et al. (Eds.): SPECOM 2013, LNAI 8113, pp. 54–61, 2013.

2   Methods

2-8 years old children's words and adults' words were analyzed. The speech material was taken from Speech corpuses INFANT.RU and CHILD.RU [12]. Speech of 8 years old children's and adult's speech were recorded.

Audio recording equipment was: recorder Marantz PMD222 (2002-2005 years), digital recorder Marantz PMD660 with a SENNHEIZER e835S external microphone (80 Hz- 14500 frequency range) (2006-2012 years).

All children were with normally development trajectory without diagnosed speech or auditory abnormalities; weight and height correspond to age norm.

2.1   Auditory Analysis

Auditory analysis of children's words from test sequences (Table 1) was carried out by adult native speakers without auditory disorders.

The words of 5-8 years old children were cut from the phrases. The adult's words were identical with 5-8 years old child's ones. All test sequences contained up to 30 words. All words were presented three times with 3 sec interval; the interval between different words was 15 sec. The loudness level of words in sequences was 40-50 dB, without normalization. The words were presented with headphones Sennheiser - HD 415 (frequency range 14 - 26000 Hz, sensitivity up to 104 dB). Adults should be to define and write the words' lexical meaning and the words' sounding letter by letter. The word's meaning was considered to be recognized correctly if 75% of the auditors defined it right.

Table 1. Experimental Test Material

Age of children	Children, n	Test sequences, n	Spectrographic analysis Words	Auditory analysis Adults
24 months	20	20	450	103
36 months	20	20	450	140
48 months	20	20	400	165
60 months	20	10	2000	165
72 months	15	5	1000	100
84 months	15	6	1500	100
96 months	14	14	420	140
Adult	4	2	160	40
Total number	128	97	6380	953

2.2   Spectrographic Analysis

The speech was analyzed in the Cool Edit sound editor. Frequency of digitization used 44100 Hz. A uniform type of quantization of signals was applied. Each speech signal was saved in a Windows PCM (wav.) format, 16 bit. Vowel duration and its stationary part, pitch value (F0) and first (F1) and second (F2) formant frequency values, were defined. A part of the spectrogram, displayed in a one type of spectrum with constant formant frequencies values and duration no less than 50 ms, and without noticeable articulation modification, was employed as a stationary part of the spectrogram. The boarders of the stationary part were defined in points of frequency changing of spectral components.

Spectral analysis based on fast Fourier transform (FFT) algorithm; data valued in Hamming window and analyzed with 512 points of the sample. The formant triangles of vowels with the tops, corresponding to F1 and F2 formant values of the vowels [a], [u], [I], with two coordinate plots F1 - F2 were built. Triangles areas were compared. The F1-F2 planar area was computed with the following formula for the area of triangles. The formula was adopted for the Russian language [10]:

$$Area = 0,5 * \{(F2[i] * F1[a] + F2[a] * F1[u] + F2[u] * F1[i]) - (F1[i] * F2[a] + F1[a] * F2[u] + F1[u] * F2[i])\};$$

where $F1[x], F2[x]$ first and second formants frequency values for the appropriate vowels.

Phonetic description of the words was made on the base of International Phonetic Alphabet (IPA) symbols.

A statistical analysis was made in Statistica 8, with using of ANOVA, Kruskal Wallis, MannWhitney, and Wilcoxon tests.

3   Results

Adults recognized the meaning of simple words of 2 years old children, consisting of one, two syllables /cot, day, mama/ only. 5% of the words from test sequence were recognized with the probability more than 0.75. Adults with the experience of interaction with children recognized more words (p<0.05 Mann-Whitney) than adults without experiences. Native speakers, having interaction experience with children and without one, recognized the word meaning of 4-5 and 8 years old children with higher probability (0.76-1.0) (Figure 1).

The lexicon of 4-7 years old consists of one till five syllable words. Amount of words with more syllables increases by 7 years that correlates with worsening of recognition of their meaning by adults (55.3%, 48.3% of words correspondingly of 6 and 7 year). The native speakers mistakes during the recognition of the meaning of 3-5 years old words were concerned with a consonant / syllable substitution, delay or replacement. As for the 5-8 years old child's words, the mistakes were primarily concerned with the words termination.

Phonetic description by IPA revealed that in 5 years old words the consonants /ʃ/, /tS/ are not formed; in 6 years - /r/, /Z/, /s/, /s/, /l/, /ts/ are not formed; the replacement of /r/ to /l/, /ʃ/ to/s/; in 6- 7 years - /tS/, /r/, /s/, /ʃ/ are not formed; the replacement of /tS/ to /t/, /r/ to /l/, /r/ to /j/; weaker /f /; in 8 years the replacement of /r/ to /l/. The phonetic description did not reveal the articulation mistakes in adults words.

The vowels' duration in 2-8 years old child's words are 204 ms (median), 212 ms, 195 ms, 137 ms, 135 ms, 129 ms, 134 ms (correspondingly for children age). The stressed vowels duration are higher than that of unstressed vowels at 3 - 8 years of age (Figure 2.A). The difference between the stationary part of the vowels and their full

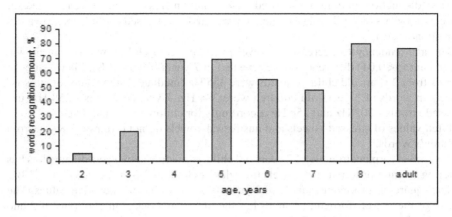

Fig. 1. Number of words recognized by native speakers with the probability 0.76-1.0 Horizontal axis: children's age; vertical axis: words, %

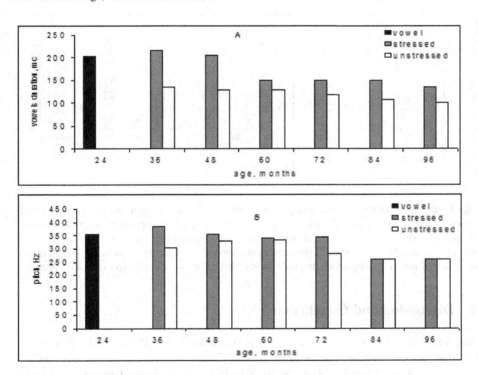

Fig. 2. Vowels' duration and pitch values of vowels from words of 2-8 years old children. Vertical axis: A – vowel duration, mc; B – frequency, Hz; horizontal axis: child's age, months. For age – 24 months – data presented for vowels; for ages 3-8 years – stressed and unstressed vowels.

duration are bigger (p<0.001) in the stressed vowels than in the unstressed ones. The maxima distinction on duration stressed vowels and unstressed ones were revealed for vowels of 3 years old children (135 mc, 105 mc median, stressed and unstressed values correspondingly).

The age tendency to decrease of vowel pitch values in child's words was shown. Significant (p<0.01) differences were revealed in 7 years (Figure 2.B). Pitch values in vowels from 2 years old children words were 355 Hz (median). Pitch values of stressed vowels in words of 3 years old children were 384 Hz, 7 years old ones - 258 Hz; unstressed vowels - 302 Hz and 258 Hz accordingly for children of 3 and 7 years.

Pitch values of stressed vowels and unstressed vowels do not differ in 7, 8 years old children's words.

The vowel formant triangle of 2 years old childrens words at two coordinate plots has differing orientation versus the vowels triangles of children 3-8 years old (Figure 3.B).

The square of a formant triangle of 2 years old vowels has the negative values. The square of the vowels formant triangles has the maximum values in childrens of 3 and 7 years old words (p<0.01). The square of the formant stressed vowels triangle from words of 8 years children is less than ones of 7 years old children.

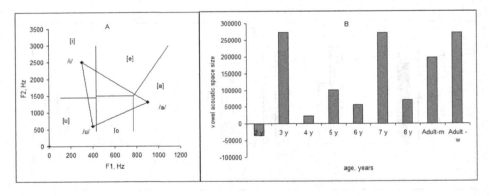

Fig. 3. The values of the formant triangle square of the vowels /a/, /u/, /i/ from the words of 2-8 year olds and adult's speech. A – the example of formant triangle of separately articulated vowels from adult's speech. On a horizontal axis – values of the first formant, Hz, on a vertical axis – the second formant, Hz. Lines specify the borders of phonemic perceptions of vowels. B – the values of square of formant triangles of stressed vowels. Vertical axis – area; horizontal – age, years.

4   Discussion and Conclusion

The ability of adult native speakers to recognize the lexical meaning of the 2-8 years old Russian child's words was demonstrated. The significant improvement in adult native speakers meaning recognition of 8 years old children's words, comparing to 2-7 years olds, was found. The expert estimation did not reveal any significant differences in word recognition between 8 years old children and adults. The auditory data confirmed the phonetic and spectrographic acoustical analysis results.

The clear articulations of vowels, defined in the area of formants triangles of vowels /a/, /i/, /u/, are mastering by 7 years of age. At 8 years of age the vowel articulation is less accurate than at 7 years, and clear consonant pronunciation is formed, according to phonetic analysis data. In recognition of a word meaning of children of 7-8 years, adults marked the mistakes that are connected with the pronouncing of the termination of a word. It is possible to explain this fact by the more complicated grammar of the child utterances, by the desire to inform quickly the listener with the significant information. Hence, with the increase in speed of the pronouncing, leading to reduced pauses and swallowing the termination of words, that is a characteristic of conjoint speech.

Age dynamics of the vowels duration and frequency are shown in Russian. Our data prove the material in different languages. A half-century ago, Peterson and Barney (1952) [11] published their classic article on vowel formant patterns in men, women, and children, showing that formant frequencies for vowels differ substantially across speakers from different age-sex groupings. In English the vowels duration and frequency dynamics were revealed between 9-12 years [12]. The maxima distinction on duration stressed vowels and unstressed ones were revealed for vowels of 3 years old children. The bases of those differences are beginning the opposition "stressedunstressed" [6] and co-articulation context [13].

In Russian, pitch values have decreased since 2-8 years child's words with significance to 7 ages. In different works the widely varying terms of degrees of pitch are specified: in English, since 5 years to 9-12 years [12]; in Korean, since 5 to 10 years [14]. In Japanese revealed a correlation between phonematic vowels' duration and vowels' acoustical space [15]. The task type correlated with pitch and volume of exhaled air at 4-5 years old children were shown [16].

The square of formants' acoustic space [10] has allowed obtaining statistical data on the areas of formant triangles of coronary vowels. The formants' triangle squares differ from children's and adults' vowels and related to the articulation skills realizing in single words and in words in phrases. The prediction from classical acoustic theory is that vowel formant frequencies decrease as the vocal tract (VT) lengthens with age [17]. The real situation includes increasing VT length [10] and heterogeneous of growth of different parts of the VT from birth to 19 years [18] and gender specific in pubertal age [19]. The VT length is longer at 7 years than at 6 years, the length and volume of nasopharynx decrease from 4 years to 7 years [20]. The significant changes of formant frequencies are revealed at the age corresponding to the greatest rate of growth of a VT [10]. Improvement of the motor control of the articulation caused by changes in the length of a VT and in a structure of a mouth at children of 7-10 years are marked [21]. These changes are connected with smaller displacement of a jaw and lips in the pronouncing [22]. The articulation model of Russian words by 8 years completely is not mastering.

Acknowledgments. This research is supported by the St. Petersburg State University (project No.1.0.133.2010), Russian Fund for Humanities (13-06-0041a), Russian Fund of Basic Research (13-06-00281 a).

References

1. Ballard, K.J., Djaja, D., Arciuli, J., James, D.J.H., van Doorn, J.: Developmental Trajectory for Production of Prosody: Lexical Stress Contrastivity in Children 3 to 7 Years and Adults. Journal of Speech, Language, and Hearing Research 55, 1716–1735 (2012)
2. Ting, H.N., Chia, S.-Y., Manap, H.H., Ho, A.-H., Tiu, K.-E., Hamid, B.A.: Fundamental Frequency and Perturbation Measures of Sustained Vowels in Malaysian Malay Children Between 7 and 12 Years Old. Journal of Voice 26(4), 425–430 (2012)
3. Scheiner, E., Hammerschmidt, K., Jrgens, U., Zwirner, P.: Acoustic Analyses of Developmental Changes and Emotional Expression in the Preverbal Vocalizations of Infants. Journal of Voice 16(4), 509–529 (2002)
4. Pols, L.C.W., Lyakso, E., van der Stelt, J., Wempe, T.G., Zajd, K.: Vowel data of early speech development in several languages. Multiling 2006 (2006), http://www.iscaspeech.org/archive/ml06/ml06_010.html
5. Lyakso, E., Gromova, A., Frolova, O., Romanova, O.: Acoustic aspect of the formation of speech in children in the third year of life. Neuroscience and Behavioral Physiology 35(6), 573–583 (2005)
6. Lyakso, E., Gromova, A.: The acoustic characteristics of Russian vowels in children of 4 and 5 years of age. Journal Psychology of Language and Communication 9(2), 5–14 (2005)
7. Lyakso, E., Kurazova, A., Gromova, A., Ostrouxov, A.: Recognition of words and phrases of 4-5-years-old children by adults. In: XI International Conference on Speech and Computer, SPECOM 2006, Saint-Petersburg, Russia, pp. 567–570 (2006)
8. Lyakso, E., Frolova, O., Grigoriev, A.: Acoustic Characteristics of Vowels in 6 and 7 Years Old Russian Children. In: Proc. International Conference INTERSPEECH 2009, Brighton, UK, pp. 1739–1742 (2009)
9. Lyakso, E.E., Frolova, O.V., Kurazhova, A.V., Gaikova, J.S.: Russian Infants and Children's Sounds and Speech Corpuses for Language Acquisition Studies. In: Proc. International Conference INTERSPEECH 2010, Makuhari, Japan, pp. 1981–1988 (2010)
10. Vorperian, H., Kent, R.D.: Vowel Acoustic Space Development in Children: A Synthesis of Acoustic and Anatomic Data. Journ. Speech Lang. Hear. Res. 50(6), 1510–1545 (2007)
11. Peterson, G.E., Barney, H.L.: Control Methods Used in a Study of the Vowels. Journ. Acoust. Soc. Am. 24(2), 175–184 (1952)
12. Lee, S., Potamianos, A., Narayanan, S.: Acoustics of Children's Speech: Developmental Changes of Temporal and Spectral Parameters. Journ. Acoust. Soc. Am. 105(3), 1455–1468 (1999)
13. Lehman, M.E.: Development differences in vowel duration in open and closed syllables. Percept. Mot. Skills 77(2), 471–481 (1993)
14. Lee, S., Iverson, G.K.: The Development of Monophthongal Vowels in Korean: Age and Sex Differences. Clin. Linguist. Phon. 22(7), 523–536 (2008)
15. Hirata, Y., Tsukada, K.: Effects of Speaking Rate and Vowel Length on Formant Frequency Displacement in Japanese. Phonetic 66(3), 129–149 (2009)
16. Brehm, S.B., Weinrich, B.D., Sprouse, D.S., May, S.K., Hughes, M.R.: An Examination of Elicitation Method on Fundamental Frequency and Repeatability of Average Airflow Measures in Children Age 4:0-5:11 Years. Journal of Voice 26(6), 721–725 (2012)
17. Fant, G.: Acoustic theory of speech production. The Hague, Mouton (1960)
18. Vorperian, H.K., Wang, S., Chung, M.K., Schimek, E.M., Durtschi, R.B., Kent, R.D., Gentry, L.R.: Anatomic Development of the Oral and Pharyngeal Portions of the Vocal Tract: An Imaging Study. The Journal of the Acoustical Society of America 125, 1666–1678 (2009)
19. Xue, S.A., Ch., R.W., Ng, L.M.: Vocal Tract Dimensional Development of Adolescents: An Acoustic Reflection Study. Intern. Journ. of Pediatric Otorhinolaryngology 74, 907–912 (2010)

20. Vorperian, H.K., Wang, S., Schimek, E.M., Durtschi, R.B., Kent, R.D., Gentry, L.R., Chung, M.K.: Developmental Sexual Dimorphism of the Oral and Pharyngeal Portions of the Vocal Tract: An Imaging Study. Journ. of Speech, Language, and Hearing Research 54, 995–1010 (2011)
21. Temple, E.C., Hutchinson, I., Laing, D.G., Jinks, A.L.: Taste development: differential growth rates of tongue regions in humans. Brain Research. Developmental Brain Research 135, 65–70 (2002)
22. Smith, A.: Development of neural control of orofacial movements for speech. In: Hardcastle, W.J., Laver, J., Gibbon, F.E. (eds.) The Handbook of Phonetic, Sciences, pp. 251–296 (2010)

Auditory and Visual Recognition of Emotional Behaviour of Foreign Language Subjects (by Native and Non-native Speakers)

Rodmonga Potapova[1] and Vsevolod Potapov[2]

[1] Moscow State Linguistic University, Institute of Applied and Mathematical Linguistics,
Moscow, Russia
RKPotapova@yandex.ru
[2] Moscow State Lomonosov University, Moscow, Russia

Abstract. The "human – human" interaction problem as a basis for "human – machine" investigations constitutes special complexity in the presence of such factors as "native language – foreign language" communication, affiliation to different ethnic cultures. In this connection we set a task of searching for key (basic) features of two-channel decoding (perceptual-auditory and perceptual-visual) of foreign language and other-cultural communication referring to the search of the solution of the verbal – non-verbal communication process modeling characterized in particular, by the final effect of interaction successfulness (consensus).

Keywords: Foreign language communication, emotive information, verbal and non-verbal communication, recognition of emotional behaviour, auditory and visual analysis.

1 Introduction

The middle and the end of the 20th century were marked by a rapid increase of the number of applied researches dedicated to the "human – machine" speech interaction (e.g. [3–6]). Above all the research was centered on issues related to formalization and algorithms of auditory image discerning processes based on the material of isolated sounds, sound combinations, order-words, word-by-word articulated phrases. Later in connection with the development of high technologies the need for decision of "human – machine" interaction problems considering multilingual, multimodal and multi-medial information appeared.

It is clear that research on the domain of "human – machine" interaction turned into scientifically interests of the specialists in the field of fundamental and applied speech studies (fundamental and applied speechology [6]).

At the same time considering *homo sapiens* as a complex biological system [1] including a number of relatively autonomous subsystems (homeostatic, motor-motional, reproductive, perceptual, cognitive, emotive, regulative) for an in-depth study of the "human – human" interaction nature the functional-substantial stratification acquires special importance:

M. Železný et al. (Eds.): SPECOM 2013, LNAI 8113, pp. 62–69, 2013.
© Springer International Publishing Switzerland 2013

- speech behaviour (the simplest: stimulus – reaction, signal – symptom),
- speech activities (coding – decoding of verbal signs in a larger communicative format),
- textual activities (creation of an integral verbal product).

Such subsystems as motor-motional, perceptual, cognitive, emotive acquire special importance in this case [8, 12]. Studying "human – human" interaction, i.e., the process of interpersonal, inter-lingual and intercultural communication, one faces a compound problem – on the one hand, the problem of mono-semantic decoding of the complex behaviour of the communication partner (an addressee) and on the other hand, the problem of semantic coding of information by the addresser, allowing centrifugal and centripetal character of physical and psychical control of speech production and speech perception in the act of communication leading to the necessity to insert the mechanisms of semantic assimilation and accommodation [2, 11, 13].

2 Investigation: Methods, Results, and Discussion

Non-verbal communication, or body language, is a vital form of communication. When people interact with others, they continuously give and receive countless wordless signals. All the people's non-verbal behaviours – the gestures we make, the way we sit, how close we stand, how much eye contact we make etc. – send out strong messages. The non-verbal signals we send either produce a sense of interest, trust, and desire for connection – or they generate disinterest, distrust and confusion. Naturally, non-verbal behaviour varies in different cultures, nations and social groups. The understanding of that depends on many factors, such as success at work, ability to communicate with other people, how information is received or, simply, on how correctly we formulate and express what we mean.

Non-verbal communication is a system consisting of a range of features often used together to aid expression. The combination of these features is often a subconscious choice made by native speakers or even sub-groups/sub-cultures within a language group. The main components of the system are:

- kinesics
- proximity (use of space)
- haptics (touch)
- eye contact (gaze)
- glance
- intonation (voice volume, speech tempo, voice timbre, loudness, melody etc.)
- vocal nuance
- mimic and body gestures
- facial expression
- pauses (silence)
- chronemics (use of time)
- sound symbols (grunting, mumbling, etc)
- clothes
- posture or position of the body
- furniture
- locomotion (walking, running, staggering, limping, etc)

These components may vary from nation to nation. A large number of research works have been carried out on the subject of intercultural non-verbal communication. Still there are certain stereotypes and prejudices in this sphere about English and American test subjects. It is generally considered that Americans are usually more outgoing, friendly and casual, with a typical smile on their faces, while English test subjects are just the opposite - reserved, prudent and formal.

The British and American people have a similar language and culture. But despite the outward similarities, the people in Great Britain and the USA have fundamentally different ways of communicating.

Thus, in England, the handshake is a common form of greeting. Also, they have a protocol of introducing people in business, with the following accepted rules: first, introduce a younger person to an older person; introduce a person of lower status to a person of higher status; when two people are of similar age and rank, introduce the one you know better to the other person. Hugging, kissing and touching are usually reserved for family members and very close friends.

Also, the British like a certain amount of personal space. One should not stand too close to another person or put his/her arm around someone's shoulder. Staring, understandably, is considered to be rude, and makes people feel uncomfortable. If you hold up two fingers in a 'v' sign and the palm faces inward, it means 'up yours'.

Whereas in America the commonly accepted non-verbal patterns of communication are different. The most common everyday rules of non-verbal communication include the following: greetings are casual and quite informal - a handshake, a smile and a 'hello'; people stand while being introduced; only the elderly, the ill and physically disabled persons remain seated while greeting someone or being introduced.

Handshakes are usually brief. Light handshakes are considered distasteful – one should use a firm grip. Eye contact is important when shaking someone's hand. It is typical to keep your distance when conversing. Americans are generally uncomfortable with same-sex touching, especially between males. Americans smile a great deal, even at strangers, and they like to have their smiles returned.

Men and women will sit with legs crossed at the ankles or knees, or one ankle crossed on the knee. It is considered rude to stare, ask questions or otherwise bring attention to someone's disability. One must arrive on time for meetings, since time and punctuality are so important to success-oriented Americans.

The experiment was carried out involving 10 test subjects both male and female aged 20-27 who speak English as a foreign language (Russian native speakers) and American English native speakers. The experiment was divided into two parts. The test subjects were given 10 short film fragments (1-2 min) taken from British and American films in the original: time period years 2001 – 2010. Each Videofile – 30s, fragments were segmented by means of Standard Program Windows Movie Maker. These fragments presented daily human situations between male and female speakers. The first part of the experiment was the perceptual-auditory analysis of communication. The test subjects should listen to the audio material of these film fragments first, *without* having a visual image. Their task was to determine the number of people involving in the communication, emotional mood and non-verbal and prosodic components of the speech.

The main part of audio experiment was to define a national identity of the speakers and ground their opinion.

The next stage was a perceptual-visual analysis. The test subjects were asked to watch the same film fragments without audio signal. Then determine the number of people involving in the communication, emotional mood, subject of the conversation, non-verbal components of the behaviour, national identity and confirmed their opinion. During the experiment the test subjects were not allowed to discuss fragments and worked without assistance.

After carrying out the experiment the results were obtained. The data after the first part of the experiment of perceptual-auditory analysis of communication showed that all informants identified the speakers' national identity correctly. The decisive factor in perception and identification was the accent of the speakers, while the prosodic characteristics did not really play the significant role. But many of the informants (listeners) paid attention to intonation and loudness of the speech, although there were minor factors for their choices.

The second part of the experiment – the perceptual-visual analysis introduced another results. The test subjects find difficulty in determing the national identity of the speakers. Each person has stereotypes in perceiving another people. The test subjects were guided by notions towards the British and American people. Almost all of them gave the same results. They considered more reserved, less emotional, stiff speakers to be the British. And more open, friendly, outgoing, emotional speakers with active mimic and gestures to be Americans.

So based on data of this experiment we can maintain the notion, that the similar nations with the similar language have fundamentally different ways of communicating. The further studies should be carried out to define other differences in body language of the British and American people.

This experiment describes the importance of comprehending non-verbal communication, the way people understand other people and communicate successfully despite the differences in culture. Most people believe that the native speakers in Britain and the USA use the same body language as a result of having cultural similarities and sharing the English language, or, to be more exact, its national-geographic variants. However, in many ways it is not so.

In our study we proceed from the assumption that, close as the British and American cultures are, historical and geographical differences are bound to have created dissimilar specific manifestations of body language.

The present study is based on the stereotypes in perceiving the British and American body language in the context of intercultural communication and the messages relevant for non-verbal understanding.

In the next stage two experiments were carried out to assess the ability of listeners to identify emotion features of verbal and non-verbal behaviour regarding foreign language communication. The experimental corpus (Talk-Shows of German TV) was analyzed by two groups of informants (Russians and Germans) on the basis of two kinds of analysis: simultaneous and successive. Our analysis has shown that the decoding of emotional behaviour of speakers by native and non-native test subjects has some differences. There are some differences regarding the kind of decoding channel too [9, 11].

The experimental investigation under consideration was carried on for a number of years step-by-step within the framework of the bilateral Russian-German project. Native speakers of Russian as well as of German were involved in this research. The experimental corpus for the research was different fragments of German TV-Talk-shows [10].

In the first stage of the research there were simultaneous performed two types of analysis – perceptual-auditory and perceptual-visual – which were based on the material of TS-fragments (time volume = 27 hours). In the experiment took part native listeners of Russian without knowledge of the German language and native listeners of German aged 18-22 (n = 35).

The two-channel analysis by listeners was made repeatedly and simultaneously (i.e. the audio and video information was given at the same time), and included answers to the questions set in a special form* (see below).

Form № 1

- 1. See a TS-fragment and recognize:
  - 1.1. number of participants
  - 1.2. subject of the TS
- 2. We ask you to recognize general emotional frame of the TS-fragment:
  - 2.1. neutral
  - 2.2. joyful-natural (free and easy)
  - 2.3. aggressive
  - 2.4. depressed (sad)
  - 2.5. agitated (strained, anxious)
  - 2.6. other types (correctly)
- 3. We ask you to recognize what means are used to express general emotional frame of TS-fragment:
  - 3.1. Intonation means
    * 3.1.1. melody
    * 3.1.2. tempo
    * 3.1.3. voice timbre ("clear", "toneless", mild (gentle)", acute etc.)
    * 3.1.4. pauses
    * 3.1.5. loudness
    * 3.1.6. other types (specify)
  - 3.2. Face and body gestures
- 4. Try to recognize what stress features (if there are any) are related to:
  - verbal (in particular, intonation)
  - non-verbal (in particular, face and body gestures)

General emotional communicative frame and also the participants had to evaluate with specific contribution of each characteristics just listed.

In the first stage of this research the following conclusions were obtained:

- The two-channel simultaneous (perceptual-auditory and perceptual-visual) decoding of identical authentic experimental material in German by Russian and German native listeners is characterized by certain discrepancy.

- For the Russian native listeners distribution of subjective evaluations regarding the prosody coding is the following: melody and melody with additional perceptual features (60%), tempo (20%), loudness (13%) and pauses (7%).

- For the German native listeners was other distribution: voice timbre and timbre with additional perceptual features (73%), melody (20%), and tempo (7%).

The general structure of divergence of the data received for both groups of informants is the following:

- The same communicative frame, taking into consideration emotionally volume and its emotive evaluation, is being decoded by auditors differently: German listeners evaluation estimated as "neutral" corresponds with Russian listeners evaluation estimated as "excited", "agitated", "aggressive".

- For Russian listeners such characteristic as "neutral" seems not to be the main for decoding, when for German listeners would be main feature.

- The feature "agitated" for German listeners corresponds with the feature "joyful" for Russian listeners.

- General emotional frame decoding of all experimental material for the Russian native listeners is characterized by a wide variety of subjective evaluations including "semi-tones" and "nuances".

- The basic feature for emotive decoding of German speech by Russians is melody itself or melody as a component in complex with other features. And vice versa emotive decoding of native speech by German native listeners is realized by means of voice timbre.

- Comparative analysis of results of the two-channel simultaneous decoding of foreign communication gives the opportunity to maintain that Russian listeners who don't speak German while defining general emotive frame in the process of foreign language communication use non-verbal information as supporting (39%) and paraverbal (paralinguistic [6]), in particular prosodic information as additional.

In the second stage of the research conditions of the experiment were changed. The participants of experiment were provided with new experimental material: TS-fragments from TV-programms selected by German colleagues with business or less emotional /sachlich kooperative Kommunikation/ communication (n = 6, time volume – 9 hours). Native speakers of Russian who don't speak German and haven't participated in any experiments earlier were taken as informants (n =15).

The experimental material was presented to the informants successively (i.e. in series):
a). visual series
b). audio-visual series
The questionnaire was greatly extended (see form N⁰ 2).
Form N⁰ 2

– 1. See TS-fragment and recognize:
  • 1.1 number of participants
  • 1.2 number of men

- 1.3 number of women
- 1.4 subject of the TS (the main problem of discussion)
  * A) business
  * B) entertaining
- 2. We ask you to recognize general emotional frame of the TS-fragment:
  - 2.1 neutral
  - 2.2 friendly (joyful-natural)
  - 2.3 agitated (strained, anxious)
  - 2.4 depressed (sad)
  - 2.5 aggressive
- 3. We ask you to recognize what means are used to express general emotional frame of TS-fragment:
  - 3.1 intonation means
    * 3.1.1 melody
    * 3.1.2 tempo
    * 3.1.3 voice tinge (clear, toneless, "mild (gentle)", acute etc.)
    * 3.1.4 pauses
    * 3.1.5 loudness
    * 3.1.6 regular rhythmic
    * 3.1.7 non-regular rhythm
  - 3.2 face and body gestures
    * 3.2.1 face motions
    * 3.2.2 eye expression
    * 3.2.3 active hand gesticulation
    * 3.2.4 moderate hand gesticulation
    * 3.2.5 absence of hand gesticulation
    * 3.2.6 body movements
    * 3.2.7 absence of body movements
- 4. We ask you what means are used:
  - 4.1 intonation (paraverbal) means
    * 4.2 speech (verbal) means
    * 4.3 Both intonation and speech

3 Conclusion

The sphere of non-verbal behaviour is rather new in science society that is why it is of great concern nowadays. One should bear in mind what non-verbal communication, or just body language, includes. And it has a number of parameters, so called signals that our body sends to our listener. These signals can be divided into two groups: intonational means and mimicry and gestures. All of our non-verbal behaviours – the gestures we make, the way we sit, how fast or how loud we talk, how close we stand, how much eye contact we make – send strong messages. The way you listen, look, move, and react tell the other people whether or not you care and how well you are listening.

The non-verbal signals you send either produce a sense of interest, trust, and desire for connection – or they generate disinterest, distrust, and confusion.

Statistical data analysis has shown:

- Evaluations of emotive information in a successive way of representing foreign language material practically coincide. At the same time transferring to sounds we observe a tendency toward more precise recognition of decoding features.

- Presence of pauses is estimated quite unequally, that from our point of view can be related to the absence of semantic information, seeing that the listeners decoded spoken foreign language perceptually without knowledge of the analyzed language.

- Along with appropriate evaluation of prosodic means (melody, timbre, level of loudness, rhythm etc.) the listeners in this stage with a high degree of accuracy managed to recognize timbre features, in particular with elements of differentiation of men and women voice timbre specificity.

- With a high degree of accuracy the participants of the experiment decoded non-verbal information (100%).

- The results of successive perceptual-auditory and perceptual-visual decoding of emotive information as a whole coincide with the results of simultaneous decoding. However successive decoding is characterized by a greater degree of accuracy, reliability and detailed elaboration.

References

1. Izard, E.E.: Die Emotionen des Menschen. Beltz, Weinheim (1981)
2. Piaget, I.: Psychologie der Intelligenz. Rascher, Zürich (1947)
3. Potapova, R.K.: Rechevoe upravlenie robotom. Radio isvjaz, Moskva (1989)
4. Potapova, R.K.: Vvedenie v lingvokibernetiku. MGLU, Moskva (1990)
5. Potapova, R.K.: Tajny sovremennogo kentavra. Rechevoe vzaimodejstvie "chelovek–maschina". Radio i svjaz, Moskva (1992)
6. Potapova, R.K.: Rech: kommunikatsija, informatsija, kibernetika, 4th edn., Moskva (2010)
7. Potapova, R.K.: Konnotativnaja paralingvistika. Triada, Moskva (1997)
8. Potapova, R.K., Potapov, V.V.: Jazyk, rech, lichnost. Jazyki slavjanskoj kultury, Moskva (2006)
9. Potapova, R.K., Potapov, V.V.: On two-channel decoding of emotive information in the act of foreign language communication. In: Proc. of the XIX Session of the Russian Acoustical Society, Nizhny Novgorod, pp. 572–575 (2007)
10. Potapova, R.K., Potapov, V.V.: Kommunikative Sprechtätigkeit. Russland und Deutschland im Vergleich. Böhlau Verlag, Köln (2011)
11. Potapova, R.K., Potapov, V.V.: Algorithm for decoding of emotive information in Russian-German speech communication. In: Proceedings of the XIIIth Intern. Conference Cognitive Modeling in Linguistics (Corfu), Kazan, pp. 332–337 (2013)
12. Potapova, R.K., Potapov, V.V.: Rechevaja kommunikacija: ot zvuka k vyskazyvaniju. Jazyki Slavjanskih Kultur, Moskva (2012)
13. Rothbaum, F., Weisz, J.R., Snyder, S.S.: Changing the world and changing the self: a two-process model of perceived control. Journal of Personality and Social Psychology 42, 5–37 (1982)

Automatic Detection of Speech Disfluencies in the Spontaneous Russian Speech

Vasilisa Verkhodanova[1] and Vladimir Shapranov[2]

[1] SPIIRAS, 39, 14th line, St. Petersburg, Russia
verkhodanova@iias.spb.su
www.spiiras.nw.ru/speech
[2] Betria Systems, Inc, 50, Building 11, Ligovskii Prospekt, St. Petersburg, Russia
equidamoid@gmail.com

Abstract. Spontaneous speech is rarely fluent due to human nature. And among other characteristics of spontaneous speech there are the speech variation and the presence of speech disfluencies such as hesitations, fillers, artefacts. Such elements are an obstacle for automatic speech processing as well as for its transcriptions processing. For automatic detection of these elements a corpus of spontaneous Russian speech was collected basing on a task methodology. Corpus was annotated taking into account such types of disfluencies as hesitations, repairs, sound lengthening, as well as artefacts. For hesitation and artefacts detection there were used such parameters as duration, energy, fundamental frequency, and other spectral characteristics.

Keywords: Speech disfluencies, hesitations, automatic speech recognition, Russian speech, Russian spontaneous speech corpus.

1 Introduction

One of the main characteristics of spontaneous speech is the presence of such phenomena as speech disfluencies: hesitations, sound lengthening, self-repairs, etc, and artefacts: cough, laugh, etc. The occurrence of these phenomena may be caused by exterior influence as well as by failures during speech act planning [1]. Hesitations are breaks in phonation that are often filled with certain sounds. They are themselves semantic lacunas and their appearance means that the speaker needs an additional time to formulate the next piece of utterance [2]. Filled pauses and lengthening help speaker to hold a conversational turn, expressing the thinking process of formulating the upcoming utterance fragment. Self-repairs appear when speakers want to change partly or entirely some piece of their utterances. Self-repairs may be online: speaker changes a piece of utterance immediately, or retrospective: speaker changes it post factum.

These phenomena are an obstacle for processing of spontaneous speech as well as its transcriptions, because speech recognition systems usually are trained on the structured data without speech disfluencies, what decreases speech recognition accuracy and leads to inaccurate transcriptions [3,4].

Nowadays there are two main types of methods of dealing with speech disfluencies: methods that process them by means of acoustic modeling and use only acoustic

M. Železný et al. (Eds.): SPECOM 2013, LNAI 8113, pp. 70–77, 2013.

parameters, such as fundamental frequency transition and spectral envelope deformation [5,6] and methods that process them by means of combined language and acoustic modeling [7,8].

There are lots of works that devoted to speech disfluences modeling within the systems of automatic speech recognition [5,7,9]. Also there are approaches that deal with speech disfluences at the stage of signal preprocessing [10], as well as speech disfluencies removal using speech transcriptions [9,11].

Thus, in [10] an algorithm, which defines and eliminates filled pauses and repetitions from the speech signal, is proposed. For detection of boundaries of filled pauses the following characteristics were applied: duration, pitch, spectral and formant characteristics. For extraction and further elimination of repetitions the proposed algorithm used duration and frequency of the repeated segments as well as the Euclidian distance between the logarithms of the Linear Predictive Coding (LPC) spectra of each pair of the voiced sections around a long pause. Also the fact that repetitions are usually accompanied by a pause was taken into account.

There are number of publications aimed to rise speech disfluencies recognition quality by means of additional knowledge sources such as different language models. In [2] three types of speech disfluencies are considered: (1) repetition, (2) revisions (content replacement), (3) restarts (or false starts). A part of Switchboard-I as well as its transcription (human transcriptions and ASR output) was taken for research. Normalized word and pause duration, pitch, jitter (undesirable phase and/or random frequency deviation of the transmitted signal), spectral tilt, and the ratio of the time, in which the vocal folds are open to the total length of the glottal cycle, were taken as the prosodic features. Also three types of language models were used: (1) hidden-event word-based language model that describes joint appearance of the key words and speech disfluencies in spontaneous speech; (2) hidden-event POS-based language model that uses statistics on part-of-speech (POS) to capture syntactically generalized patterns, such as the tendency to repeat prepositions; (3) repetition pattern language model for detection of repetitions.

This paper is organized as follows: in the section 2 the methodology for corpus recording and the collected corpus description are given. Section 3 is devoted to description of the method of speech disfluencies and artefacts detection. In section 4 the experimental results of hesitations, sound lengthening and breath are presented.

2   Corpus of Russian Spontaneous Speech

Nowadays for studying the speech disfluencies corpora with Rich Transcriprion [12] are used. As example such corpus as Czech Broadcast Conversation MDE Transcripts [13] may be cited. This corpus is a transcripts with metadata of the files in Czech Broadcast Conversation Speech Corpus [14], and its annotation contains such phenomena as background noises, filled pauses, laugh, smacks, etc [15].

For our purposes a corpus of spontaneous Russian speech was collected based on the task methodology: map-tasks and appointment-task. So that the recorded speech is informal, unrehearsed and is the result of direct dialogue communication, what makes it spontaneous [16]. For example, in Edinburgh and Glasgow was collected HCRC corpus, which consists of only map-task dialogs [17], and half of the another corpus, corpus of German speech Kiel, consists of appointment tasks [18].

Map task dialogs in the collected corpus represented a description of a route from start to finish, basing on the maps. Pair of participants had a map which had various landmarks drawn on it. One participant also had a route marked on their map. And the task was to describe the route to the other participant, who had to draw this route onto their own map. After fulfilling this task participants switched their roles and dialog continued. For dialogs based on appointment task, a pair of participants tried to find a common free time for: a) telephone talk (at least 15 minutes), b) meeting (1 hour) based on their individual schedules. For our investigation several pairs of maps of varied difficulty were created. For the criterion for difficulty the number of unmatched landmarks was used. An example of difficult maps is shown on the Figure 1. Participants could not see maps or schedules of each other. Due to maps and schedules structure participants had to ask questions, interrupt and discuss the route or possible free time. This resulted in speech disfluencies and artefacts appearance.

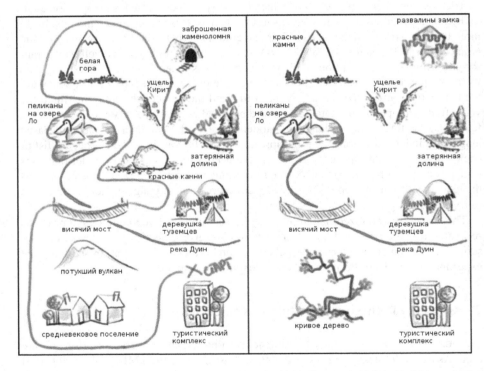

Fig. 1. An example of maps with the route (left) and without the route (right), used in map-task dialogs recording

The recorded corpus consists of 18 dialogs from 1.5 to 5 minutes. Recording was performed in the sound isolated room by means of two tablets PCs Samsung Galaxy Tab 2 with Smart Voice Recorder. Sample rate was 16kHz, bit rate - 256 Kbit/s. All the recordings were made in St. Petersburg in the end of 2012 - beginning of 2013.

Table 1. The distribution of several hesitations (hes.) and lengthenings (len.) among the speakers of different specializations (h - humanitarians, t - technicians)

Phenomena	Speakers											
	h1	h2	h3	h4	h5	h6	t1	t2	t3	t4	t5	t6
Breath	27	27	29	22	14	14	26	11	2	3	20	70
hes. [ə]	25	7	5	7	1	11	5	1	34	18	2	10
hes. [m]	3	6	1	1	1	2	6	4	4	8	3	3
hes. [ɐ]	1	1	2	6	6	2	16	11	2	0	5	4
hes. [əm]	2	1	0	0	2	0	0	0	1	2	0	2
len. [ɐ]	1	7	0	3	10	1	8	1	2	9	4	5
len. [i]	1	7	4	3	4	3	8	1	4	3	3	2
len. [ə]	0	1	1	0	0	0	0	1	3	2	0	2
len. [ɔ]	2	0	0	1	3	0	3	1	0	1	0	2
len. [s]	1	1	1	2	0	0	4	0	0	0	0	0
len. [m]	0	1	0	0	0	0	4	0	1	0	0	1
len. [u]	1	1	1	0	0	0	1	0	0	0	0	1
len. [ʃ]	0	0	0	0	1	0	1	0	0	0	0	0
len. [v]	0	0	0	2	0	0	0	2	1	0	0	0

Participants were students: 6 women speakers and 6 men speakers from 17 to 23 years old with technical and humanitarian specialization (Table 1).

Corpus was manually annotated in the Wave Assistant [19] on two levels: those disfluencies and artefacts that were characteristic for one speaker were marked on first level, those that were characteristic for the other speaker - on the second level. During annotation 1042 phenomena such as filled pauses (for example [ə], [ɐ] hesitations), artefacts (as laugh, breath), self-repairs and false-starts as well as words-fillers were marked.

3   Method of Speech Disfluencies and Artefacts Detection

In this research we have confined ourselves to the most frequent elements in speech disfluencies - filled pauses (hesitations or hesitational pauses) and hesitational sound lengthening, and in artefacts - breath. The basic idea of our method is to find acoustical features of hesitations, sound lengthening and breath in speech signals by using spectrum analysis. Our method assumes that a filled pauses and lengthenings contains a continuous voiced sound of an unvaried phoneme, due to this the neighbouring instantaneous spectra are similar. As the measure of their similarity we have used a cross correlation procedure. As for lengthening of unvoiced fricatives, each can be characterized by wide bands of certain frequencies, while spectrum of breath is similar to the spectrum of white noise with occasional peaks in the low-frequency regions.

In the following, we describe the main procedure of our method (Figure 2). First step was to calculate Fourier transform to acquire spectrogram with the window size of 512 samples and with the step - 128 samples. To estimatea amplitude signal was divided into overlapping frames, where the difference of maximum and minimum in each frame is taken as the amplitude in correspondent moment of time.

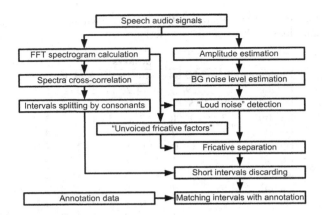

Fig. 2. Scheme of hesitations and breath detection method, where FFT - fast Fourier transform, BG noise - background noise

Then the acquired dependence of amplitude and time was smoothed with the Gauss smoothing. Standard deviation of the Gaussian filter is selected as equal to half of characteristic length of silence intervals. Minimum of this range is taken as background noise level.

For the loud noise detection there were taken intervals, where voice was absent and signal amplitude minimum in 2-3 times exceeded the background noise amplitude.

The absence of voice was estimated by means of the following expression:

$$\frac{\sqrt{\overline{x_n^2} - \overline{x}_n^2}}{\overline{x}_n},$$

where x_n - samples from low-frequency part of instantaneous spectrum.

Intervals with the voice have peaks on spectrum, what leads to numerator increase in this ratio. Thus, the biggest value (<1) of this ratio corresponds to the unvoiced intervals.

The idea of fricative factors is based on that lengthenings of unvoiced fricatives are characterized by wide band (bands) of certain frequencies in the spectrum. The situation of such bands for each unvoiced fricative sound is independent from the speaker.

At this stage to detect unvoiced fricative lengthenings the following temporal series are computed: the ratio of mean value for instantaneous spectrum samples in the band to mean value for samples of the spectrum. Those intervals where the series value exceeds a certain constant (more than 3) presumably contain the sound in question.

For fricatives separation the following actions were performed. For the found intervals values of "fricative factors" were examined by turns to detect among these intervals those that are corresponding to consonant lengthenings. The rest of the found elements were considered as breath.

For every pair of neighboring instantaneous spectra the maximum of their ross-correlation function was computed: $c_t = \max(\text{x-corr}(X_n, X_{n-1}))$, where x-corr is the cross-correlation function, X_n, X_{n-1} - the neighboring instantaneous spectra. The obtained value ct characterizes the constancy of the spectrum (an example is shown on Figure 3).In advance the following normalization was performed:

$$\sum_{n=0}^{N-1} x_n{}^2 = 1,$$

where x_n - instantaneous spectrum samples.

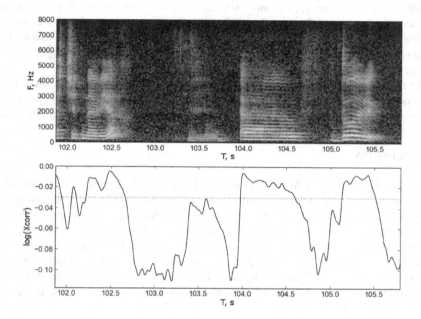

Fig. 3. The upper part of the figure represents the spectrogram, the lower - the logarithm of maximum of cross-correlation function for the neighboring samples (c_t)

Signal is then splitted into intervals, where $c_t > C_{min}$, with c_t described above and C_{min} being a threshold (0.97). The short intervals, shorter than 200ms, are discarded. For each of the found intervals the matching mark in annotation was searched. The case is considered matching, when the length of common part of a mark and an interval exceeded the value of 0.6 of length of both mark and the interval.

4 Experimental Results

A filled pauses, sound lengthening and breath detection system based on the above method has been implemented and tested on a collected Russian spontaneous speech corpus. The accuracy of voiced filled pauses and lengthening detection was 79%. System also has found those lengthening that were missing in the annotation as well as the parts of laryngealized filled pauses and lengthening. Their duration was not enough to overcome the threshold for correctly found elements. So that when solving the problem of laryngealized sounds the detection accuracy will rise up to 87%. As for accuracy of detection unvoiced fricative lengthening and breath - it was 66%.

It is worth listing the problems that appeared during the experiments. One of them is the problem of borders between sounds: fragments that consist of several sounds were detected as one lengthening. This is possible to solve by a) trying to find another criteria for delimiting sounds, b) trying to reduce the influence of main max-imum in spectrum on the value of cross-correlation.

Another problem is laryngealization, which, according to Merriam-Webster dictionary, is an articulation with laryngeal modification, that is produced by or with constriction of the larynx. The possible solutions are: a) to try to enlarge the window size for the purpose of clicks smoothing, b) to use the auto correlation function for laryngealized signal parts processing.

And two related problems - noises and overlappings, which is almost impossible to solve if not recording the data in the perfect conditions. For example the paper riffle sometimes is very similar to lengthening of a /s/ consonant and is detected in-correctly.

5   Conclusion

In this paper the method of filled pauses, sound lengthening and breath detection by using the spectrum analysis is presented. For the experimental data the corpus of spontaneous Russian speech was collected and annotated taking account of speech disfluencies and artefatcts. As an estimation of detection working we have performed the matching with the annotation marks. The accuracy of voiced filled pauses and lengthening detection was 79%. And accuracy of detection unvoiced fricative lengthening and breath was 66%. Solving of the laryngealized sounds problem may rise the detection accuracy up to 87%, what is planned to be implemented in the future work as well as other listed problems.

Acknowledgments. This research is supported by the grant of Russian Foundation for Basic Research (project N° 12-06-31203) and the Committee on Science and Higher Education of the Administration of St. Petersburg.

References

1. Podlesskaya, V.I., Kibrik, A.A.: Speech disfluencies and their reflection in discourse transcription. In: Proceedings of VII International Conference on Cognitive Modelling in Linguistics, Varna, Bulgaria, vol. 1, pp. 194–204 (2004)
2. Clark, H.H., Fox Tree, J.E.: Using uh and um in spontaneous speaking. Cognition 84, 73–111 (2002)
3. Verkhodanova, V.O., Karpov, A.A.: Speech disfluencies modeling in the automatic speech recognition systems. The Bulletin of University of Tomsk 363, 10–15 (2012) (in Rus.)
4. Kipyatkova, I., Karpov, A., Verkhodanova, V., Zelezny, M.: Analysis of Long-distance Word Dependencies and Pronunciation Variability at Conversational Russian Speech Recognition. In: Proceedings of Federated Conference on Computer Science and Information Systems, FedCSIS 2012, Wroclaw, Poland, pp. 719–725 (2012)
5. Masataka, G., Katunobu, I., Satoru, H.: A real-time filled pause detection system for spontaneous speech Recognition. In: Proceedings of the 6th European Conference on Speech Communication and Technology, Eurospeech 1999, Budapest, Hungary, pp. 227–230 (1999)

6. Veiga, A., Candeias, S., Lopes, C., Perdigão, F.: Characterization of hesitations using acoustic models. In: Proceedings of the 17th International Congress of Phonetic Sciences, ICPhS XVII, Hong Kong, China, pp. 2054–2057 (2011)
7. Liu, Y., Shriberg, E., Stolcke, A.: Automatic Disfluency Identication in Conversational Speech Multiple Knowledge Sources. In: Proceedings of the 8th European Conference on Speech Communication and Technology, Eurospeech 2003, Geneva, Switzerland, pp. 957–960 (2003)
8. Liu, Y., Shriberg, E., Stolcke, A., et al.: Enriching Speech Recognition with Automatic Detection of Sentence Boundaries and Disfluencies. IEEE Transactions on Audio, Speech and Language Processing 1(5), 1526–1540 (2006)
9. Lease, M., Johnson, M., Charniak, E.: Recognizing disfluencies in conversational speech. IEEE Transactions on Audio, Speech and Language Processing 14(5), 1566–1573 (2006)
10. Kaushik, M., Trinkle, M., Hashemi-Sakhtsari, A.: Automatic Detection and Removal of Disfluencies from Spontaneous Speech. In: Proceedings of the 13th Australasian International Conference on Speech Science and Technology (SST), Melbourne, Australia, pp. 98–101 (2010)
11. Snover, M., Dorr, B., Schwartz, R.: A lexically-driven algorithm for disfluency detection. In: Proceedings of the Human Language Technology Conference of the North American Chapter of the Association for Computational Linguistics, HLT-NAACL-Short 2004, Boston, Massachusetts, USA, pp. 157–160 (2004)
12. Liu, Y.: Structural Event Detection for Rich Transcription of Speech. PhD thesis, Purdue University and ICSI, Berkeley, 253 p. (2004)
13. Corpus "Czech Broadcast Conversation MDE Transcripts". In: LDC, http://www.ldc.upenn.edu/Catalog/CatalogEntry.jsp?catalogId=LDC2009T20 (accessed May 5, 2013)
14. Corpus "Czech Broadcast Conversation Speech". In: LDC, http://www.ldc.upenn.edu/Catalog/CatalogEntry.jsp?catalogId=LDC2009S02 (accessed May 5, 2013)
15. Kolář, J., Švec, J., Strassel, S., et al.: Czech Spontaneous Speech Corpus with Structural Metadata. In: Proceedings of the 9th European Conference on Speech Communication and Technology, INTERSPEECH 2005, Lisbon, Portugal, pp. 1165–1168 (2005)
16. Zemskaya, E.A.: Russian spoken speech: linguistic analysis and the problems of learning, Moscow (1979) (in Rus.)
17. Anderson, A., Bader, M., Bard, E., Boyle, E., Doherty, G.M., Garrod, S., Isard, S., Kowtko, J., McAllister, J., Miller, J., Sotillo, C., Thompson, H.S., Weinert, R.: The HCRC Map Task Corpus. Language and Speech 34, 351–366 (1991)
18. Kohler, K.J.: Labelled data bank of spoken standard German: the Kiel corpus of read/spontaneous speech. In: Proceedings of Fourth International Conference on Spoken Language, ICSLP 1996, vol. 3, pp. 1938–1941 (1996)
19. Wave Assistant, the speech analyzer program by Speech Technology Center, http://www.phonetics.pu.ru/wa/WA_S.EXE (accessed January 5, 2013)

Automatic Morphological Annotation in a Text-to-Speech System for Hebrew

Branislav Popović[1], Milan Sečujski[1], Vlado Delić[1], Marko Janev[2], and Igor Stanković[3]

[1] University of Novi Sad, Faculty of Technical Sciences, Novi Sad, Serbia
{bpopovic,secujski,vdelic}@uns.ac.rs
[2] Serbian Academy of Sciences and Arts, Mathematical Institute, Belgrade, Serbia
markojan@uns.ac.rs
[3] Brest National Engineering School, European Center for Virtual Reality, Brest, France
stankovic@enib.fr

Abstract. The paper presents the module for automatic morphological annotation within a text synthesizer for Hebrew, based on an efficient combination of two approaches. The first approach includes the selection of lexemes from appropriate lexica, while the other approach involves automatic morphological analysis of text input using a complex expert algorithm relying on a set of transformational rules and using 6 types of scoring procedures. The module operates on a set of 30 part-of-speech tags with more than 3000 corresponding morphological categories. The paper discusses the advantages of the proposed method in the context of an extremely morphologically complex language such as Hebrew, with particular emphasis given to the relative importance of individual scoring procedures. When all 6 scoring procedures are applied, the accuracy of 99.6% is achieved on a corpus of 3093 sentences (55046 words).

Keywords: part-of-speech tagging, speech synthesis, Hebrew.

1 Introduction

Morphological annotation, or part-of-speech (POS) tagging, is one of the well known challenges of computational linguistics, which finds its use in a number of tasks related to natural language processing [1]. Its accuracy can vary depending on a number of factors including the actual complexity of the language in question as well as the number of tags that the POS tagger is expected to operate upon. Within text-to-speech synthesis, the primary purpose of POS tagging is to determine the correct pronunciation of a word, defined by the string of phonemes/allophones and the position(s) and type(s) of stress. In this paper we describe a POS tagger used within text-to-speech synthesis in Hebrew, which is an environment where the accuracy of the tagger is of critical importance.

The remainder of the paper is organized as follows. Section 2 provides an overview of the principal sources of ambiguity in Hebrew. In Section 3 the basics of the proposed POS tagger are presented, with a detailed description of the scoring procedures given in Section 4. Section 5 presents the results of the measurements of tagging accuracy on a previously unseen corpus of text. Finally, Section 6 provides the conclusions and gives an outline of our future work.

M. Železný et al. (Eds.): SPECOM 2013, LNAI 8113, pp. 78–85, 2013.

2   Sources of Ambiguity in Hebrew

Hebrew is a West Semitic language of the Afro-Asiatic language family. In the last two centuries it was revived as a spoken and literary language, with about 5.3 million speakers worldwide, mainly in Israel. Classical Hebrew comprises several evolving and overlapping dialects and is used for prayer or study in Jewish communities around the world. On the other hand, Modern Israeli Hebrew is one of the two official languages of Israel, the other one being Arabic. Modern Israeli Hebrew has a range of properties which drastically contribute to lexical and morphological ambiguity, and therefore the design of a speech synthesis system and the development of speech technologies in general [2]. The phonology, the syllabic structure and the stress patterns are unique to Modern Hebrew. The traditional biblical system in which one-to-one correspondence existed between the graphemes and the phonemes has given way to a more ambiguous one. The meaning of a word is carried not only by its phonological content, but also by its stress. The stress is ultimate or penultimate in Hebrew words and inflections following biblical patterns, although some words exhibit a stress on the antepenultimate syllable, or even further back, which often occurs in loanwords and affixes combined with the traditions of various Jewish communities. Specific rules relate the location of the stress to the length of the vowels in the last syllable. It is not uncommon to find pairs of words containing the same string of phonemes, but pronounced differently, the only difference being the stress.

The Hebrew language belongs to the group of *abjad* languages. Each symbol commonly stands for a consonant. Vowels can be indicated by the use of "weak consonants" serving as vowel letters (e.g. the letter *vav* indicates that the preceding vowel is either /o/ or /u/, *yodh* indicates an /i/, whereas *aleph* indicates an /a/). Another way to indicate the vowels is by using a set of diacritical symbols called *niqqud*. Niqqud is seldom used in order to represent vowels or distinguish between alternative pronunciations of letters in Hebrew alphabet, except in specialized texts such as dictionaries, poetry, or texts for children or new immigrants. Abjad languages, including Hebrew, suffer from very loose spelling rules. For a number of words there can be more than one acceptable spelling, which is a very serious source of ambiguity. The problem has been aggravated by the revival of the Hebrew language in the late 19th century, which has left many unresolved issues [3]. Namely, a majority of Hebrew speakers were previously native speakers of European languages and thus accustomed to the Latin alphabet, which has led to the development of two parallel spelling systems. The first one assumes that vowel indicators are used according to the historic rules, while in the second one vowel indicators are used excessively. Finally, a vast majority of Hebrew speakers today commonly make spelling errors, which constitute a great source of ambiguity in Hebrew and have to be accepted as a part of standard inventory.

As to morphology, Hebrew exhibits a pattern of stems consisting typically of consonantal roots from which nouns, adjectives, and verbs are formed in various ways. It uses a range of very productive prefixes and a multitude of suffixes, that may have various grammatical roles (e.g. articles, prepositions, diminutives), which dramatically increases the number of possible morphological interpretations of each surface word form [4], making statistically oriented *N*-gram based language models impossible for practical use in POS tagging. There is also a significant freedom in the word order, and the syntactic structure of the sentence can be considered as highly flexible. One commonly encounters sentences where several orders of words can be considered equivalent, i.e. having different word order without the influence on meaning, even though particular choices in word ordering can indicate specific literary styles or genres. This is another source of ambiguity for automatic morphological annotation of text.

3   Morphological Annotation

The complexity of a number of tasks related to natural language processing directly corresponds to the complexity of the morphology of the language [5]. A lexicon should contain entries representing each and every possible surface word form. However, the surface form of a word is rarely a sufficient source of information as to how the word should be read or annotated. Words are modified in order to express a wide range of grammatical categories. In case of Hebrew, together with the use of prefixes and suffixes, this results in extremely large vocabularies. It is possible to derive several hundreds of morphological forms from a single lemma in Hebrew. The number of entries undermines the practical usability of the system and makes it difficult to obtain the accurate speech synthesis. A number of morphological and syntactical ambiguities have to be resolved in order to pronounce a word correctly.

The text preprocessing module is charged with conversion of a plain text into a suitable format. It firstly performs sentence and word segmentation. Thereafter, elements such as abbreviations, dates and numbers, punctuation and special characters, web addresses and other non-orthographic expressions are expanded into full orthographic words. The text is further submitted to automatic morphological annotation, with the aim of assigning part-of-speech tags as well as additional morphological information that may be of interest to any subsequent phase of automatic prosody generation. Preprocessing is partly revisited after the annotation, in order to take into account possible changes in the morphological tags of words in particular contexts. The morphological analysis begins by assigning an empty array of "readings" to every surface word form in a sentence. The term reading here denotes a morphological interpretation of a surface word form and its phonological representation. It consists of a particular inflected form of a word, together with the corresponding lemma, values of part-of-speech and corresponding morphological categories, its pronunciation and the position and type of stress. During the evaluation process, an evaluation score is assigned to each of the readings of a word token, with the aim of selecting the reading which is most likely to be correct.

The system presented in this paper uses a combination of the morphology-based method and the lexicon-based method. The morphology-based method involves an automatic morphological analysis of the input text string, as well as generation of appropriate readings by using a complex expert algorithm relying on a set of transformational rules. Even a small fault in the generation module may cause the exclusion of many readings. This is a recursive process, employing a large number of iterations. The use of the morphology-based method reduces the initialization time and the number of inflected morphological forms in the lexicon by two orders of magnitude. The lexicon-based method constitutes a search for a particular input word and a retrieval of a block of all the possible readings from the lexica which contain morphological paradigms of particular lemmas and are generated from the dictionary. Although this approach greatly increases the accuracy, the total number of retrieved readings can still be very high, bearing in mind the language particularities. For that reason, the number of entries in the lexicon is obtained as a tradeoff between the speed and accuracy. Combining the advantages of both approaches, enables the use of the software component within real-time applications.

3.1   Lexicon-Based Method

The lexicon-based method presumes the selection of appropriate lexemes, by using a set of lexica. The lexica contain morphological paradigms of particular lemmas and are derived by scanning all the dictionary entries and generating from each one the full range of derived forms. The input word is searched in all of the lexica and a block of all the possible readings is retrieved. The process requires a heavy generation module where every possible correctly formed text string associated with the Hebrew language has to be included, as well as every possible register, source or style. The lexicon of foreign words in Hebrew transcription contains entries in common use, with or without common Hebrew alternatives, as well as overly technical terms and transliterations of foreign words. The lexicon of frequent foreign words contains entries without the common Hebrew transliteration. Foreign words may not be attached possessive suffixes, but otherwise behave like any other Hebrew words. Hebrew is still in the middle of its self-defining process and many tests we see are full of errors. Some of these forms have become so common that ignoring them would be a mistake. The process should allow the same pronunciation of words with several different forms, as well as different pronunciation of homonyms. Various other types of words should also be included, such as proper names or onomatopoeic words, although they are not usually a part of standard dictionaries. As mentioned before, Hebrew has a multitude of prefixes and a very productive suffixes, both of which are a great source of polymorphism, although not every combination is valid. A majority of such prefixes and suffixes are analyzed in real time, thus an unnecessary explosion of the lexicon size is avoided. The information contained in the lexica should be the smallest possible, allowing proper lexical identification.

3.2   Morphology-Based Method

The morphology-based method involves the application of transformational rules, defined in the form of complex tree structures. Words are filtered in order to remove diacritical signs and analyzed recursively by being disassembled into morphemes. Every word is analyzed from right to left in a forward procedure, and then from left to right in a backward procedure. Each iteration potentially generates a number of readings, depending not only on the current iteration, but according to the left and right context of the word, bearing in mind all the restrictions that apply due to the previously removed morphemes. The aim is to correctly identify the surface form as a particular inflected form of a particular lemma by using morphological patterns. Verb patterns and noun patterns are used in the process of building the word's transcription. Readings are filtered according to their niqqud. If no readings are found in the lexicon, readings are predicted based on their input form, again by using a set of morphological rules including diacritical signs. The method allows the analysis of a sentence in real time, while the number of surface forms in the dictionary has been reduced by several orders of magnitude, therefore drastically reducing the initialization time, without any noticeable influence on accuracy. The number of surface forms in the dictionary has been determined as a tradeoff between processing time and accuracy. The system supports more than 30 POS tags with more than 3000 corresponding morphological categories. Fig. 1. represents the readings for a selected word. In this case, readings are generated by disassembling the prefixes during the forward procedure, and then the suffixes during the backward procedure. Readings are additionally evaluated according to their contexts.

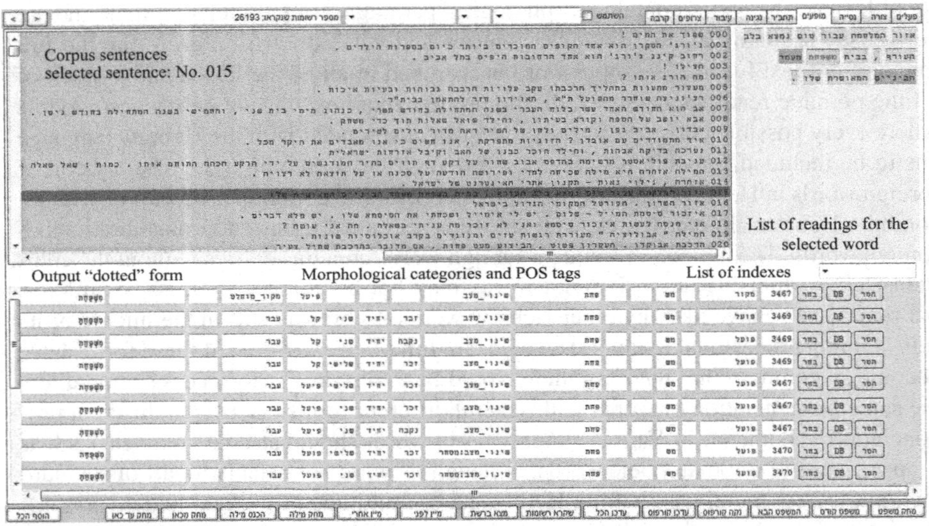

Fig. 1. Generation of readings following the morphology-based method

4   Evaluation Procedures

The evaluation module consists of a set of disambiguation tools, divided into individual scoring procedures, used for the evaluation of particular readings in order to select the most likely one.

Syntactic score. The scoring of syntactic structures assigns syntactic indexes to words using a set of predefined statistical rules. Each syntactic index contains the identification, the number of context windows, the index of the first window, the frequency, and a key containing the indexes of part-of-speech and morphological categories. The algorithm is coupled with an accurate comparison mechanism in order to allow the use of existing indexes in order to project on unfamiliar ones. The aim is to establish the similarity measure between the syntactic structure of the input sentence and the predefined syntactic structures. A syntactic score indicates the level of compatibility of a certain reading to the previously specified syntactic environment.

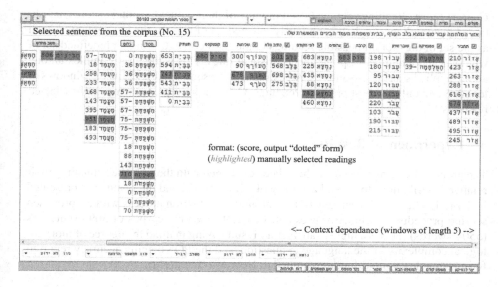

Fig. 2. Evaluation scores for an example sentence

Semantic score. In case of the scoring of semantic structures an analogous method is used. The structures represent semantic relations instead of syntactic ones and the index is built over semantic attributes. The challenge is to build the most convenient set of indexes, and to determine the collection of a minimal number of morphological descriptors covering at the same time the maximum number of words.

Proximity score. There are three types of proximity rules. *Generic to generic* refers to the assignment of a relationship between linguistic items of non-specific identity. The attributes that can be used in composing these rules may be of grammatical and/or semantic nature. *Specific to generic* attach a generic rule to a specific word, while *specific to specific* relate two specific words. Rules are generated in the form of lists, containing sets of values coupled with specific morphological categories. The effect of proximity scoring is limited only to the words and entities for which proximity rules have been defined.

Full-niqqud score. Full-niqqud scoring is a type of scoring developed exclusively for Hebrew in order to determine how close a certain reading of a word is to the most commonly used spelling version. Diacritics are used in order to represent vowels or distinguish between alternative pronunciations or acceptable spellings.

Frequency score. Scoring of readings according to their frequency in standard texts is used in cases when other scoring procedures have assigned approximately equal scores to multiple readings, thus serving as an efficient tie-breaker. Such a procedure usually serves as a baseline for establishing the performance of more sophisticated morphological annotation procedures and it would clearly be highly inaccurate on its own.

Context score. Readings are evaluated in view of their context. Context scores are obtained in compliance with the previously selected set of tags for the left context, as well as the set of tags for all possible readings in the right context, using a predefined set of windows and a number of predefined statistical rules. This is the most complex among all the applied scoring procedures. An example is presented in Fig. 2, using windows of length 5 and only the best previous readings. Green color represents manually selected readings.

5   Experimental Results

The proposed scoring procedures have been examined with the aim of establishing their relative contributions to overall accuracy of POS tagging, and the results are presented in Table 1. The overall accuracy of the automatic annotation process with all proposed scoring procedures included was established at 99.6% on a corpus of 3093 sentences (55046 words). This is a highly satisfactory result having in mind the degree of morphological complexity of the language in question, and the POS tagging accuracy reported for machine learning techniques applied to Hebrew (cf. e.g. [6]).

Table 1. The overall accuracy of evaluation procedures [%]

Scoring	Status								
Syntactic	-	on	-	-	-	-	on	on	on
Semantic	-	-	on	-	-	-	on	on	on
Proximity	-	-	-	on	-	-	on	-	on
F. Niqqud	-	-	-	-	on	-	-	-	on
Context	-	-	-	-	-	on	-	on	on
Frequency	on	-	-	-	-	-	-	-	on
Nouns	13.3	88.4	71.8	32.1	31.9	35.5	98.7	99.4	99.4
Verbs	14.9	94.1	68.3	68.3	41.8	40.1	99.2	99.3	99.6
Adverbs	11.0	91.8	94.6	19.5	19.3	23.2	99.8	99.7	99.8
Corpus	32.1	92.3	85.9	44.7	45.1	46.9	99.3	99.4	99.6

6   Conclusion

In this paper we have presented a POS tagger for the Hebrew language, which combines a lexicon-based approach with an approach involving automatic morphological analysis of text using a complex expert algorithm relying on a set of transformational rules. The surprisingly high accuracy of this POS tagger once again confirms well known facts - that the role of a human in the process of building a successful tagger is still indispensable, and that this process requires a great deal of expert knowledge of the phonology, morphology and syntax of the language in question. Our future work will be oriented on syntactic parsing of Hebrew, with the aim of further increasing the accuracy of the described tagger, but also of modeling other aspects of speech communication such as spoken language understanding and dialogue management.

Acknowledgments. This research work has been supported by the Ministry of Education, Science and Technological Development of the Republic of Serbia, and it has been realized as a part of the research project TR 32035.

References

1. Manning, C., Schütze, H.: Foundations of statistical natural language processing. MIT Press, Cambridge (2000)
2. Aronoff, M., Rees-Miller, J.: Morphophonemics of modern Hebrew. Wiley-Blackwell, San Francisco (2003)
3. Fellman, J.: Concerning the "revival" of the Hebrew language. Anthropol. Linguist. 15(5), 250–257 (1973)
4. Lembersky, G., Shacham, D., Wintner, S.: Morphological disambiguation of Hebrew: A case study in classifier combination. Nat. Lang. Eng. Available on CJO 2012 (2012)
5. Wintner, S.: Hebrew computational linguistics: Past and Future. Artif. Intell. Rev. 21(2), 113–138 (2004)
6. Bar-Haim, R., Sima'an, K., Winter, Y.: Part-of-speech tagging of modern Hebrew text. Nat. Lang. Eng. 14(2), 223–251 (2008)

Comparative Study of English, Dutch and German Prosodic Features (Fundamental Frequency and Intensity) as Means of Speech

Anna Moskvina

Moscow State Linguistic University, Moscow, Russia
annmoskvina90@yandex.ru

Abstract. This paper reports on a comparative analysis of specific prosodic features (fundamental frequency and intensity) used as a means of speech influence in Germanic languages (English, Dutch, German,). The aim of the study is to compare the prosodic patterns of the languages mentioned above in order to find out whether these patterns are similar or they have some differences that are used only in a particular language. The conducted experiment included two types of analysis: acoustic analysis and perceptual analysis. The results obtained during the acoustic analysis supervised by R.K. Potapova testify to the fact that the languages use different prosodic features as a means of speech influence.

Keywords: prosodic patterns, fundamental frequency, intensity, duration, accentuation, temporal characteristics, utterance.

1 Introduction

The investigation of speech influence is of great importance nowadays, as a life of modern man is constantly influenced and threatened by others. Showing some emotions while transmitting information helps to affect people's opinion, believes, will and behaviour. One of the most effective and elusive ways of speech influence is by using prosody.

Every language is known to possess its own prosodic peculiarities that are revealed in speech melody, types of accent, in specific tone structures. Prosody is a compulsory element of any speech unit and plays an active part in organisation of oral texts and their components [3].

At present several terms like "prosody", "prosodic" and "prosodemic" can be found [6]. Prof. Potapova understands "prosody" as a term that is related to a physiological means of speech realisation. For this reason according to Prof. Potapova to study prosody implies to analyse fundamental frequency (Hz), level of intensity (dB) and temporal characteristics (msec). The same approach is used at the present study.

For now it is still not thoroughly examined how the interaction of interparalinguistic means form connotation. Comparative studies are even rarer [8]. That is the reason why the aim of this study was to compare and to analyse the prosodic features and characteristics (such as F0 and intensity) of English, Dutch and German languages. There are a number of papers devoted to the prosody of only one or two of the languages

M. Železný et al. (Eds.): SPECOM 2013, LNAI 8113, pp. 86–91, 2013.

mentioned above: Dutch [1,2]; Russian and German – [5,9]; German – [10], though the comparative study of these three Germanic languages is especially seldom [4].

Though all the languages mentioned above belong to the same language family (Germanic languages) it is obvious that they should differ in use of prosody. This paper attempts to analyse these differences and to establish the possibility to recognise speech influence in a foreign language by people who have been studying it for several years as well as by those, who do not know it at all, that is why no native speakers have taken part in the experiment.

2   Material and Method

For the analysis of the prosodic features used as means of speech influence in different Germanic languages (English, Dutch, German) several samples of spontaneous speech (interviews, only male speakers) were chosen according to the communicative situation. Each participant was aiming to make his opponent change his/her mind.

On the whole 60 samples (20 for English, 20 for Dutch and 20 for German) were chosen. Each sample was numbered and lasted no longer than 1 minute. All the samples were recorded in wav format, mono signal.

Firstly a perceptual analysis was conducted. Only those who have been studying English (and/or German) for several years and showed at least intermediate language competence took part in it (all in all 15 subjects). The task was to fill in the questionnaire with different characteristics and speech peculiarities of each speaker, emotions, evoked in the subjects by utterances and temporal boundaries of samples, where according to the subject they could perceive speech influence. Each subject worked on his own without consulting others.

Then all the questionnaires were examined and the samples where the subjects detected speech influence were put under acoustic analysis. Each phrase then was divided into syntagmas. Here syntagma is understood as elementary constituent segment within speech. Each syntagma has an accented apex that makes its semantic centre [7]. All measurements were conducted with the help of Praat versio 4.0.52 (measurements of intensity) and **ZsignalWorkshop** (fundamental frequency measurement) programs. Frequency range of syntagmas in relative units was calculated by the following:

$$N = 12 \cdot \log_2 \left(\frac{F_N}{F_{ля}} \right) \tag{1}$$

Where N stands for the number of semitones by which the note of the sound under analysis with the frequency FN distinguishes from the note A of the first octave.

Experimental basis for English was samples from analytical talk-show HARDTalk. The following speakers (all used British pronunciation) were chosen:

David Harvey – Anglo-American geographer, one of the founders of so called "radical geography", a leading social theorist;
Douglas Carswell – a British Conservative Party politician, a Member of Parliament;
George Galloway – a British politician, author, journalist, and broadcaster, and the Respect Member of Parliament (MP) for Bradford West;

Hugh Hendry – the founding partner and, at various times, the chief investment officer, chief executive officer and chief portfolio manager of Eclectica Asset Management;

David Millar – a Scottish road racing cyclist riding for Garmin-Sharp;

Nick Clegg – a British politician, Deputy Prime Minister of the United Kingdom and Lord President of the Council;

Clinton Richard Dawkins – an English ethologist, evolutionary biologist and author;

Nigel Paul Farage – a British politician and leader of the UK Independence Party (UKIP) since 2010.

Experimental basis for German was samples taken from the political talk-show AnnaWill. The following speakers were chosen:

Cem Özdemer – a German politician. He is co-chairman of the German political party Alliance '90/The Greens;

Detlaf Gürtler – journalist;

Klaus Kocks – a German economist, PR-manager, journalist;

Peter Zudeich – a German journalist;

Wolfgang Grupp – a German entrepreneur.

Experimental basis for Dutch was samples taken from several political interviews. The following speakers were chosen:

Alexander Pechtold – a Dutch politician, a representative of the Democratic Party;

Carlo – a Dutch journalist;

Mark Rutte – a Dutch politician, the Prime Minister of the Netherlands, the Leader of the People's Party for Freedom and Democracy (Volkspartij voor Vrijheid en Democratie –VVD);

Geert Wilders – a Dutch politician and the founder and leader of the Party for Freedom;

Marcel van Dam – a former Dutch politician and television presenter.

For acoustic analysis phrases chosen by the subjects were cut into segments, each no more than 10 msec at the average, with the help of the program Soundforge 8.

The following acoustic characteristics were examined:

1. fundamental frequency:
   - absolute values of F0 (Hz) within each syllable;
   - frequency interval within the syllables and between them;
   - frequency range of the syntagmas (in absolute and relative units).
2. intensity:
   - absolute maxima within each syllable [8].

3   Results

At the perceptive analysis 60 samples were offered for audition. These were 20 samples in English, 20 samples in German and 20 samples in Dutch. After the audition only those samples that were chosen by the subjects as they contained cases of speech influence (according to the questionnaires filled by the subjects) underwent acoustic analysis. If the sample was described as containing cases of speech influence by more than 10 subjects for English it was examined acoustically further. The problem with German and Dutch samples was that not all the subjects could fill the questionnaires as they did not know any of these languages and even were not able to distinguish speech. As a result only 7 subjects filled the questionnaires for Dutch and German and if the sample was described as containing cases of speech influence by more than 5 subjects this sample was examined further. All in all 14 English samples were chosen for acoustic analysis, 11 German and 6 Dutch samples. After the acoustic analysis the following results were obtained.

3.1 Results for English Language

Fundamental Frequency. All the speakers had approximately the same fundamental frequency that was situated within the boundaries of 80 Hz (the lowest F0) up to 150 (Hz), when the speaker was emotionally calm and up to 250 (Hz) when the speaker was excited. When the speaker wants to transmit relevant information, the one that must be heard by the opponent, the Brits raise the F0 sharply as well as they change the intensity. The beginning of each syntagma, that precedes the main accent, is pronounced 1-1,5 tone lower than in usual state and about 4-5 tones lower, than the accent peak of the whole syntagma, when the speaker is excited. Nevertheless sometimes the difference between the accent peak and the syllables surrounding it approached 14 or even 22 semitones. Probably this occurs due to the individual peculiarities of the speaker.

Intensity. Within the whole utterance the average change of intensity approximately equals 3,8 dB, besides within every syntagma these changes do not exceed 2-3 dB.

3.2 Results for German Language

Fundamental Frequency. Every speaker had approximately the same quite high fundamental frequency. It was situated within the boundaries of 150 Hz and 230-250 Hz, though in some cases there were rises up to 300 Hz. Results show that Germans in order to make an accent peak in the syntagma (while talking to the opponent or showing one's disapproval) raise the fundamental frequency significantly. There are sudden changes up to 8-9 tones both within the syntagmas and at their boundaries.

Intensity. Results of acoustic analysis showed that intensity practically does not change by the German speakers. Within the syntagma, at the boundaries and within the whole utterance the change in intensity does not exceed no more than 1 or 2 dB.

3.3 Results for Dutch Language

Fundamental Frequency All the speakers were chosen so that they had approximately the same fundamental frequency. It was situated within the boundaries of 150 Hz (the lowest measured frequency) and 270-300 Hz. As in German the fundamental frequency had the tendency to rise abruptly when the accent peak must have been marked out.

The beginning of each syngama as a rule started with a lower frequency, at the end of the syntagma fundamental frequency did not go down, as it was needed for preservation of rhythm. Both within the syntagma the frequency changed for several semitones (minimal change equalled 3-4 semitones, maximal change – 6-8, average change – 3,75 semitones).

Intensity. Acoustic analysis of this prosodic characteristic showed that the changes of intensity within the syntagma and at the boundaries approximately equalled 5-6dB, on average – 4,25 dB.

4   Discussion

This paper is devoted to the study of prosodic peculiarities of English, Dutch and German languages. Aim of the work was to compare prosodic means of speech influence on the basis of three Germanic languages and to investigate whether these means are similar or they are specific for each language.

Acoustic analysis showed that for English language both changes of fundamental frequency and intensity are equally important, as they help to accentuate separate words and even word combinations.

In German language the most relevant prosodic means of speech influence is the change of fundamental frequency, as intensity stays the same within the whole utterance.

In Dutch sufficient change of fundamental frequency is used though in smaller degree than in English and German. Changes of intensity within syntagmas and at their boundaries are also used.

The fact that for acoustic analysis only 14 of 20 samples for English, 11 from 20 for German and 6 from 20 for Dutch were chosen by the subjects shows that language competence plays a very important role in perceiving a foreign language and as a result in detecting speech influence.

Results of the acoustic analysis of a larger set partly confirmed the results obtained during the similar research conducted in 2011 [4] and made the situation with Dutch language more exact. For German language the changes of fundamental frequency are most important when a person resorts to speech influence. Changes of fundamental frequency and intensity are used equally in English for speech influence while the most important for Dutch is the change in intensity.

5   Conclusion

The results gained in the course of the experiment show that different languages (English, German, Dutch), though they belong to the same language family (Germanic languages) do have and use particular prosodic patterns that vary from language to language though some similarities can also be found. The correlation of the use of the change in the fundamental frequency, intensity and temporal characteristics also vary from language to language.

The present study is only one of the first studies that focus not only on one particular language but on the comparison of some of languages. It should be remembered that, however, the results of this research are still only preliminary. Much work should be done as in these paper just utterances of males and only interviews were taken into consideration. Other kinds of oral speech should be studied. None of the subjects was a native speaker, so the results should be testifies on new subjects (native speakers) as well. And their number should be enlarged in order to get more reliable and profound findings.

References

1. Gussenhoven, C.: Prosodic Typology and Transcription: A Unified Approach. Oxford University Press, Oxford (1998)
2. Hirst, D., Di Cristo, A., 'T Hart, J.: Intonation in Dutch. In: Intonation Systems: A Survey of Twenty Languages. Cambridge University Press, Cambridge (2008)
3. Moroz, N.U., Blokhina, L.P.: Problems of prosodic interference under conditions of bilingualism. In: Topical Problems of Applied and Experimental Linguistics, Rema, Moscow, pp. 178–190 (2008) (in Russian)
4. Moskvina, A.: Prosodic features as means of speech influence (comparative study of English, German and Dutch). In: Proc. 14th International Conference SPECOM 2001, Kazan, pp. 213–217 (2011)
5. Potapova, R.K.: Comparative paraverbalics and its prosodic correlates. In: Comparative Studies of the Languages of the World, vol. (3), pp. 252–258. Institut jasikoznanija RAN, Moscow (2009) (in Russian)
6. Potapova, R.K.: Syllabic phonetics of Germanic languages. Visshaya shkola, Moscow (1986) (in Russian)
7. Potapova, R.K., Lindner, G.: Peculiarities of German pronunciation. Visshaya shkola, Moscow (1991) (in Russian)
8. Potapova, R.K., Potapov, V.V.: Language, speech, personality. Yasiki slavjanskih kultur, Moscow (2006) (in Russian)
9. Potapova, R.K., Potapov, V.V.: Kommunikative Sprechtatigkeit. Russland und Deutschland im Vergleich. Buhlau Verlag, Koln (2011) (in German)
10. Schwitalla, J.: Gesprochenes Deutsch. Eine Einführung, Erich Schmidt Verlag (1997) (in German)

Covariance Matrix Enhancement Approach to Train Robust Gaussian Mixture Models of Speech Data

Jan Vaněk, Lukáš Machlica, Josef V. Psutka, and Josef Psutka

University of West Bohemia in Pilsen, Univerzitní 22, 306 14 Pilsen
Faculty of Applied Sciences, Department of Cybernetics
{vanekyj,machlica,psutka_j,psutka}@kky.zcu.cz

Abstract. An estimation of parameters of a multivariate Gaussian Mixture Model is usually based on a criterion (e.g. Maximum Likelihood) that is focused mostly on training data. Therefore, testing data, which were not seen during the training procedure, may cause problems. Moreover, numerical instabilities can occur (e.g. for low-occupied Gaussians especially when working with full-covariance matrices in high-dimensional spaces). Another question concerns the number of Gaussians to be trained for a specific data set. The approach proposed in this paper can handle all these issues. It is based on an assumption that the training and testing data were generated from the same source distribution. The key part of the approach is to use a criterion based on the source distribution rather than using the training data itself. It is shown how to modify an estimation procedure in order to fit the source distribution better (despite the fact that it is unknown), and subsequently new estimation algorithm for diagonal- as well as full-covariance matrices is derived and tested.

Keywords: Gaussian Mixture Models, Full Covariance, Full Covariance Matrix, Regularization, Automatic Speech Recognition.

1 Introduction

Gaussian mixture models (GMMs) are very popular models of multivariate probabilistic distributions in various domains, including speech and speaker recognition domains. For given training data set, one is confronted with three mutually dependent problems:

- How complex the model should be? How many Gaussians? Diagonal- or full- covariance matrix?
- How to estimate model parameters to fit also to unseen data?
- Is the model numerically stable? Variances may go approach zero and full-covariance matrices may be ill-conditioned.

The problem with numerical stability can be handled in relatively easy way. In the case of low variances, the problematic model component can be simply discarded or a minimum variance threshold can be specified. The threshold is usually a fixed fraction of the global variance of the entire data set [1]. From the other hand, the threshold introduces an additional prior, in the form of a magic number, into the estimation algorithm and it may be dubious. In the case of full-covariance matrices, smoothing or shrinkage

M. Železný et al. (Eds.): SPECOM 2013, LNAI 8113, pp. 92–99, 2013.

methods can be used [2], [3]. They are based on the lowering of the off-diagonal values of the covariance matrix.

Choosing a proper model complexity is the main challenge [4–8]. It is the trade-off between an accurate training data fit and a generalization ability to unseen data. The trade-off can be handled easily if one knows both information. But, in our case, we have only the first half: the training data. The generalizations ability to unseen data can be only estimated.

The first class of solutions involves penalization of the training data fit by the model complexity. The most popular criteria are Bayesian information criterion (BIC) [9] and Akaike's information criterion (AIC) [10]. BIC and AIC penalize the mean of the log-likelihood of training data by the number of model parameters. BIC penalization depends moreover on a number of training data samples. These criteria may work nicely in most cases. However, they depend on the log-likelihood of the training data. It means that they depend also on a way how the minimum variance is handled. In the case of outliers, the variance will go to zero and the log-likelihood will go to infinity. An extreme example is the mixture model of Dirac functions placed on locations of training data samples. This model is completely incorrect, but it gives the best BIC and AIC. Additional weak point in BIC is the number of samples. The samples are assumed mutually independent, but it is not true in most of real cases (e.g. speech data). This may be solved by a tunable gain of the penalization part in the BIC, but it brings an additional magic constant into the training set-up.

In the second class of solutions an unseen-data performance is estimated via cross-validation technique. In the simplest case, the available data are split into two parts - training and development. The training part is used to train the model parameters and the development part is used to evaluate the model performance. In a more complex case - the true cross-validation - data are split into more parts and an one-leave-out approach with all combinations is used. The cross-validation works well on real data, but it has also disadvantages. The first one is much higher computational requirements, which grow with the number of data splits. The second disadvantage resides in fact that the result varies with the number of splits and data distribution between these parts.

The approach proposed in this paper is based on an assumption that the training data and the testing data are generated from the same source distribution. When this is not true, one should use an appropriate normalization and/or adaptation technique to compensate for the difference as much as possible. The key part of the approach is to use a criterion based on the source distribution rather than the training data itself. Naturally, the source distribution is unknown. But, we are able to modify the estimation procedure in order to fit the distribution better despite the fact that it is unknown. Based on a criterion, we have derived how the covariance matrices need to be enhanced, and we have proposed a new estimation algorithm for diagonal as well as full covariance matrices. Also, a very useful feature of the algorithm is the ability to leave out the redundant Gaussians. Therefore, the final GMM has an optimal number of components. Moreover, such enhanced full covariance matrices are well-conditioned. Thus, this feature prevents numerical stability issues. The proposed approach may be understood also as the extreme case of cross-validation, where each data sample forms a new part.

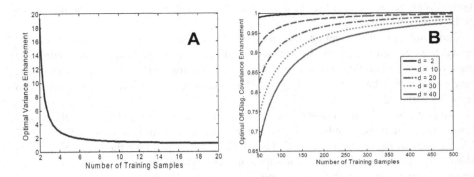

Fig. 1. Fitted functions of the ratio between the optimal estimate of variance of the source-distribution and the optimal estimate of variance (Figure A) and covariance (Figure B) of training data for various numbers of training samples

2   Robust GMM Training

2.1   Estimation of Single Gaussian Model

Assume we have i.i.d. random data set $X = \{x_1, x_2, \ldots, x_n\}$ sampled from univariate normal distribution $\mathcal{N}(\mu, \sigma^2)$ (the real-speech data case will be discussed later in the paper). The Maximum Likelihood (ML) estimates of sample mean $\hat{\mu}$ and sample variance $\hat{\sigma}^2$ are given by the well-known formulas:

$$\hat{\mu} = \frac{1}{n} \sum_{i=1}^{n} x_i \tag{1}$$

$$\hat{\sigma}^2 = \frac{1}{n} \sum_{i=1}^{n} (x_i - \hat{\mu})^2 \tag{2}$$

From Central Limit Theorem, it can be derived that the estimate of the sample mean $\hat{\mu}$ has normal distribution $\mathcal{N}(\mu, \frac{\sigma^2}{n})$ and the estimate of the sample variance $\hat{\sigma}^2$ has Chi-square distribution with variance equal to $\frac{2\sigma^2}{n-1}$. These estimates give the best value of the ML criterion for the training data set X. On the other hand, these estimates are not optimal, and they do not achieve the best value of the ML criterion for unseen data generated from the source distribution $\mathcal{N}(\mu, \sigma^2)$.

We performed a very large amount of Monte Carlo simulations for various lengths of data sets, and we have found out that the ML estimate of the optimal variance of the source distribution should have a higher value. The difference grows especially for data sets containing few samples. We fitted a function of the ratio between the optimal estimate of variance of the source-distribution and the optimal estimate of variance of training data. The function is given in dependence on the number of training samples and it is shown in Figure 1 A. The ratio function can be used to enhance the variance estimate $\hat{\sigma}^2$ given by the equation (2). The enhanced variance estimate $\tilde{\sigma}^2$ is calculated in following way:

$$\tilde{\sigma}^2 = \hat{\sigma}^2 \left(1 + \frac{1}{n - 1.25}\right)^{3.5} \tag{3}$$

In the multivariate case, assuming a diagonal covariance matrix, the same variance enhancement can be used for individual dimensions. The variance enhancement also handles numerical stability issues. The enhanced estimate cannot be close to zero even for outliers, because the enhanced variance grows fast when only a few samples are available.

In the case of multivariate data and full covariance model, the covariance matrix should be enhanced in the same way - by multiplication with the coefficient from equation (3). Moreover, the off-diagonal part of the matrix need to be corrected. We performed some additional Monte Carlo simulations to fit the optimal function for the off-diagonal part. The optimal correction coefficient was found in the interval $\langle 0, 1 \rangle$. It means that for small training sets some suppression of the off-diagonal elements is needed. This is similar to smoothing and shrinkage methods [2], [3]. The optimal value of the correction coefficient depends on the number of training samples n and on the number of dimensions d. The fitted functions are shown in Figure 1 B. The enhanced estimate of the off-diagonal element $\hat{s}_{ij}$ of the covariance matrix, which was enhanced by equation (3) already, is

$$\tilde{s}_{ij} = \hat{s}_{ij} \left[1 - \left(\frac{d}{d - 1 + n}\right)^{1.4}\right]. \tag{4}$$

Covariance matrix enhanced this way is also well-conditioned. The Monte Carlo simulation and the fit was done for dimensions in range from 2 to 50. Therefore, the fit may be inaccurate in cases with significantly higher dimensions.

2.2 Real Speech Data

Real speech data (e.g. MFCC or PLP vectors augmented by delta and acceleration coefficients) are not i.i.d.. Subsequent feature-vectors are mutually dependent. This is the consequence of the speech processing itself. There is an overlap of the FFT window and the delta and acceleration coefficients are computed from neighbouring feature-vectors. Also, the speech production is continuous, i.e. time dependent. It means that n used in formulas (3) and (4) cannot be directly the number of feature-vectors.

An number of independent feature-vectors $\tilde{n}$ needs to be estimated too from the given data set of n real feature-vectors. For such an estimation we used a normalized mean of absolute differences of consecutive feature-vectors:

$$\tilde{\delta} = \frac{1}{d} \sum_{j=1}^{d} \frac{1}{n\hat{\sigma}_j} \sum_{i=2}^{n} |x_{ij} - x_{i-1,j}|. \tag{5}$$

In the case of dependent data, the difference $\tilde{\delta}$ is smaller than for the independent data. We simulated various filter lengths and many filter shapes (e.g. Hamming, Blackman,

Triangle, Rectangular) to analyze a relation between the data dependency influenced by the filter and the difference $\tilde{\delta}$. The relation depends mainly on the filter length. The dependence on the filter shape is minor. Again, we fitted a function to estimate the number of independent feature-vectors $\tilde{n}$ from the difference $\tilde{\delta}$ and the number of feature-vectors n:

$$\tilde{n} = 1 + (n - 1)0.7\tilde{\delta}^3. \tag{6}$$

2.3 Enhanced Gaussian Mixture Models

In the case of GMM, the above described approach can be used for individual components. The optimality is not ensured since the overlap of Gaussian components is ignored. All the estimates are calculated incorporating the posterior probability of the individual Gaussian components. Instead of the number of feature-vectors n, the sum of posteriors is used in the equations (3), (4), and (5). Only in the equation (6) the sum of posterior square roots is used.

2.4 Training Procedure

We use a modified Expectation-Maximization (EM) algorithm. We modified the estimation equations as described above. The iterative training converges in most cases, but the convergence is not assured. Appropriate number of iterations is higher in comparison with the classic EM algorithm. Some model components may be found redundant during the iterations. This means that other components comprise most of the data from the redundant component. The redundant component should be discarded since its estimates become very inaccurate. Discarding the redundant component naturally produces a model with an optimal number of components.

The modified EM algorithm does not converge to a global optimum alike the classic EM. The initial seed is important. According to our experiments, starting with a single component followed by subsequent split of the component with highest weight results to a reliable final model. However, it is a very time-consuming method when dealing with large datasets, where a random initialization of all the components gives a model in much shorter time. In that case, we recommend to try out several random initializations and select the model witch gives the best value of the ML criterion. The individual random initializations may vary in the number of components, but the proposed algorithm provides (after a few iterations) their optimal subset. Hence, the redundant ones will be discarded.

3 GMM Estimator Software

We incorporated previous methods of the covariance matrix enhancement into our GMM estimator software. The GMM estimator supports diagonal and full covariance matrices and it is developed for processing of very large datasets. It uses CUDA GPU acceleration (if available) [11], [12] or multi-threaded SSE implementation in all other case. It is free for academic use. More information is available at http://www.kky.zcu.cz/en/sw/gmm-estimator.

4 Speech Recognition Results

We employed the proposed GMM training approach into an acoustic model training. For this paper, we choose a ML trained triphone Hidden Markov Model (HMM) baseline where each tied-state has a uniform number of components with diagonal covariance matrices. We used this model to label all the training feature-vectors with tied-state labels. Each state was then trained as an independent GMM. On the end, we collected all the GMMs and constructed a new HMM.

We compared models with diagonal as well as full covariance matrices. Three variants were assumed. We tested various uniform numbers (each HMM state has same number of components) of components (i.e. 2, 4, 8, 16, 32) and kept the best performing ones: 16 components for diagonal covariance models and 8 components for full covariance models. We did not use Speaker adaptive training, discriminative training, nor adaptation, in order to keep the influence of the modelling approach evident. Summary of the compared models:

- Diagonal covariance HMM with uniform number of components per state, 16 components used (denoted as *Diag_16G*), trained by classical EM algorithm.
- Enhanced diagonal covariance HMM with the target number of components equal to 16, but in one third of states some of the components were marked as redundant and left out (marked as *Diag_16G_Enh*).
- Enhanced diagonal covariance HMM with variable number of components, the largest component was split until the ML criterion grew (marked as *Diag_Vari_Enh*).
- Full covariance HMM with uniform number of components per state equal to 8 (marked as *Full_8G*) trained by classical EM algorithm. 10% of the states was not able to be trained with full covariances because of ill-conditioning. These states was replaced by enhanced GMMs from the following model.
- Enhanced full covariance HMM with target number of components equal to 8, but one half of states had some components redundant (marked as *Full_8G_Enh*).
- Enhanced full covariance HMM with variable number of components, the largest component was split until the ML criterion grew (marked as *Full_Vari_Enh*).

4.1 Test Description

A corpus *Bezplatne Hovory* was chosen as a data source for the experiments. It is a *Switchboard* like telephone speech corpus, recorded at 8kHz in Czech language. It contains spontaneous speech with unlimited vocabulary, hence it is hard to get high recognition accuracy compared to some domain specific corpora.

280h of speech were selected for training and other 2h were selected for tests. Feature vectors were standard PLPs with delta and acceleration coefficients followed by the Cepstral Mean Subtraction. Total dimension of the vectors was 36.

Czech language belongs to flexible languages, therefore the vocabulary used needs to be extremely large in order to carry most of the pronounced words. Since less than 5 million words from the training set transcriptions do not suffice for such a task, a language model was trained from distinct text sources. Next, 200 million words mainly from internet forums and blogs were mixed with training set transcriptions in the ratio

Table 1. Recognition results

Model	#States	#Gaussians	#Gaussians/#States	WER[%]
Diag_16G	4104	65,654	16.0	45.24
Diag_16G_Enh	4104	54,444	13.3	45.02
Diag_Vari_Eng	4104	108,422	26.4	44.69
Full_8G	4104	32,809	8.0	42.73
Full_8G_Enh	4104	28,246	6.9	41.89
Full_Vari_Enh	4104	29,870	7.3	40.81

1:3. Resulted trigram back-off language model contained 550k words (650k baseforms). Kneser-Ney smoothing was used. A perplexity of the test set was 102 with 1.17% of OOV words.

The results of the speech recognition are shown in Table 1. Most interesting is the last column: Word Error Rate (WER). The full covariance models perform better than diagonal ones in this task. The full covariance models are also more sensitive to the selected training algorithm. The enhanced training procedure with variable number of components per state gave best results for both diagonal and full covariance models. The middle column with a total number of Gaussians is also of interest. It illustrates how many redundant Gaussians were present in the uniform models. The full covariance model with variable number of components *Full_Vari_Enh* performed better by 4.5% absolutely, when compared to the baseline diagonal model *Diag_16G*.

The overall WERs are somewhat high. This is caused by the difficulty of the task - spontaneous telephony speech with unlimited vocabulary, which contains also slang and expressive words. We needed to add more than a half million of words to the vocabulary in order to carry the speech variability. We also did not use any adaptation nor discriminative training techniques to keep the influence of the training method evident. Merging the enhanced covariances, discriminative training and adaptation is going to be the focus of our future research.

5   Conclusions

The approach of covariance matrix enhancement was proposed and described in this paper. It handles all the most problematic issues from the GMM training: optimal model complexity, unseen data, numerical stability. The key idea is to move the focus of ML criterion from the training data to the source distribution of the data. The covariance matrix needs to be enhanced to get an optimal ML criterion. We performed a very large set of Monte Carlo simulations to get the optimal enhancement of a covariance matrix.

The proposed approach was incorporated into our high-performance GMM training software, which is free for use for research community. Finally, we successfully tested the new approach incorporating it to the training of acoustic models for ASR. The significant reduction of WER was achieved using the covariance matrix enhancements.

Acknowledgments. This research was supported by the Technology Agency of the Czech Republic, project No. TA01011264.

References

1. Young, S., et al.: The HTK Book (for HTK Version 3.4), Cambridge (2006)
2. Diehl, F., Gales, M.J.F., Liu, X., Tomalin, M., Woodland, P.C.: Word Boundary Modelling and Full Covariance Gaussians for Arabic Speech-to-Text Systems. In: Proc. INTER-SPEECH 2011, pp. 777–780 (2011)
3. Bell, P., King, S.: A Shrinkage Estimator for Speech Recognition with Full Covariance HMMs. In: Proc. Interspeech 2008, Brisbane, Australia (2008)
4. Bell, P.: Full Covariance Modelling for Speech Recognition. Ph.D. Thesis, The University of Edinburgh
5. Lee, Y., Lee, K.Y., Lee, J.: The Estimating Optimal Number of Gaussian Mixtures Based on Incremental k-means for Speaker Identification. International Journal of Information Technology 12(7), 13–21 (2006)
6. Figueiredo, M.A.T., Leitão, J.M.N., Jain, A.K.: On Fitting Mixture Models. In: Hancock, E.R., Pelillo, M. (eds.) EMMCVPR 1999. LNCS, vol. 1654, pp. 54–69. Springer, Heidelberg (1999)
7. Mclachlan, G.J., Peel, D.: On a Resampling Approach to Choosing the Number of Components in Normal Mixture Models. Computing Science and Statistics 28, 260–266 (1997)
8. Paclík, P., Novovičová, J.: Number of Components and Initialization in Gaussian Mixture Model for Pattern Recognition. In: Proc. Artificial Neural Nets and Genetic Algorithms, pp. 406–409. Springer, Wien (2001)
9. Schwarz, G.E.: Estimating the dimension of a model. Annals of Statistics 6(2), 461–464 (1978)
10. Akaike, H.: On entropy maximization principle. In: Applications of Statistics, pp. 27–41. North-Holland, Amsterdam (1977)
11. Machlica, L., Vanek, J., Zajic, Z.: Fast Estimation of Gaussian Mixture Model Parameters on GPU using CUDA. In: Proc. PDCAT, Gwangju, South Korea (2011)
12. Vanek, J., Trmal, J., Psutka, J.V., Psutka, J.: Optimized Acoustic Likelihoods Computation for NVIDIA and ATI/AMD Graphics Processors. IEEE Transactions on Audio, Speech and Language Processing 20(6), 1818–1828 (2012)

Dealing with Diverse Data Variances
in Factor Analysis Based Methods

Lukáš Machlica

University of West Bohemia in Pilsen, Univerzitní 22, 306 14 Pilsen
Faculty of Applied Sciences, Department of Cybernetics
machlica@kky.zcu.cz

Abstract. Probabilistic Linear Discriminant Analysis (PLDA) and the concept of i-vectors are state-of-the-art methods used in the speaker recognition. They are based on Factor Analysis, in which a data covariance matrix is decomposed in order to find a low dimensional representation of given feature vectors. More precisely, the Factor Analysis based methods seek for directions/subspaces in which the projected (overall/between/within) variance is highest. In order to train models related to individual methods, development speech corpora comprising various acoustic conditions are utilized. The higher are the variations in some of these acoustic conditions, the more will the model tend to reflect them. Strong data variations in some of the development corpora may suppress conditions present in other corpora. This can lead to poor recognition when acoustic variations in test conditions significantly differ. In this paper techniques alleviating such effects are investigated. The idea is to use several background and i-vector models related to different parts of development data so that several i-vectors are extracted, processed and handed over to the PLDA modelling. PLDA model is then used to utilize all the extracted information and provide the verification result.

Keywords: speaker recognition, PLDA, i-vector, factor analysis, decomposition.

1 Introduction

Nowadays Factor Analysis (FA) does play a crucial role in the speaker recognition. It was introduced to the speaker recognition community with a method called Joint Factor Analysis (JFA) [1], which was further adjusted to the concept of identity vectors (i-vectors) [2]. Both techniques operate with SuperVectors (SVs), which are high dimensional mappings of a feature vector set extracted from a speech recording. In fact, supervectors are concatenated relevant statistics representing the distribution of feature vectors in the feature space. To extract such statistics Gaussian mixture model is used. It is trained on a huge amount of development data, and it defines operating conditions of interest. Since SVs are of significantly high dimension, which is often higher than the number of involved speakers, it can be anticipated that a lot of redundancies will be present in a SV. Now, methods like JFA and i-vectors come in handy.

I-vector can be thought of as a low dimensional representation of a speaker's feature dataset. Since usually only one i-vector is extracted per recording it is sometimes denoted as the speaker print related to a recording. The difference from JFA is that JFA

M. Železný et al. (Eds.): SPECOM 2013, LNAI 8113, pp. 100–107, 2013.

tries to decompose a SV to a speaker and channel part, but this is not the case in the concept of i-vectors. In i-vectors the channel and the speaker part is not distinguished. In order to perform verification of two given i-vectors frequently Probabilistic Linear Discriminant Analysis (PLDA) model [3] is used, which is also based on FA. PLDA performs a decomposition of the i-vector space to a speaker and channel dependent part. Hence, instead of dealing with channel space directly in high dimensions utilizing JFA, the channel effects are treated in the low dimensional i-vector space utilizing PLDA. The main reason is that in [4] it was found that the channel space treated in JFA does still contain a lot of information concerning the identity of a speaker. PLDA is used as a back end not only in i-vector based system, but also in speaker recognition systems based e.g. on adaptation matrices [5,6].

FA is closely related to the eigenvector decomposition of a covariance matrix [7]. In both cases subspaces, in which the projected variance is highest, are searched for. In FA in addition a noise term is assumed and the estimated subspace reflects also the magnitude of present noise. Therefore the resulting subspace in the case of JFA, i-vectors or PLDA does reflect mainly those development conditions, which variabilities are highest. If operating conditions during the use of the system are extensive this may decrease its performance. The idea is to define several operating conditions using several UBMs and utilize several decompositions of the supervector space. The connection between these conditions is made in the i-vector space, where a correspondence to some of the operating conditions is evaluated, and an adjusted i-vector is proposed uniting all the information related to distinct operating conditions.

The article is organized as follow. At first, short introduction to the background model is made in Section 2 and main variables are defined. Next, the concept of supervectors and i-vectors are presented in Section 3 and Section 4, respectively. The new training regime and adjusted i-vectors are described in Section 6. Experiments along with the set up of the system are described in Section 7. Results are presented on NIST SRE 2010. Last section is devoted to the conclusion, where possible directions for future work are indicated.

2   Universal Background Model (UBM)

Universal background model is a Gaussian Mixture Model (GMM) trained on a huge background set of feature vectors from many speakers recorded on several channels. It is a crucial part of a speaker recognition system since it delimits the parts of the acoustic space, in which the speaker recognition does take place. It is specified by a set of parameters $\lambda = \{\omega_m, \mu_m, C_m\}_{m=1}^M$ consisting of weights ω_m, means μ_m and covariance matrices C_m of respective Gaussians.

3   Supervectors

Supervectors (SVs) used in the concept of i-vectors are derived from UBM and from a given feature set $X_s = \{x_{st}\}_{t=1}^{T_s}$ of speaker s, $x_{st} \in \mathbb{R}^D$. SVs consist of zero and first order statistics

$$f_{sm}^0 = \sum_t \gamma_m(x_{st}), \quad f_{sm}^1 = \sum_t \gamma_m(x_{st})x_{st} \tag{1}$$

related to individual speakers and Gaussians $m = 1, \ldots, M$ in the UBM, and $\gamma_m(x_t)$ is the probability of feature vector x_t occupying m^{th} Gaussian in the UBM given as

$$\gamma_m(x_t) = \omega_m \mathcal{N}(x_t; \mu_m C_m)/p(x_t|\lambda), \quad p(x_t|\lambda) = \sum_{i=1}^{M} \omega_i \mathcal{N}(x_t; \mu_i, C_i). \quad (2)$$

Since feature vectors not aligned to Gaussians have $\gamma_m(x_t) = 0$, only feature vectors close to operating conditions, defined by the development data used to train the UBM, are taken into account. Therefore the UBM does not only the clustering of the feature space, it also excludes some of the feature vectors related to acoustic conditions not seen during its training. Now, the supervector $\psi_s \in \mathbb{R}^{DM}$ is easily constructed by concatenating the statistics extracted for each Gaussian, thus

$$\psi_s = [(f_{s1}^1/f_{s1}^0)^{\text{T}}, \ldots, (f_{sM}^1/f_{sM}^0)^{\text{T}}]^{\text{T}}. \quad (3)$$

Note that $\hat{\mu}_{sm} = f_{sm}^1/f_{sm}^0$ is the maximum likelihood estimate of the mean μ_m of mth Gaussian given the dataset X_s.

4   I-vectors

In simple terms, the idea of i-vectors is to find a low dimensional representation of ψ_s, which is most responsible for variations in the high dimensional SV space. For this purpose a FA based model

$$\psi_s = m + Tw_s + \epsilon, \quad (4)$$
$$w_s \sim \mathcal{N}(0, I), \quad \epsilon \sim \mathcal{N}(0, \Sigma) \quad (5)$$

is used, where $m \in \mathbb{R}^{DM}$ is the mean of ψ_s (it is usually replaced by the supervector constructed from UBM means), $T \in \mathbb{R}^{DM \times K}$ is a low rank matrix of rank $\leq K$, $w_s \in \mathbb{R}^K$ is the i-vector and $\epsilon \in \mathbb{R}^{DM}$ is a residual noise term normally distributed with diagonal covariance matrix Σ. The matrix T is trained on a set of SVs extracted individually from each recording of each speaker. Since no relation is made between SVs of one speaker, the i-vector space contains both speaker and channel variabilities. Therefore T is often denoted as the total variability space matrix. In fact, the estimation process is an extension to an ordinary FA training algorithm, where in addition dimensions related to individual Gaussians are weighted, for details see [2].

Note that since (5) is a FA model and the estimation is related to a decomposition of a covariance matrix, columns of T form a basis of the subspace in which the variations of SVs are highest. In relation to the estimation procedure of T it is possible that T will reflect in greater extent the channel or noise variations rather than the variation in speakers.

5   Probabilistic Linear Discriminant Analysis (PLDA)

PLDA is a generative model based on FA and can be expressed as

$$w_{sh} = m_w + Fz_s + Gr_{sh} + \epsilon, \quad (6)$$
$$z_s, r_{sh} \sim \mathcal{N}(0, I), \quad \epsilon \sim \mathcal{N}(0, S), \quad (7)$$

where the indexes s and h refer to speakers and sessions of a speaker, m_w is the mean of w_{sh}, columns of F span the between-speaker space (speaker identity space), z_s of dimension D_z are coordinates in this space and they do not change across sessions of one speaker, columns of G span the channel space, r_{sh} of dimension D_r are the session dependent speaker factors, and ϵ is a residual noise factor following normal distribution with diagonal covariance S. Since PLDA model incorporates individual models representing the channel and the speaker variabilities, two covariance matrices are decomposed in the estimation phase, namely the between and the within speaker covariance matrix [8].

5.1 Verification

In the verification stage one can ask for probabilities $p(w|z_s, \theta)$, $\theta = \{m_w, F, G, S\}$ is the set of model parameters, w is i-vector extracted from speaker in question and z_s is the speaker identity factor from (7) of a reference speaker s. However, if only one i-vector per speaker is available, the estimate of z_s gets not very accurate. It is more convenient to integrate all latent parameters out and use the log-likelihood ratio of the form

$$\text{LLR}(w_1, w_2) = \log p(w_1, w_2|\theta) - \log p(w_1|\theta) - \log p(w_2|\theta) \qquad (8)$$

instead. Thus, the question stated is whether two i-vectors w_1 and w_2 share the same identity given the subspaces generated by F and G.

6   Dealing with Diverse Data Variances

In [9] authors proposed a system suitable for multiple acoustic conditions. More precisely, two significantly different sound environments were dealt with, namely telephone and microphone speech. The main motivation was the insufficient amount of microphone data to train a reliable i-vector system. Hence, two i-vector extractors were trained and the resulting subspaces were merged. Dividing the speech data according to telephone and microphone conversations is evident. However, variety of conditions exists in telephone speech only.

In order to allow higher flexibility of a speaker recognition system in a variety of acoustic environments, several modifications to the training procedure are made:

1. Multiple acoustic conditions are defined utilizing multiple UBMs. Each UBM is trained from a different development set, which should reflect different impacts of telephone channels on available recordings.
2. A set of statistics for each recording is extracted for each UBM. These statistics express the exposure to different acoustic conditions, and SVs are constructed for each set of statistics.
3. Multiple i-vector extractors (total variability space matrices T and diagonal covariance Σ given in (5)) are trained. One i-vector model is trained from supervectors related to recordings from which the respective UBM, used to extract these SVs, was estimated. Thus, several speaker prints per recording are obtained in relation to a specific acoustic environment.

4. For each development recording all possible i-vectors are extracted.
5. In order to combine resulting i-vectors a new i-vector $\boldsymbol{v}$ is composed as

$$\boldsymbol{v} = [p_1\boldsymbol{w}_1^{\mathrm{T}}, p_2\boldsymbol{w}_2^{\mathrm{T}}, \ldots, p_N\boldsymbol{w}_N^{\mathrm{T}}]^{\mathrm{T}}, \tag{9}$$

where N is the number of trained UBMs and i-vector extractors, p_n is the probability of a set of feature vectors (used to extract i-vector $\boldsymbol{w}_n$) in the respective UBM.

6. New i-vectors are then used as input to the PLDA estimation procedure, and a PLDA model is trained.

Note that since the new i-vector $\boldsymbol{v}$ is a concatenation of i-vectors, in the PLDA modelling phase the covariance of respective i-vectors is computed. Thus, distinct i-vectors are correlated, and resulting PLDA subspaces reflect strongest differences between them. Loosely speaking, directly in the PLDA modelling informativeness of respective i-vectors $\boldsymbol{w}_n$ is assessed. The extraction process of an i-vector $\boldsymbol{v}$ is depicted in Figure 1.

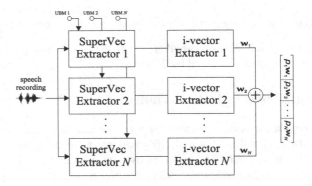

Fig. 1. Extraction of one i-vector $\boldsymbol{v}$ given in (9)

7   Experiments

The experiments aim to demonstrate that splitting the development dataset and separately train several i-vector extractors for telephone conditions will make the speaker recognition system more flexible in these conditions. Such an assumption is based on the fact that FA methods search for subspaces where the data variance in the development set is highest. Following experiments were proposed in order to demonstrate these effects. Let us first describe the set up of the system.

The experiments were carried out on male telephone conversation speech, and NIST SRE 2010 corpora with 74 762 trials in total was used for evaluation of the performance of the speaker recognition system.

7.1 Feature Extraction

The feature extraction was based on Linear Frequency Cepstral Coefficients (LFCCs), Hamming window of length 25 ms was used, the shift of the window was set to 10 ms, 25 triangular filter banks were spread linearly across the frequency spectrum, and 20 LFCCs were extracted, delta coefficients were added leading to a 40 dimensional feature vector. Also the Feature Warping (FW) normalization procedure was applied utilizing a sliding window of length 3 seconds. Just before FW a simple voice activity detection was carried out. It is based on detection of energies in filter banks located in the frequency domain. Local SNRs were estimated for each feature vector as a mean value of SNRs in each of the filter-banks, and global SNR was represented as a mean value of local SNRs computed across whole utterance. Feature vectors with local SNR lower than the global SNR were marked as non-speech.

7.2 System Set-up

Development corpora NIST SRE 2004 (NIST04), NIST SRE 2005 (NIST05), NIST SRE 2006 (NIST06), Switchboard 1 Release 2 (SW1), Switchboard 2 Phase 3 (SW2), Switchboard Cellular Audio Part 1 and Part 2 (SWC) and Fisher English Training Speech Part 1 and Part 2 (FSH) were used. The overall number of male speakers in NIST04, NIST05, NIST06 was 465 with approximately 8 session for each speaker, in SW1, SW2, SWC 659 male speaker with approx. 11 sessions were present, and in FSH the number of speakers was 1612 with at most 3 sessions each. The data source of all the recordings was telephone conversation and the duration of each recording including the silence was approx. 5 minute, but in FSH the length of recordings varied from 6 to 12 minutes.

The number of Gaussians in the UBM was set to 1024. The size of the total variability space matrix T was set to $(1024 * 40) \times 400$, hence 400 dimensional i-vectors were extracted. In order to train i-vector extractor 7 Maximum Likelihood (ML) and 1 minimum divergence iterations were carried out. The i-vectors where normalized to unit lengths at the end [10]. In case of PLDA 20 ML iterations were performed.

7.3 Dealing with Diverse Data Variances

At first, the development data were divided to three sets according to the corpus they belong to so that 3 data clusters were obtained: NIST = {NIST04, NIST05, NIST06}, SWB = {SW1, SW2, SWC} and the last cluster contained all the data from FSH. In the future more sophisticated method should be developed to cluster the data according to acoustic/channel conditions, but it is out of scope of this paper. Next, three UBMs were trained (UBM$_{\text{NIST}}$, UBM$_{\text{SWB}}$, UBM$_{\text{FSH}}$) from respective datasets. Statistics (1) were extracted for each UBM and all the development data, and supervectors (3) were constructed. Statistics related to individual UBMs should reflect those acoustic conditions, which were used (in form of a training set) to train respective UBMs.

Next, three i-vector extractors were trained: IV$_{\text{NIST}}$, IV$_{\text{SWB}}$, IV$_{\text{FSH}}$, i.e. IV$_{\text{NIST}}$ was trained from SVs extracted from data cluster NIST using UBM$_{\text{NIST}}$, etc. Finally, for all development recordings i-vectors were extracted utilizing each UBM and each IV.

Hence, for each recording 3 i-vectors were available. A new i-vector v was constructed as described in Section 6, hence

$$v = [p_{\text{NIST}} w_{\text{NIST}}^{\text{T}}, \ p_{\text{SWB}} w_{\text{SWB}}^{\text{T}}, \ p_{\text{FSH}} w_{\text{FSH}}^{\text{T}}]^{\text{T}}, \tag{10}$$

where $p_{\text{NIST}}, p_{\text{SWB}}, p_{\text{FSH}}$ are the probabilities of feature vectors, extracted from a single recording from which the i-vector w was computed, in the respective UBM. Now the dimension of the new i-vector v become $3 * 400 = 1200$. To train the PLDA model all the i-vectors v extracted from all the development corpora were utilized.

Table 1. Equal Error Rates (EERs) and minimum of the Decision Cost Function (DCF) on NIST SRE 2010

	baseline	IV$_{\text{NIST}}$	IV$_{\text{SWB}}$	IV$_{\text{FSH}}$	v_{200}	v_{800}
EER[%]	8.42	8.53	7.47	7.68	7.05	6.84
minDCF	0.0455	0.0482	0.0434	0.0456	0.0417	0.0416

Results are given in Table 1. Equal Error Rate (EER) along with minimum of the Decision Cost Function (minDCF) are reported. To compute the value of minDCF $C_{\text{Miss}} = 10$, $C_{\text{FA}} = 1$, $P_{\text{Target}} = 0.01$. The baseline system is a i-vector and PLDA based system, where all the development data (NIST + SWB + FSH) were used to train one UBM, one i-vector extractor and one PLDA model. Also results when only one from NIST, SWB, FSH development datasets was used to train the whole system are given. In all the cases the dimension of the session space formed by columns of G in the PLDA model was set to the dimension of the input i-vector (thus $G \in \mathbb{R}^{400 \times 400}$ or $G \in \mathbb{R}^{1200 \times 1200}$). The dimension of the between speaker subspace formed by columns of F was set to $D_z = 200$, but since the new i-vector v is of higher dimension also higher dimensions were tried out and the results for $D_z = 800$ are also reported – these are the results for v_{200} and v_{800}. The dimensions were determined experimentally and values for stable regions (change in dimension causes insignificant changes in system performance) were used.

After examination of the results we can see that the baseline system was outperformed already in cases when only a part of the development set was utilized. Best results are obtained for the SWB dataset. Hence, one can judge the suitability of a given corpus for given task. However, this cannot be anticipated and in praxis it is not possible to rely only on one specific corpus. When the new i-vectors are used the speaker recognition system performs best. Moreover, slightly increasing the dimension of the latent variable in the PLDA model, further decreases the error rates. Hence, 19% relative improvement was achieved on the EER, and also the minimum DCF decreased from 0.0455 to 0.0416.

8   Conclusions

In this paper the influence of development corpora on the speaker recognition was investigated. The focus was laid on state-of-the-art methods based on factor analysis.

It was shown how to incorporate several development corpora more efficiently utilizing several UBMs and i-vector extractors. The development data were divided to clusters without any elaborate method. Yet, the system's performance increased. This is the task intended for future work. In fact, none methods exist, which would point out some of the parts of acoustic space, e.g. most responsible for speaker changes (special phonetic events) or mostly vulnerable to channel or noise corruption, already in the UBM modelling stage. All of these issues are usually handled in consequent phases, but it would be of interest to pre-highlight such areas.

Acknowledgements. This research was supported by the Technology Agency of the Czech Republic, project No. TA01030476.

References

1. Kenny, P.: Joint Factor Analysis of Speaker and Session Variability: Theory and Algorithms. Centre de Recherche Informatique de Montréal, CRIM (2006)
2. Dehak, N., Kenny, P., Dehak, R., Dumouchel, P., Ouellet, P.: Front-End Factor Analysis for Speaker Verification. IEEE Transactions on Audio, Speech and Language Processing (2010)
3. Prince, S., Elder, J.: Probabilistic Linear Discriminant Analysis for Inferences About Identity. In: IEEE 11th International Conference on Computer Vision, pp. 1–8 (2007)
4. Dehak, N.: Discriminative and Generative Approaches for Long- and Short-term Speaker Characteristics Modeling: Application to Speaker Verification. Ph.D. thesis, École de Technologie Supérieure, Université du Québec (2009)
5. Scheffer, N., Lei, Y., Ferrer, L.: Factor Analysis Back Ends for MLLR Transforms in Speaker Recognition. In: Interspeech 2011, pp. 257–260 (2011)
6. Garcia-Romero, D., Zhou, X., Zotkin, D., Srinivasan, B., Luo, Y., Ganapathy, S., Thomas, S., et al.: The UMD-JHU 2011 speaker recognition system. In: IEEE International Conference on Acoustics, Speech and Signal Processing (ICASSP), pp. 4229–4232 (2012)
7. Machlica, L., Zajc, Z.: Factor Analysis and Nuisance Attribute Projection Revisited. In: Interspeech 2012 (2012)
8. Machlica, L., Zajíc, Z.: An Efficient Implementation of Probabilistic Linear Discriminant Analysis. In: ICASSP 2013 (2013)
9. Senoussaoui, M., Kenny, P., Dehak, N., Dumouchel, P.: An i-vector Extractor Suitable for Speaker Recognition with both Microphone and Telephone Speech. In: Proc. IEEE Odyssey Workshop, Brno, Czech Republic (2010)
10. Garcia-Romero, D., Espy-Wilson, C.Y.: Analysis of I-vector Length Normalization in Speaker Recognition Systems. In: Interspeech, pp. 249–252 (2011)

Detection of the Frequency Characteristics of the Articulation System with the Use of Voice Source Signal Recording Method

Vera Evdokimova[1], Karina Evgrafova[1], Pavel Skrelin[1], Tatiana Chukaeva[1], and Nikolay Shvalev[2]

[1] Russia,Saint-Petersburg State University, Universitetskaya emb.,11
`{postmaster,evgrafova,skrelin,chukaeva}@phonetics.pu.ru`
`www.spbu.ru`
[2] Russia, Saint-Petersburg, Mariinsky Theatre, Teatralnaya square, 1
`dr-nix99@mail.ru`
`www.mariinsky.ru/en`

Abstract. The given research is aimed at registering and analysing speech signal obtained through a microphone placed in the proximity of the vocal folds and comparing it with the output speech signal. The external microphone was located near the lips of the subject. The internal one was located in the proximity of the subjects's vocal folds by a phoniatrician with the use of special medical equipment. The speech signal containing isolated vowels and connected speech was registered synchronously through both microphones. The main interest of the paper is the acoustic characteristics of these signals, mainly, the vowel formant structure. Besides, the non-linearity of the vocal tract system was considered. The new method of obtaining frequency characteristics of the articulation system is used. The coprocessing of several acoustic realizations helps to elaborate the methods of discrimination and modeling the transfer functions of the voice source and filter components of the vocal tract. The speech signals that are influenced at different levels by two parts of the vocal tract are processed. It allows constructing the vowel formant structure of frequency constituents and their variations.

Keywords: phonetics, voice source signal, system of articulation, formants.

1 Introduction

The traditional approach to phonetic research of the vocal tract assumes that there are several successive stages of speech production which are initialization, phonation, articulation and radiance of speech signal. The phonation stage provides the input signal to the filter component of the vocal tract. This input signal contains the fundamental frequency and its high harmonics. The voice signal goes through the filter component – a set of pharynx, nasal and oral cavities. The voice source signal is the strongest acoustic signal in the human vocal tract. Almost all the internal organs are parts of the bio-mechanical oscillating system that generates the voice signal. This signal is individual and optimized by nature [1–4, 8]. The periodic sequence of lung pressure differences in larynx is called the glottal wave [5, 6]. The frequency of these pulses corresponds to the

M. Železný et al. (Eds.): SPECOM 2013, LNAI 8113, pp. 108–115, 2013.
© Springer International Publishing Switzerland 2013

fundamental frequency in speech signal. Some of the traditional theories are described bellow.

The fact of the interaction between the two parts of the vocal tract does not make the traditional linear source–filter theory completely consistent. Obtaining the vocal fold signal detached from the influence of the articulation system and analysing its nature is an important up-to-date problem for different fields of speech science and speech technology. There exist different voice source models that are applied to the majority of linguistic research and speech technology applications.

The LF-model (Lilencrants and Fant) of the voice source was one the first models of the vocal tract. It was developed in the 80-s by G. Fant [5, 6]. It described the glottal wave as a sequence of pulses of the given shape. Their shape is similar to the experimentally measured shape of glottal pulses. The spectral density of voice source from the experiments was the pattern for the choice of shape of the glottal pulses. The voice source constituents were obtained from the signal using the inverse filtering. Comparing the model with the pattern showed that the voice signal can be modeled successfully by the derivative of glottal wave function. The glottal wave curve differed greatly from the ideal sinusoid because of the high harmonics of pitch. The choice of these four parameters provided for the production of an individual voice source characteristic. The improved quality of the speech synthesis system based on the LF-model was caused by the fact that not only the pitch but also its high harmonics were taken into account. The basis of interference of voice and filter components was maintained in the model. The intensity of glottal flow, phoneme durations, and fundamental frequency were set as time functions for phoneme production. The LF-model imitated the voice signal and worked well for a predefined voice of text-to-speech synthesis system. However, it is more complicated to use it for real time analysis of voice. In this case the problem is solved by the determining of the LF-model parameters. It is a very complicated task which requires many calculations.

Apart from LF-model, there exist biomechanical models of the voice source and the vocal folds. Single-mass models could be more precisely termed single degree-of-freedom vibration models for the vocal folds because each vocal fold is modeled with a single mass-spring system. Generally, it is assumed that the mass-spring systems modeling each vocal fold are identical and the glottal flow is assumed to be the same on the either side of the glottal center-line [15, 12]. These models are of particular interest theoretically because they must explain the net work done on the vocal folds by air flow in 1 cycle in terms of asymmetries between opening and closing phases in air flow conditions. That is, the flow asymmetries between the opening and closing phases of the vocal folds cannot be the result of asymmetries in the vocal fold geometry. This is in contrast to the two-mass model which explains net energy input into the vocal folds using asymmetries in vocal fold geometry between opening and closing. The two-mass vocal fold model introduced by Stevens [4] consists of two pairs of masses, larger ones representing the inferior part of the vocal folds, and smaller ones representing the superior part of the vocal folds. The model is symmetric, i.e., there is no differentiation between the masses of the left and right side. The whole process of the excitation function computation is described in Chapter 2 of [4].

The source–filter interactions that involve changes in vocal fold vibration have been demonstrated by investigators [14, 16–18, 7]. However, the data presented are sometimes fragmentary and inconsistent. In the traditional models the filter cannot influence the source to produce new frequencies or change the overall energy level of the source. Titze [13, 14] showed that this assumption is generally not valid. However, under certain conditions it is an appropriate simplification. The main Titze's goal was to determine the proportion of irregularities that are due to nonlinear source–tract interactions and to provide a theoretical framework for the bifurcation phenomena in vocal fold vibration with a nonlinear source–filter construct.

Our research is aimed at registering and analysing the signal obtained through the microphone placed in the proximity of the vocal folds (Microphone Internal - MI) and comparing it with the output speech signal (Microphone External - ME). Besides, the non-linearity of the vocal tract system is considered. The main interest of the paper is the acoustic characteristics of these signals, mainly, the vowel formant structure.

2   Method

The subject of the experiment, a female native speaker of Russian, was asked to pronounce the 6 isolated Russian vowels /a/, /e/, /i/, /ɨ/, /o/, /u/ for 1 second several times and several utterances. The overall length of the speech signal was 15 minutes. In all, the subject produced 178 Russian vowel stimuli. The recordings were made in the recording studio at the Department of Phonetics, Saint-Petersburg State University. Multichannel recording system Motu Traveler and WaveLab program were used. The recordings had a sample rate of 32000 Hz and a bitrate of 16 bits. Two microphones were used during the recording. The capacitor microphone AKG HSC200 was placed in the output of the speakers mouth (ME). The miniature microphone QueAudio (d=2.3 mm, waterproof) was located in the proximity of the speaker's vocal folds (MI) with the use of special medical equipment. This procedure was performed by a phoniatrician.

3   Perceptive and Acoustic Analysis

The stimuli were presented to phoneticians. The signals obtained through the both microphones were listened to and compared in order to find out if vowels recorded through the internal microphone could be identified . The results of the perceptive analysis showed that the open Russian vowel /a/ is easy to identify. It is not also difficult to recognise the vowels /e/ and /o/. The vowels /i/ and /u/ had much more problems with identification . In some cases the vowel /ɨ/ was not identified as certain Russian vowel.

The spectral characteristics of the vowels were obtained in order to compare the frequency constituents of both signals.

Fig.1-2 show examples of spectral densities of the 6 Russian vowels from the material. There are two curves in each picture. The solid line shows the spectral density of ME signal and the dashed line shows the spectral density of MI signal.

The analysis of the vowel spectra shows that the signal from MI contains the frequency constituents of the vowel formants (resonance frequencies of the set of pharynx,

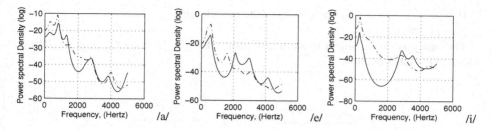

Fig. 1. Spectral densities for Russian vowels /a/, /e/, /i/

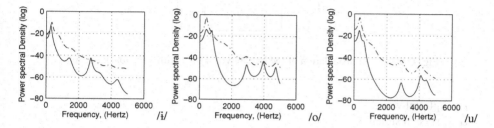

Fig. 2. Spectral densities for Russian vowels /ɨ/, /o/, /u/

nasal and oral cavities) However, the frequency constituents are weakened. It can be assumed that it is caused by the reflection of the acoustic energy from the articulation system backwards. As well as this, the plots show that the signals can be very different for the two microphones. For example, see the plot for the vowel /ɨ/ (fig.2).

4   Vocal Tract Modeling

The human vocal tract is usually regarded as a unified dynamic system consisting of two concatenated parts which are the voice source and filter component which have their own dynamic characteristics. The both parts are non-separable and interact.

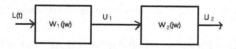

Fig. 3. Dynamic system of the human vocal tract consisting of two parts

$L(t)$ – air flow pressure from the respiratory apparatus (the lungs),

$W_1(j\omega)$ – frequency characteristics of the source component that includes trachea, larynx and the vocal chords,

$U_1(t)$ – output acoustic signal of the source component that includes the pitch ant its high harmonics, also it includes a lot of other frequencies which were reduced on that stage,

$W_2(j\omega)$ – frequency characteristics of the articulation,

$U_2(t)$ – speech signal.

The analysis of the signal made by MI made it possible to correct this model by adding a feedback section.

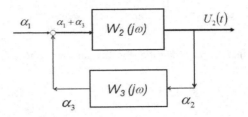

Fig. 4. System of articulation of the human vocal tract with a feedback section

α_1 – glottal wave,

α_2 – speech signal,

$U_2(t)$ – output speech signal,

α_3 – reflected backwards acoustic energy,

$W_2(j\omega)$ – frequency characteristics of the articulation,

$W_3(j\omega)$ – frequency characteristics of the feedback section.

Equivalent logarithmic amplitude-frequency characteristics of the feedback section (ELAFFS) for the above vowels are on the following plots:

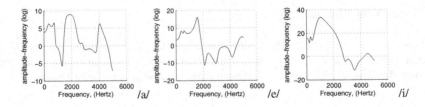

Fig. 5. ELAFFS for the feedback section for Russian vowels /a/, /e/, /i/

The shape of the ELAFFS shows that the main function of the feedback section is to weaken the constituents of the formants.

4.1 Constructing the Formant Structure of the Vowels

This dynamic system consisting of two parts (see fig.7) can be presented [9],[10]:

$$U_1(t) = W_1(j\omega)L(t), \qquad U_2(t) = W_2(j\omega)U_1(t) \qquad (1)$$

Let us find the spectral densities of the signals:

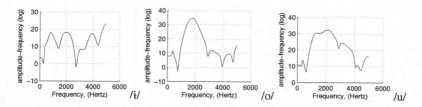

Fig. 6. ELAFFS for the feedback section for Russian vowels /i/, /o/, /u/

$$S_{U_1}(w) = [W_1(j\omega)]^2 S_L(\omega) \tag{2}$$

$$S_{U_2}(w) = [W_2(j\omega)]^2 S_{U_2}(\omega) \tag{3}$$

$S_{U_2}(\omega)$, $S_{U_1}(\omega)$, $S_L(\omega)$ – spectral densities of the U_2, U_1, L signals.

The procedure of detecting the parameters of the equivalent transfer functions by processing the real speech data and processing the obtained spectral densities of the U_2 signal for the vowels is considered bellow.

The co-processing of several acoustic realizations helps to elaborate the methods of discrimination and modeling the transfer functions of the voice source and filter components of the vocal tract. It is important to process the speech signals that have different levels of influence of the two parts of the vocal tract. The transfer functions of the voice source and system of articulation can be obtained through processing the experimental speech data.

In order to get an adequate division of the voice source and filter components the described method must take into account not only the main phonetic laws but also the particular qualities of the mathematic procedures application. The use of non-parametric methods in spectral density estimation, particularly, the standard procedure of the periodogram estimation leads to the irregularity of the lines in the spectral density $S_{U_20}(\omega)$ That can lead to the mistakes in calculations. It seems more convenient to use the parametric methods of signal processing for solving this task. In this case the spectral analysis becomes the optimization task, the search of the parameters of the model to make it as close as possible to the real speech signal [11]. It allows modeling the amplitude-frequency characteristics of the source and filter components of the vocal tract. These amplitude-frequency characteristics describe the dynamics of the system and can be used as a starting material for solving the problem of modeling of these parts of the vocal tract.

The coprocessing of several acoustic realizations helps to elaborate the methods of discrimination and modeling the transfer functions of the voice source and filter components of the vocal tract for vowels and to obtain the formant structure. It is important to process the speech signals that have different levels of influence of the two parts of the vocal tract. The examples of it are the coprocessing of rather long utterance and several pitch periods of a vowel. As a result, the transfer function of the system of articulation and particularly the vowel formant structure (Fig.7) can be obtained.

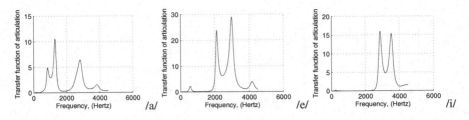

Fig. 7. Amplitude-frequency characteristic of the speech signal obtained from the ratio (6), filter component transfer function $|W(j\omega)|$ of the stressed vowels /a/, /e/, /i/ (30 ms). The formant structure is well-defined.

Conclusions

The new method of synchronous recording of the speech signal by placing the microphone near the vocal chords gives an opportunity to investigate and correct the model of the source-filter model. The results of the experiment confirm the work of the feedback section and the reflection of the acoustic energy from the filter component backwards. The proposed method gives the opportunity of automatic discrimination of the formant structure of the vowels by processing the real speech data. The constructed model of the filter part of the vocal tract completely corresponds to the basic phonetic statements and can be used for solving the specific problems of speech technologies such as automatic speech recognition and high-quality speech synthesis system elaboration.

References

1. Bondarko, L.V.: Phonetics of Russian modern language, SPbSU (1998) (in Russian)
2. Kodzasov, S.V., Krivnova, O.F.: General Phonetics, Moscow (2001)
3. Fant, G.: Acoustic Theory of Speech Production. Mouton, Netherlands (1960)
4. Stevens, K.N.: Acoustic Phonetics. The MIT Press, Cambridge (1998)
5. Fant, G.: The voice source in connected speech. Speech Communication 22 (1997)
6. Fant, G., Liljencrants, J., Lin, Q.: A four-parameter model of glottal flow. STL-QPSR (2-3) (1985)
7. Flanagan, J.L.: Source-system interaction in the vocal tract. Ann. N.Y. Acad. Sci. 155, 9–17 (1968)
8. Flanagan, J.L.: Speech Analysis, Synthesis, and Perception. Springer, New York (1972)
9. Bessekersky, V.A., Popov, E.P.: Automatic control theory systems, Moscow, Nauka (1972) (in Russian)
10. Evdokimova, V.V.: The use of vocal tract model for constructing the vocal structure of the vowels. In: SPECOM 2006, Saint-Petersburg, June 25-29, pp. 210–214 (2006)
11. Sergienko, A.B.: Digital signal processing, Moscow (2003) (in Russian)
12. Howe, M.S., McGowan, R.S.: On the single-mass model of the vocal folds. Fluid Dyn. Res. 42, 015001 (2010), doi:10.1088/0169-5983/42/1/015001
13. Titze, I.R.: Non-linear source-filter coupling in phonation: Theory. J. Acoust. Soc. Am. 123, 2733–2749 (2008), doi:10.1121/1.2832337
14. Titze, I.R., Riede, T., Popolo, P.: Nonlinear source-filter coupling in phonation: Vocal exercises. J. Acoust. Soc. Am. 123, 1902–1915 (2008), doi:10.1121/1.2832339

15. Zanartu, M., Mongeau, L., Wodicka, G.R.: Influence of acoustic loading on an effective single mass model of the vocal folds. J. Acoust. Soc. Am. 121, 1119–1129 (2007), doi:10.1121/1.2409491
16. Hatzikirou, H., Fitch, W.T.S., Herzel, H.: Voice instabilities due to source-tract interactions. Acta Acust. Acust. 92, 468–475 (2006)
17. Miller, D.G., Schutte, H.K.: 'Mixing' the registers: Glottal source or vocal tract? Folia Phoniatr Logop 57, 278–291 (2005)
18. Mergell, P., Herzel, H.: Modeling biphonation — The role of the vocal tract. Speech Commun. 22, 141–154 (1997), doi:10.1016/S0167-6393(97)00016-2

Encoding of Spatial Perspectives
in Human-Machine Interaction

Milan Gnjatović and Vlado Delić

Faculty of Technical Sciences, University of Novi Sad,
Trg Dositeja Obradovića 6, 21000 Novi Sad, Serbia
milangnjatovic@yahoo.com, vdelic@uns.ac.rs

Abstract. A spatial context is often present in speech-based human-machine interaction, and its role is especially significant in interaction with robotic systems.
Studies in the cognitive sciences show that frames of reference used in language
and in non-linguistic cognition are correlated. In general, humans may use multiple frames of references. But since the visual sensory modality operates mainly
in a relative frame, most of users normally and preferably use relative reference
frame in spatial language. Therefore, there is a need to enable dialogue systems
to process dialogue acts that instantiate user-centered frames of reference. This
paper introduces a cognitively-inspired, computational modeling method that addresses this research question, and illustrates it for a three-party human-machine
interaction scenario. The paper also reports on an implementation of the proposed model within a prototype system, and briefly discusses some aspects of the
model's generalizability and scalability.

Keywords: Human-machine interaction, spatial perspective, relative frame of
reference, focus tree, cognition.

1   Introduction

Spatial thinking is closely related to language. In his well-known work, Levinson [1]
distinguishes between three major types of frame-of-reference systems that humans use,
and shows that frames of reference used in language and in non-linguistic cognition are
correlated. This is an important guideline for research in the field of human-machine
interaction (HMI). A spatial context is often present in HMI, whether it is a simple
display with a graphical interface, or a set of physical objects in interaction with a
robotic system. Therefore, it is crucial that a frame of reference used by the system
is correlated to a frame of reference selected by the user. Another insight comes from
developmental psychology and relates to the question of how humans partition and
conceptualize space. Studies of language acquisition show that humans partition space
into discrete basic spatial categories [2–4]. For example, a relation between two objects
in space may fall in one of the following spatial semantic categories: containment (i.e.,
object A is in object B), support and contiguity (i.e., object A is on object B), occlusion
(i.e., object A is under object B), etc. (cf. [2, pp. 149-161] and [5, pp. 252-254]). This
insight leads to the second important guideline. A computational model that addresses
the research question of modeling spatial perspectives in HMI can be built around a
final set of spatial semantic categories.

M. Železný et al. (Eds.): SPECOM 2013, LNAI 8113, pp. 116–123, 2013.
© Springer International Publishing Switzerland 2013

The presented work incorporates these insights into the focus tree model of attentional information in task-oriented HMI, introduced by Gnjatović and colleagues [6, 7]. The focus tree is a cognitively-inspired model that addresses the research question of robust automatic processing of different syntactic forms of spontaneously uttered users' commands with no explicit syntactic expectations. Its various adaptations were successfully applied in several prototypical dialogue systems with diverse domains of interaction that include spatial contexts [5, 8, 9] or quasi-pictorial mental representations that serve as a non-linguistic contexts shared between the user and the system [10, 11]. However, the focus tree does not allow descriptions in multiple frames of reference, e.g., in interaction scenarios that involve users with different spatial perspectives. This paper proposes an extension of the focus tree model to address the research question of processing users' commands in such scenarios, and reports on its implementation within a prototype conversational agent integrated with a robotic system.

2   Basic Notions

(i) Relative reference frame. Three major reference frames in Levinson's conceptualization of spatial perspectives are: relative (i.e., viewer-centered), intrinsic (i.e., object-centered), and absolute (i.e., environment-centered). The intrinsic system projects out a search domain from a named facet of a landmark object, the relative system imports the observer's bodily axes and maps them onto the ground object, and the absolute system uses a fixed set of bearings or a conceptual "slope" to define a direction from a ground object [1, p. 76]. One of the reasons why humans use multiple frames of reference may lie in the fact that the spatial representations specialized to the different sensory modalities (e.g., vision, touch, etc.) each have their own native frames of reference. It is important to note that vision operates mainly in a relative frame [1, p. 25] (cf. also [12]). The point of departure for this paper is that most of users normally and preferably use relative reference frames in spatial language. Therefore, the systems should be able to process dialogue acts that instantiate user-centered frames of reference.

(ii) The interaction scenario. The dedicated interaction scenario for the prototype system is inspired by a therapeutic interaction between the language therapist and the child with receptive language difficulties. In one of the commonly used therapeutic exercises, the child and the therapist share a linguistic and a spatial contexts. The spatial context consists of a set of objects placed on a table. During the interaction, the therapist utters various commands for the child to perform simple manipulations of those objects. The role of the child is to interpret these verbal stimuli and to perform the therapist's commands. This paper additionally extends the scenario. It introduces a scenario of a three-party interaction between the therapist, the child and the robotic system. The task of the robotic system in this scenario is to support the child to correctly interpret and perform the therapist's commands. We select this interaction scenario for two reasons. First, it does not include information related to an underlying task structure or an intentional structure of the therapist. The manipulation of the objects is not a goal by itself, as opposite to the case of solving a graphical puzzle. The therapist does not instruct commands in order to place objects in some specific position, but only to expose the child to examples of verbal stimuli that relate to fundamental spatial relations. It is

clear that information on specific rules of the task or on predicted intentions of the therapist would significantly support the processing of the therapist's commands. Therefore, such information was deliberately excluded from the interaction scenario in order to illustrate robust processing of the therapist's commands that relies solely on linguistic and attentional information. And second, this scenario involves the verbal and spatial contexts shared between the participants, which makes it appropriate for demonstrating the concept of spatial perspective in HMI.

3   Extending the Focus Tree

Forcing humans to use absolute directions in cases when it is more natural to use coordinates based on their body schemata (e.g., left and right, etc.) would impose a cognitive overhead. They would have to invest a significant conscious effort to maintain accurate mental maps and to constantly update their positions and orientations on them (cf. also [1, pp. 21,49]). Therefore, this background calculation is performed by the system. The system sets four directions on two orthogonal axes that correspond with the directions *forward*, *backward*, *leftward* and *rightward* in the system-centered frame of reference (Fig. 1a). The origin of the system's coordinate system is positioned at the center of the table, so that the x-axis is parallel to one edge of the table, and the y-axis with another edge of the table. This coordinate system is used for determining positions of the objects and the human participants. The position of an object is defined in an absolute manner. An object may be positioned anywhere in the working frame of the system (i.e., the table), and its position is determined by x and y coordinates of the object's center (Fig. 1b). In contrast to this, the human participants may take only four discrete positions in this coordinate system, each of which is determined by one side of the table (Fig. 1c).

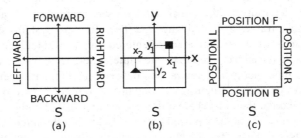

Fig. 1. (a) The system-centered spatial perspective. (b) Absolute positioning of the objects. (c) Four possible discrete positions of the human participants. The position of the system is denoted as S.

An instance of the focus tree, introduced by Gnjatović and colleagues, that represents the spatial context in the system-centered frame of reference is given in Fig. 2. Each node in the focus tree represents a semantic entity from the spatial context. Thus, the meaning of this focus tree is following: there are two objects on the table (the square and the triangle), and each of them can be pointed to (action *Show*) or translated in the horizontal plane of the table (action *Move*) along the four directions—*forward* (↑),

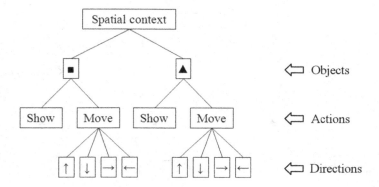

Fig. 2. Focus tree representing the spatial context in the system-centered frame of reference

backward ($\downarrow$), *leftward* ($\leftarrow$) and *rightward* ($\rightarrow$). During the course of interaction, each of these semantic entities may come into the focus of attention. At every moment of interaction, the current focus of attention is placed on exactly one node.

However, this focus tree is not appropriate for representing the spatial context in the observed interaction scenario. Let us assume that the system is located at Position B, the child at Position R (cf. Fig. 1), and that the therapist instructs the child to move the square rightward. The instructed direction is determined in the child-centered reference frame which is not the same as the system-centered reference frame. In order that the system can correctly interpret this command in its relative reference frame (i.e., move the square forward), it must have information on the position of the child with respect to itself. In addition, the system must have information to whom the therapist's command is addressed. If the therapist had instructed the system, instead of the child, to move the square rightward, the command could have been interpreted directly in the system-centered reference frame. Therefore, the focus tree given in Fig. 2 needs to be extended to include information on relative reference frames of all relevant participants, and on the participants' mutual positions.

The extended focus tree is given in Fig. 3. For the purpose of easier representation, and without loss of generality, we consider here the positions of the system and the child, while we abstract away from the position of the therapist. The spatial context is represented as a composite of the relative spatial perspectives of all relevant participants. In comparison with the initial focus tree, the extended tree contains one additional level, that we refer to as *Observers*. The nodes at this level (*System* and *Child*) relate to the participants. Another difference is that the terminal nodes that represent directions in the distinct spatial perspectives are interrelated (these relations are represented by dashed lines in Fig. 3). For example, the meaning of the relation between the node representing the direction *rightward* ($\rightarrow$) in the child-centered reference frame and the node representing the direction *forward* ($\uparrow$) in the system-centered reference frame is that these two directions coincide. This is in line with the starting assumption that the system is located at Position B, and the child at Position R. In other words, the relations between the terminal nodes encapsulate information on the mutual position between the child and the system.

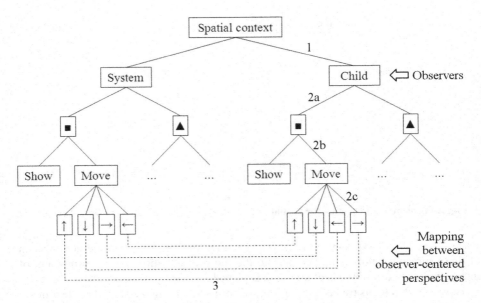

Fig. 3. A simplified version of the extended focus tree

4   The Prototype System

We report an improvement of the prototype system initially developed by Gnjatović et al. [8]. It integrates an anthropomorphic robotic arm (ABB IRB 140), a dialogue system and a visual system. The spatial context shared between the user and the system consists of a set of wooden objects, placed on a table, that differ in base, height, size and color. The system is able to recognize the objects on the table, determine their positions, interpret the user's commands, and perform requested manipulation of the objects.

Implementation of the extended focus tree model within the dialogue system improved primarily the natural language understanding and dialogue management modules. This is illustrated in the interaction fragment given in Fig. 4. At the start of the fragment, the current focus of attention is placed on the root node of the tree. In the first dialogue act (Therapist₁), the therapist explicitly utters the name of the child (denoted as ≪C≫). This keyword is assigned only to node *Child*, so the system places the focus of attention on this node (cf. the edge marked with number 1 in Fig. 3). It means that the following dialogue act will be mapped onto the subtree determined by node *Child* as its root node. This is an important restriction for the system. It is clear that the therapist refers to the child in the second command (Therapist₂). However, from the system's point of view, this command addresses neither the child nor the system explicitly. In order that the system can infer to whom the therapist's command is addressed, it must take the history of interaction into account, which is summarized in the current focus of attention (cf. [13, p. 177]). Since the mapping of this command is—at the moment— restricted to the subtree determined by node *Child*, the system infers that this command refers to the child. Furthermore, the command contains three keywords: *the square, move*, and *right*—ordered from the most general to the most specific. In general, the keyword *square* is assigned to two nodes marked with ■ in the focus tree. Still, the introduced restriction implies that the focus of attention must be transited to node ■ that is a child of the node that carries the current focus of attention. In a similar manner, the mapping of two other keywords is restricted to subtrees determined by actual foci of attention. Thus, the focus of attention after the command is processed will be placed on the terminal node marked with → (cf. the edges marked with number 2 in Fig. 3).

Therapist$_1$:	Hi, ≪C≫.
Therapist$_2$:	Move the square to the right.
Child$_3$:	(no response)
Therapist$_4$:	≪S≫, do it.
System$_5$:	(moves the square rightward, in the child-centered frame of reference)
Therapist$_6$:	Move the square to the right.
System$_7$:	(moves the square rightward, in the system-centered frame of reference)

Fig. 4. Interaction fragment, translated from Serbian to English. The nonverbal dialogue acts are underlined.

Since the child does not respond to this command (Child$_3$), the therapist asks the system to do it (Therapist$_4$). This dialogue act fits well in the dialogue context—it contains two forms of anaphoric cohesion [14, pp. 316,322]: an ellipsis-substitution (verb *do*), and a reference (pronoun *it*)—but does not carry explicit information what the system is expected to do. However, the terminal node that carries the current focus of attention is related with terminal node ↑ in the subtree determined by node *System* (cf. the dashed line marked with number 3 in Fig. 3). As already discussed, the direction *rightward* in the child-centered reference frame coincides with the direction *forward* in the system-centered reference frame. Since the system is supposed to perform the therapist's command, it moves the square along the direction *forward* in its frame of reference. The focus of attention is transited to terminal node ↑ in the subtree determined by node *System*.

Finally, command Therapist$_6$ is, at the surface level, the same as command Therapist$_2$. However, the system interprets this command with respect to the current focus of attention. Therefore, the command is performed in the system-centered frame of reference.

5   Discussion and Conclusion

In the observed scenario, the objects can be moved over the surface of the table. Consequently, we considered the research question of how to specify directions on the horizontal plane in a computationally appropriate manner, such that search domains can be reliably projected off a ground object. The research focus on the horizontal plane was an intentional choice. While perceptual cues for the vertical plane provide a good universal solution to one axis (e.g., there is a fixed direction provided by gravity), there is no simple solution to the linguistic description of horizontal spatial patterns [1, pp. 35,76].

The proposed extension of the focus tree represents a cognitively-inspired modeling method for linguistic encoding of frame-of-reference information, aimed at enabling dialogue systems to process dialogue acts that instantiate user-centered frames of reference. For the purpose of illustration, we specified four directions in the horizontal plane of the table. But in some other interaction scenarios we might need a more fine-grained partition of the horizontal plane. In a general case, we may use n directions represented by vectors in the horizontal plane that start from the same point C (e.g., the center of the table) and are oriented $\frac{360}{n}$ degrees from each other. Every rotation of these vectors by $\frac{360}{n}$ degrees around point C in the horizontal plane represents a possible spatial perspective that the users or the system may take during the interaction. Thus, in this case, the model differentiates between n distinct spatial perspectives in the horizontal plane. It is important to note that these changes can be incorporated in the proposed model by simple modification of the tree topology, while all underlying algorithms related to processing of the user's verbal commands remain the same.

Acknowledgments. The presented study is performed as part of the projects "Design of Robots as Assistive Technology for the Treatment of Children with Developmental Disorders" (III44008) and "Development of Dialogue Systems for Serbian and Other South Slavic Languages" (TR32035), funded by the Ministry of Education, Science and Technological Development of the Republic of Serbia. The responsibility for the content of this paper lies with the authors.

References

1. Levinson, S.C.: Space in Language and Cognition: Explorations in Cognitive Diversity. Cambridge University Press (2003)
2. Bowerman, M.: The origins of children's spatial semantic categories: cognitive vs. linguistic determinants. In: Gumperz, J.J., Levinson, S.C. (eds.) Rethinking Linguistic Relativity, pp. 145–176. Cambridge University Press (1996)
3. Bowerman, M., Choi, S.: Space under construction: Language-specific spatial categorization in first language acquisition. In: Gentner, D., Goldin-Meadow, S. (eds.) Language in Mind, pp. 387–427. MIT Press, Cambridge (2004)
4. Gentner, D., Bowerman, M.: Why some spatial semantic categories are harder to learn than others: The typological prevalence hypothesis. In: Guo, J., Lieven, E., Budwig, N., Ervin-Tripp, S., Nakamura, K., Ozcaliskan, S. (eds.) Crosslinguistic Approaches to the Psychology of Language: Research in the Tradition of Dan Isaac Slobin, pp. 465–480. Psychology Press, New York (2009)
5. Gnjatović, M., Delić, V.: Attention and linguistic encoding of motion events in human-machine interaction. In: Halupka-Rešetar, S., Marković, M., Milicćev, T., Milićević, N. (eds.) Selected Papers from SinFonIJA, pp. 237–257. Cambridge Scholar Publishing (2012)
6. Gnjatović, M., Janev, M., Delić, V.: Focus Tree: Modeling Attentional Information in Task-Oriented Human-Machine Interaction. Applied Intelligence 37(3), 305–320 (2012)
7. Gnjatović, M., Delić, V.: A Cognitively-Inspired Method for Meaning Representation in Dialogue Systems. In: Proc. of the 3rd IEEE International Conference on Cognitive Infocommunications, Kosice, Slovakia, pp. 383–388 (2012)

8. Gnjatović, M., Tasevski, J., Nikolić, M., Mišković, D., Borovac, B., Delić, V.: Adaptive Multimodal Interaction with Industrial Robot. In: Proc. of the IEEE 10th Jubilee International Symposium on Intelligent Systems and Informatics (SISY 2012), Subotica, Serbia, pp. 329–333 (2012)

9. Gnjatović, M., Rösner, D.: Adaptive Dialogue Management in the NIMITEK Prototype System. In: André, E., Dybkjær, L., Minker, W., Neumann, H., Pieraccini, R., Weber, M. (eds.) PIT 2008. LNCS (LNAI), vol. 5078, pp. 14–25. Springer, Heidelberg (2008)

10. Gnjatović, M., Suzić, S., Morošev, M., Delić, V.: A Prototype Conversational Agent Embedded in Android-Based Mobile Phones. In: Proc. of the TELFOR 2012, Belgrade, Serbia, pp. 1444–1447 (2012)

11. Gnjatović, M., Pekar, D., Delić, V.: Naturalness, Adaptation and Cooperativeness in Spoken Dialogue Systems. In: Esposito, A., Esposito, A.M., Martone, R., Müller, V.C., Scarpetta, G. (eds.) COST 2102 Int. Training School 2010. LNCS, vol. 6456, pp. 298–304. Springer, Heidelberg (2011)

12. Struiksma, M.E., Noordzij, M.L., Postma, A.: Reference frame preferences in haptics differ for the blind and sighted in the horizontal but not in the vertical plane. Perception 40(6), 725–738 (2011)

13. Grosz, B., Sidner, C.: Attention, Intentions, and the Structure of Discourse. Computational Linguistics 12(3), 175–204 (1986)

14. Halliday, M.: An Introduction to Functional Grammar, 2nd edn. Edward Arnold, London (1994)

Evaluation of Advanced Language Modeling Techniques for Russian LVCSR

Daria Vazhenina and Konstantin Markov

Human Interface Laboratory, The University of Aizu, Japan
{d8132102,markov}@u-aizu.ac.jp

Abstract. The Russian language is characterized by very flexible word order, which limits the ability of the standard n-grams to capture important regularities in the data. Moreover, it is highly inflectional language with rich morphology, which leads to high out-of-vocabulary (OOV) word rates. In this paper, we present comparison of two advanced language modeling techniques: factored language model (FLM) and recurrent neural network (RNN) language model, applied for Russian large vocabulary speech recognition. Evaluation experiments showed that the FLM, built using training corpus of 10M words was better and reduced the perplexity and word error rate (WER) by 20% and 4.0% respectively. Further WER reduction by 7.4% was achieved when the training data were increased to 40M words and 3-gram, FLM and RNN language models were combined together by linear interpolation.

Keywords: language modeling, Russian language, factored language models, recurrent neural network, inflectional languages.

1 Introduction

Although the underlying speech technology is mostly language-independent, differences between languages with respect to their structure and grammar have substantial effect on the automatic speech recognition (ASR) systems performance. Research in the ASR area has been traditionally focused on several main languages, such as English, French, Spanish, Chinese or Japanese, and some other languages, especially eastern European languages, have received much less attention.

The Russian language belongs to the Slavic branch of the Indo-European group of languages, which are characterized by complex mechanism of word-formation and flexible word order. Word relations within a sentence are marked by inflections and grammatical categories such as gender, number, person, case, etc. [1]. Sentence structure is not restricted by hard grammatical rules as in the English, German or Arabic languages. These two factors greatly reduce the predictive power of the conventional n-gram language models (LMs).

Regardless, in current Russian large vocabulary continuous speech recognition (LVCSR) systems conventional n-grams are usually used [2,3,4]. An improved bi-gram was proposed in [5] where the counts of some of the existing n-grams are increased after syntactic analysis of the training data. Long-distance dependencies between words are

M. Železný et al. (Eds.): SPECOM 2013, LNAI 8113, pp. 124–131, 2013.

identified and added as new bi-gram counts. This allowed to reduce the word error rate of a speech recognition system with dictionary of 208K words from 58.4% to 56.1%.

Recently, for the Arabic, which is also highly inflectional language, it was proposed to incorporate word features, called factors, into the language model [6]. This factored language model (FLM) implements a back-off procedure by excluding factors one by one or even several factors at a time without taking into account factor's distance from the predicted word. This improves the robustness of the probability estimates for rarely observed word n-grams. Using this model, relative WER reduction of 3.4% was achieved for Arabic LVCSR system with 70K vocabulary size [7]. For the Turkish language, it was reported that the FLM reduced the WER by 1.7% relative for a 200K words ASR system [8].

For the Czech language, which is also morphologically rich, implementation of neural network (NN) based language models was presented in [9]. Using such 4-gram LM for the Czech lecture recognition task, WER relative improvement of 15% was obtained. To be able to use larger context, LM based on recurrent neural network (RNN) was proposed in [10]. RNN LMs allow effective processing of arbitrary length sequences, which overcomes the main n-gram drawback - dependency on only few consecutive words.

This paper describes our implementation of the FLM and RNN LM for Russian LVCSR with vocabulary of 100K words. We investigated the influence of different factors for the FLM and different size of the RNN hidden and output layers on the language model performance. Both language modeling techniques are implemented using n-best re-scoring. Best, in terms of WER, was the interpolation of the conventional 3-gram LM with both the FLM and RNN LM.

2   Factored Language Models

In the factored language model (FLM), it is proposed to include word features, called factors, in the standard n-gram language model. Factors of a given word can be any grammatical information about the word, such as its lemma, stem, root, ending, part-of-speech, etc. In the FLM, word sequence $W = \{w_1, w_2...w_t\}$ is represented by a sequence of K factors for each word w_i, $f_i^{1:K} = \{f_i^1, f_i^2...f_i^K\}$. A probabilistic language model is estimated over the factor vectors. Using n-gram-like formula, the general model takes the following form $P(f_t^{1:K}|f_{t-1}^{1:K}, f_{t-2}^{1:K}...f_{t-n+1}^{1:K})$, which can be simplified to $P(f_t|f_1, f_2...f_m)$, where $f_t = w_t$ and $\{f_i\}, i = 1...m, m \leq K * (n-1)$ is any combination of factors. If an n-gram of word or factor is not sufficiently observed, generalized back-off procedure is used. As shown on Fig.1(b), during the back-off any factor can be dropped at each step in any order. This flexible back-off procedure is the main advantage of the FLM.

In order to obtain a good FLM performance, we need to tune its parameters: the combination of conditioning factors (factor set) and the back-off tree. In [6], two ways were proposed to optimize these parameters: manually choose the factor set and fix the back-off tree based on linguistic knowledge [8]; automatically determine optimal parameters using genetic algorithm (GA) [6,7].

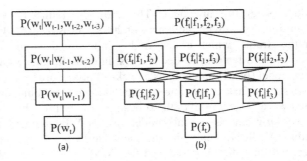

Fig. 1. *N*-gram and FLM back-off trees. (a) Standard *n*-gram back-off path has strict order of dropping words, (b) In the FLM case, any factor may be dropped at each step resulting in many possible paths.

In [6], it was demonstrated that the factor set and back-off tree optimized using GA can perform better than hand-selected ones. In addition, relative WER reductions presented in [6] and [7] were higher than those reported in [8].

The genetic algorithm for FLM optimization seeks the optimal factor set and back-off tree based on minimizing the model perplexity over some test set. This procedure produces many FLMs and those with the lowest perplexity are further evaluated on speech test data.

3   Recurrent Neural Network

The main advantage of the RNN LM over conventional *n*-gram and feed-forward NN LM is the ability to store arbitrary long history of given word [10].

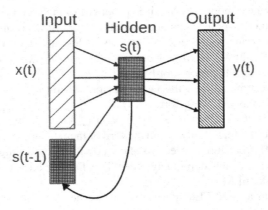

Fig. 2. Recurrent neural network architecture for language modeling

The RNN used in our experiments is shown in Fig.2 and has three layers. An 1-of-N vector representation x(t) of the current word is fed to the input layer, which also takes the output s(t-1) of the hidden layer. This recurrent feedback stores the word history information in the hidden layer. The output layer gives the probability distribution of the next word y(t) and therefore uses neurons with softmax activation function. The size of the input and output layers is defined by vocabulary size, but the size of the hidden layer is a free parameter, which has to be determined experimentally.

Learning of the weight matrix between the hidden and the output layer is the most time consuming part in the NN training. To reduce the computational complexity, it was proposed to factorize the output layer using classes [11]. Words are mapped into classes with frequency binning, which proportionally assigns words to classes based on their frequency. Thus, the number of classes becomes another free parameter of the model.

4 Language Resources

Our text corpus contains 41M words with vocabulary size of about ∼100K words. This corpus was assembled from recent news articles published by freely available Internet sites of several on-line Russian newspapers for the years 2006-2011. We split our corpus into 40M words train set and a test set consisting of 1M words. For the first experiments with FLM and RNN LM 10M words were separated from the full train set and used as small train set.

Word features for the FLM were obtained using the TreeTagger tool [12] with tagset described in [13]. This tool annotates words with lemma and morphological tag, which contains detailed grammatical information about the word, such as POS category, gender, number, case, etc.

In addition to the word, lemma and morphological tag factor types, we use two extra: POS category and gender-number-person factor, which contains important grammatical information for the word relations in a sentence. The list of all factor types, we experimented with, is shown in Table 1.

Table 1. Factor types for the Russian language used in the experiments

Factor type	Description	Size
W	word	99 958
L	lemma	23 742
T	morphological tag	819
G	gender, number and person	30
P	part-of-speech (POS) category	10

The LM training corpus is preprocessed so that every word is replaced with a vector of all factor types. For instance, word 'брэнды' (brands) is replaced with the vector {W-брэнды:P-N:T-Ncmpnn:L-брэнд:G-MP}.

5   Experiments

5.1   Speech Database and Feature Extraction

In our experiments, we used the SPIIRAS [14] and GlobalPhone [3] Russian speech databases. Speech data are collected in clean acoustic conditions. In total, there are 28671 utterances pronounced by 165 speakers (86 male and 79 female) with duration of about 38 hours. Speech test data consist of 10% of the GlobalPhone recordings pronounced by 5 male and 5 female speakers not used for acoustic model (AM) training.

The speech signal was coded with energy and 12 MFCCs and their first and second order derivatives. The AM consists of 5342 tied states with 16 mixture GMMs as output models. Our speech decoder (Julius ver. 4.2 [15]) produces 500-best hypothesis list, which we use for re-scoring by the selected FLMs.

The FLMs we built using SRILM toolkit (v.1.5.11) [16]and the RNN LMs were implemented using the RNNLM toolkit (v.0.3b) [11].

5.2   Experimental Results

To determine parameters of the FLM and RNN LM, we used the small train set of 10M words, which speeds up this step. As a baseline LM, we use conventional 3-gram trained on same train data using Kneser-Ney discount. Its perplexity is 537 and the word error rate is 35.4%.

FLM Evaluation

First, we evaluated each factor type from Table 1 individually. For this reason, we built several small FLMs using the word and one of the other factor types for time context 1 and 2 corresponding to 2-gram and 3-gram contexts respectively. In other words, train FLMs, which model probability distributions $p_k(w_t|w1, f_k1, w2, f_k2)$ for $k = 1...K$. On this step, we set back-off path manually, in a manner similar to the conventional 3-gram back-off path, which has two possible variations:

- Back-off path 1: Drop the words in time distance order: $w2, w1$, then drop factors in the same order: f_k2, f_k1.
- Back-off path 2: First drop the most distant word and factor $w2, f_k2$, then less distant ones $w1, f_k1$.

The performance of these FLMs presented in Table 2 shows that the back-off path has big influence on the perplexity. Since factors G and P showed the perplexity worse than baseline in both cases, we choose to continue with L and T factor types only.

Then, using GA, we find the optimal factor set and back-off trees for factor types W, L and T using time context 1, 2 and 3. In Table 3, results obtained using FLMs with lowest perplexities are presented. The best perplexity was achieved using the largest model F1, which is a significant 19.9% reduction relative to the baseline. Using model F3 with longer context, the lowest WER was achieved. However, the biggest relative WER reduction of 6.9% is obtained by the interpolated with 3-gram model F2, which is built with quite small factor set and not highly branched back-off tree. So, we chose this model for further experiments.

Table 2. Perplexities of FLMs built from the small training set with different back-off paths. The baseline perplexity is 537.

Factor types	Back-off path 1	Back-off path 2
WL	611	525
WT	685	488
WG	988	714
WP	652	549

Table 3. Performance of FLMs built using most effective factors

Model	Factors (# back-off tree nodes)	FLM		3-gram + FLM		
		perpl.	WER,%	Int.coef	perpl.	WER,%
3-gram				1.0	537	35.4
F1	W1,L1,T1,W2,L2,T2 (55)	430	34.5	0.51	437	33.3
F2	W1,L1,T1,L2,T2 (20)	440	34.4	0.45	445	**33.0**
F3	W1,L1,T1,L2,T2,T3 (43)	460	**34.0**	0.43	463	33.4

RNN LM Evaluation

To determine main parameters of RNN LMs: the number of hidden nodes and the number of word classes, we trained several models using the small train set. Perplexity and WER of those models were much higher than baseline, about 1100 and 38% respectively. However, when interpolated with the baseline 3-gram, their performance improved significantly. In Table 4, we summarize results obtained from the 3-gram and RNN LM interpolation. The interpolation coefficient (Int.coef.) was manually tuned for each model.

Table 4. Performance of the RNN LM interpolated with 3-gram. The baseline perplexity is 537 and the WER is 35.4%.

# hidden nodes	# classes								
	150			500			1000		
	Int.coef	perpl.	WER,%	Int.coef	perpl.	WER,%	Int.coef	perpl.	WER,%
100	0.68	466	33.5	0.64	470	33.3	0.68	503	33.3
150	0.67	474	33.6	0.67	457	33.3	0.66	462	**33.1**
200	0.69	454	33.3	0.77	458	33.5	0.64	471	34.1
250	0.81	459	33.9	0.63	469	33.5	0.67	459	33.5

Perplexity of all interpolated models is lower than the baseline and is in the same range as of the FLM. The best relative WER improvement of 6.5% was obtained using 150 hidden nodes and 1000 classes. These parameters were chosen for the further experiments.

Results Using the Full Training Set

After defining optimal parameters for both LM types, the 3-gram and FLM (F2) models were re-trained using all training text. On the other hand, the RNN model with 150 hidden nodes and 1000 classes (h-150, c-1000) was updated with one more iteration using the full train data. Using the full training set, the baseline 3-gram LM perplexity became 293 and the word error rate - 33.9%. In the Table 5, results obtained using the new models and their interpolations are presented. While FLM model WER improved, the result of its interpolation with the 3-gram did not change. However, in terms of WER, performance of the stand-alone RNN model improved significantly from 38.3% to 32.9%. The best WER relative improvement of 7.4% was achieved by the linear interpolation of all the 3 models.

Table 5. Performance of FLM and RNN LMs built using all train data

#	Model	Int.coef.	perpl.	WER, %
1	3-gram	1.0	293	34.0
2	FLM (F2)	1.0	242	33.7
3	(1) + (2)	0.55 + 0.45	241	33.0
4	RNN (h-150, c-1000)	1.0	393	32.9
5	(1) + (4)	0.49 + 0.51	244	31.9
6	(2) + (4)	0.6 + 0.4	215	32.0
7	(1) + (2) + (4)	0.3 + 0.4 + 0.3	216	**31.5**

6   Conclusions

This paper presents implementation of some advanced language modeling techniques such as factored language model and recurrent neural network language model for Russian speech recognition task. We evaluate those models and present the results obtained using small and large training sets. Obtained WER relative improvement of 7.4% is quite high, in comparison to improvements achieved for other morphologically rich languages such as Arabic and Turkish using advanced language modeling techniques [7,8].

Factored language models seems to be able to capture additional information and improve LM probability estimates, when the amount of training data is limited. On the other hand, RNN LM evaluation showed significant improvement applying large training set.

References

1. Cubberley, P.: Russian: a linguistic introduction. Cambridge University Press (2002)
2. Whittaker, E.W., Woodland, P.C.: Comparison of language modelling techniques for Russian and English. In: Proc. ICSLP (1998)
3. Stuker, S., Schultz, T.: A grapheme based speech recognition system for Russian. In: Proc. SPECOM, St. Peterburg, Russia, pp. 297–303 (September 2004)

4. Vazhenina, D., Markov, K.: Phoneme set selection for Russian speech recognition. In: Proc. IEEE NLP-KE, Tokushima, Japan, pp. 475–478 (November 2011)
5. Karpov, A., Kipyatkova, I., Ronzhin, A.: Very large vocabulary ASR for spoken Russian with syntactic and morphemic analysis. In: Proc. InterSpeech, pp. 3161–3164 (August 2011)
6. Kirchhoff, K., Vergyri, D., Bilmes, J., Duh, K., Stolcke, A.: Morphology-based language modelling for conversational Arabic speech recognition. Computer Speech and Language 20(4), 589–608 (2006)
7. El-Desoky Mousa, A., Schluter, R., Ney, H.: Investigations on the use of morpheme level features in language models for Arabic LVCSR. In: Proc. ICASSP, Kyoto, Japan, pp. 5021–5024 (March 2012)
8. Sak, H., Saraclar, M., Gungor, T.: Morphology-based and sub-word language modelling for Turkish speech recognition. In: Proc. ICASSP, Dallas, USA, pp. 5402–5405 (March 2010)
9. Mikolov, T., Kopecky, J., Burget, L., Glembek, O., Cernocky, J.: Neural network based language models for highly inflective languages. In: Proc. ICASSP, Taipei, Taiwan, pp. 4725–4728 (April 2009)
10. Mikolov, T., Karafiat, M., Burget, L., Cernocky, J., Khudanpur, S.: Recurrent neural network based language model. In: Proc. InterSpeech, Makuhari, Japan, pp. 1045–1048 (September 2010)
11. Mikolov, T., Kombrink, S., Burget, L., Cernocky, J., Khudanpur, S.: Extentions of recurrent neural network language models. In: Proc. ICASSP, Prague, Czech Republic, pp. 5528–5531 (May 2011)
12. Schmid, H.: Probabilistic part-of-speech tagging using decision trees. In: Proc. NeMLaP, Manchester, UK, pp. 44–49 (1994)
13. Sharoff, S., Kopotev, M., Erjavec, T., Feldman, A., Divjak, D.: Designing and evaluating Russian tagsets. In: Proc. LREC, Marrakech, pp. 279–285 (May 2008)
14. Jokisch, O., Wagner, A., Sabo, R., Jaeckel, R., Cylwik, N., Rusko, M., Ronzhin, A., Hoffmann, R.: Multilingual speech data collection for the assessment of pronunciation and prosody in a language learning system. In: Proc. SPECOM, St. Petersburg, Russia, pp. 515–520 (June 2009)
15. Lee, A., Kawahara, T.: Recent development of open-source speech recognition engine Julius. In: Proc. APSIPA ASC, Sapporo, Japan, pp. 131–137 (October 2009)
16. Stolcke, A.: SRILM - an extensible language modeling toolkit. In: Proc. ICSLP, vol. 2, pp. 901–904 (2002)

Examining Vulnerability of Voice Verification Systems to Spoofing Attacks by Means of a TTS System

Vadim Shchemelinin[1] and Konstantin Simonchik[2]

[1] National Research University of Information Technologies, Mechanics and Optics,
St. Petersburg, Russia
www.ifmo.ru
[2] Speech Technology Center Limited, St. Petersburg, Russia
{shchemelinin, simonchik}@speechpro.com
www.speechpro.com

Abstract. This paper examines the method of spoofing text-dependent voice verification systems based on the most popular TTS approaches: Unit Selection and HMM. Research of this method shows the possibility of achieving a false acceptance error of 98%-100% if the duration of the TTS database is sufficiently large. A distinctive feature of the method is that it can be fully automatical if used in conjunction with a speech recognition system.

Keywords: spoofing, speech synthesis, unit selection, HMM, speaker recognition.

1 Introduction

Speaker verification systems have become widespread in recent time. They are used in different areas of our lives: forensic research, physical access control systems, banking, as well as on the web. The two main roles that such systems have in every-day life are usability enhancement and security. So to perform its functions a voice verification system has to have high robustness, especially if it is used for access to a bank account or personal information [1]. However, as will be demonstrated below, state-of-the-art verification systems are vulnerable to spoofing by means of automatic Text-to-Speech (TTS) systems. This paper examines a method of spoofing [2] a text-dependent verification system based on i-vectors [3]. Recent NIST SRE 2012 competitions [5] showed that the field is currently dominated by systems based on representing a speaker voice model in the total variability space, so they were chosen as the subject of our research.

Different spoofing methods are known. For example, [6] describes methods based on Replay attack, Cut and paste, Handkerchief tampering and Nasalization tampering. In our case spoofing is performed using a hybrid TTS method that combines Unit Selection and Hidden Markov Models (HMM), which can be considered the best TTS method to date [12].

The paper reports research into the dependence of verification robustness on the volume of the speech database used for TTS. We aim to determine the minimal length of speech recordings that is necessary to significantly reduce verification robustness.

M. Železný et al. (Eds.): SPECOM 2013, LNAI 8113, pp. 132–137, 2013.

2   Description of Our Methods and Systems

2.1   The Voice Verification System

In our experiments we used i-vector based speaker recognition system [3], [4].

We used special signal preprocessing module, which included energy based voice activity detection, clipping [7], pulse and multi-tonal detection. The front-end computes 13 mel-frequency cepstral coefficients, as well as the first and second derivatives, to yield a 39 dimensional vector per frame. The derivatives are estimated over a 5-frame context. To obtain these coefficients, speech samples are pre-emphasized, divided into 22ms window frames with a fixed shift of 11ms, and each frame is subsequently multiplied by a Hamming window function.

We also applied a cepstral mean subtraction (CMS) and did not apply Feature Warping [8] for the cepstral coefficients.

We used a gender-independent universal background model (UBM) with 512 - component gaussian mixture model (GMM), obtained by standard ML-training on the telephone part of the NISTs SRE 1998-2010 datasets (all languages, both genders) [9], [10].

In our study we used more than 4000 training speakers in total. We also used a diagonal, not a full-covariance GMM UBM.

The i-vector extractor was trained on more than 60000 telephone and microphone recordings from the NIST 1998-2010 comprising more than 4000 speakers voices.

The main expression defining the factor analysis of the GMM parameters with the aim of lowering data dimensionality is given below:

$$\mu = m + T\omega + \epsilon,$$

where μ is the supervector of the GMM parameters of the speaker model,
m is the supervector of the UBM parameters,
T is the matrix defining the basis in the reduced feature space,
ω is the i-vector in the reduced feature space, $\omega \in N(0, 1)$,
ϵ is the error vector.
LDA matrix was trained on the same data from the NIST 1998-2010.

2.2   The TTS System

For the modeling of a spoofing attack we used a TTS system developed by Speech Technology Center Limited, (STC Ltd.) [11] based on two most popular approaches:

1. The Unit Selection algorithm (speech element selection). This approach makes it possible to synthesize speech with maximum naturalness, given an accurately segmented voice database of a large size (10 hours and more). On the other hand, the second approach, which produces synthesized speech that is less natural, has the advantages presented below.
2. Statistical models (HMM TTS), which produce synthesized speech that is less natural, but smoother, without detectable phone boundaries (pitch or energy leaps) which are usual for concatenative synthesis. In addition, the HMM-based method

provides an easy way to modify voice characteristics by using speaker adaptation/interpolation techniques. Finally, applying the HMM-based speech synthesis method makes it possible to create a new TTS voice in much less time and to reduce the memory size required for storing the voice data.

Experiments [12] show that the naturalness of speech synthesized by the hybrid TTS system is increased compared to systems based only on Unit Selection or hidden Markov models. A detailed description of the TTS system is given in [12].

2.3 The Method of Spoofing the Verification System

In this paper we propose to explore the method of spoofing a text-prompted verification system using TTS technology.

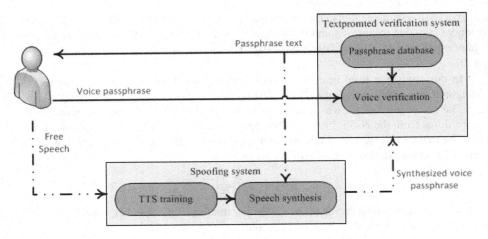

Fig. 1. Scheme of spoofing a text-prompted verification system using TTS technology

The method is based on creating a TTS voice based on previously recorded free speech of a verification system customer. In the process of text-prompted verification, the text of the passphrase is received and it is then synthesized with the customers voice. A detailed scheme of the spoofing procedure is shown in Figure 1.

3 Experiments with Verification System Spoofing

3.1 Speech Database

In our experiment we used a Russian speech database with 7 speakers (2 men and 5 women) whose voices were used for creating a TTS system. Examples of passphrases include: "City of Ekaterinburg, Railway Station street, 22, Railway Station"; "pay three roubles and publish an ad in the bulletin", etc. It is important to note that the recorded phrases were not included in the TTS database. In total, 63 phrases by different speakers were recorded.

3.2   The Influence of TTS Material on Verification Robustness

The aim of our experiments was to establish a dependence of the false acceptance (FA) verification error on the duration of speech material used for creating the synthesized voice.

For the experiments we used the previously described voice verification system. The system thresholds were calibrated using a YOHO speech database [13] consisting of 138 speakers (male and female) each of whom pronounced a "Combination lock" phrases of the form "36-24-36", with about 1.5-2 seconds of pure speech. Only one passphrase was used for enroll and one for the verification.

Two verification system thresholds were set:

1. A threshold based on Equal Error Rate (EER), so-called ThresholdEER. EER was estimated as 4% on the YOHO database.
2. A threshold with the likelihood of false acceptance not higher than 1% (Threshold-FA1). This threshold is usually used in systems where it is necessary to provide maximum defense against criminal access.

Then, for each speaker, attempts to access the system were made using a TTS voice that was created using the speech material of this speaker. The length of speech material for TTS varied from 1 minute to 4 hours of speech. The experimental results are presented in Figure 2.

Additionally, Table 1 shows FA values for the verification system thresholds that we are examining. As can be seen from the table, if the TTS database is 8 minutes or longer, verification system robustness decreases dramatically. If the database is large (4 hours of speech), synthesized speech is virtually indistinguishable from the original speech of a living human from the point of view of the verification system.

Table 1. FA verification error for different amounts of data for the TTS system

Length of speech data for TTS	FA for ThresholdEER (%)	FA for ThresholdFA1 (%)
1 minute	8 (12.7%)	1 (1.5%)
3 minutes	22 (34.9%)	5 (7.9%)
8 minutes	28 (44.4%)	12 (19.1%)
30 minutes	35 (55.6%)	15 (23.8%)
4 hours	63 (100%)	62 (98.4%)

Based on these results, we can conclude that the proposed spoofing method not only significantly reduces verification system robustness, but also circumvents such an additional defence as the liveness detector. If the verification system gives the user a password as a sound message, it is possible to use an automatic speech recognition (ASR) system to make the spoofing process fully automatical. In contrast to spoofing methods by speech feature conversion [14,15], this method used together with ASR can exclude the participation of a human from the dialog with the verification system. Using a hybrid of TTS and ASR technologies for an automatic spoofing system is the subject of our further research.

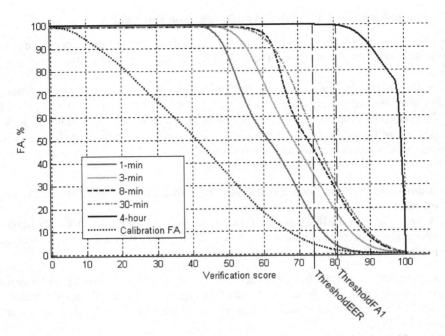

Fig. 2. FA diagrams for spoofing the verification system based on different volumes of free speech used for TTS

4   Conclusions

This paper analyzes the robustness of contemporary verification methods against spoofing using a hybrid TTS system based on Unit Selection and HMM technologies. As shown by our experiments, by using even 8 or more minutes of TTS speech data-base it is possible to significantly reduce verification robustness, while if the database is increased to 4 hours the verification system virtually does not distinguish the syn-thesized signal from the customers voice.

An important characteristic of the method is the possibility to make it fully automatic if it is integrated with an ASR system.

References

1. Matveev, Y.N.: Biometric technologies of person identification by voice and other modalities, Vestnik MGTU. Priborostroenie. Biometric Technologies, Special Issue 3(3), 46–61 (2012) (Rus.)
2. Wu, Z., Kinnunen, T., Chng, E.S., Li, H., Ambikairajah, E.: A Study on spoofing attack in state-of-the-art speaker verification: the telephone speech case. In: Proc. APSIPA ASC 2012, Hollywood, USA, pp. 1–5 (December 2012)
3. Kenny, P.: Bayesian speaker verification with heavy tailed priors. In: Proceedings of the Odyssey Speaker and Language Recognition Workshop, Brno, Czech Republic (June 2010)

4. Simonchik, K., Pekhovsky, T., Shulipa, A., Afanasyev, A.: Supervized Mixture of PLDA Models for Cross-Channel Speaker Verification. In: 13th Annual Conference of the International Speech Communication Association, Interspeech 2012, Portland, Oregon, September 9-13 (2012)
5. The NIST Year 2012 Speaker Recognition Evaluation Plan (2012), http://www.nist.gov/itl/iad/mig/upload/NIST_SRE12_evalplan-v17-r1.pdf
6. Villalba, J., Lleida, E.: Speaker verification performance degradation against spoofing and tampering attacks. In: FALA 2010 Workshop, pp. 131–134 (2010)
7. Aleinik, S., Matveev, Y., Raev, A.: Method of evaluation of speech signal clipping level. Scientific and Technical Journal of Information Technologies, Mechanics and Optics 79(3), 79–83 (2012) (Rus.)
8. Pelecanos, J., Sridharan, S.: Feature warping for robust speaker verification. In: Proc. Speaker Odyssey, the Speaker Recognition Workshop, Crete, Greece (2001)
9. Matveev, Y.N., Simonchik, K.K.: The speaker identification system for the NIST SRE 2010. In: The 20th International Conference on Computer Graphics and Vision, GraphiCon 2010, Conference Proceedings, St. Petersburg, Russia, September 20-24 (2010)
10. Kozlov, A.V., Kudashev, O.Y., Matveev, Y.N., Pekhovsky, T.S., Simonchik, K.K., Shulipa, A.K.: Speaker recognition system for the NIST SRE 2012. In: SPIIRAS Proceedings, vol. 25(2), pp. 350–370 (March 2013)
11. Chistikov, P.G., Korolkov, E.A.: Data-driven Speech Parameter Generation for Russian Text-to-Speech System. Computational Linguistics and Intellectual Technologies. Papers from the Annual International Conference "Dialogue", 1 of 2(11(18)), 103–111 (2012)
12. Chistikov, P.G., Korolkov, E.A., Talanov, A.O.: Combining HMM and unit selection technologies to increase naturalness of synthesized speech. In: Dialog 2013 (2013)
13. Campbell, J., Higgins, A.: "YOHO Speaker Verification database", http://www.ldc.upenn.edu/Catalog/catalogEntry.jsp?catalogId=LDC94S16
14. Wu, Z., Chng, E.S., Li, H.: Speaker verification system against two different voice conversion techniques in spoofing attacks, Technical report, http://www3.ntu.edu.sg/home/wuzz/
15. Kinnunen, T., Wu, Z.-Z., Lee, K.A., Sedlak, F., Chng, E.S., Li, H.: Vulnerability of Speaker Verification Systems Against Voice Conversion Spoofing Attacks: the Case of Telephone Speech. In: Proc. ICASSP 2012, Kyoto, Japan, pp. 4401–4404 (March 2012)

Exploiting Multiple ASR Outputs
for a Spoken Language Understanding Task

Marcos Calvo, Fernando García, Lluís-F. Hurtado,
Santiago Jiménez, and Emilio Sanchis

Departament de Sistemes Informàtics i Computació
Universitat Politècnica de València, València, Spain
{mcalvo,fgarcia,lhurtado,sjimenez,esanchis}@dsic.upv.es

Abstract. In this paper, we present an approach to Spoken Language Understanding, where the input to the semantic decoding process is a composition of multiple hypotheses provided by the Automatic Speech Recognition module. This way, the semantic constraints can be applied not only to a unique hypothesis, but also to other hypotheses that could represent a better recognition of the utterance. To do this, we have developed an algorithm to combine multiple sentences into a weighted graph of words, which is the input to the semantic decoding process. It has also been necessary to develop a specific algorithm to process these graphs of words according to the statistical models that represent the semantics of the task. This approach has been evaluated in a SLU task in Spanish. Results, considering different configurations of ASR outputs, show the better behavior of the system when a combination of hypotheses is considered.

Keywords: Combination of multiple outputs, graph of words, graph of concepts, Spoken Language Understanding.

1 Introduction

Speech-driven human-computer interaction systems are becoming day after day more important in our lives. In many of these systems, an Automatic Speech Recognizer (ASR) is used as a front-end when the user speaks. However, an important drawback of this approach is that the errors that are generated in this first stage are impossible to be recovered afterwards, as the corresponding information is lost. This is the case of Spoken Language Understanding (SLU) systems [1], where the ASR output is processed by a semantic decoder, in order to obtain the meaning of the utterance. One possible solution for this problem is to integrate in a whole model all the knowledge sources that take part in the process (acoustic, lexical, syntactic and semantic) and apply all the linguistic constraints at once. Unfortunately, this solution generates an excessively large search space, increasing this way the difficulty of the task. Also, in this unified model, the different individual models should be properly weighted during its combination, in order to improve the performance of the system. The computation of these weights makes the application of the unified model even harder. For this reason, a more realistic option is to use a modular sequential architecture, in which the information that is transmitted from one module to the following one is a set of hypotheses, instead of just one hypothesis.

M. Železný et al. (Eds.): SPECOM 2013, LNAI 8113, pp. 138–145, 2013.

It is possible that the ASR provides a set of hypotheses to the following modules by means of a variety of mechanisms. One of these mechanisms is that the output of the ASR is a word lattice, which can be weighted with acoustic or language model probabilities, or even with some kind of confidence measure. Another option is to combine multiple sentences provided either by a single ASR (n-best list) or by several ASRs working in parallel, in order to exploit the benefits of each of them. For this approach, there are also several ways to carry out this combination. One of them is to use a voting algorithm, like ROVER [2], to obtain a new output that is made of segments corresponding to the original sentences. Another option is to build a graph of words, which can represent as well a reasonable generalization of the input sentences, if a Grammatical Inference algorithm is used. For this work, we have developed a Grammatical Inference algorithm based on the ClustalW [3] Multiple Sequence Alignment (MSA) algorithm. The ClustalW MSA algorithm was originally used for aligning biosequences, but has also been successfully used in other fields like Machine Translation [4,5].

Once the graphs of words are generated, it is necessary to develop a semantic decoder that is able to process these structures. This semantic decoder can be based on a statistical modelization of the semantics of the task [6]. Nevertheless, there is not many work done in SLU using graphs of words as input [7], as many of the SLU models assume that the input is a single sentence which is completely known when applying the semantic model.

Our goal in this work is to present an approach to SLU that takes advantage of multiple hypotheses provided by the ASR module, in any of the forms mentioned above, and exploit them by using graphs of words as the input to the semantic decoding module. For the SLU module, we have developed a specific Dynamic Programming (DP) algorithm for semantic decoding, which combines the weighted input graph with a set of Stochastic Finite State Automata (SFSA) that modelize the semantics of the task. To evaluate this approach, we have performed a set of experiments with the DIHANA task [8]. This is a SLU task in Spanish designed for being integrated in a telephonic Spoken Dialog System where the goal of the user is to request information about train fares and timetables. The statistical semantic model was automatically learned from the training set of the DIHANA corpus, which is segmented and labeled in terms of concepts.

2   Architecture of the SLU System

In this work, we have addressed the problem of exploiting the combination of multiple ASR outputs for SLU by means of a decoupled modular architecture (Figure 1), which is composed of the following modules:

1. A first module dedicated to Automatic Speech Recognition. We will consider three kinds of different ASR outputs: a word lattice weighted with acoustic probabilities, a n-best list provided by a single ASR, and a set of 1-best decodifications provided by several ASR working in parallel.
2. The second module is based on the idea of Grammatical Inference of generating a language that generalizes a set of positive samples provided as its input. Thus, this module takes a set of sentences and outputs a graph that represents a generalization

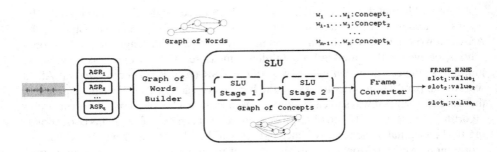

Fig. 1. Scheme of the architecture of our system

of the language represented by the individual sentences. The input sentences are either the n-best decodifications provided by an ASR, or the set of 1-best provided by several ASRs. As a lattice is itself a graph, if the output of the ASR is a word lattice this step can be skipped.

3. Then, the semantic decoding is carried out by means of a SLU module that is able to deal with graphs of words. For this system, we have developed a semantic decoding methodology that works in two stages. The first one takes as input a graph of words and a set of SFSA that modelize the lexical structures attached to each concept, and outputs a graph of concepts, which represents matchings between sequences of words and concepts. This graph of concepts is processed in a second stage, which also takes as input another SFSA that represents how the concepts are concatenated. The output of this module is the best sequence of concepts, as well as the underlying sequence of words and its segmentation in terms of the concepts.

4. Finally, the relevant semantic information is extracted and converted into a frame representation.

3   The Graph of Words Builder Module

The goal of this module is to generate a weighted graph of words from the outputs supplied by one or more ASRs. This graph represents a set of recognition alternatives that are a generalization of the individual transcriptions of the utterance. This way, the following modules can search among these alternatives for the most accurate sentence according to their specific constraints. It is also convenient that the words that appear in the graphs have associated some kind of weight, which is usually the normalized acoustic or language model probability, or a confidence measure. In our case, we have considered two ways for obtaining these graphs:

1. The output of the ASR is the lattice generated by the Viterbi algorithm, and the weights are the normalized acoustic probabilities associated to the words. In this case, it is not necessary any algorithm to generate the graph of words because it is supplied by the ASR.
2. The output of the ASR module is a set of sentences (i.e., a n-best list or a set of 1-best from different ASRs). In this case, a graph of words is estimated from these

alternative hypotheses. One of the advantages of building a graph of words is that it can represent an extra-language of structures similar to the original sentences, which is a Grammatical Inference process.

This way, we have an homogeneous mechanism of communication between modules, and the same algorithms can tackle with the lattices supplied in the case 1, and with the graphs generated in the case 2.

The algorithm proposed in this work for generating the graphs of words consists of two phases. In the first phase a multi-sentence alignment is performed. To do this, an adaptation of the ClustalW [3] MSA is used. This algorithm finds the best multiple alignment that minimizes the total number of edit errors (substitution, insertion and deletion of words) among all the sentences. Then, the second phase consists in finding the synchronization points in the alignment, generating nodes in these points, and creating the arcs (labeled with the words and weighted with the normalized counters) that represent alternative paths [6]. Figure 2 shows an example of a graph generated using this method. As it is shown, this graph represents not only the input sentences, but also an extra-language of sentences of similar characteristics. For example, the correct sentence *me puede decir horarios de trenes a Alicante* (could you tell me train timetables to Alicante) was not among the candidates provided, but can be recovered using this mechanism.

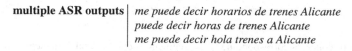

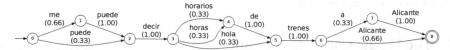

Fig. 2. Graph of words built from multiple ASR outputs

4   The SLU Module

We propose an understanding system that is able to deal with graph of words, where each arc is labeled with a word and a probability. This SLU system works in two stages. The first stage converts a graph of words into a graph of concepts using the information represented in a set of Stochastic Finite State Automata. Each of these automata modelizes a bigram Language Model that represents the lexical structures associated with a concept, as well as their probabilities. The second stage searches for the best path in the graph of concepts, according to a bigram Language Model of sequences of concepts represented as another SFSA. The final result is the best sequence of concepts, as well as the underlying sequence of words and its segmentation in terms of the concepts. Both stages are based on Dynamic Programming algorithms.

The graph of concepts obtained as the output of the first stage (see Figure 3) is the result of finding, for each concept c and each pair of nodes i, j, the sequence of words

W induced by a path from i to j in the graph of words that maximizes the product
of the probability of the path and the probability of W according to the SFSA of c.
Consequently, each arc in the graph of concepts is labeled with a sequence of words and
a concept associated to it, and is weighted with the product of the probabilities provided
by both the graph and the SFSA. Thus, a graph of concepts is a compact representation
of the semantics of the segments of words contained in the graph of words. Once the
graph of concepts is built, it is easy to find the path of maximum probability that goes
from the start to the ending node, taking into account a Language Model of sequences
of concepts.

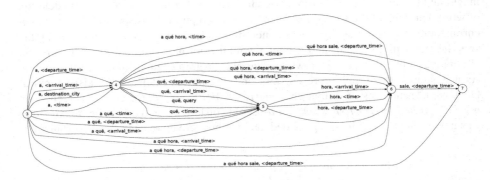

Fig. 3. Graph of concepts corresponding to the segment "a qué hora sale" (*which is the departure
time*), built from a graph of words

5   The Frame Converter Module

This last module converts the segmentation provided by the SLU module into a frame
representation of the semantics. The operations performed in this module are: the deletion of irrelevant segments (such as courtesies), the reordering of the relevant concepts
and attributes that appeared in the segmentation following an order which has been
defined a priori, the automatic instantiation of certain task-dependent values, etc.

Table 1 shows an example of an ideal situation where the input utterance is correctly
recognized, then the SLU module provides the correct semantic segmentation, and finally the frame converter outputs the correct frame representation.

6   Experiments and Results

To evaluate the proposed architecture, we have performed a set of experiments using
the DIHANA task [8]. The goal of this task is to use a Spoken Dialog System by phone
to request information about railway timetables and fares. This task has a corpus of
900 dialogs of spontaneous telephonic speech in Spanish, which was acquired by 225
speakers using the Wizard of Oz technique, amounting to a total of 6, 229 user turns.
This set of turns was split into a subset of 4, 889 utterances for training and 1, 109 for

Table 1. Example of the outputs of the SLU (semantic segmentation) and Frame Converter modules

Input utterance	*hola buenos días quería saber los horarios de trenes para ir a Madrid* *(hello good morning I'd like to know the train timetables to go to Madrid)*
Semantic segments	*hola buenos días* : courtesy *quería saber* : query *los horarios de trenes para ir* : <time> *a Madrid* : destination_city
Frame	(TIME?) DEST_CITY : Madrid

test. The orthographic transcriptions of all the user turns are available in this corpus, and are semi-automatically segmented and labeled using a set of 30 concepts.

For this experimentation, we used the HTK, Loquendo and Google ASRs. For HTK, both the Language and Acoustic Models of the ASR were trained with the training set. For Loquendo, only the Language Model was trained this way. No information of the task was provided to the Google ASR. The WERs obtained for the test set considering the 1-best output of each of the ASRs individually are: 17.85 for HTK, 17.90 for Loquendo and 29.45 for Google. The WER obtained for the Google ASR is higher than the rest because it is a general purpose ASR, without any knowledge of the task, while the others have some information about it.

We performed four types of SLU experiments, depending on the way that the ASR hypotheses are supplied:

1. Three experiments, one for each ASR, using the 1-best of each ASR separately. These experiments constitute the baselines.
2. Using a word lattice generated by HTK.
3. Taking the 3, 5 and 20-best hypotheses provided by the Google ASR, and combining them in a graph of words.
4. Taking the 1-best decodifications provided by the three ASRs, and combining them in a graph of words.

Two measures were used to evaluate each of the configurations:

- The Concept Error Rate (CER), which corresponds to errors in the output of the SLU module.
- The Frame-Slot Error Rate (FSER), which corresponds to errors in the slots of the frames in the final output of the system.

The results obtained are shown in Table 2. It must be noted that FSER is lower than CER because some concepts are not relevant for the final semantic representation. For example errors in the concept *courtesy* are not transmitted to the corresponding frame. Also, the results for the Google ASR are worse because it is a general purpose ASR, without any knowledge of the task.

These results show that all the experiments performed with multiple ASR outputs outperform the corresponding baseline. Also, they confirm the hypothesis that the combination of several sentences in a graph of words by means of a Grammatical Inference

Table 2. Results obtained using the different compositions of ASR outputs, as well as the individual 1-bests

Input graphs of words	CER	FSER
HTK 1-best	17.72	13.02
Loquendo 1-best	18.29	11.94
Google 1-best	25.80	23.38
HTK word lattice	14.23	11.19
Google 3-best	20.04	18.65
Google 5-best	18.92	17.74
Google 20-best	18.37	17.27
HTK + Google + Loquendo 1-bests	12.85	8.87

algorithm generates new sentences, belonging to the inferred extra-language, that can lead to an improvement of the semantic output.

7   Conclusions

In this work, we have presented an approach to SLU that takes advantage of multiple hypotheses generated by the ASR phase. We have developed a Grammatical Inference algorithm to generate a language representing different recognition alternatives of the uttered sentence (graph of words), and also a methodology to analyze this graph of words according to the statistical semantic model. Results, considering a task of an information system about train timetables and fares, show that adequately combining these hypotheses the behavior of the system can be improved. This means that some recognition alternatives generated by the Grammatical Inference algorithm are more adequate for the semantic model, and lead to a best semantic decodification. As future work, we want to perform some experiments with other corpora, and also research other algorithms to generate the graphs of words.

Acknowledgements. This work is partially supported by the Spanish MICINN under contract TIN2011-28169-C05-01, and under FPU Grant AP2010-4193.

References

1. Tür, G., Mori, R.D.: Spoken Language Understanding: Systems for Extracting Semantic Information from Speech, 1st edn. Wiley (2011)
2. Fiscus, J.G.: A post-processing system to yield reduced word error rates: Recognizer output voting error reduction (ROVER). In: Proceedings of the 1997 IEEE Workshop on Automatic Speech Recognition and Understanding, pp. 347–354. IEEE (1997)
3. Larkin, M.A., Blackshields, G., Brown, N.P., Chenna, R., McGettigan, P.A., McWilliam, H., Valentin, F., Wallace, I.M., Wilm, A., Lopez, R., Thompson, J.D., Gibson, T.J., Higgins, D.G.: ClustalW and ClustalX version 2.0. Bioinformatics 23, 2947–2948 (2007)

4. Sim, K.C., Byrne, W.J., Gales, M.J.F., Sahbi, H., Woodland, P.C.: Consensus network decoding for statistical machine translation system combination. In: IEEE Int. Conference on Acoustics, Speech, and Signal Processing (2007)
5. Bangalore, S., Bordel, G., Riccardi, G.: Computing Consensus Translation from Multiple Machine Translation Systems. In: Proceedings of IEEE Automatic Speech Recognition and Understanding Workshop (ASRU 2001), pp. 351–354 (2001)
6. Calvo, M., Hurtado, L.-F., García, F., Sanchís, E.: A Multilingual SLU System Based on Semantic Decoding of Graphs of Words. In: Torre Toledano, D., Ortega Giménez, A., Teixeira, A., González Rodríguez, J., Hernández Gómez, L., San Segundo Hernández, R., Ramos Castro, D. (eds.) IberSPEECH 2012. CCIS, vol. 328, pp. 158–167. Springer, Heidelberg (2012)
7. Hakkani-Tür, D., Béchet, F., Riccardi, G., Tür, G.: Beyond ASR 1-best: Using word confusion networks in spoken language understanding. Computer Speech & Language 20, 495–514 (2006)
8. Benedí, J.M., Lleida, E., Varona, A., Castro, M.J., Galiano, I., Justo, R., López de Letona, I., Miguel, A.: Design and acquisition of a telephone spontaneous speech dialogue corpus in Spanish: DIHANA. In: Proceedings of LREC 2006, Genoa, Italy, pp. 1636–1639 (2006)

Fast Algorithm for Automatic Alignment
of Speech and Imperfect Text Data

Natalia A. Tomashenko and Yuri Y. Khokhlov

Speech Technology Center, Saint-Petersburg, Russia
{tomashenko-n,khokhlov}@speechpro.com
www.speechpro.ru

Abstract. A solution to the problem of fast single-pass alignment of speech with imperfect transcripts is introduced. The proposed technique is based on constructing a special word network for segmentation. We examine robustness and segmentation quality for different types of errors and different levels of noise in the text, depending on the parameters of network tuning. Experiments showed that with properly selected parameters the algorithm is robust to noise of any type in transcripts. The proposed approach has been successfully applied to the task of creating movie subtitles.

Keywords: speech segmentation, imperfect transcriptions, speech-text alignment, closed caption.

1 Introduction

The problem of producing speech segmentation based on inaccurate text data is important for many applications of speech processing, such as lightly-supervised acoustic model training [1][2], multimedia indexing systems that provide web access to television and radio programs [3], automatic annotation and segmentation of audio books for TTS [4]-[6], generating closed-captions for television programs, indexing presentation videos [7], etc.

The main difficulty in the task of speech segmentation has two sources. The first one is the poor quality of available transcriptions, when they do not correspond exactly to the audio content. Such approximate transcriptions contain errors in the text, deletions of certain words, or even parts of the text, insertion in the text of words that are not spoken, changes in the word order, etc. The second source of difficulty is related to characteristics of audio files; for example, it includes long audio files (typically half an hour and more), disfluencies, repetitions, overlapping speech from simultaneous speakers, emotional speech, background noises, music and other non-speech events. A traditional approach to segmentation, such as forced-alignment with Viterbi algorithm, fails to work under these conditions.

In this paper we describe a solution to the problem of fast, single-pass alignment of speech with imperfect transcripts. The motivation for solving this problem was to develop a program for fast creation of subtitles for television programs and series from available scripts.

M. Železný et al. (Eds.): SPECOM 2013, LNAI 8113, pp. 146–153, 2013.
© Springer International Publishing Switzerland 2013

Many methods were proposed in the literature for aligning speech with synchronized or imperfect transcripts [1]-[11]. What most of these previous approaches have in common is the fact that they are applied in a multi-pass manner and require a long processing time, thereby making them inapplicable to our problem.

In this paper we propose an algorithm for word segmentation of long audio files in case of approximate transcripts. The proposed algorithm provides accurate word segmentation of television programs and movies based on scripts (when no time-stamps are available). The algorithm has two main advantages in comparison to similar systems. The first one is relatively high speed of performance and the fact that it can be done in a single pass. The second advantage is the simplicity of its implementation.

2   Automatic Alignment of Speech and Imperfect Transcriptions

2.1   Problem Description

The aim of our work is to produce word segmentation for the audio file of a TV program or a movie from a text script of this file. The script is an approximate transcript of what is really said in the audio file, however there may be deletions or insertions of words or utterances. The audio file contains different noises, laughter, shouting, songs, background music, etc, which are not recorded in the original text file. The obtained word segmentation is then used to build subtitles for the program, so it is important to get accurate boundaries for the maximum number of words in the text file. For the words whose boundaries were not found by the algorithm, positions are roughly estimated by interpolation.

2.2   Related Work

In [3], P.J. Moreno et al proposed an algorithm for recursive alignment of long audio streams to their text transcriptions. The main idea is based on finding well synchronized areas, called islands of confidence.

The ASR output is compared with the original text by means of dynamic programming (DP) algorithm and anchor words are found. These anchors are used to partition the text and the audio into unaligned and aligned segments. The algorithm is launched recursively on unaligned parts until it reaches the convergence point, and for each part, a specific language model is estimated. This method obtains good results, however it involves several iterations, and the reported speed, depending on the quality of the original signal, ranges from 1 to 5 RTF, which is too slow for our task. The methodology of comparing the ASR result with the approximate transcriptions by means of the DP algorithm is also presented in other studies on the subject of alignment of speech and imperfect text data [2][5][8]. At the recognition stage a language model is often used which is derived from a generic large language model and "biased" towards the text that is being aligned [3][4][9][10]. In [7] the idea of speech-text alignment with DP is employed on the phonemic level: first, vowels and fricatives are detected in the text and speech, and then DP is used for their alignment.

Methods based on recognition and DP alignment are reliable but have a number of drawbacks. First, when applying the DP algorithm, the output from an ASR system is needed for the complete recording. For very long audio files (one hour or more), this process may take a lot of time. Second, DP alignment may fail when dealing with repeating words and phrases.

We introduce a fast segmentation algorithm which can be executed in a single pass. The algorithm is simple to implement and is based on constructing a special word network for segmentation. Unlike many other approaches, no language models are required in this case. The proposed idea of using a special word network, which makes it possible to skip unspoken words from the original text during the segmentation, is similar to the one proposed in [11], where segmentation is done by means of a special graph, called "skip network" and with grapheme-based acoustic models. In [11] the authors use segmentation for acoustic model training, so they use strict selection of data during segmentation and additional passes to estimate the confidence measure with different skip-networks, as well as a separate pass with a background model; only 55% of speech was harvested with 99% word accuracy. The speed of the algorithm is not reported. For us, however, speed is a crucial factor. In our work, the graph has a different, slightly more complex topology and is applied to acoustic models of triphones. In our work a word network is constructed in such a way that additional passes for selecting correct segments are not required. Through the use of a special filler model (FM) in the graph we can perform reliable segmentation in a single pass.

2.3   Word Network for Segmentation

We construct the segmentation network using original transcripts in such a way that during the segmentation process, all words are aligned in the same sequence as they are in the original text with the possibility of removing those words from the text that are not contained in the audio. Moreover, words from the audio that are not transcribed in the original text are automatically skipped during the segmentation. The ability to bypass non-speech material and the utterances for which there are no corresponding words in the original text is realized through the use of a special filler model.

For the construction of this network, we use a filler model, illustrated in Fig.1.a. The aim of the filler model is to absorb silence, fragments of speech that are not present in the text file, and various non-speech events during the segmentation. These models are added between pairs of small sequences of words. In order to be able to regulate the garbage model ability to absorb sound fragments not present in the text, it is given a weight that is added (on each vector) to the logarithm likelihood of the corresponding hypothesis in the process of decoding.

The entire text is divided into small word sequences (WS). The length of every WS is approximately determined by the number of phonemes in it; so that the number of phonemes in the WS exceeds a chosen threshold (we use the value 20). Then, for each WS, a subnetwork, illustrated in Fig.1.b, is constructed. Between pairs of words in a WS a filler model is added.

A network which is used for the segmentation of the whole text is schematically shown in Fig.2. The network requires for all words in the text to occur in exactly the same sequence as they appear in the original text. The words that are present in the text but not contained in audio are automatically skipped during the segmentation. Audio fragments that do not match the original text are also absorbed by FM. However, this

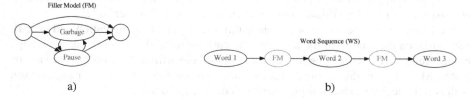

Fig. 1. a) Filler Model. b) Subnetwork for Word Sequence.

works only within certain limits, determined by the number of skips, a skip penalty and the weight of the garbage model in FM. An appropriate choice of these parameters makes it possible to achieve optimal speed and high quality of segmentation. The skip number of the network depicted in Fig.2 equals 2. This means that starting from some WS, we may skip no more than two following WSs in the process of segmentation. In practice, the optimal number of skips is determined by the maximum length of the text fragment that has no match in the audio file. This type of network produces alignment with a much tighter constraint than that imposed by biased LM [11], therefore it results in a more accurate segmentation.

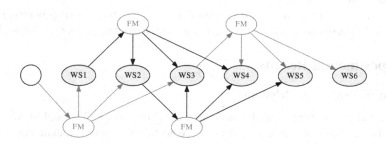

Fig. 2. Skip-network for Segmentation: skip number=2

The goal of this paper is to examine robustness and segmentation quality for different types of errors and different levels of noise in text, depending on two main parameters of network tuning: garbage model weight and WS skip number.

3   Experimental Setup

To evaluate the performance of the proposed approach we use five 45-minute audio files of a TV series. The audio material is complicated from the acoustic point of view: it contains fragments of songs, music, emotional speech, shouting, various background noises, overlapping speech from simultaneous speakers.

Acoustic models were built on a 148 hour speech corpus consisting of TV programs and movies. 55-dimensional tandem LCRC features with CMN were used. The garbage model is a 1-state global HMM with 35 Gaussians, it is trained on all the speech data of the corpus. The pause model is a 1-state HMM with 470 Gaussians. Triphone models are 3-state, with 5161 tied states and (on average) 27 Gaussians per state.

We examined the behavior of the algorithm (accuracy of segmentation and speed), depending on the quality of the texts and the parameters of the network (skip, garbage model weight). The corresponding transcriptions were artificially corrupted at various levels. Manually produced word segmentation was used as reference for comparison with automatically produced segmentation in these experiments.

There were 4 series of experiments:

1. Existing texts were artificially corrupted by **deletions**, with a constant % of corruption (WER between noisy texts and exact transcripts = 15%) and different lengths of the omitted word sequences. We examined the dependence of segmentation quality in this case on the garbage model weight (4.1).
2. Existing texts were corrupted by **deletions**, as in the previous case. However, here we examined the influence of **corruption level** on the obtained segmentation quality. Deletions in text files must be dealt with by the filler model, so this parameter is important here (4.1).
3. Existing texts were corrupted by **insertions** with a constant corruption level (WER = 15%) and different lengths of the inserted word sequences. The possibility of omitting the words absent from the audio file during segmentation is determined by the skip number (4.2).
4. Practical implementation of the proposed algorithm in the task of generating subtitles. WER between available texts and the exact transcript is about 2-3% (4.3).

4   Experimental Results

4.1   Experiments with Deletions

Results of the experiments with deletion noise are shown in Fig.3, a) and b). To mesure the segmentation performance we use the word accuracy metric, calculated as follows:

$$Accuracy = (Corr - Ins)/N, \tag{1}$$

where N is the number of words in the text used for segmentation, $Corr$ is the number of words that were aligned within the 1 second of true alignment and Ins is the number of insertions.

4.2   Experiments with Insertions

To mesure the segmentation performance in experiments with insertions, we modifed word accuracy metric: N in (1) was replaced by N_o, where N_o is the number of words in the original (clean) text. Results of the experiments with insertion noise are shown in Fig.4. The three lines correspond to different lengths of inserted word sequences (corruption level is 15%): 3, 9 and 15 words. The longer the maximum length of the inserted word sequence, the greater the value of the skip number should be.

Table 1 summarizes our experiments in Section 4.1-4.2. The table shows segmentation accuracy values under optimal parameters. In experiments 1-4 the skip number is 2. In experiments 5-7 the garbage model weight is 1.5.

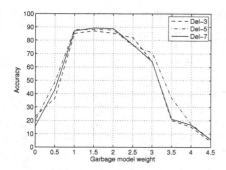
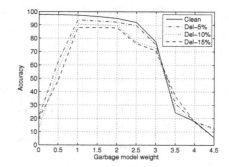

a) Noise level 15%. The three lines correspond to different lengths of the deleted word sequences: 3, 5, 7 consecutive words.

b) The four lines correspond to different corruption levels of the original text by word deletions: clean, 5%, 10%, 15%. The length of the deleted word sequences is 7.

Fig. 3. Dependence of accuracy on garbage model weight. Skip=2.

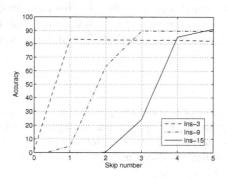

Fig. 4. Dependence of segmentation accuracy on the skip number. Garbage model weight=1.5.

4.3 Practical Implementation in Generating Subtitles

It was important to obtain accurate segmentation for a maximum number of words from the original text, so segmentation was performed in three steps:

1. Segmentation using the graph presented in Figure 2. At this stage the FM parameters are selected in such a way that only very reliable fragments are segmented.
2. In the second step, segmentation is performed only for the fragments that were not segmented at the first stage, and the garbage model weight is reduced. This means that alignment is performed under stricter conditions, so after the second step more words are segmented.
3. In the last step, boundaries are found for the words that were not segmented at the previous stages, using interpolation from adjacent words. It is important to note that all three steps can in practice be implemented in one pass, that is, it is not necessary to process the whole file in order to begin the second and third steps.

Table 1. Segmentation accuracy values under optimal parameters

Num	Text Errors, %	Text Errors, type	Sequences	Best Param	Accuracy
1	0	–	–	0	97.8
2	5	deletions	7	1.5	93.8
3	10	deletions	7	1.5	91.1
4	15	deletions	3, 5, 7	1.5	88.1
5	15	insertions	3	1	83.5
6	15	insertions	9	3	89.9
7	15	insertions	15	5	91.3

Deviations of the automatically segmented boundaries from manual segmentation with optimal parameters (skip=2, garbage model weight = 0.9) are the following. After the first step: word accuracy = 96.8% (we considered words as correctly segmented if the deviation of their boundaries from manual segmentation did not exceed 1 second). After all the steps: the amount of words with boundaries deviating from manual segmentation by no more than 1 second is 99.2%. This percentage is calculated with respect to only those words that are present in both the audio and the original text. The speed of the first step of the algorithm is 0.01 RTF, of all three steps 0.015 RTF.

5   Conclusions

The paper presented an effective method for speech alignment with imperfect text transcripts. The main advantages of this approach are simplicity of implementation, high segmentation accuracy, high speed (0.01 RTF) and the possibility to use it in streaming mode. Using texts with artificially added noise, we studied the effect of the algorithm parameters on the quality of segmentation.

Experiments showed that with properly selected parameters the algorithm is robust to noise of any type in transcripts (insertions or deletions). The segmentation accuracy is 88-91%, provided that WER between noisy and ideal transcripts does not exceed 15%. Moreover it is possible to choose parameters that are optimal for all texts, with varying degrees of accuracy and different types of errors.

Applying this approach in the practical task of creating movie subtitles, under conditions of slightly inaccurate texts (WER=3%), we used extra segmentation passes and obtained the following result: 99.2% of the words (that are present in both the audio and the original texts) are within 1 second of the true alignment.

In future work we plan to develop an algorithm for the automatic evaluation of the reliability of segmented fragments.

References

1. Pitz, M., Molau, S., Schluter, R., Ney, H.: Automatic transcription verification of broadcast news and similar speech corpora. In: Proc. DARPA Broadcast News Workshop, Herndon, VA, pp. 157–159 (1999)

2. Lamel, L., Gauvain, J.L., Adda, G.: Lightly supervised acoustic model training. In: Proc. ISCA ITRW ASR 2000 (2000)
3. Moreno, P., Joerg, C., Van Thong, J.-M., Glickman, O.: A recursive algorithm for the forced alignment of very long audio segments. In: Proc. ICSLP 1998, Sydney, Australia, pp. 2711–2714. IEEE Press (1998)
4. Braunschweiler, N., Gales, M.J.F., Buchholz, S.: Lightly supervised recognition for automatic alignment of large coherent speech recordings. In: Proc. of INTERSPEECH 2010, 11th Annual Conference of the International Speech Communication Association, pp. 2222–2225 (2010)
5. Boeffard, O., Charonnat, L., Maguer, S., Lolive, D., Vidal, G.: Towards Fully Automatic Annotation of Audiobooks for TTS. In: Proc. LREC (2012)
6. Katsamanis, A., Black, M.P., Georgiou, P.G., Goldstein, L., Narayanan, S.: SailAlign: Robust long speech-text alignment. In: Proc. of Workshop on New Tools and Methods for Very-Large Scale Phonetics Research (2011)
7. Haubold, A., Kender, J.R.: Augmented segmentation and visualization for presentation 2005, pp. 51–60. ACM Press, Singapore (2005)
8. Hazen, T.J.: Automatic Alignment and Error Correction of Human Generated Transcripts for Long Speech Recordings. In: Interspeech. IEEE Press, Pittsburgh (2006)
9. Lecouteux, B., Linarés, G., Nocéra, P., Bonastre, J.-F.: Imperfect transcript driven speech recognition. In: Proc. Interspeech (2006)
10. Placeway, P., Lafferty, J.: Cheating with Imperfect Transcripts. In: Proceedings ICSLP (1996)
11. Stan, A., Bell, P., King, S.: A grapheme-based method for automatic alignment of speech and text data. In: Proc. IEEE Workshop on Spoken Language Technology (2012)

GMM Based Language Identification System Using Robust Features

Sadanandam Manchala[1] and V. Kamakshi Prasad[2]

[1] Kakatiya University, Warangal, Andhra Pradesh, India
sadanb4u@yahoo.co.in
[2] Jawaharlal Nehru Technological University Hyderabad, Andhra Pradesh, India
kamakshiprasad@jntuh.ac.in

Abstract. In this work, we propose new features for the GMM based spoken language identification system. A two stage approach is followed for extraction of the proposed new features. MFCCs and formants are extracted from huge corpus of all languages under consideration. In the first phase, MFCCs and formants are concatenated to form the feature vector. K clusters are formed from these feature vectors and one Gaussian is designed for each cluster. In the second phase, these feature vectors are evaluated against each of the K Gaussians and the returned K probabilities are considered as the elements of the proposed new feature vector, thus forming a K-element new feature vector. This proposed method for deriving new feature vector is common for both training and testing phases. In the training phase, K-element feature vectors are generated from the language specific speech corpus and language specific GMMs are trained. In testing phase, similar procedure is followed for extraction of K-element feature vector from unknown speech utterance and evaluated against language specific GMMs. Usefulness, the language specific apriori knowledge is used for further improvement of recognition performance. The experiments are carried out on OGI database and the LID performance is nearly 100%.

Keywords: Keywords-Language Identification, LID, MFCC, Formants using LPC and new feature set.

1 Introduction

Automatic language identification (LID) is the task of classifying an unknown utterance of speech from a list of languages. These systems are very useful in several applications like call routing systems, language translation, spoken document retrieval and front-end processing in multilingual systems etc. [1–3]. It is also a topic of great interest in the areas of intelligence and security for information distillation. The communication among humans is established by speech, wherein the information to be conveyed is embedded in the sequence of sound units produced. These basic sound units are normally referred to as phonemes. The sequences of phonemes used for communication are governed by the rules of the language.

There are several cues to identify the spoken language like phonemes, prosody, phonotactics, syntax and structure etc [4]. Among those cues, one of the important cues

M. Železný et al. (Eds.): SPECOM 2013, LNAI 8113, pp. 154–161, 2013.

is acoustic phonetic for the LID task. While the term acoustic refers to physical sound patterns, the term phonotactic refers to the constraints that determine permissible syllable structures in a language. We can consider acoustic features as the proxy of phonetic repertoire and call it acoustic-phonetic features. On the other hand, we see phonotactic features as the manifestation of the phonotactic constraints in a language [5, 6]. The type of perceptual cues that human listeners use is always the source of inspiration for automatic spoken language recognition [7].

The acoustic LID approach aims at capturing the essential differences among languages by modeling the distribution of spectral vectors directly [8]. These systems use acoustic features like Mel frequency cepstral coefficients, shift delta cepstral coefficients, perceptual linear production (PLP) features, Formants etc., which are extracted directly from speech signals. A GMM is used to approximate the acoustic-phonetic distribution of a language. It is generally believed that each Gaussian density in a GMM captures some broad phonetic classes [9]. Sound frequencies are different in different languages and this difference is characterized by acoustic features like Mel frequency cepstral coefficients and delta cepstral coefficients [10, 11]. T. Nagarajan [12] proposed VQ based LID using several statistical methods using MFCCs and used usefulness parameter to improve LID performance.

The acoustic characteristics of the phonemes are closely related to the manner in which they are produced. The phonemes that are produced depend on the type of excitation and the shape of the vocal tract system. As the basic sound units are characterized by a set of formant frequencies which correspond to the resonances of the vocal tract system, formants are one of the major acoustical cues for the identification of language from speech. Formant frequencies have rarely been used as acoustic features for language recognition, in spite of their phonetic significance.

State-of-the-art formant estimators locate candidate peaks of the spectra from short-time analysis of speech and perform temporal tracking. Traditional formant frequency estimation methods are based on spectral analysis and peak picking techniques. The characteristics of phonemes are generally manifested in spectral properties of speech signal and formants are best choice to represent the acoustic features of basic sound units which are useful for LIDs [13]. Formants are extracted using linear prediction coefficients (LPC) and these formants have the information about different sounds [14, 15].

In this paper, we propose new features to implement LID system using conventional features MFCCs and formants. MFCCs and formant features are extracted from speech utterance and then concatenated. New features are derived using concatenated features using Gaussians. Language dependent GMMs are created one for each language using new features. In the testing phase, the new feature vectors of unknown utterance are evaluated against GMM of under considering languages. A language is hypothesized based on apriori knowledge of specific language. The steps followed in the implementation of LID system is explained in the following sections.

2   Feature Extraction

The performance of any LID system depends on the type of feature vectors and the classifier used. If the feature vectors do not represent underlying phonetic content of the speech, the system will perform poorly irrespective of the classifier used. The fundamental cue to recognize the spoken language is the frequency of occurrence of basic sound units is different in different languages [12]. In short-term speech processing, it is very likely that most of the cues of basic sound units are covered in a short-term window. Hence there is a close resemblance between basic sound units and derived feature vectors. This has motivated us to explore new features. In earlier systems, phonemes are described with the acoustic features. The acoustic features are represented well with MFCC. But the state of art LID systems gave the poor results for tonal languages with only MFCC features. This has motivated us to form the features by combining MFCCs and formants. In VQ based LID systems, for each feature vector only one code book index is considered, discarding second best and third best indices etc. But these cues are also very important in making comprehensive decisions. Hence it is proposed to use k-best alternatives in decision making process instead of a single code book index.

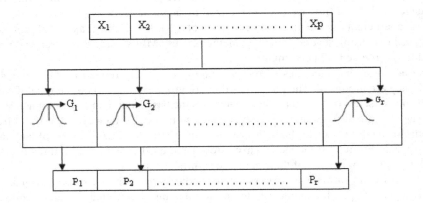

Fig. 1. HMM based LID using new features and usefulness

In this work, p-dimensional MFCC features and q-formant frequencies are extracted from speech signal and concatenated them to form (p+q)-dimensional feature vectors. These feature vectors are grouped into clusters using clustering algorithm. One Gaussian is formed for each cluster. These combined features are passed through all Gaussians and calculated probability using probability density function of the respective Gaussians. The probabilities of Gaussians are treated as coefficients of new feature vectors. Each feature vector (p+q-demensional) is transformed into a r-dimensional new feature vector as described in Fig.1. This proposed method for the derivation of new features is used in both training and testing phases of LID system. In training phase, new features are extracted from huge corpus of language specific speech for each language. In testing phase, new features are extracted from unknown utterance of speech.

3   Design of Text-Independent LID Using Proposed Model

In the proposed model, GMM based LID is implemented using i) new feature vector derived from MFCC and formant feature vectors of short-term speech signal and

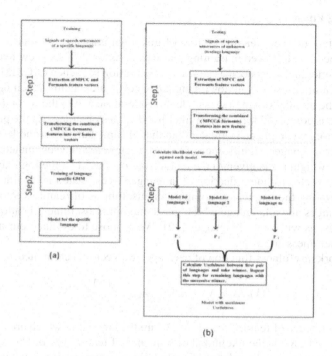

Fig. 2. Schematic digram of proposed LID

ii) usefulness of new feature vectors. It consists of two phases namely training phase and testing phase. Each spoken language is represented by distinct one GMM, which is parameterized by the mean vectors, covariance matrices and mixture weights from all component densities.

3.1 Training Phase

The training phase involves two steps. In the first step, consider a huge speech corpus consisting of speech of 25 minutes duration for each language. P-dimensional MFCC feature vectors and r-dimensional formants are extracted from each of the listed languages by applying overlapped windowing and LPC spectrum. These p-dimensional MFCC feature vectors and q-dimensional formants are concatenated. These concatenated feature vectors are grouped into clusters hyper space and one Gaussian is formed for each cluster.

In the second step, (p+q)-dimensional feature vectors are extracted from the language specific corpus as specified in the above step and transform all concatenated feature vectors into r-dimensional new feature vectors using the method discussed in section 2. These new feature vectors are used as training set of GMM. GMMs are trained one for each language using Baum-Welch re-estimation algorithm. The abstract flow diagram of training phase of the proposed language identification system is illustrated in Fig.2(a).

3.2 Testing Phase

In the first step, the new feature vectors of unknown utterance of speech are derived using the procedure followed in training phase as in figure 2. These new feature vectors of unknown utterance of speech are used as observation sequence of GMM.

The speech utterance of unknown language is evaluated against each of M GMMs, where M is the number of languages under consideration and in the second step useful-ness measure is computed for a pair of likelihood values obtained. As the probability of a feature vector in a language is greater than that of some languages and lesser than that of some other languages, significance of feature vector cannot be estimated in isolation. In such case, weightage is given to the feature vectors based on the log likelihood ratio of the feature vector for identification of language. To estimate the significance of fea-ture vector among the languages, compute the usefulness of feature vector between a pair of languages and a language which gives maximum usefulness is allowed for fur-ther comparisons with other languages [12]. We propose to evaluate our new features using this usefulness criterion.

In this work, usefulness function of each spectral vector is computed,

$$U(V_k, \lambda_i)/\lambda_j = P(V_k/\lambda_i)log\frac{P(V_k/\lambda_j)}{P(V_k/\lambda_i)} \tag{1}$$

where V is sequence of feature vector, λ_i, λ_j are the languages which are considered in training and $P(V/\lambda_i)$ is the likelihood of sequence of feature vector V in λ_i Language.

In the second step, the likelihood of each derived feature vector is calculated against each GMM. The usefulness of all feature vectors for a pair of languages is calculated using eqn-1. The Language which gives maximum usefulness of all feature vectors will be allowed to further comparisons with other language one at a time. This process is repeated for all languages under consideration. If the considered languages are M, then the number of comparisons is (M-1) only. In this process, after the comparison of all languages, the language which gives max usefulness in the last comparison is identi-fied as the recognized language. The abstract flow diagram of the steps involved in the testing phase of the proposed language identification system is illustrated in Fig.2(b).

4   Experimental Setup

OGI database has been used for the study [16]. 25 minutes duration of speech is used for each language. Features are extracted using overlapping window and LPC spectrum. In this work 12 dimensional (p=12) MFCC feature vectors and five formants (q=5) are extracted from short-time windowed speech signal. The number of Gaussians is chosen as 15 (r=15) so that each of the concatenated feature vectors (p+q-demsional) is transformed into 15 dimensional (r=15) new feature vectors. Gaussian mixture models with varying number of mixtures 8, 16 and 32 are implemented using new features. Testing is performed for different utterances of 1s, 2s and 3s duration using the proposed method.

5 Results

The performance of language identification for OGI database using MFCC feature vectors for different duration of test utterances and varying number of mixtures of GMM using usefulness value is depicted in Table 1. The performance is measured in terms of percentage of correct identification of test samples from the given test samples..

Table 1. LID performance (using MFCC) in % using usefulness for OGI database

Language	Performance (%) for 8 mixtures			Performance (%) for 16 mixtures			Performance (%) for 32 mixtures		
	1 sec	2 sec	3 sec	1 sec	2 sec	3 sec	1 sec	2 sec	3 sec
English	75	76	81	77	77	81	78	79	82
French	74	77	79	76	79	79	77	81	82
Farsi	65	67	66	69	70	71	70	72	74
German	72	75	78	75	77	73	77	78	79
Mandarin	4	6	8	8	10	12	11	13	15
Spanish	16	19	21	22	23	25	42	45	53
Japanese	13	15	13	11	14	11	12	12	13
Korean	10	16	36	21	33	32	35	46	48
Tamil	79	81	80	80	82	81	80	80	81
Vietnam	80	82	83	84	82	84	82	83	84
Average	48.8	51.4	54.5	52.3	54.7	54.9	56.4	58.9	61.1

The performance of language identification for OGI database using new feature vectors for different duration of test utterances and varying number of mixtures of GMM using usefulness value is depicted in Table 2

Table 2. LID performance (using new features) in % using usefulness for OGI database

Language	Performance (%) for 8 mixtures			Performance (%) for 16 mixtures			Performance (%) for 32 mixtures		
	1 sec	2 sec	3 sec	1 sec	2 sec	3 sec	1 sec	2 sec	3 sec
English	100	100	100	100	100	100	100	100	100
French	99	99	100	99	100	100	100	100	100
Farsi	85	89	93	85	90	95	97	97	99
German	94	95	98	95	95	99	95	97	99
Mandarin	82	84	86	88	90	92	90	94	96
Spanish	86	89	89	89	90	92	92	95	99
Japanese	90	90	93	90	94	94	94	96	99
Korean	81	86	86	91	93	95	95	96	98
Tamil	99	99	100	100	100	100	100	100	100
Vietnam	85	85	90	100	100	100	100	100	100
Average	90.1	91.9	93.5	93.7	95.2	96.7	96.3	97.5	98.8

Table 3. LID performance using new features and Usefulness for OGI database

	8 mixtures	16 mixtures	32 mixtures
IR	91.5	95.2	98.8
FRR	9.2	4.9	1.8
FAR	13.5	8.6	3.4

The performance of LID system is also referred in terms of Identification Rate (IR), False Acceptance Rate (FAR) and False Rejection Rate (FRR). IR is the percentage of test utterances that in certain languages and classified as "true" for those languages. FAR is the percentage of test utterances that are not in certain languages but classified them as "true" for those languages. FRR is the percentage of test utterances that in certain languages but classified as "false" for those languages. The performance of LID in terms of IR, FAR, FRR for different duration of test utterances and varying number of Mixtures of GMM using likelihood value and usefulness is depicted in Table 3.

6   Conclusions

In this paper, a new GMM based approach has been proposed for text independent language recognition using new feature vectors derived from MFCC feature vectors and formants. Formants are extracted using LP spectrum of speech signal. LID system is developed using Gaussian mixture model with different mixtures. Formant and MFCC feature vectors represent the acoustic features of speech signals so that LID performance is improved. Usefulness of new feature vectors has been considered to improve the language recognition performance. The average recognition performance of this text independent LID system is achieved more for 32 mixtures for OGI languages is 98.8%.

References

1. Zissman, M.A.: Overview of Current Techniques for Automatic Language Identification of Speech. In: Proceedings of the IEEE Automatic Speech Recognition Workshop, pp. 60–62 (December 1995)
2. Waibel, A., Geutner, P., Tomokiyo, L.M., Schultz, T., Woszczyna, M.: Multilinguality in speech and spoken language systems. Proc. IEEE 88(8), 1181–1990 (2000)
3. Sugiyama, M.: Automatic language recognition using acoustic features. In: Proc. IEEE Int. Conf. Acoust., Speech, and Signal Processing, pp. 813–816 (May 1991)
4. Zissman, M.A.: Comparison of Four Approaches to Automatic Language Identification of Telephone Speech. IEEE Trans. Speech and Audio Proc. SAP-4(1), 31–44 (1996)
5. Martin, A.F., Garofolo, J.S.: NIST speech processing evaluations: LVCSR, speaker recognition, language recognition. In: Proc. IEEE Workshop on Signal Processing Applications for Public Security and Forensics, pp. 1–7 (2007)
6. Kirchhoff, K.: Language characteristics. In: Schultz, T., Kirchhoff, K. (eds.) Multilingual Speech Processing. Elsevier (2006)
7. Zhao, J., Shu, H., Zhang, L., Wang, X., Gong, Q., Li, P.: Cortical competition during language discrimination. NeuroImage 43, 624–633 (2008)

8. Torres Carrasquillo, P.A., Reynolds, D.A., Deller Jr., J.R.: Language identification using Gaussian mixture model tokenization. In: Proc. IEEE Int. Conf. Acoust., Speech, and Signal Processing, vol. 1, pp. 757–760 (2002)
9. Muthusamy, Y.K., Barnard, E., Cole, R.A.: Automatic language identification: A Review/Tutorial. IEEE Signal Processing Magazine (October 1994)
10. Nakagawa, S., Suzuki, H.: A New Speech Recognition Method Based on VQ-Distortion Measure and HMM. In: Proc. Int. Conf. ASSP, pp. 673–679 (April 1993)
11. Torres-Carrasquillo, P.A., Singer, E., Kohler, M., Greene, R., Reynolds, D.A., Deller Jr., J.R.: Approaches to language identification using Gaussian mixture models and shifted delta cepstral features. In: Proc. ICSLP, pp. 89–92 (2002)
12. Nagarajan, T., Murthy, H.A.: Language identification using spectral vector distribution across the languages. In: Proceedings of Int. Conf. Natural Language Processing (December 2002)
13. Yegnanarayana, B.: Formant extraction from linear prediction phase spectrum. J. Acoust. Soc. Amer. 63, 1638–1640 (1978)
14. Bruce, I.C., Karkhanis, N.V., Young, E.D., Sachs, M.B.: Robust formant tracking in noise. In: ICASSP (2002)
15. Bruce, I.C., Mustafa, K.: Robust formant tracking for continuous speech with speaker variability. IEEE Trans. ASSP 14(2), 435–444 (2006)
16. OGI Multi Language Telephone Speech (January 2004),
    http://www.cslu.ogi.edu/corpora/mlts/

Hierarchical Clustering and Classification of Emotions in Human Speech Using Confusion Matrices

Manuel Reyes-Vargas[1], Máximo Sánchez-Gutiérrez[1], Leonardo Rufiner[2],
Marcelo Albornoz[2], Leandro Vignolo[2],
Fabiola Martínez-Licona[1], and John Goddard-Close[1]

[1] Universidad Autonoma Metropolitana, Electrical Engineering Depto., Mexico City, Mexico
[2] Centro de I+D SINC(i), Universidad Nacional del Litoral / CONICET, Argentina
{manuel.reyesvargas,edmax86,lrufiner,albornoz.marcelo,
leandro.vignolo}@gmail.com, {fmml,jgc}@xanum.uam.mx

Abstract. Although most of the natural emotions expressed in speech can be clearly identified by humans, automatic classification systems still display significant limitations on this task. Recently, hierarchical strategies have been proposed using different heuristics for choosing the appropriate levels in the hierarchy. In this paper, we propose a method for choosing these levels by hierarchically clustering a confusion matrix. To this end, a Mexican Spanish emotional speech database was created and employed to classify the 'big six' emotions (anger, disgust, fear, joy, sadness, surprise) together with a neutral state. A set of 14 features was extracted from the speech signal of each utterance and a hierarchical classifier was defined from the dendrogram obtained by applying Wards clustering method to a certain confusion matrix. The classification rate of this hierarchical classifier showed a slight improvement compared to those of various classifiers trained directly with all 7 classes.

Keywords: Emotional speech, confusion matrix, hierarchical clustering.

1 Introduction

Speech communication provides the most significant information for humans through the emission of thoughts, ideas and even emotions. Due to the dynamic nature of the speech signal it has high levels of variability: speech production depends on the location and movement of the elements of the vocal tract and the face, and variations of parameters such as local accents, social status or personal style [1]. In this process, the emotional state which is expressed in the spoken words, enhances the message's content. It has been claimed that words account for less than 10% of the meaning of the message for the listener [2], so the analysis of features like prosody, rhythm or voice quality has become important.

Emotions are hard to define in theory, although features like time durations and intensity are most useful in the identification of emotions like joy, anger, and sadness, even though differences in perception between different people may arise. In trying to differentiate emotions, efforts have also focused on describing them in terms of activation and valence indexes, where the amount of energy needed to express the emotion

M. Železný et al. (Eds.): SPECOM 2013, LNAI 8113, pp. 162–169, 2013.

and its correlates to the nervous system are studied [3,4]. This leads to a representation of the archetypal emotions as a kind of elemental emotions palette, similar to the case of the primary colors [5]; these elemental emotions are anger, disgust, fear, joy, sadness and surprise, and the different combinations of them give rise to a wider variety of emotional states. Although most of the natural emotions expressed in speech can be clearly identified by a human, automatic classification systems still display significant limitations on this task. In this paper, automatic classification of Mexican Spanish emotional speech is undertaken, using a hierarchical classifier which is defined from a confusion matrix using Wards method. This gives a method for defining the hierarchies found in the classifier.

In the last few years, several emotional speech databases have been created for purposes such as emotion recognition and expressive speech synthesis, human emotion perception, or to produce virtual teachers [6]. Most of them are recorded in English, but there are also a few in German [7] and Spanish [8], where the recordings may contain natural speech, acted speech, or both. Limitations of these databases have often been reported when they are perceptually tested by humans because of factors such as the poor emotional simulation, the variable quality of the recordings, and the lack of phonetic transcriptions of the phrases. In the particular case of Spanish, the reported databases represent the Spanish language as spoken in Spain, and the creation of databases with different variants of the Spanish language is important in order to obtain a better understanding of the emotional content of speech.

The characteristics which are most commonly extracted from the speech signal for analysis purposes are derived from fundamental frequency, the time durations of phonemes, syllables, or words, energy and formants [9]. By using features which are based on these characteristics it has been possible to identify in general most of the big six emotions in English and Spanish [10]. Some other parameters, as well as variations of the previously mentioned ones, have been applied to the classification of emotions. In [11], pitch based features were used to recognize emotions in German with reasonably good results for six emotions with a Bayesian classifier. Time level recognition has been utilized for classification with support vector machines [12], and the influence of speaking rate in speech emotion recognition has been studied in [13], as well as Gaussian mixture models to classify natural, acted and mixed emotional speech [14]. There are approaches that focus on the search for the optimal set of features including acoustic and linguistic ones [15], or by creating a hybrid system that includes neural networks, fuzzy systems and genetic algorithms [16]. Hierarchical emotion recognition schemes are a novel set of methods for the analysis of the speech signal. Some works use a binary decision tree approach with acoustic features [17], prosodic, spectral and glottal flow features [18], or multiple feature methods [19]. The choice of hierarchical levels tends to be heuristically motivated. Clustering techniques for a hierarchical conversion has been used for speech synthesis [20].

In this paper a Mexican Spanish emotional speech corpus was created, influenced by [21,22], and used to classify the big six emotions. Considering the variety of possible feature selection and classification systems, our approach uses 14 features together with a hierarchical binary classifier. The hierarchical levels are found by applying Wards method to a certain confusion matrix.

2   Methods

A Mexican Spanish emotional speech database was created and a set of features were defined, in order to classify the six emotions of anger (a), disgust (d), fear (f), joy (j), sadness (sa), surprise (s) and a neutral state (n).

2.1   Data

A Mexican male professional speaker recorded three sets of speech data. Each set had 40 words selected from the Swadesh list for Spanish [23], and 40 sentences that included each word. Swadesh, originally devised by the linguist Morris, contains words that are present in almost all languages and form the basis for communication between humans. The sets of selected words included nouns (numbers, colors, animals, body parts, etc), pronouns and verbs.

The sentences were based on each word of the list and contained the complete structure: subject, verb and predicate. Although there are some emotional speech databases that aim to be phonetically balanced (using nonsense phrases) [8], in our case the objective of using these sentences was to allow the speaker to express himself better in terms of the emotions considered; this was previously agreed on with him. The texts that were recorded belonged to segments from Benito Prez Galdoses novel "Fortunata y Jacinta" (Fortunata and Jacinta), Miguel de Cervantes Saavedra's short novel "La espaola inglesa" (The Spanish English) and Octavio Paz's poem "Primer da" (First day). The texts had around 450 words on average and did not contain any dialog; the poem has 94 words. The recordings were carried out on a desktop PC using the Speech Filing System Version 4.8 [24] with a sampling frequency of 16 KHz; the amplitude and noise levels were controlled by the speaker.

2.2   Features and Classification

14 features were extracted from the speech signal of each utterance using the averages of the first 12 MFCC, fundamental frequency F0 and log energy coefficients. A total of 1562 examples were obtained. Our objective was to form and test a hierarchical binary classifier on the seven emotion classes contained in our data. In order to do this we had to decide how to form the binary hierarchy, and then which binary classifiers to employ at each juncture. The way we automatically found the hierarchy was to first train a classifier using the seven classes, and then apply Ward's hierarchical clustering method to the resulting confusion matrix. The corresponding dendrogram provides the hierarchy. This idea was proposed in [25], for the automatic generation of topic hierarchies.

The Ward's method is one of the hierarchical clustering methods most used in the literature [26,27]. It is a greedy, agglomerative hierarchical method, that determines a diagram, called a dendrogram, that shows the sequence of mergings of clusters into larger clusters. It seeks to form the partitions in a manner that minimizes the loss of information associated with each merging. The information loss is quantified in terms of an error sum of squares criterion, so Wards method is often referred to as the minimum variance method. We used the usual euclidean distance measure for determining the inter-class similarity. Finally, support vector machines (SVM) were taken as the binary classifiers at each juncture.

3   Results

Firstly, we obtained the cross validation error rate, using ten partitions, for several classifiers and all seven emotion classes. The results are shown in Table 1. Here we can observe that the best classifier, SVM, achieves a classification rate of 34.7%. We used Weka [28] to obtain these results, where J48 is a version of Quinlan's C4.5 algorithm, k-NN refers to k nearest neighbors, MLP to a multilayer perceptron. The parameters employed for SVM were a radial basis function kernel with gamma = 0.1, and C=100. In the case of the MLP, the parameters were the standard ones used in Weka.

Table 1. Classification rates with all of the 7 emotions

Classifier	% Error Rate
J48	51.34
1-NN	50.83
3-NN	48.98
5-NN	45.71
7-NN	43.79
SVM	34.7
MLP	37.45

We took the confusion matrix of the worst classifier, J48, as shown below in Table 2, and applied Ward's hierarchical method to it. The idea of using the worst classifier was to emphasize the differences that occur in the confusion matrix. We also tried, however, confusion matrices from the other classifiers and got similar results in terms of the dendrograms.

Table 2. Classification rates with all of the 7 emotions

	Neutral	Joy	Sadness	Anger	Fear	Disgust	Surprise
Neutral	120	2	47	4	34	35	1
Joy	6	136	0	29	5	12	55
Sadness	42	1	110	0	63	26	1
Anger	1	41	2	139	1	3	16
Fear	34	4	58	0	70	33	4
Disgust	29	7	43	2	35	84	24
Surprise	2	58	2	21	3	16	101

The dendrogram given by Ward's method is shown in figure 1. We can see that the clusters which are obtained are successively: {a,j,s} and {d,n,sa,f}, {a} and {j,s}, {d} and {n,sa,f}, {n} and {sa,f}.

Rearranging the confusion matrix according to the clusters {a,j,s} and {d,n,sa,f}, gives the confusion matrix shown in Table 3. We can observe that a certain order has been brought to this table where lower values are found in the lower left and upper right submatrix blocks, something difficult to perceive in Table 2.

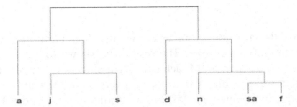

Fig. 1. Dendrogram obtained from a confusion matrix using Ward's method

The initial separation with Ward's method gives the following two clusters: {f,sa,n,d} and {j,s,a}. We also applied the clustering technique of k-means, with k=2, and in this case got the clusters: {n,sa,f}, {j,a,d,s}; as we can observe, the emotion disgust changes from one cluster to the other. We can ask what difference this makes in terms of the classification.

To try to answer this, we treated the data as two, two-class problems, with the classes formed in each case by the two different partitions which we found using Ward's method and k-means. We then found the cross validation rates for the classifiers given in Table 4.

Table 3. Rearranged confusion matrix of J48

	Fear	Sadness	Neutral	Disgust	Joy	Surprise	Anger
Fear	70	58	34	33	4	4	0
Sadness	63	110	42	26	1	1	0
Neutral	34	47	120	35	2	1	4
Disgust	35	43	29	84	7	24	2
Joy	5	0	6	12	136	55	29
Surprise	3	2	2	16	58	101	21
Anger	1	2	1	3	41	16	139

Table 4. Classification rates with two 2-class problems given by the clustering

Classifier	% Error Rate {n,sa,f,d}, {j,a,s }	% Error rate {n,sa,f},{j,a,d,s}
J48	5.7	12.48
1-NN	7.1	13.12
3-NN	6.34	11.14
5-NN	6.53	10.37
7-NN	5.76	10.24
SVM	3.27	9.86
MLP	4.55	10.76

We see that the error rate was worse for each classifier. This suggests that the choice of clustering method employed, and hence also the hierarchical classifier constructed, will make an important difference to the result.

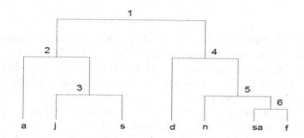

Fig. 2. Hierarchical classifier obtained from the dendrogram in Figure 1

Finally, from the dendrogram, we obtain the following binary hierarchical classifier, shown in figure 2. The numbers signify a different SVM binary classifier in each juncture where: 1 separates the classes formed by {a,j,s} and {d,n,sa,f}, 2 separates the classes formed by {a} {j,s}, etc. In total we have a hierarchical classifier formed using 6 binary classifiers. The error rate obtained using this classifier was 33.59%.

4   Conclusions

In this paper, we have applied Ward's hierarchical clustering method to a confusion matrix which we obtained from a classifier employed on the 7 class problem of a Mexican Spanish emotional speech database. We then used the corresponding dendrogram to define a hierarchical classifier, placing a binary SVM at each juncture. This gave a more principled way of defining the hierarchical structure of the classifier. We have seen that the choice of dendrogram, and so the hierarchy obtained, is important in defining the resulting classifier, as using a different clustering method (the 2-means algorithm) to cluster the confusion matrix produced worse classification results. Finally, the hierarchical classifier was applied to the 7 class problem and produced slightly better results than all of the other classifiers. It should be noted that very little parameter tuning was done to the binary classifiers, only binary SVM classifiers were applied at each juncture, and the same number of data features was used at all levels of the hierarchical classifier. It is to be expected that classification results could be improved by taking some of these factors into consideration and the authors hope to do this, as well as employing other emotional speech databases, in future work.

Acknowledgement. This work was supported by the SEP and CONACyT, through the Program SEP-CONACyT CB-2012-01, No.182432, and by the UAM, in Mexico, as well as CONICET, UNL, and UNER from Argentina.

References

1. Benzeghiba, M., De Mori, R., Deroo, O., et al.: Automatic speech recognition and speech variability: A review. Speech Communication 49, 763–786 (2007)
2. Mehrabian, A.: Communication without words. Psychology Today 2, 53–56 (1968)
3. Williams, C., Stevens, K.: Vocal correlates of emotional states. In: Speech Evaluation in Psychiatry. Grune and Stratton (1981)
4. Fernandez, R.: A computational model for the automatic recognition of affect in speech. Ph.D. Thesis, Massachussetts Institute of Technology (2004)
5. Cowie, R., Douglas, E., Tsapatsoulis, N., Kollias, S., Fellenz, W., Taylor, J.: Emotion recognition in human-computer interaction. IEEE Signal Process. Mag. 18, 32–80 (2001)
6. Ververdis, D., Kotropoulos, C.: A Review of Emotional Speech Databases. Department of Informatics, Aristotle University, Greece (2003)
7. Burkhardt, F., Paeschke, A., et al.: A database of German emotional speech. In: Proceedings of the Interspeech, Lisbon, pp. 1517–1520 (2005)
8. Barra-Chicote, R., Montero, J.M., Macias-Guarasa, J., Lufti, S., Lucas, J.M., Fernandez, F., D'haro, L.F., San-Segundo, R., Ferreiros, J., Cordoba, R., Pardo, J.M.: Spanish Expressive Voices: Corpus for Emotion Research in Spanish. In: Proc. of 6th International Conference on Language Resources and Evaluation (LREC 2008), Morocco (2008)
9. Ei Ayadi, M.: Survey on speech emotion recognition: Features, classification schemes, and databases. Pattern Recognition 44, 572–587 (2011)
10. Muñoz, A., Jiménez, F.: La expresion de la emocón a traés de la conducta vocal. Revista de Psicología General y Aplicada 43, 289–299 (1990)
11. Yang, B., Lugger, M.: Emotion recognition from speech signals using new harmony features. Signal Processing 90, 1415–1423 (2010)
12. Schuller, B., Rigoll, G.: Timing levels in segment-based speech emotion recognition. In: Proceedings of Interspeech, Pittsburg, pp. 1818–1821 (2006)
13. Phlilippou-Hübner, D., Vlasenko, B., Böck, R., Wendemuth, A., von Guericke, O.: The performance of the speaking rate parameter in emotion recognition from speech. In: Proceedings of IEEE International Conference on Multimedia and Expo, Melbourne, pp. 248–253 (2012)
14. Sungrack, Y., Chang, Y.: Loss-scaled large-margin Gaussian mixture models for speech emotion classification. IEEE Transactions on Audio, Speech and Language Processing 20, 585–598 (2012)
15. Batliner, A., Stedi, S., Schuller, B., et al.: Whodunnit - searching for the most important feature types signaling emotion-related user states on speech. Computer and Speech Language 25, 4–28 (2011)
16. Gharavian, D., Scheikhan, M., Nazeriech, A., Garoucy, S.: Speech emotion recognition using FCBF feature selection method and GA-optimized fuzzy ARTMAP neural network. Neural Computer & Applications 21, 2115–2126 (2012)
17. Lee, C., Mower, E., Busso, C., Lee, S., Narayanan, S.: Emotion recognition using hierarchical decision tree approach. Speech Communication 53, 1162–1171 (2011)
18. Giannoulis, P., Potamianos, G.: A hierarchical approach with feature selection for emotion recognition from speech. In: Proceedings of the Eighth International Conference on Language Resources and Evaluation, Istanbul, pp. 1203–1206 (2012)
19. Albornoz, E., Milone, D., Rufiner, H.: Spoken emotions using hierarchical classifiers. Computer Speech and Language 25, 556–570 (2011)
20. Chung-Hsien, W., Chi-Chun, H., Chung-Han, L., Mai-Chun, L.: Hierarchical prosody conversion using regression-based clustering for emotional speech synthesis. IEEE Transactions on Audio, Speech and Language Processing 18, 1394–1405 (2010)

21. Vaughan, B., Cullen, C.: Emotional speech corpus creation, structure, distribution and re-use. In: Young Researchers Workshop in Speech Technology (YRWST 2009), Dublin (2009)
22. Van Eyne, F., Gibbon, D. (eds.): Lexicon Development for Speech and Language Processing. Springer (2000)
23. Swadesh lists for Spanish, http://en.wiktionary.org/wiki/Appendix:Spanish_Swadesh_list
24. Speech Filing System, University College London, http://www.phon.ucl.ac.uk/resource/sfs/
25. Godbole, S.: Exploiting Confusion Matrices for Automatic Generation of Topic Hierarchies and Scaling Up Multi-Way Classifiers. Technical report, IIT Bombay (2002)
26. Everitt, B.S., Landau, S., Leese, M., Stahl, D.: Cluster Analysis. John Wiley & Sons Inc. (2011)
27. Gan, G., Ma, C., Wu, J.: Data Clustering Theory, Algorithms, and Applications. ASA-SIAM Series on Statistics and Applied Probability. SIAM, Philadelphia (2007)
28. Hall, M., Frank, E., Holmes, G., Pfahringer, B., Reutemann, P., Witten, I.H.: The WEKA Data Mining Software: An Update. SIGKDD Explorations 11 (2009)
29. van der Maaten, L.J.P., Hinton, G.E.: Visualizing High-Dimensional Data Using t-SNE. Journal of Machine Learning Research 9, 2579–2605 (2008)

Improvements in Czech Expressive Speech Synthesis in Limited Domain*

Martin Grůber and Jindřich Matoušek

Department of Cybernetics, Faculty of Applied Sciences
University of West Bohemia, Czech Republic
{gruber,jmatouse}@kky.zcu.cz
http://www.kky.zcu.cz

Abstract. In our recent work, a method on how to enumerate differences between various expressive categories (communicative functions) has been proposed. To improve the overall impact of this approach to both the quality of synthetic expressive speech and expressivity perception by listeners, a few modifications are suggested in this paper. The main ones consist in a different way of expressive data processing and penalty matrix calculation. A complex evaluation using listening tests and some auxiliary measures was performed.

Keywords: expressive speech synthesis, unit selection, target cost, communicative functions.

1 Introduction

At present, research in the field of expressive speech is very interesting topic for many scientists. The reason is that naturally sounding speech can be used in various complex systems, especially when considering dialogue systems focused on human-computer interaction. For such systems that attempt to "replace" a human in personal dialogues, there is even more need for incorporating expressivity in speech. Current TTS systems are for sure able to produce high quality speech. However, without any sign of expressivity the listeners (human partners in dialogues) always know that they are communicating with just a machine "pretending" to be a human.

To synthesize expressive speech, an expressivity description has to be designed. Many approaches have been suggested in the past. Continuous descriptions using multidimensional space with several axes to determinate "expressivity position" were described e.g. in [1]. Another option is a discrete division into various groups, for emotions e.g. happiness, sadness, anger, joy, etc. [2]. The discrete description is the most commonly used method and various sets of expressive categories are used, e.g. dialogue

* This work was supported by the European Regional Development Fund (ERDF), project "New Technologies for Information Society" (NTIS), European Centre of Excellence, ED1.1.00/02.0090. The access to computing and storage facilities owned by parties and projects contributing to the National Grid Infrastructure MetaCentrum, provided under the programme "Projects of Large Infrastructure for Research, Development, and Innovations" (LM2010005) is highly appreciated.

M. Železný et al. (Eds.): SPECOM 2013, LNAI 8113, pp. 170–180, 2013.

acts [3], emotion categories [4] or categories like good news and bad news [5]. The systems dealing with expressive speech synthesis are often focused on a specific limited domain, e.g. [6].

In our work, we restricted the domain to conversations between seniors and a computer. As the topic for these discussions, personal photographs were chosen since the work started as a part of a major project whose aim was to develop a virtual senior companion with an audiovisual interface [7] (the more detailed background is described in [8–10]). Such a companion should help the elderly people when they are alone and want to talk to someone.

To describe expressivity within our limited domain, we decided to employ a set of so-called communicative functions (see Section 2). Even though the set is not a general solution for the expressivity description issue, a similar approach (with different expressive categories) might be used when designing a dialogue system for a different domain.

Since our current neutral TTS system ARTIC [11] is a data-driven system based on a unit selection method with a huge neutral speech corpus, there was a need to collect expressive data, i.e. an expressive speech corpus. It can be merged with the neutral one to obtain a robust system being able not only to produce expressive speech but also to keep the ability of synthesizing general texts. The description of the expressive speech corpus recording process and its annotation in terms of expressivity (communicative functions) can be found e.g. in [10]. The modifications of the unit selection algorithm that were performed to enable expressive speech synthesis are described in [9, 12]. The modifications mainly consisted in an adjustment of a target cost function. In the unit selection approach, the target cost is used to measure a suitability of a speech unit (a candidate) from a unit inventory (a database of candidates) for a target utterance (an utterance that is requested to be synthesized; it consists of so-called target units) in terms of prosodic features. One of the features is named communicative function (hereinafter referred to as CF), and a penalty is given to a candidate if its CF label does not meet the target unit requirement. In our recent work [12], suggestions about the penalty settings have been presented and in the current work we try to improve these settings to obtain synthetic speech of a better quality and with more expressed expressivity.

To evaluate achieved results, listening tests were performed to asses both the synthetic speech quality and the expressivity perception by listeners. In addition, overall impression of the expressive speech synthesis system was evaluated in dialogues from our limited domain.

The paper is organized as follows. The expressivity description and the set of CFs is briefly described in Section 2, short background of the target cost calculation is shown in Section 3. Modifications in expressive data processing and acoustic penalty matrix calculation (when compared to [12]) are presented in Section 4 and an evaluation is shown in Section 5. Conclusions are outlined in Section 6.

2   Communicative Functions

In the first phases of our research in this field, a set of CFs was designed to describe expressive categories appearing in the given dialogues of the limited domain. The set of CFs was inspired by dialogue acts proposed in [13] and more detailed description is in [9, 12, 14]. The process of expressive corpus recording and annotation is presented in [8] or [10]. Thus, in this work we present only a list of used CFs labels along with their relative occurrence in the expressive corpus:

- DIRECTIVE (2.4%)
- REQUEST (4.4%)
- WAIT (0.7%)
- APOLOGY (0.6%)
- GREETING (1.4%)
- GOODBYE (1.6%)
- THANKS (0.7%)
- SURPRISE (4.2%)

- SAD-EMPATHY (3.4%)
- HAPPY-EMPATHY (8.6%)
- SHOW-INTEREST (34.9%)
- CONFIRM (13.2%)
- DISCONFIRM (0.2%)
- ENCOURAGE (29.4%)
- NOT-SPECIFIED (7.4%)

Most of the CFs were detected only sparsely in the expressive corpus. Since we need to create a robust TTS system, all the CFs must be used. There might be some mistakes when representing distinctions between the sparsely appearing CFs but we believe that this effect does not influence the overall synthetic speech quality so much. Nevertheless, only the most appearing CFs are used for an evaluation to avoid result distortions caused by usage of not very well represented expressive categories.

It should be noted that the sum of all relative occurrence rates is greater than 100% in our case. This is caused by the fact that during the expressive corpus annotations by CFs, the annotators were allowed to label any sentence from the corpus with more than one CF if necessary. Thus, this is also reflected in the final annotations [12]. However, such sentences have been omitted from the experiments.

Speech units coming from the original neutral speech corpus were marked as *NEU-TRAL* for the further processing. It should represent neutral speaking style (i.e not expressing any kind of expressivity).

3   Target Cost for Expressive Speech

In the unit selection method, target cost C^t is a function that is used to measure a suitability of a speech unit u for a target unit t in terms of prosodic features. The target cost can be calculated as follows:

$$C^t = \frac{\sum_{j=1}^{n} w_j \cdot d_j}{\sum_{j=1}^{n} w_j},$$

(1)

where C^t is the target cost of candidate u for target unit t, n is a number of features under consideration, w_j is a weight of *j-th* feature and d_j is an enumerated difference between *j-th* feature of candidate u and target unit t. The differences of particular features (d_j) will be further referred to as penalties.

For synthesis of expressive speech, the set of prosodic features is extended so it includes the feature of CF. This means that a measure enumerating a difference (penalty) between various CFs must be developed. In our recent work [12], a penalty matrix determining such penalties has been proposed. It is based on:

1. perceptual similarities revealed during annotation of expressive speech corpus [8] – perceptual penalty matrix **P**;
2. acoustic analysis that was performed on this corpus [15] – acoustic penalty matrix **A**.

Coefficients m_{ij} of the final penalty matrix **M** are calculated as

$$m_{ij} = \frac{w_p \cdot p_{ij} + w_a \cdot a_{ij}}{w_p + w_a}, \tag{2}$$

where p_{ij} and a_{ij} represent coefficients from matrices **P** and **A**, w_p and w_a are corresponding weighs.

Several combinations of weighs w_p and w_a were examined. Finally, $w_p = 3$ and $w_a = 1$ setting was used. Using this setting, the best results were achieved when subjectively comparing resulting synthetic speech. We also believe that the perceptual part should be emphasized.

In this work, more acoustic data preprocessing techniques were employed and more enhanced description of acoustic parameters was used to improve the acoustic penalty matrix **A**.

4 Acoustic Penalty Matrix Enhancement

To enhance the acoustic penalty matrix (when comparing with [12]), data coming from the acoustic analysis of expressive speech [15] were preprocessed using outliers detection techniques. To describe various acoustic parameters such as $F0$, phoneme duration and RMS values, several statistical characteristics were employed.

4.1 Outliers Detection

Results of the acoustic analysis of all voiced segments from the expressive speech corpus (in terms of various CFs) were used to create an acoustic penalty matrix. For these segments, 3 acoustic parameters were measured: $F0$, phoneme duration and RMS. It means that each voiced segment is represented by a 3 dimensional vector. For outliers detection, technique [16] based on Wilks method [17] was used. Using this approach, the outliers can be identified in a multidimensional space. The detected outliers were removed. Thus, for each CF a representative set of data was available.

4.2 Statistical Characteristics

After outliers removal, the probability distribution of values of each acoustic parameter (in terms of various CFs) was described using 4 statistical measures: mean, standard deviation, skewness and kurtosis (only mean was used in [12] but results of expressive speech acoustic analysis [15] suggest that other statistical measures might be influenced by expressivity too, as confirmed also by other studies [18, 19]). For each CF we obtained a 12-dimensional feature vector x_i (3 acoustic parameters × 4 statistical characteristics), where i represents i-th CF.

4.3 Enumerating Differences

To enumerate differences between various CFs, suppression of absolute differences of various statistical characteristics of various acoustic parameters was needed. Thus, normalization was applied to the feature vectors as follows:

$$\forall i : \mathbf{x}_i^N = \frac{\mathbf{x}_i - \min_\mathbf{x}}{\max_\mathbf{x} - \min_\mathbf{x}}, \tag{3}$$

where $\mathbf{x}_i$ is a feature vector representing i-th CF, $\min_\mathbf{x}$ is a vector consisting of minimal values of all $\mathbf{x}_i$ and $\max_\mathbf{x}$ is a vector consisting of maximal values of all $\mathbf{x}_i$. Resulting values of vectors $\mathbf{x}_i^N$ are in the range of $\langle 0, 1 \rangle$.

To find coefficients a_{ij} of the acoustic penalty matrix $\mathbf{A}$, Euclidean distance was used. The calculation of coefficients was performed in two steps:

1. Obtaining coefficients a'_{ij} as the Euclidean distance of normalized feature vectors:

$$\forall i, j : a'_{ij} = d(\mathbf{x}_i^N, \mathbf{x}_j^N), \tag{4}$$

where i and j represent i-th and j-th CF, $\mathbf{x}_i^N$ is the normalized feature vector obtained from (3) and d represents the Euclidean distance;
2. Normalization of coefficients a'_{ij} to get the values into the range $\langle 0, 1 \rangle$ again:

$$\forall i, j : a_{ij} = \frac{a'_{ij}}{\max_{a'}}, \tag{5}$$

where i and j represents i-th and j-th CF and $\max_{a'}$ is maximum value of all a'_{ij}. This is the same normalization as (3) but the $\min_{a'}$ can be omitted since it is always 0.

The perception penalty matrix $\mathbf{P}$ remains the same as proposed in [12]. The final penalty matrix $\mathbf{M}$ is then created as described in Section 3 using matrices $\mathbf{P}$ and $\mathbf{A}$ and keeping the same weighs. An excerpt from the matrix $\mathbf{M}$ is depicted in Table 1.

5   Evaluation

To evaluate an impact of our modifications on synthetic expressive speech, several views were used. At first, isolated utterances were presented to listeners for evaluation in terms of speech quality and expressivity perception. Next, part of dialogues between a computer and a human in two versions (expressive vs. neutral speech synthesis for the computer responses) were created and presented to listeners to obtain their preferences.

5.1   Isolated Utterances

Seven CFs (including *NEUTRAL*) were selected from the whole set to evaluate the performance of expressive speech synthesis. The selection was necessary for two reasons. First, some of the CFs occurred only sparsely in the expressive corpus and thus the

Table 1. Excerpt from the final penalty matrix **M**

	CONFIRM	ENCOURAGE	HAPPY EMPATHY	NOT SPECIFIED	SAD EMPATHY	SHOW INTEREST	NEUTRAL
CONFIRM	0.00	0.71	0.40	0.48	0.41	0.50	0.72
ENCOURAGE	0.50	0.00	0.35	0.31	0.39	0.14	0.55
HAPPY-EMPATHY	0.25	0.24	0.00	0.21	0.29	0.27	0.58
NOT-SPECIFIED	0.26	0.12	0.15	0.00	0.22	0.13	0.46
SAD-EMPATHY	0.28	0.26	0.33	0.28	0.00	0.25	0.67
SHOW-INTEREST	0.53	0.15	0.43	0.27	0.41	0.00	0.45
NEUTRAL	0.72	0.55	0.58	0.46	0.67	0.45	0.00

coefficients of the penalty matrix might be a little distorted. Next, there are two main requirements for the listening tests that must be met: sufficient number of examples for each CF and sufficient number of listeners. Thus, there is a need to reduce the number of test queries to an acceptable level. However, full final penalty matrix was used during the synthesis (not only the excerpt shown in Table 1), i.e. speech units labelled with any CF (all speech units from both corpora) could be used to produce synthetic speech.

The following CF labels were used when synthesizing expressive speech for the evaluation: *SHOW-INTEREST, ENCOURAGE, CONFIRMATION, HAPPY-EMPATHY, SAD-EMPATHY* (that was chosen mainly to complete the set with supposedly contradictory pair of happy vs. sad empathy). We also used *NOT-SPECIFIED* and *NEUTRAL* which usage is assumed to produce neutral speech.

The evaluation is divided into two parts: synthetic speech quality and expressivity perception. In both parts, 13 listeners assessed 30 utterances (4 for each CF and 2 natural neutral utterances – to compare the synthetic speech quality with the natural speech).

The test stimuli were the same for both parts and were prepared as follows: random sentences with required CFs were selected from the corpora and content (text) of these sentences was modified — similar meaning was retained. This approach ensures that the sentences will be really synthesized and not only replayed. Before the synthesis, each sentence was tagged with the required CF label.

In addition, two auxiliary measures were employed to evaluate the speech quality and the expressivity perception. The first one is relative ratio of so-called "smooth joints". Smooth joint is a concatenation of two speech units that were originally adjacent in a speech corpus. The next one is relative ratio of speech units used for the synthesis being labelled with such CF that is required to be synthesized (hereinafter referred to as RRSU measure).

Speech Quality. During the listening test, the listeners were asked to assess the synthetic speech quality using 5-point MOS scale. In the following evaluation, we would like to present the comparison with the previous system presented in [12] which is called as *baseline system.*

The results of two independent evaluations are presented in Table 2: evaluation performed for the new system proposed in this work and former evaluation of baseline system from [12]. In addition to the absolute values of MOS score (mean values of all CFs in evaluation), a relative comparison with natural speech is presented in both cases. It allows us to compare results of various MOS tests.

Table 2. Results of MOS test

Settings	new system	natural speech	baseline system	natural speech
MOS Score	3.5	4.6	3.4	4.7
Relative	69%	100%	65%	100%

We might conclude that the synthetic speech quality has improved from 65% (for the baseline system) to 69% (for the new proposed system). The difference is statistically significant – confirmed by ANOVA test (with $\alpha = 0.05$).

The auxiliary measure of relative ratio of smooth joints in synthetic speech is shown in Table 3. We can observe an improvement in smoothness when compared with the baseline system for almost all CFs. This is consistent with results of MOS evaluation.

Table 3. Relative occurrence of "smooth joints" in the resulting synthetic speech

CF label	new system	baseline system
CONFIRM	80%	80%
ENCOURAGE	76%	70%
HAPPY-EMPATHY	77%	67%
SAD-EMPATHY	80%	69%
SHOW-INTEREST	82%	75%
mean	**79%**	**72%**
NOT-SPECIFIED	82%	82%
NEUTRAL	82%	not available

Expressivity Perception. Beside the speech quality evaluation, the listeners were asked to mark if they are able to perceive any kind of expressivity in the presented utterances. They were not instructed to mark any specific CF since the main objective of the test was just to generally evaluate a difference in speech perception when comparing an expressive TTS and a neutral (mainstream) TTS approach. This way we also tried to avoid any forced-choice evaluation. The listeners were provided with a few samples of expressive and neutral sentences to outline a definition of expressivity in speech. The results of the evaluation are shown in Table 4.

The mean value of expressivity perception ratio is 54%, the mean value of auxiliary RRSU measure is 50%. It is remarkable that the expressivity perception ratio of 42% was achieved in natural neutral utterances. This could mean that utterances in neutral corpus are not expressively neutral as it was supposed or that the listeners are very

Table 4. Expressivity perception ratios and values of RRSU measure in terms of various CFs

CF label	expressivity perception	unable to decide	RRSU measure
CONFIRM	69%	4%	75%
ENCOURAGE	42%	8%	68%
HAPPY-EMPATHY	50%	10%	35%
SAD-EMPATHY	63%	4%	33%
SHOW-INTEREST	46%	4%	40%
mean	**54%**	**6%**	**50%**
NOT-SPECIFIED	10%	0%	4%
NEUTRAL	15%	0%	100%
natural speech	42%	4%	–

sensitive in expressivity perception. For synthetic neutral speech, the results mean that the listeners perceived almost no expressivity. It can be also observed that the RRSU measure does not correspond with the expressivity perception very much.

The value 4% of RRSU for *NOT-SPECIFIED* was further inspected. We found out that for synthesis of sentences tagged with this CF, speech units coming from neutral corpus (labelled with *NEUTRAL*) were mostly selected. This might suggest that these two CFs are very similar (neither should express any kind of expressivity).

To prove that the results are different from those that would be achieved by chance, several measures were used: precision, recall, F1 measure and accuracy. These are often used in classification tasks to evaluate classifiers. However, the listeners can be also viewed as classifiers classifying into two classes: perceive or do not perceive expressivity ("unable to decide" responses were not considered here). Thus, these measures were calculated for our results and for results of a random simulation. We simulated a situation when the listeners evaluate the listening test randomly. The measured values are shown in Table 5.

It can be concluded that the results achieved using the listening test are above the chance level. It means that the expressivity is quite recognizable in the synthetic speech.

Unlike the speech quality evaluation, comparison with [12] is not possible for expressivity perception because of missing results in that previous work. On the other hand, a comparison of RRSU measures would be distorted since in [12] different penalty

Table 5. Measures for classification of expressivity in synthetic speech; comparison of the real results and the results achieved by the random simulation

measure	listeners	simulation
precision	0.92	0.72
recall	0.58	0.50
F1 measure	0.71	0.59
accuracy	0.66	0.50

matrix coefficients were used (not in range of $\langle 0, 1 \rangle$ and thus influencing the target cost calculation significantly).

5.2 Dialogues

For evaluation of an overall impact of synthetic expressive speech in dialogues, test stimuli were prepared as follows:

- 6 parts of natural dialogues[1] between a human and a computer avatar (approximately 1 minute in length) were randomly selected (referred to as *mini-dialogues*);
- texts of avatar responses were extracted from the mini-dialogues and were modified in order to avoid just replaying from the corpus during the following synthesis;
- the modified texts were synthesized using neutral TTS system ARTIC [11] and the new system proposed in this work;
- the original avatar responses in mini-dialogues were replaced by the newly synthesized utterances producing two versions for each mini-dialogue: one with neutrally synthesized responses and one with expressively synthesized responses.

Each mini-dialogue contained 4 avatar responses in average expressing various CFs, mostly *SHOW-INTEREST* or *ENCOURAGE*. However, all CFs in evaluation were used at least once. The mini-dialogues (both version at once) were then presented to listeners to mark which version is more pleasant, more natural and preferred. The results are shown in Table 6.

Table 6. Evaluation of expressive speech synthesis in dialogues

synthesis method	preference
neutral	8 %
expressive	83 %
unable to decide	9 %

The expressive speech were much more preferred to the neutral one (83%). This result is one of the most important findings since the expressive speech synthesis proposed in this work is supposed to be used in similar dialogues.

6 Conclusions and Future Work

In this work, improvements in Czech expressive speech synthesis in limited domain were shown in comparison with neutral synthesis and with our previous work in this field. Benefits of the penalty matrix coefficients calculation enhancement were presented in the form of listening test results and an auxiliary measure. The results show that the proposed system improved the synthetic speech quality when compared to the

---

[1] The process of natural dialogues collection is described e.g. in [10].

previous work and that expressive speech is preferred to the neutral one by listeners in dialogues.

For the future work, other modifications of penalty matrix approach should be considered. The main challenge for the near future is to create a phoneme-dependent acoustic penalty matrix since differences of acoustic parameters might vary in terms of various phonemes or phoneme groups (like vowels/consonants).

References

1. Russell, J.A.: A circumplex model of affect. Journal of Personality and Social Psychology 39, 1161–1178 (1980)
2. Cornelius, R.R.: The science of emotion: Research and tradition in the psychology of emotions. Prentice-Hall, Englewood Cliffs (1996)
3. Syrdal, A.K., Conkie, A., Kim, Y.J., Beutnagel, M.: Speech acts and dialog TTS. In: Proceedings of the 7th ISCA Speech Synthesis Workshop – SSW7, Kyoto, Japan, pp. 179–183 (2010)
4. Zovato, E., Pacchiotti, A., Quazza, S., Sandri, S.: Towards emotional speech synthesis: A rule based approach. In: Proceedings of the 5th ISCA Speech Synthesis Workshop – SSW5, Pittsburgh, PA, USA, pp. 219–220 (2004)
5. Hamza, W., Bakis, R., Eide, E.M., Picheny, M.A., Pitrelli, J.F.: The IBM expressive speech synthesis system. In: Proceedings of the 8th International Conference on Spoken Language Processing – ISCLP, Jeju, Korea, pp. 2577–2580 (2004)
6. Krstulovic, S., Hunecke, A., Schroder, M.: An HMM-based speech synthesis system applied to German and its adaptation to a limited set of expressive football announcements. In: Proceedings of Interspeech, Antwerp, Belgium, pp. 1897–1900 (2007)
7. Ircing, P., Romportl, J., Loose, Z.: Audiovisual interface for Czech spoken dialogue system. In: IEEE 10th International Conference on Signal Processing Proceedings, Beijing, China, pp. 526–529. Institute of Electrical and Electronics Engineers, Inc. (2010)
8. Grůber, M., Matoušek, J.: Listening-test-based annotation of communicative functions for expressive speech synthesis. In: Sojka, P., Horák, A., Kopeček, I., Pala, K. (eds.) TSD 2010. LNCS, vol. 6231, pp. 283–290. Springer, Heidelberg (2010)
9. Grůber, M., Tihelka, D.: Expressive speech synthesis for Czech limited domain dialogue system – basic experiments. In: IEEE 10th International Conference on Signal Processing Proceedings, Beijing, China, vol. 1, pp. 561–564. Institute of Electrical and Electronics Engineers, Inc. (2010)
10. Grůber, M., Legát, M., Ircing, P., Romportl, J., Psutka, J.: Czech Senior COMPANION: Wizard of Oz data collection and expressive speech corpus recording and annotation. In: Vetulani, Z. (ed.) LTC 2009. LNCS, vol. 6562, pp. 280–290. Springer, Heidelberg (2011)
11. Tihelka, D., Kala, J., Matoušek, J.: Enhancements of Viterbi search for fast unit selection synthesis. In: Proceedings of Interspeech, Makuhari, Japan, pp. 174–177 (2010)
12. Grůber, M.: Enumerating differences between various communicative functions for purposes of Czech expressive speech synthesis in limited domain. In: Proceedings of Interspeech, Portland, Oregon, USA, pp. 650–653 (2012)
13. Syrdal, A.K., Kim, Y.J.: Dialog speech acts and prosody: Considerations for TTS. In: Proceedings of Speech Prosody, Campinas, Brazil, pp. 661–665 (May 2008)
14. Grůber, M., Hanzlíček, Z.: Czech expressive speech synthesis in limited domain: Comparison of unit selection and HMM-based approaches. In: Sojka, P., Horák, A., Kopeček, I., Pala, K. (eds.) TSD 2012. LNCS, vol. 7499, pp. 656–664. Springer, Heidelberg (2012)

15. Grůber, M.: Acoustic analysis of Czech expressive recordings from a single speaker in terms of various communicative functions. In: Proceedings of the 11th IEEE International Symposium on Signal Processing and Information Technology, pp. 267–272. IEEE (2011)
16. Trujillo-Ortiz, A., Hernandez-Walls, R., Castro-Perez, A., Barba-Rojo, K.: MOUTLIER1: Detection of outlier in multivariate samples test. A MATLAB file (2006) (online; cited October 29, 2012)
17. Wilks, S.S.: Multivariate statistical outlier. The Indian Journal of Statistics 25(4), 407–426 (1963)
18. Přibil, J., Přibilová, A.: Statistical analysis of spectral properties and prosodic parameters of emotional speech. Measurement Science Review 9, 95–104 (2009)
19. Přibil, J., Přibilová, A.: Statistical analysis of complementary spectral features of emotional speech in Czech and Slovak. In: Habernal, I., Matoušek, V. (eds.) TSD 2011. LNCS, vol. 6836, pp. 299–306. Springer, Heidelberg (2011)

Improving Prosodic Break Detection
in a Russian TTS System

Pavel Chistikov and Olga Khomitsevich

Speech Technology Center Ltd.,
4 Krasutskogo street, St. Petersburg, Russia, 196084
{chistikov, khomitsevich}@speechpro.com
http://www.speechpro.com

Abstract. We propose using statistical methods for predicting positions and durations of prosodic breaks in a Russian TTS system, in order to improve on a baseline rule-based system. The paper reports experiments with CART and Random Forests (RF) classifiers. We used CART to predict break durations inside and between sentences, and compared the results of CART and RF for predicting break positions inside sentences. We find that both classifiers show an improvement over the baseline system in predicting break positions, with RF showing the best results. We also observe good results in experiments with predicting break durations. To increase the naturalness of synthesized speech, we included probability-based break durations into a working Russian TTS system. We also built an experimental system with probability-based break placement in sentence parts without punctuation marks, which was evaluated higher than the baseline system in a pilot listening experiment.

Keywords: phrasal breaks, prosodic breaks, prosodic boundaries, pauses, speech synthesis, TTS, text-to-speech, statistical models.

1 Introduction

Correct prosodic segmentation in a Text-to-Speech system is necessary for achieving natural-sounding synthesized speech. If a sentence is sufficiently long, it is usually divided into prosodic phrases, which are normally separated by pauses[1]. This makes speech both more natural and more intelligible, since ambiguous constructions can be made clear by the use of pauses.

Many TTS systems rely solely on punctuation to mark prosodic breaks. However, large chunks of uninterrupted speech between punctuation marks can sound monotonous and difficult to understand, which raises the problem of finding appropriate places for breaks inside them. A different problem is present in a language like Russian, where punctuation is traditionaly used for some expressions that are not separated by pauses

---

[1] Throughout this paper, we only take into account prosodic breaks that are accompanied by a pause of non-zero length. Prosodic breaks without a pause are possible and are in fact found in our Russian database, however in read speech they mostly mark "minor" boundaries, so we decided not to model them in synthesized speech.

M. Železný et al. (Eds.): SPECOM 2013, LNAI 8113, pp. 181–188, 2013.
© Springer International Publishing Switzerland 2013

in natural speech (e.g. words like "maybe" or "of course"). Consequently, a more complicated break placement system is needed to achieve natural prosody in synthesized speech.

Additionaly, a TTS system must determine the length of prosodic breaks between phrases in the synthesized sentences as well as between the sentences. The easiest method is to rely on constants, but this means simplifying the behavior of human speakers since pause duration can vary significantly in real speech, so a method for computing various break durations for different contexts is needed [1].

The way natural speech is segmented prosodically depends on various factors. A major factor is syntactic structure: prosodic breaks often fall between syntactic constituents, so that syntactic structure can be seen as "mapped" onto prosodic phrases [2, 3]. However, the length of the sentence, semantics of certain words, and other features also play a role [4]. In a TTS system, these factors can be captured either by rigid rules defining which words in the synthesized sentence should be followed by a pause [5, 6], or by statistical models trained on large speech corpora and predicting probabilities of prosodic breaks [7, 8].

The Russian TTS system that we are working with uses a rule-based algorithm for placing prosodic breaks and constants for determining pause duration [9]. These methods work reasonably well; however, as with any algorithm developed by experts, it is extremely difficult to take into account all the complicated cases present in real texts. In addition, developing such a system for a new TTS language is very time-consuming. Machine learning methods have the advantage of being easy to train, given adequately labeled speech corpora. They are also expected to emulate the behavior of real speakers, rather than reflecting an expert's knowledge. In this paper, we take the existing algorithm for prosodic break detection as a baseline and examine ways of improving synthesized speech by use of statistical methods of prosodic analysis.

2   CART and RF Classifiers

We experimented with two classifiers for predicting break position and duration: CART [10] and Random Forests (RF) [11]. The CART classifier can be used for predicting both break placement and break duration: the classifier predicts a break duration for every position in the sentence, with breaks placed where the duration exceeds zero or a predetermined threshold. We also used CART for predicting break duration only; in this case, the classifier yields a predicted break duration for every position where a break was placed at a previous stage. The Random Forests classifier was used for break placement only because of the different principle of its work.

CART is a recursive partitioning method based on minimization of partition goodness criterion (1):

$$G(C_1, C_2) = \frac{D(C_1)T(C_1) + D(C_2)T(C_2)}{T(C_1) + T(C_2)}, \tag{1}$$

where

$$D(C) = \frac{2\left(\sum_{i=1}^{|C|} \sum_{j=1}^{|C|} d(U_i, U_j)\right)}{|C|^2 - |C|}, \tag{2}$$

$$T(C) = \frac{1}{2}\left(|C|^2 - |C|\right),\tag{3}$$

$|C|$ is a size of cluster C, $d(U, V)$ is a distance between U and V vectors, the stop criterion is the minimal number of items in the cluster (in our work this number is 3).

Random Forests classify data using a given set of features by means of a hierarchy (a "tree") of queries, based on the predictive value of each feature at each point. The classifier is capable of processing large amounts of training data. The leaves of each tree in the forest store the class distribution of all samples falling into the corresponding region of the feature space, which then serve as predictors for test samples. In our system, we use a forest containing 100 trees, and the probabilistic value is calculated by dividing the number of trees classifying the target class by the total number of trees. Each tree is built on the basis of 60% of randomized training data. This prevents the data from being dependent on noise in the training set. The parameters of the classifier were chosen by using a grid search method to maximize the result quality.

3   Experimental Setup

In our experiments we used a large high-quality database originally recorded as the Unit Selection speech database for a TTS system and consisting of read speech by nine speakers (four male and five female). The texts read by the speakers were contemporary Russian works of fiction as well as newspaper articles on the topics of politics and technology. The database comprises over 50 hours of speech, which contain over 38000 phrasal breaks. It was divided into a training set and a test set.

When training the break placement model, we only took into account intra-sentential breaks, assuming that sentence boundaries are already known. The speech database consists of read speech, and the speakers generally marked sentence boundaries in the material with a pause when reading the text (the text was read in chunks consisting of several sentences or paragraphs). In our experiments, the text was broken into sentences by the normalization process of the TTS engine, which is done with a high degree of accuracy. As for break duration, both sentence-internal and sentence-external break durations were used for training.

We used the following features for classification:

- Punctuation: the punctuation mark on the current word as well as two preceding and two following words.
- Word and syllable count: the number of words and syllables in the sentence, the number of words and syllables from the previous break to the current word, from the current word to the end of the sentence, etc.
- Grammatical form. Since using all morphological features of Russian words would result in an enormous number of tags, too large for the classifier to cope with, we decided to limit the grammatical features to part of speech and case. We also use the information on whether or not the word is a proper noun (name, geographical location, etc). This information is calculated using a speech synthesis engine which includes a morphological vocabulary.

- Agreement features: whether or not the grammatical form of the current word matches that of the following word and the second word on the right.
- Capitalization of the first letter of the current word and the two preceding and two following words.

Both in model training and testing, homonym resolution is necessary to minimize the number of errors due to incorrect feature calculation. We use homonym resolution provided by the TTS system, which labels 96% of homonyms correctly [12].

4   Results for Break Placement

In Table 1 we present the results for automatic break placement (CART and Random Forests) compared to the results of the baseline rule-based algorithm that is implemented in the standard version of the TTS system we are working with. The test set contained 47819 junctures (word pairs inside sentences) and 6186 phrase breaks (with 264336 junctures and 32630 breaks in the training set).

Table 1. Results of automatic break detection

	Baseline TTS	CART	Random Forests
Correct junctures	43254 (90%)	44358 (93%)	44865 (94%)
Correct breaks	5042 (82%)	5176 (84%)	4695 (76%)
FA	3421 (55%)	2451 (40%)	1463 (24%)
FR	1144 (18%)	1010 (16%)	1491 (24%)
Recall	82%	84%	76%
Precision	60%	68%	76%
F-score	69%	75%	76%

In this table, "correct junctures" denote the number of correctly identified breaks or non-breaks among all word pairs in the data, while "correct breaks" denote the proportion of correctly identified breaks; these measures were used in [7] and are given here for comparison, along with FA (False Alarms), FR (False Rejections) and the F-score. The results of both classifiers show an improvement on the baseline system: they yield a higher F-score, and the rates of FA to FR errors are more balanced. CART shows a higher percentage of correct breaks due to a lower level of False Rejection errors; however, the RF classifier gives the highest percentage of correct junctures. The F-scores of CART and RF are not very different (we plan to perform tests in our future work to determine whether the difference is statistically significant). However, importantly, RF can be tuned during testing by adjusting the probability threshold which signals the presence of a break after a word, so that we can achieve an equal count of FA and FR errors. Overall, RF can be considered the best-performing model.

The results of the classifier also compare favorably with those reported in the literature. For instance, for English [7] reports up to 91.1% correct junctures and the F-score of up to 71.9; [8] improves their result and attains the F-score of 74.4.

5   Results for Break Duration

Apart from predicting break placement and break duration simultaneously, we trained a CART model to predict break durations separately; that is, given a predetermined position for a prosodic break, the model predicts the break duration for this position. The model is trained on the duration of the breaks found in the training set; during testing, the classifier makes a prediction for each break position found in the test dataset. We can use a model trained in this way to combine break duration prediction with a rule-based break placement model or with the results of RF, which may be preferable because it turns out that CART's performance in predicting break positions is inferior to that of RF, and because RF is easier to tune in order to change the frequency of breaks in the speech; this gives our prosodic phrasing model a greater flexibility.

In our experiments we first trained the classifier to predict the lengths of all prosodic breaks in the dataset: both those inside sentences and between sentences. Then we decided to divide the two tasks, namely, predicting sentence-internal vs. sentence-external breaks. It should be noted that in spontaneous speech, sentences are not easy to detect, and such an approach would probably fail; in that case it would probably be more productive to distinguish between types of breaks such as long and short breaks. However, since we were dealing with read speech, we felt that speakers were aware of sentences in the text and marked them prosodically, and we wished to imitate this effect in synthesized speech.

We tested the performance of break duration prediction using the NRMSD (Normalized Root-Mean-Square Deviation) measure, similar to the method found in [1]. The results are given in Table 2.

Table 2. NRMSD results for break duration prediction

	Sentence-external breaks	Sentence-internal breaks
General model	0.25	0.23
Specialized models	0.19	0.16

This table presents results for the general model (modeling all breaks in the dataset) and the specialized models (two separate models for sentence-external and sentence-internal breaks). We can see that the specialized models give a better approximation both for sentence-internal and sentence-external breaks.

6   Integration in the TTS System

As was mentioned above, the baseline Russian TTS system uses a rule-based algorithm for break placement, and constants for break duration. Breaks are divided into four types according to length: one type of inter-sentential breaks and three types of intra-sentential breaks. This does not provide much variation in speech rhythm, so we decided to include probability-based break duration prediction into the system. The first model that we implemented inserted statistically predicted break durations into the positions where the rule-based model predicted a break (of any type); this was done using separate models for inter-sentential and intra-sentential breaks. This experiment received positive reviews from listeners.

We next experimented with integrating the probability-based break placement model into the existing TTS system. The baseline system works as follows: first, breaks are inserted in places of punctuation marks, with some exceptions where punctuation marks are purely traditional and do not signify a pause. Then, if a chunk of speech between two breaks exceeds a certain threshold number of words, rules are applied in order to attempt to segment it with breaks (based on superficial syntactic analysis). We decided to replace the second part of the algorithm with a probabilistic method, leaving the first in place. So the general principle of break placement in the system remains the same: first, punctuation is taken into account, and then long word sequences that are still left without breaks are dealt with. Of course, it is also possible to only rely on the statistical model for break placement, without any artificially imposed restrictions, however we felt that it would make the system less predictable and so less suitable for practical applications.

We then had to decide whether to choose CART or RF for break placement. One obvious advantage of CART is the small size of the model, which is an important consideration for an applied TTS system. However, as was shown in Table 1, the RF model shows slightly higher accuracy in predicting phrase breaks. Moreover, even when we tune the RF model by reducing the probability threshold that signifies the presence of a break, so that FA-type errors exceed in number FR-type errors the way they do in the CART results, the RF results still seem more accurate to the listener than the results of CART. This effect cannot be observed from automatic testing. The problem here is that the automatic testing process considers all breaks (and non-breaks) in the reference material to be the only correct variant, disregarding the fact that a sentence can often be segmented prosodically in more than one way. This means that not all errors are equally important: in some positions a prosodic break is completely impossible while in others it could be placed. It turns out that CART makes significantly more serious errors than RF, although this can only be established by a human expert listening to the synthesized speech. Specifically, the errors made by CART often include breaks inside syntactically linked phrases: after prepositions, conjunctions and other function words typically linked to the following word; between a modifier (adjective, adverb, etc) and a noun or verb it modifies; inside a complex noun phrase; etc. These error types are almost entirely absent from RF results.

Additionally, as already mentioned, RF is a more flexible model because it can be tuned in order to increase or decrease the number of breaks in synthesized speech, which may be useful in practical cases of TTS applications; for instance, increasing the number of breaks results in a perceived slowing down of speech.

To sum up, in our experimental system we decided to use the RF model to define prosodic break positions in long word sequences without punctuation marks. Comparing the results of this new system to the baseline is not easy, and a complex evaluation procedure of the Mean Opinion Score (MOS) type is needed, which will be the subject of our future research. However, we have conducted a pilot test to determine listeners' preferences. We chose 25 sentences from a base of texts used normally to test the

TTS system; the sentences contained large word sequences uninterrupted by punctuation marks, and they were segmented in differing ways by the baseline system and the experimental system. 18 Russian speakers were asked which variant of break placement they liked more; 10 of them reported they preferred the new system, with 4 preferring the other variant and 4 undecided.

7 Conclusions

In this paper we have examined a probability-based approach to prosodic break detection in a Russian TTS system. Experimental results show that break placement models based on CART and RF classifiers give more accurate test results than the baseline rule-based algorithm. The CART model displays more errors than the RF model, and these errors are typically less acceptable for the listener, such as breaks inside syntactically closely linked phrases, so we decided to use the RF in an experimental break assignment model for an existing TTS system. This system was positively evaluated by listeners.

We also experimented with CART-based prediction of pause durations. We found that predicting break duration works better if sentence-internal and sentence-external breaks are modeled separately. This model was judged to produce more natural synthesized speech and has been included in a new version of the TTS system to replace the old constant-based system.

References

1. Parlikar, A., Black, A.W.: Modeling Pause-Duration for Style-Specific Speech Synthesis. In: Proceedings of Interspeech, Portland, OR, USA, pp. 446–449 (2012)
2. Bachenko, J., Fitzpatrick, E.: A computational grammar of discourse-neutral prosodic phrasing in English. Computational Linguistics 16(3), 155–170 (1990)
3. Tepperman, J., Nava, E.: Where should pitch accents and phrase breaks go? A syntax tree transducer solution. In: Proceedings of Interspeech, Florence, Italy, pp. 1353–1356 (2011)
4. Zellner, B.: Pauses and the temporal structure of speech. In: Keller, E. (ed.) Fundamentals of Speech Synthesis and Speech Recognition, pp. 41–62. John Wiley, Chichester (1994)
5. Abney, S.: Parsing by chunks. In: Berwick, R.C., Abney, S.P., Tenny, C.L. (eds.) Principle-Based Parsing: Computation and Psycholinguistics, vol. 44, pp. 257–278. Springer (1991)
6. Atterer, M.: Assigning Prosodic Structure for Speech Synthesis: A Rule-based Approach. In: Proceedings of Speech Prosody, Aix-en-Provence, pp. 147–150 (2002)
7. Black, A.W., Taylor, P.: Assigning phrase breaks from part-of-speech sequences. Computer Speech & Language 12(2), 99–117 (1998)
8. Busser, B., Daelemans, W., Bosch, A.V.D.: Predicting phrase breaks with memory-based learning. In: 4th ISCA Tutorial and Research Workshop (ITRW) on Speech Synthesis, pp. 29–34 (2001)
9. Khomitsevich, O.G., Solomennik, M.V.: Automatic pause placement in a Russian TTS system [Avtomaticheskaja rasstanovka pauz v sisteme sinteza russkoj rechi po tekstu]. In: Komp'iuternaia Lingvistika i Intellektual'nye Tehnologii: Trudy Mezhdunarodnoj Konferentsii "Dialog 2010" [Computational Linguistics and Intellectual Technologies: Proceedings of the International Conference "Dialog 2010"], pp. 531-537 (2010) (in Russian)
10. Loh, W.-Y.: Classification and Regression Tree Methods. In: Encyclopedia of Statistics in Quality and Reliability, pp. 315–323. Wiley (2008)

11. Breiman, L., Cutler, A.: Random Forests, http://www.stat.berkeley.edu/ ~breiman/RandomForests/cc_home.htm
12. Khomitsevich, O.G., Rybin, S.V., Anichkin, I.M.: Linguistic analysis for text normalization and homonymy resolution in a Russian TTS system [Ispol'zovanie lingvisticheskogo analiza dlja normalizatsii teksta i snjatija omonimii v sisteme sinteza russkoj rechi]. In: Izvestija vuzov. Priborostroenie. Tematicheskij vypusk "Rechevye informatsionnye sistemy" [Instrument making. Thematic issue Speech information systems], vol. 2, pp. 42–46 (2013) (in Russian)

Investigation of Forensically Significant Changes of Acoustic Features with Regard to Code-Switching (on the Basis of Russian and German)

Tatiana Platonova[1] and Anna Smolina[2]

[1] Department of Applied and Experimental Linguistics,
Moscow State Linguistic University,
119992 st. Ostozhenka 38, Moscow, Russia
`tanya_platonova@mail.ru`
`www.linguanet.ru`
[2] STEL Computer Systems Ltd., 105082 st. B. Pochtovaya 55/59, Moscow, Russia
`smolina_aa@stel.ru`
`www.speech.stel.ru`

Abstract. The investigation of the phenomenon of code-switching presents great scientific interest nowadays. An explosive development of info-communication technologies and the growth of the international crime made it crucial to create multilingual systems, capable of speaker identification with regard to code-switching. That task is obviously impossible without a thorough study of speaker identification and code-switching on the basis of different languages. The paper focuses on the investigation of changes of the speaker's specific speech features under the conditions of switching from the native language to a foreign one. The conducted experiment was based on the material in Russian and German languages and included two types of analysis: acoustic analysis and perceptual analysis. The results of the experiment testify to the fact that the situation of code-switching has an impact on certain speech features. For instance, the mean fundamental frequency tends to decrease, speech melody becomes uneven, speech tempo slows down, duration of pauses increases, the articulation becomes tenser and distinct. At the same time it was found out that some characteristics of the speakers voice were not subjected to any changes.

Keywords: code-switching, speaker identification, Russian language, German language.

1 Introduction

Speaker identification has become one of the most topical linguistic trends in the modern world. There are several reasons for this. First of all, the amount of theoretical knowledge as well as powerful computing technologies make it possible to develop advanced systems of speaker identification and put them into practice [9]. Besides, due to the growth of crime and the appearance of its new forms, practical need for such systems cannot be overestimated.

Speaker identification becomes possible because of the unique character of the voice biometrics, which (like fingerprints or retina) is never exactly the same from person to

M. Železný et al. (Eds.): SPECOM 2013, LNAI 8113, pp. 189–194, 2013.

person. Speech signal is individualized during all stages of its formation [13]. Different people have different structure and functioning of vocal apparatus and nervous system in the first place. But our speech is a complex phenomenon; it reflects the interaction of biological, physical, psychological processes and serves as a means of communication at the same time [7]. Thus its peculiarity is the result of both individuality of human body organization and specificity of the surrounding community. Each person, being a part of a certain nation and culture, inherits a worldview inherent to all speakers of a certain language. All the knowledge about the world is stored in the language; it forms the personality of native speakers and conditions their outlook, way of life, etc. That is why, according to I. Khaleeva, "the content of speakers personality is influenced by the peculiarities of his or her native language" [6, p. 23].

In the course of studying a foreign language one comes to know a new way of life, another worldview, etc. The process of studying a foreign language "makes a person to exist in two different sociocultural communities at the same time, speculating over their divisions" [6, p. 58]. The interaction of the native and foreign languages forms a new, specific outlook, which, without a doubt, has a great impact on the persons speech performance in general. Therefore the knowledge of a foreign language becomes an important individual characteristic that should be taken into account during speaker identification.

Nowadays criminal law experts have to process a considerable number of phonograms that contain foreign language material. Although some positive results have been gained with regard to speaker identification on the basis of the Russian language in our country, the development of methods of speaker identification on the basis of other languages, such as English, German, French, is in the initial stage [5].

As such, the problem of the identification of a speaker, who uses a foreign language, by an expert, who learned it as a second language or does not know it at all, is of the utmost scientific interest. One of the first investigators of the problem was K. Thompson. His experiments demonstrated that the knowledge of the language does have a considerable influence in the situation of speaker identification: the English-speaking experts recognized better those subjects, who spoke without a foreign accent [10].

The first study of the role of the linguistic competence in the process of speaker identification in Russia was performed at Moscow State Linguistic University. The conducted experiment testifies to the fact that an expert, who has a good command of a foreign language, can better identify speakers who use it [12].

An explosive development of info-communication technologies and the growth of the international crime made it crucial to create multilingual systems capable of speaker identification with regard to code-switching. There are several definitions of the term "code-switching". In its narrow meaning code-switching involves the use of words from two different languages within a single discourse or within a single utterance [4]. In general it can be regarded as the mixing of words, phrases and sentences from two distinct grammatical (sub)systems across sentence boundaries within the same speech event [1] (i.e. the term is employed not only to describe the use of more than one language, but the use of more than one style within an utterance or discourse as well [3]). However, it is the process of switching from one language to the other that presents a considerable problem for speaker identification, since it has a certain impact on individual vocal features.

Although it is hardly possible to challenge the importance of this problem in the modern world, the influence of code-switching on speaker identification has not been much studied yet by either foreign or Russian researchers. First investigations on the topic were conducted in the USA and Germany. Prosodic features such as fundamental frequency, intensity and temporal characteristics were closely examined. The investigations gave the opportunity to figure out the features that change due to the difference of articulators tension and places of articulation in different languages (for example some falling of voice pitch when switching from Russian to German was observed) [5].

In Russia the only previous research on the effect of code-switching on speaker identification was performed at the Department of Applied and Experimental Linguistics of Moscow State Linguistic University in 2004. It was aimed at determining possible changes of some prosodic features for both read and semi-spontaneous speech under conditions of switching from Russian to English. The results of the investigation show that it is possible to identify a speaker who switches from Russian to English, though one should take into account the changes that some characteristics of voice (such as voice pitch, speech tempo, voice strength, type of articulation) are subjected to [10].

The aim of the study described in this paper was to define the changes of prosodic features entailed by code-switching and, if possible, to find some invariable characteristics or general changes that take place in the speech of Russian native speakers when they switch to German.

2 Materials and Methods

The material for the experiment was recorded with the help of six Russian native speakers who had studied German for at least three years. The material for the recording was a fragment taken from "Stationschef Fallmerayer" by Joseph Roth (volume = 269 words) and its translation into Russian (volume = 235 words) by M. Shchyolkova. Both texts were unknown to the speakers. The subjects read the text in L1, then in L2 and then retold it in the same way. Then they made up dialogs based on the text, during which they switched randomly from L1 to L2 and vice versa. All these types of speech behavior were recorded with the help of Wavelab lite 2.6 computer program. Recording parameters were 48 kHz, 16-bit, Mono.

In the course of the experiment two types of analysis were carried out - acoustic and perceptual. During the acoustic analysis (for details see [8, p. 335]) the mean fundamental frequency was measured and analyzed for each speaker in both languages (Russian, German) separately for different types of speech. The perceptual analysis included two stages. Thirteen Russian native speakers who have not studied German took part in the first stage. Their task was to listen to the three recorded types of speech (read, semi-spontaneous and spontaneous speech) and determine such specific features of each speaker as voice pitch, speech melody, speech tempo, speech breathing, duration of pauses, ways of their filling, type of articulation, accentuation (rhythmical pattern), voice strength and voice timbre using a questionnaire designed by R. K. Potapova (for details see [13, p. 104].

The second stage of the perceptual experiment was aimed at testing the consistency of the results gained during the first stage. Twelve Russian native speakers who have not studied the German language took part at this stage. Their task was the same: the subjects were to listen to the recorded material and evaluate the individual vocal characteristics of the speakers.

3 Results

The results of both acoustic and perceptual analysis were interpreted and compared separately for the three examined types of speech (reading, retelling and dialog) in both languages. It must be mentioned that since the spontaneous speech with regard to code-switching was studied for the first time, it was of the greatest interest during the investigation. That is why particular attention was paid to the dialogs.

As it has been already pointed out, the mean fundamental frequency was measured during the first part of the research. It was observed that this parameter tends to decrease in the situation of code-switching. The tendency is especially clear in the case of the read speech and dialogs. These results correspond with those obtained during the investigation of the phenomenon accomplished in the USA and Germany (for details see [5]), as well as those received in the researches conducted at the Department of Applied and Experimental Linguistics at Moscow State Linguistic University (for details see [10]). Basing on the data for both English and German it may be suggested that the mean fundamental frequency should not be considered an unalterable characteristic of the speaker. The decrease of the mean fundamental frequency may be caused by dissimilarity of Russian and German articulatory patterns, first of all by labialization of German consonants and the differences in rhythmical structures and intonation contours of the two languages. Yet this hypothesis should be tested.

The comparison of the results gained during the two stages of the perceptual analysis made it possible to draw the following conclusions:

1. Speech melody tends to become carved in the German language; this is especially clear in read speech and dialogs (the subjects on both stages of the perceptual experiment pointed out that the change took place in 66.7% of cases).
2. Speech tempo tends to slow down, particularly in retold speech (this is characteristic for 66.7% of the subjects).
3. The duration of pauses increases; the tendency is connected with the previous one and manifests itself best in dialogs (in the speech of 66.7% of the subjects).
4. Articulation becomes more tense and distinct, particularly in retold speech (the articulation alters in 66.7% of cases).
5. Speech breathing data are controversial – according to the first stage of the analysis it becomes irregular and uncomfortable in dialogs, while the second stage subjects decided that this change occurs in read and retold speech.
6. The situation of code-switching has no impact on rhythmical patterns; however, this parameter vary with the type of speech.
7. The ways of filling pauses undergo no changes; this result fits in with the one obtained in the experiment with the English language (see [13]). It could be consequently concluded that every person has his or her own way of filling pauses that remains unchanged in the situation of switching from the native language to a foreign one. That fact may be of use for speaker identification.

8. The behavior of the other parameters (i.e. voice pitch, voice strength and voice timber) is not clear. Further investigations are needed to throw light on it. It must be pointed out, that according to the researches the phenomena of switching from Russian to English and to German exert similar influence on speech tempo, the duration of pauses and ways of the filling.

However, the tendency discovered for articulation in the present study contradicts the results received in 2004. The reason for this is likely to be the difference between the English language and the German language. German sounds are articulated with more tension, greater air pressure than Russian sounds, which, for instance, manifests itself in a stronger aspiration of plosive consonants and a greater noise intensity of fricative sounds. Hence, the articulation of the speaker switching from Russian to German becomes more tensed.

4   Conclusion

Speaker identification appears to be top priority for applied linguistics in the modern world. Although in Russia and abroad there are reliable methods that provide a means for speaker identification on the basis of one language, it is obviously not enough. The explosive development of info-communication technologies (e.g. Internet) as well as the process of international integration and thereupon emerging problems cause the need to create multilingual systems capable of speaker identification with regard to code-switching. To fulfill this task a thorough investigation of the phenomenon of code-switching on the basis of different languages must be carried out.

In view of this the present experiment was conducted. The goal was to study the behavior of the specific prosodic features in the speech of Russian native speakers when they switch to German. According to the observations made in the cause of the research the mean fundamental frequency decreases, speech melody becomes more curved, speech tempo slows down, articulation becomes tense, the duration of pauses increases, while the ways of their filling along with accentuation undergo no evident changes. It must still be emphasized that the present findings should be considered preliminary. The influence of the phenomenon of code-switching on speaker identification has not been completely studied yet. To throw light on the problem and get more reliable results subsequent experiments should be planned with more subjects, other foreign languages and a more detailed acoustic analysis involved.

References

1. Ayeomoni, M.O.: Code-Switching and Code-Mixing: Style of Language Use in Childhood in Yoruba Speech Community. Nordic Journal of African Studies 15(1), 90–99 (2006)
2. Blohina, L.P., Potapova, R.K.: Methodical recommendations. The way to analyze prosodic characteristics of the speech, MSPIFL publishing office, 84 p. (1977) (in Russian)
3. Lyu, D.-C., Lyu, R.-Y., Chiang, Y.-C., Hsu, C.-N.: Speech Recognition on Code-Switching among the Chinese Dialects. In: International Symposium on Chinese Spoken Language Processing, ISCSLP 2004, Hong Kong, pp. 1105–1108 (2006)

4. Chan, J.Y.C., Ching, P.C., Lee, T., Meng, H.M.: Detection of language boundary in Code-Switching Utterances by Biphone Probabilities. In: International Symposium on Chinese Spoken Language Processing, ISCSLP 2004, Hong Kong, pp. 293–296 (2004)
5. Isakova, E.E.: Speaker identification under the condition of code-switching (English and Russian languages). In: Khitina, M.V. (ed.) Topical Issues of Experimental and Applied Linguistics, Rema, pp. 94–107 (2008) (in Russian)
6. Khaleeva, I.I.: The foundations of the theory of teaching foreign languages (professional training of translators). Visshaya shkola (1989) (in Russian)
7. Mihailov, V.G., Zlatoustova, L.V.: The alteration of speech parameters. Radio i svyaz (1987) (in Russian)
8. Platonova, T.S., Smolina, A.A.: Speaker identification with regard to code-switching (on the basis of Russian and German languages). In: 14th International Conference SPEECH and COMPUTER, SPECOM 2011, Kazan, pp. 333–337 (2011) (in Russian)
9. Potapova, R.K., Potapov, V.V.: Language, Speech, Personality. Languages of Slavonic Culture (2006) (in Russian)
10. Potapova, R.K., Statsenko, O.N., Isakova, E.E.: Speaker Identification Considering Code-Switching (Russian and English languages). In: 10th International Conference SPEECH and COMPUTER, SPECOM 2005, Patas, pp. 559–561 (2005)
11. Potapova, R.K.: Subject-oriented perception of foreign speech. Vorposiyazikoznaniya, pp. 46–65 (2005) (in Russian)
12. Potapova, R.K.: To the problem of the influence of forensic experts language competence on speaker identification. In: Theory and Practice of Speech Investigations (APCO 1999): Conference Proceedings (1999) (in Russian)
13. Statsenko, O.N.: Speaker identification with regard to switching from native language to a foreign one and vice versa (on the basis of Russian and English languages): Ph.D. thesis - Moscow, 148 p. (2007) (in Russian)

LIMA: A Spoken Language Identification Framework

Amalia Zahra and Julie Carson-Berndsen

CNGL, School of Computer Science and Informatics, University College Dublin
amalia.zahra@ucdconnect.ie, julie.berndsen@ucd.ie

Abstract. This paper presents LIMA, the <u>L</u>anguage <u>I</u>dentification for <u>M</u>ultilingual <u>A</u>SR, which is a web-based parameterisable spoken language iden-tification framework. LIMA is a novel system which facilitates a personalised experience for the user who can tailor the system to evaluate different LID tech-niques with varied parameterisations across a range of languages. A number of standard LID techniques have been implemented in the system, together with a novel technique based on unique n-phones. By way of illustration of the system, evaluation results for one particular parameterisation of the system are presented.

Keywords: spoken language identification, system prototype development, personalisation.

1 Introduction

Spoken language identification (henceforth called LID) is the task of identifying the lan-guage of an unknown speech utterance. It typically serves as a front-end to other tasks. For instance, the telephone company AT&T provides the *Language Line* interpreter ser-vice that routes an incoming call to a human operator who is fluent in the corresponding language. The police emergency call 911 also offers such a service in the effort to handle emergency cases from foreign people in the United States. As the needs of international communication grow rapidly, LID plays an increasingly important role. For example, LID as a front-end component of a multilingual automatic speech recognition (ASR) system offers increased system flexibility with regard to expansion to additional lan-guages. Rather than developing ASR systems which can deal with multiple languages, such as the ATR multilingual speech-to-speech translation system presented in [1] , an LID component can be coupled with multiple monolingual speech recognisers which can be selected according to the language hypotheses provided by the LID system. Thus effort can be focussed on achieving high quality and robustness in monolingual ASR.

A number of studies have been carried out with respect to the functionality of an LID component to assist a multilingual ASR system [2,3]. In [2], an LID component was developed to identify Tamil and Hindi speech before being passed to an ASR system, while the study in [3] included more languages (i.e. 6 languages) and was designed to be employed in mobile devices. Both studies implement the same idea of identifying the language of an unknown speech utterance prior to recognising the words with a monolingual speech recogniser.

LIMA is an LID system designed as a front-end for monolingual speech recognisers, offering similar functionality to that of the aforementioned components.

M. Železný et al. (Eds.): SPECOM 2013, LNAI 8113, pp. 195–202, 2013.

However, LIMA introduces further flexibility to users in terms of the language set to be included in the task, the input mode, the LID technique and its parameters. For those users who want to use the system for the purposes of simply identifying the language of an unknown speech utterance, standard input parameters can be chosen. For those users who wish to undertake more in-depth evaluation across a number of techniques, it is possible to personalise the system to account for specific requirements and obtain more insights about the results and techniques employed. Currently, the system is in the state of a prototype, which opens many opportunities to more functionalities.

The remainder of this paper is structured as follows. Section 2 presents the LIMA interface and discusses the various components of the system. Section 3 outlines the LID techniques implemented in LIMA and by way of illustration of the value of the system, the outputs for one particular data set and parameterisation of the system are presented. Finally, Section 4 concludes with some directions for future work.

2   The LIMA Interface

LIMA[1] is an LID framework that allows users to personalise the LID experience through parameterisation of inputs to and outputs of the system. It is designed to be easily extended through a web-based interface. LIMA is presented to the user following sign-in as two screens which are captured as two web pages that perform LID tasks. The first page is a form which is shown in Fig. 1 (subsection 2.1) that allows the user to choose required inputs and specify parameters. This is followed by the second page shown in Fig. 2 (subsection 2.2) that presents the summary of the user inputs and the LID outputs according to the parameterisation.

2.1   Inputs and Parameters

Figure 1 shows that the page is divided into two columns. The left column ("Settings") contains a form that allows users to enter three types of basic information prior to specifying the follow-up parameters. Firstly, the input mode (1) has to be selected among the three modes: a speech file (in *wav* format), live speech, or a folder of speech files.

The next step is to select a number of target languages to be included in the task (2). There are 21 languages currently covered in the system: Arabic, Bengali, Chinese Cantonese, Chinese Mandarin, Chinese Min, Chinese Wu, English, Farsi, French, German, Hindustani, Indonesian, Italian, Japanese, Korean, Russian, Spanish, Tagalog, Tamil, Thai, and Vietnamese. The user is asked to select at least two target languages.

The final step in the left column is to select the LID technique(s) to be applied (3). The techniques are categorised into two types: phonetic or acoustic-based. The selection of multiple techniques allows for a comparison of the results given by the corresponding techniques. Once all these basic inputs have been assigned, the user can specify the parameters required by each of the selected techniques by clicking the button in the left column.

---

[1] http://muster.ucd.ie/~amalia/lima (login information can be obtained by contacting the author).

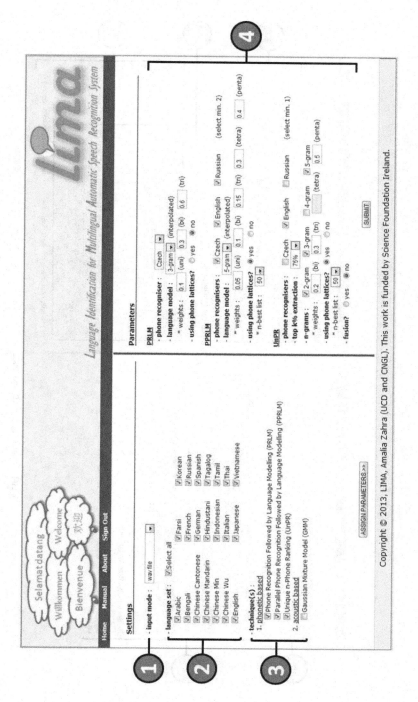

Fig. 1. The LIMA first main page

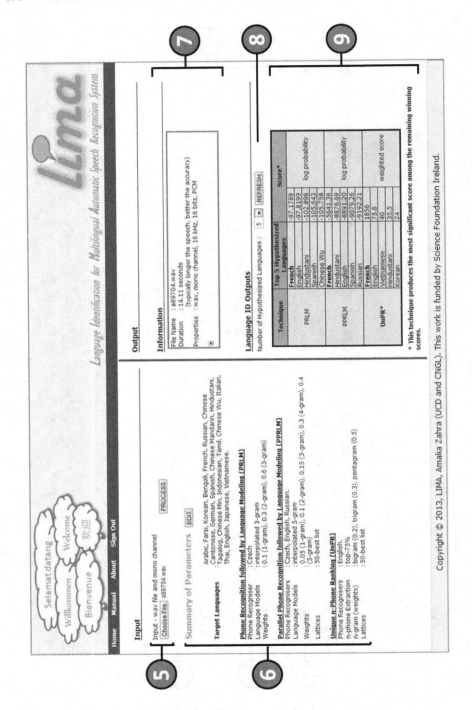

Fig. 2. The LIMA second main page

The content of the form displayed in the right column ("Parameters") (4) depends on the technique(s) selected in the left column. In the example shown in Fig. 1, three techniques are selected: phone recognition followed by language modelling (PRLM) [4], parallel phone recognition followed by language modelling (PPRLM) [4,5], and unique n-phone ranking (UnPR) [6]. Thus, the parameters presented in the right column are those required for each technique respectively. The parameters include the language of the phone recogniser(s), the type of language model (LM), the weights assigned for interpolated LMs, and whether lattices are utilised, followed by the size of the n-best list generated from those lattices. For UnPR, there is a slight difference in terms of the n-gram distribution used and the amount of top n-phones extracted. These inputs relate to the procedure carried out in UnPR [6].

2.2 Summary and Outputs

Once the necessary fields in the page shown in Fig. 1 have been assigned, the next steps are presented in the page shown in Fig. 2. Similar to the previous web page, this page is also divided into two columns: left ("Input") and right ("Output"). The input column allows the user to input a speech utterance(s) (5), either as a single speech file, live speech, or a folder of speech files, depending on the type of input specified by the user previously. The example shown in Fig. 2 allows users to submit a single speech file. The property of the file currently allowed by LIMA is *wav* format and mono channel. This column also displays a summary of all the parameters (6) that have been specified previously. This allows the user to verify them again prior to LID processing. If there are a number of parameters that need to be modified, the user can click the edit button to return to the previous page.

When every input has been verified, the LID task is then performed and the outputs are presented in the right column. LIMA firstly presents some information related to the unknown speech utterance (7), such as file name, duration of the file, its property, and a player to play the utterance. Also if there is error with respect to the speech utterance (e.g. format), the error message will be displayed in this area.

As mentioned earlier, the number of hypothesised languages to be displayed can be determined by the user, which is up to 21 languages (8). This is followed by a table presenting the LID output of each LID technique selected by the user (9), which is a list of hypothesised languages of the speech utterance and their corresponding scores. In the example shown in Fig. 2, 5 of 21 hypothesised languages are listed, ranked based on the log probability scores (PRLM and PPRLM) or the weighted scores (UnPR) (i.e. the speech input is French). Furthermore, the system highlights which technique produces the most confident decision based on the level of significance of the winning score compared to the other winning scores of the remaining techniques.

LIMA provides an experimental framework which is suitable for a range of users, from those who want to identify the language of a single speech utterance, to those who are more familiar with the parameters and wish to compare and contrast several identification techniques across a range of languages to investigate which technique is best suited to a particular purpose. The language candidates displayed allow users to get more insights about the unknown speech, not just the top hypothesis of each technique. The scores given for each language candidate provide an indication as to the distance between the score of a particular language and the scores of the remaining languages. This aspect of LIMA is currently being extended to provide the user with a more personalised and comprehensive LID experience to include the language family, visualisation of the scoring, and classification as to whether the language is tonal or non-tonal, for example. The interface is designed to allow straightforward incorporation of new LID techniques.

While this section has described the LIMA interface, the next section will now explain the techniques employed by the system.

3   LID Techniques

Currently, three phonetic-based LID techniques have been fully implemented. They are phone recognition followed by language modelling (PRLM), parallel phone recognition followed by language modelling (PPRLM), and unique n-phone ranking (UnPR). In this paper, these phonetic-based techniques use the phone recognisers developed by Brno University [7]. PRLM and PPRLM have been widely used in phonetic-based LID [4,5,8,9]; while UnPR [6] is a novel technique that achieves promising accuracy and runs faster than the other two techniques. One acoustic-based LID technique, the Gaussian mixture model (GMM) technique [10] has also been implemented for a reduced number of languages but is not discussed further here. This section briefly describes the phonetic techniques and presents their accuracies for an optimum parameterisation of the system.

The first step during the LID in PRLM [4] is to decode an unknown speech utterance using a phone recogniser to obtain a corresponding phone sequence. This phone sequence is then passed to a maximum-likelihood based classifier, where the language model (LM) likelihoods are computed over up to 21 (based on the number of languages chosen) discriminative n-grams. The LM that produces the highest likelihood will determine the hypothesised language of the unknown speech.

PPRLM [4] implements a similar idea to PRLM except that it utilises multiple phone recognisers and takes the average likelihood from a set of likelihoods produced by the phone recognisers. This average is subsequently the basis of the maximum-likelihood based classification.

UnPR [6] also utilises at least one phone recogniser to generate phone sequences. However, the novelty in this approach lies in the way the phone sequences are processed to perform LID tasks. The key idea of UnPR is to use a list of ranked unique n-phones to each target language while other phonetic-based techniques [5,8,11] include all the n-grams even though they overlap between languages. Moreover, the value of n for the unique n-phone list varies in order to take the context of various lengths of phone sequences into account. These unique n-phones are then sorted based on their numbers of occurences in the training set and its top-$k\%$ are extracted to form a list that is considered as the discriminative factor that distinguishes one language from the remaining languages in the target set. This list is used in a weighted sum scoring to obtain a score for an unknown speech utterance given each possible language in the target set. Finally, a maximum-score based classifier is employed to decide the hypothesised language of the speech utterance.

All three phonetic techniques can be performed utilising phone lattices. Therefore, an option to include lattices is provided by LIMA, complemented with an additional option to select the size of the n-best list generated from the lattices.

Using the 2007 NIST Language Recognition Evaluation Test Set [12], 80% for training and 20% for testing, the best LID accuracies achieved for this data set by implementing PRLM, PPRLM, and UnPR are shown in Table 1. Note that the parameters for each of these accuracies are different since different techniques have different optimum sets of parameters, as determined following previous experimentation with the system. The results presented here are based on the evaluations on three speech lengths: 3s, 10s, and 30s.

Table 1. LID accuracies over 21 languages

LID Technique	Parameters	Duration		
		3s	10s	30s
PRLM	phone recogniser: English language model: interpolated 5-gram using a phone lattice with 50-best list	97%	97.2%	93.6%
PPRLM	phone recognisers: Czech, English, and Russian language model: interpolated 5-gram using a phone lattice with 50-best list	97.9%	96.2%	94.3%
UnPR	phone recognisers: Czech, English, and Russian n-grams: bigram, trigram, and pentagram using all unique n-phones (100%) using a phone lattice with 30-best list applying fusion	97%	96.4%	95.8%

Table 1 shows that the accuracies achieved by the three techniques are comparable. However, while it would be expected that the longer the speech segment, the more accurate the LID system, the table shows that here there is a performance degradation for longer speech segments. From a number of random checks on several speech samples, it was found that the longer speech samples in this data set contain more noise (e.g. fillers) than shorter ones. However, a more thorough investigation of this is required.

4   Conclusion and Future Work

A web-based system for spoken LID, namely LIMA, was introduced in this paper. It is designed to allow users to perform LID evaluations and offers various types of flexibility to users in terms of the language set to be included, the input mode, the LID technique to be applied and the parameters which can be chosen. Regular users use LIMA simply to perform LID for an unknown speech utterance while more advanced users may use LIMA as an LID experimentation and evaluation platform.

Future work includes the integration of additional LID techniques and visualisations of some of the statistics associated with the results which may provide more insights into the benefits of a particular technique for a specific application. Finally, in order to evaluate LIMA as a front-end to a multilingual speech recognition system, a number of monolingual speech recognisers will be integrated which use the LID outputs for identifying which recogniser to use.

Acknowledgment. This research is supported by the Science Foundation Ireland (Grant 07/CE/I1142) as part of the Centre for Next Generation Localisation (www.cngl.ie) at University College Dublin (UCD). The opinions, findings, and conclusions or recommendations expressed in this material are those of the authors and do not necessarily reflect the views of Science Foundation Ireland.

References

1. Nakamura, S., Markov, K., Nakaiwa, H., Kikui, G., Kawai, H., Jitsuhiro, T., Zhang, J.S., Yamamoto, H., Sumita, E., Yamamoto, S.: The ATR multilingual speech-to-speech translation system. IEEE Transactions on Audio, Speech, and Language Processing 14(2), 365–376 (2006)
2. Kumar, C.S., Haizhou, L.: Language identification for multilingual speech recognition systems. In: 9th Conference Speech and Computer, SPECOM (2004)
3. Hategan, A., Barliga, B., Tabus, I.: Language identification of individual words in a multilingual automatic speech recognition system. In: IEEE International Conference on Acoustics, Speech and Signal Processing (ICASSP), pp. 4357–4360 (2009)
4. Zissman, M.A.: Comparison of four approaches to automatic language identification of telephone speech. IEEE Transactions on Speech and Audio Processing 4, 31–44 (1996)
5. Matějka, P., Schwarz, P., Černocký, J., Chytil, P.: Phonotactic language identification using high quality phoneme recognition. In: Proceedings of Eurospeech, vol. 5 (2005)
6. Zahra, A., Carson-Berndsen, J.: Unique n-phone ranking based spoken language identification. In: 5th IEEE International Conference on Computational Intelligence, Communication Systems and Networks (CICSyN), pp. 239–244 (2013)
7. Schwarz, P., Matějka, P., Černocký, J.: Hierarchical structures of neural networks for phoneme recognition. In: IEEE International Conference on Acoustics, Speech and Signal Processing (ICASSP), pp. 325–328 (2006)
8. Wang, L., Ambikairajah, E., Choi, E.H.C.: Multi-lingual phoneme recognition and language identification using phonotactic information. In: 18th International Conference on Pattern Recognition, vol. 4, pp. 245–248 (2006)
9. Suo, H., Li, M., Liu, T., Lu, P., Yan, Y.: The design of backend classifiers in pprlm system for language identification. In: IEEE Third International Conference on Natural Computation (ICNC), vol. 1, pp. 678–682 (2007)
10. Torres-Carrasquillo, P.A., Singer, E., Kohler, M.A., Greene, R.J., Reynolds, D.A., Deller Jr., J.R.: Approaches to language identification using Gaussian mixture models and shifted delta cepstral features. In: Proceedings of International Conference on Spoken Language Processing (ICSLP), vol. 2, pp. 89–92 (2002)
11. Deng, Y., Liu, J.: Automatic language identification using support vector machines and phonetic n-gram. In: Proceedings of International Conference on Audio, Language and Image Processing (ICALIP), vol. 1, pp. 71–74 (2008)
12. Martin, A., Le, A.: 2007 NIST language recognition evaluation test set. Catalog LDC2009S04 (2009), http://www.ldc.upenn.edu/Catalog/catalogEntry.jsp?catalogId=LDC2009S04

Language Identification System for the Tatar Language

Aidar Khusainov and Dzhavdet Suleymanov

[1] Kazan (Volga region) Federal University, Kazan, Russia
khusainov.aidar@gmail.com
http://kpfu.ru
[2] Institute of Applied Semiotics, Tatarstan Academy of Sciences, Kazan, Russia
dvdt.slt@gmail.com
http://ips.antat.ru

Abstract. This paper describes a speech identification system for the Tatar, English and Russian languages. It also presents a newly created Tatar speech corpus, which is used for building a language model. The main idea is to investigate the potential of basic phonotactic approaches (i.e. PRLM-approach) when working with the Tatar language. The results indicate that the proposed system can be successfully employed for identifying the Tatar, English and Russian languages.

Keywords: language identification, speech corpus, the Tatar language.

1 Introduction

Nowadays it becomes more and more obvious that creating and using speech technologies starts playing an important role in many areas of life. Different types of speech analysis systems can now be effectively used in call-centers, dictation automation, during the search through big audio-data archives, in device controlling, etc. All these applications motivate researchers to develop such kind of systems for languages, which have important regional significance, for instance, for the Tatar language.

Nevertheless, in real-world situations these call-centers and speech assistant programs are used by people who speak different languages. Therefore, it is important to have the possibility of differentiating the speech utterances according to their language. This is why the task of automatic language identification is so topical nowadays.

When choosing the basic approaches for our investigation, we took into consideration the fact that there was no corpus for the spoken Tatar language. PRLM (phone recognition followed by language modeling) approach requires only one-language phoneme recognizer. In our system the recognizer is built for the English language, because there are well-developed annotated English corpora.

Basing on the observation above, we have focused our research on creating a language identification system for the English, Russian and Tatar languages. This requires building a corpus of the Tatar speech.

The structure of the rest of this paper is as follows: in Section 2 we discuss the structure of the language identification system, including the characteristics of the corpora and the features of language models. In Section 3 we describe the realization aspects of the system. Section 4 deals with experimental results we have achieved. The summary of this work can be found in Section "Conclusion and perspectives".

M. Železný et al. (Eds.): SPECOM 2013, LNAI 8113, pp. 203–210, 2013.

2 Language Identification System

2.1 Structure

Research in automatic spoken language identification has a history of more than 30 years. Numerous techniques and algorithms have been invented, and we have chosen one of them phone recognition followed by language modeling (PRLM). This choice was motivated by low requirements of this approach to speech materials.

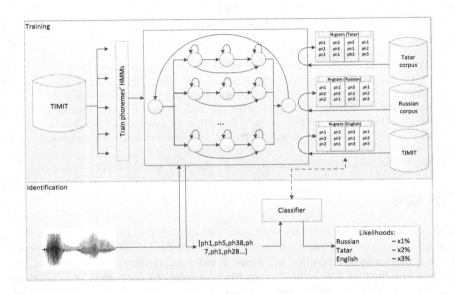

Fig. 1. Structure of PRLM-based language identification system

As the term suggests, PRLM approach has two main parts: the phone recognizer and language modeling (generally n-gram models). Records from the training parts of speech corpora in each language are tokenized by a phone recognizer, which is built for the English language. The resulting phone sequence is used to estimate the language model for each language.

During the recognition, the same phone recognizer tokenizes the utterance. Then the system calculates the probability that this phone sequence belongs to each of the three languages. The language model with the highest probability is selected as result of the identification process. The structure of a PRLM-based language identification system is shown in Fig.1. The main parts of the proposed system are as follows:

1. Speech corpora of the English, Tatar and Russian languages,
2. English acoustic model,
3. Phonotactic models of the English, Tatar and Russian languages,
4. Classifier.

2.2   Corpora

There are two different applications of speech corpora to the language identification task. Firstly, phonetically labeled speech corpus is required to build an English phoneme recognizer. Secondly, the Tatar, Russian and English corpora are used to build statistical models of languages based on probabilities of phoneme sequences in these languages.

For the first mentioned subtask, the TIMIT corpus has been used. Acoustic models have been built for each of 62 phonemes. Every phoneme is represented by a 3-state left-to-right hidden Markov model (HMM), as shown in Fig. 2. The distribution of features in HMM state is a mixture of 8 Gaussians.

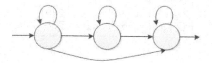

Fig. 2. HMM phoneme

For the second subtask, we need speech corpora of three languages: for the English we use the TIMIT corpus with VoxForge project corpus, for the Russian only VoxForge project corpus.

For the Tatar language we have created a test corpus, which contains speech records of 6 speakers. Most utterances have been taken from classical Tatar literature and modern magazines and newspapers. On the whole the corpus contains 10 hours of speech.

Additionally, files in all corpora were divided into training and testing parts. The training parts are used to form language models, while the testing parts are employed to calculate the correctness of language identification. Some additional information about the corpora is shown in Table 1.

Table 1. Information on the speech corpora

Parameter	English	Russian	Tatar
Number of files	14900	2914	4925
Total duration	15:41:36	9:39:33	9:52:35
Average file duration	0:00:04	0:00:12	0:00:07
Number of short files	13837	1952	4381
Number of long files	1063	962	544
Testing part	100	100	100
Short files	50	50	50
Long files	50	50	50

2.3   Language Models

In this work we use phonotactic information about the languages in order to identify the language. So, the phoneme recognizer plays an essential role: it converts training speech corpora into sequences of English phonemes. These sequences are then analysed to accumulate statistical information about each language. Statistical models are represented by n-gram models.

Table 2 presents the information about the Tatar, English and Russian n-gram models.

Table 2. Information on the language models

Number	English	Russian	Tatar
1-gram	62	62	62
2-gram	3309	3262	2701
3-gram	54323	45451	35742

According to the limit of the corpora size, the developed language models cant be complete. Thus, there will be unseen n-grams with zero probability. As the probability of the entire speech utterance is calculated as multiplication of separate n-grams, this can lead to the situation, in which even one unseen n-gram zeroes out the total utterance probability. To overcome this drawback we used Katz's back-off model, where 3-grams case probabilities are estimated according to the following options:

$$P^*(w_i|w_{i-1}, w_{i-2}) = \begin{cases} \frac{C(w_{i-2}w_{i-1}w_i)}{C(w_{i-2}w_{i-1})} & r > k, \\ d_r \frac{C(w_{i-2}w_{i-1}w_i)}{C(w_{i-2}w_{i-1})} & 0 < r < k, \\ \alpha(w_{i-1}w_{i-2})P(w_i|w_{i-1}) & r > 0, \end{cases}$$

where $C(*)$ number of *-sequence, d_r - the discount rate and α - normalization coefficient. The parameter k selects one of the three approaches; value of k is set to 1.

3   Realization

The main components of the language identification program are as follows:

– English phoneme recognizer,
– Language models,
– Classifier.

Building acoustic models for English phonemes, recognizing training and testing parts of speech corpora and building n-gram language models for the Tatar, Russian and English languages is effectuated using the hidden Markov model toolkit (HTK). The developed c#-programming module called LI_Core has made it possible to create and adjust HTK scripts.

Diagrams of major core classes are presented in Fig. 3.

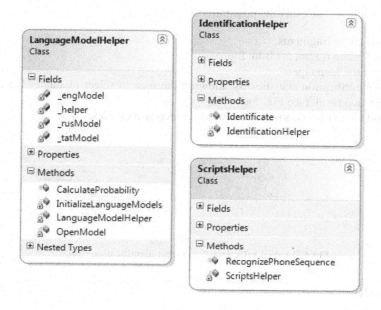

Fig. 3. Diagrams of core classes

Additionally, for experimental purposes a user interface has been developed. The main user form can be seen in Fig. 4.

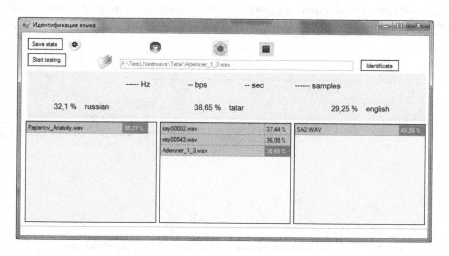

Fig. 4. Main user form

This form gives the users the possibility to:

– Record audio fragments,
– Upload audio fragments from file,
– Identify the language,
– Form identification statistics by allowing the user to select manually the correct recognition result (see Fig. 5),
– Extend the existing corpora by newly recorded speech files.

Fig. 5. Manual selection of a correct identification result

4   Results

To evaluate the quality of the developed language identification system, we have worked out a testing subcorpus for each of the analyzed languages.

This testing corpus contains three hundred records with duration from 3 seconds to 2 minutes each. The variety in duration gives us the possibility to detect the relation between the quality of identification results and audio files duration. It is obvious that longer audio files contain more language specific information and give better identification results. This dependency is shown in Fig. 6.

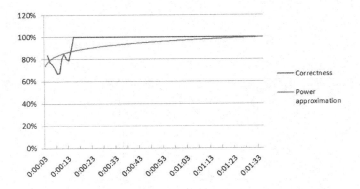

Fig. 6. Correlation between audio files duration and identification results

On the whole, the language identification system has shown 83 percent correctness on the testing corpus. Nevertheless, this quality varies from language to language. As can be seen in Table 3, the average quality for the Russian and English languages identification exceeds the same value for the Tatar language by 37%. This can be explained by the fact that the number of speakers in the Tatar corpus is insufficient (6 speakers, to compare: in the Russian corpus — 110, in the English one — 1228) and that the records of different speakers have different duration.

Table 3. Language identification results

Correctness	English	Russian	Tatar
Short files	96%	96%	50%
	81%		
Long files	88%	100%	66%
	85%		
Total	83%		

5   Conclusion and Perspectives

We have presented a language identification system, which can distinguish among the Tatar, English and Russian speech utterances. We have used HTK toolkit and our own-developed program tools to provide the possibility for recording audio files and identifying languages. In order to include the Tatar language into this system, the experimental corpus of spoken Tatar language has been created. It contains about 10 hours of 6 speakers voice records.

Experimental results have led us to the conclusion that standard PRLM-approach is well suited for work with the Tatar language, but the quality of the system can be significantly improved by a more representative corpus of Tatar speech with more speakers.

In the future we intend to improve the proposed identification module and to use it as the first stage in the complex Tatar speech analysis system.

References

1. Zissman, M.: Comparison of four approaches to automatic language identification of telephone speech. IEEE Transactions on Speech and Audio Processing 4 (1996)
2. Zissman, M., Singer, E.: Automatic language identification of telephone speech messages using phoneme recognition and n-gram modeling. In: Proc. ZCASSP 1994, vol. 1, pp. 305–308 (1994)
3. Lopes, C., Perdigao, F.: Phone recognition on TIMIT database. Speech Technologies, 285–302 (2011)
4. Young, S.: The HTK book (for HTK version 3.4) (2009)
5. Niesler, T., Willett, D.: Language identification and multilingual speech recognition using discriminatively trained acoustic models. In: ISCA Workshop on Multilingual, Speech and Language Processing, Stellenbosch, South Africa (2006)
6. Khusainov, A., Suleymanov, D.: Speech analysis platform prototype for Tatar language. Open Semantic Technologies for Intelligent Systems, Minsk, Belarus (2013)
7. Khusainov, A.: An overview of speech recognition approaches. In: Proceedings of the 14th International Conference "Speech and Computer", Kazan, Russia (2011)

8. Karpov, A., Kipyatkova, I., Ronzhin, A.: Very Large Vocabulary ASR for Spoken Russian with Syntactic and Morphemic Analysis. In: Proceedings INTERSPEECH 2011 International Conference, ISCA Association, Florence, Italy, pp. 3161–3164 (2011)
9. Karpov, A., Kipyatkova, I., Ronzhin, A.: Speech Recognition for East Slavic Languages: The Case of Russian. In: Proceedings of the 3rd International Workshop on Spoken Languages Technologies for Under-resourced Languages, SLTU 2012, Cape Town, RSA, pp. 84–89 (2012)
10. Matejka, P.: Phonotactic Language Identification using High Quality Phoneme Recognition. In: Proc. Eurospeech, Portugal (2005)
11. Martin, A., Le, A.: The Current State of Language Recognition: NIST 2005 Evaluation Results. In: IEEE Odyssey 2006, Puerto Rico (2006)
12. Gauvain, J., Messaoudi, A., Schwenk, H.: Language Recognition using Phone Lattices. In: Proc. ICSLP 2004 (2004)
13. Wong, K.-K., Siu, M.-H.: Automatic language identification using discrete hidden markov model. In: Proc. ICSLP, Jeju, Korea (2004)
14. Reynolds, D., Campbell, W., Shen, W., Singer, E.: Automatic Language Recognition Via Spectral and Token Based Approaches. Springer Handbook of Speech Processing, ch. 41, pp. 811–824 (2008)
15. Yonghong, Y., Barnard, E., Vermeulen, P.: Development of an Approach to Language Identification Based on Language-dependent Phone Recognition (1995)
16. Li, H., Ma, B., Lee, K.A.: Spoken Language Recognition: From Fundamentals to Practice. Proceedings of the IEEE 101(5), 1136–1159 (2013)
17. Kirchhoff, K., Schultz, T.: Language characteristics. In: Multilingual Speech Processing, Amsterdam, The Netherlands (2006)
18. Ambikairajah, E., Li, H., Wang, L., Yin, B., Sethu, V.: Language identification: A tutorial. IEEE Circuits Syst. Mag. 11(2), 82–108 (2011)

Language Model Comparison
for Ukrainian Real-Time Speech Recognition System

Mykola Sazhok[1,2] and Valentyna Robeiko[2]

[1] Hlushkov Institute of Cybernetics,
Kyiv, Ukraine
mykola@cybermova.com
[2] International Research/Training Center for Information Technology and Systems,
Kyiv, Ukraine
{sazhok,valia.robeiko}@gmail.com

Abstract. This paper describes a real-time speech recognition system for Ukrainian designed basically for text dictation purpose targeting moderate computation requirements. The research is focused on language model parameter estimation. As a Slavonic language Ukrainian is highly inflective and tolerates relatively free word order. These features motivate transition from word- to class-based statistical language model. According to our experimental research, class-based LMs occupy less space and potentially outperform a 3-gram word-based model. We also describe several tools developed to visualize HMMs, to predict word stress, and to manage cluster-based language modeling.

Keywords: language models, speech recogntition, real-time, Ukrainian.

1 Introduction

Specific features of Slavonic languages are high inflectiveness and relatively free word order, which leads to rapid growth of the recognition vocabulary (6–8 times larger for same domain in English) and weakening of the language model prediction force. Therefore, the applicability of conventional methods and algorithms to Slavonic languages looks rather unpromising that is the reason of search for alternative to conventional recognition schemes, particularly considering word composition by the acoustic phoneme decoding output [1]. However, the potential of the recognition scheme having been developed for decades still remains uncovered [2].

The open question is limits of the vocabulary used in the speech-to-text system based on the conventional recognition scheme provided that the system shows real-time performance on a computational platform available for an ordinary user.

Therefore we aimed to build a real-time system that could be exploited on a contemporary personal computer for speech-to-text conversion like a dictation machine.

The system operating conditions must meet potential user's expectations. A recognition vocabulary should cover arbitrary speech with OOV $< 1\%$ and means to update the vocabulary must be provided. Acoustically, the system must be able to process the speech of every adequate user. In advance prepared speech, read text and spontaneous utterances should be recognized on a similar level of accuracy. The system must provide

M. Železný et al. (Eds.): SPECOM 2013, LNAI 8113, pp. 211–218, 2013.
© Springer International Publishing Switzerland 2013

an ability for the user to dictate in conditions of home and office, inside and perhaps outside.

In our previous work [3] we described a speech-to-text system that operated in real time with a 100k vocabulary tightly covering common and news domains (politics, economics, culture, education, sports, and weather). Nevertheless we have to work with a vocabulary for million words to reach the desired OOV for the arbitrary speech.

In this paper we explain assumptions concerning language distinctions on acoustical, phonetic and lexical levels, try to clear a prospective to attain the necessary vocabulary size, describe respective developed tools and discuss experimental results.

2   Speech-to-Text System Structure

The basic speech-to-text conversion system structure is shown in Fig. 1. The real-time component implements *Decoder* that refers to *Data and Knowledge Base* developed off-line by means beside the illustrated components.

To create a speech recognition system we developed several data and program resources and used the toolkits available on Internet.

A real time component takes the *Input Speech Signal* from an available source (microphone, network or file system). *Voice Activity Detector* suggests beginnings of speech segments for *Pre-processor* that extracts acoustic features from. The system uses mel-frequency cepstral coefficients with subtracted mean and accomplished with energy and dynamic components (delta and delta-delta coefficients). *Decoder* compares an input segment with model signal hypotheses, being generated in accordance to acoustic and language models, using a conservative strategy of non-perspective hypotheses rejection [4]. The output, presented as a confusion network, is passed to *Decision Maker* that forms a *Recognition Response* considering the history and performing necessary mappings to symbols and actions.

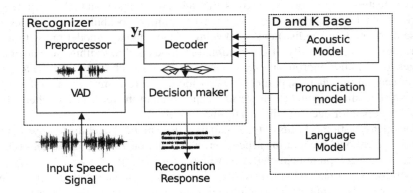

Fig. 1. General structure for a basic speech-to-text system

Acoustic model is developed on a 40 hour subset of the AKUEM speech corpus [5],[6]. The basic phoneme alphabet consists of 56 phonemes including stressed and unstressed versions for 6 vowels. The reason we distinguish them is discussed in the next chapter. Currently, HMMs built for context-independent phonemes contain from 8 to 32 Gaussians.

Pronunciation Model provides *Decoder* with word pronunciation transcriptions that are formed off-line by Grapheme-to-phoneme module implementing a multilevel multi-decision symbol conversion technique based on describing the regularities of relation between orthographic and phonemic symbols [7]. An expert formulates about 40 find-replace-and-step rules of grapheme-to-phoneme mapping partially counting for individual speaker peculiarities and co-articulation and reduction of sounds in a speech flow. The rules are adjusted so that on average each word produces about 1.2 transcriptions. The same algorithm with another rules allows for converting numbers, abbreviations and symbolic characters to word sequences. The vocabulary for the entire system consists of a frequency dictionary extracted from the large text corpus and supplementary vocabularies covering speech corpus, social and local dialects, proper names, abbreviations, etc. Taking a specified amount of top-frequent words from the system vocabulary a recognition vocabulary is formed.

Language Model is created proceeding from the recognition vocabulary and a text corpus subset consisting of sentences containing below the specified portion of OOV words. The basic text corpus is derived from a hypertext data downloaded from several websites containing samples of news and publicity (60%), literature (8%), encyclopedic articles (24%), and legal and forensic domain (8%). To be noted that the data downloaded from news websites contains numerous user comments and reviews, which we consider as text samples of spontaneous speech. The text filter, used for text corpus processing, provides conversion of numbers and symbolic characters to relevant letters, removing improper text segments and paragraph repetitions. Total size of the basic text corpus is 2 GB that includes 17.5 million sentences that is a list of words containing above 275 million items and forming a vocabulary of more than two million words.

For the recognition vocabulary of 100 000 words, 88.5 million distinct 3-grams are detected in the subset of the basic text corpus after removing sentences containing more than 20% or at least three running unknown words. This sub-corpus is used for language modeling and referred as 250 M corpus. Consequently, we found out OOV words occupy 2.5% of all words that is about twice less than in the Ukrainian arbitrary text for the specified vocabulary size. To model spontaneous speech characteristics a class of transparent words is introduced to the recognition vocabulary. It contains non-lexical items like pause fillers and emotion and attitude expressions (laugh, applauds, etc.).

Applying language modeling tool [8] we have received a text file in ARPA format that occupies 5 GB reduced to 1.2 GB by a module of the decoder tool [4].

The real-time modules are used to build a basic speech-to-text conversion system for experimental research and trial operation. Graphical user interface integrated with the basic system allows for demonstrating continuous speech recognition for wide domain in real time, using a contemporary notebook [3].

Further, we consider a transition from word- to class-based statistical language model in order to move towards a vocabulary that provides the desired OOV for the arbitrary speech.

3   Class-Based LM Development

As a Slavonic language, Ukrainian is highly inflective, the number of word forms per dictionary entry accedes 12 that is about 6 times more than for English. Therefore, to build an adequate language model a 6 time larger vocabulary is required. Moreover, relatively free word order is normative that leads to perplexity and data sparsity growth. Analysis of these features motivates a transition from word- to class-based statistical language model that operates with transition probability and membership probability [9].

Word clustering procedure tries to maximize the perplexity improvement criterion

$$F_{\mathbf{G}} = \sum_{g,h \in \mathbf{G}} C\left(g,h\right) \log C\left(g,h\right) - 2 \sum_{g \in \mathbf{G}} C\left(g\right) \log C\left(g\right) \tag{1}$$

where (g, h) means a class g follows a class h from the set of equivalence classes $\mathbf{G}$ and function $C(\cdot)$ counts its argument occurrence in the training corpus. An exchange algorithm described in [9] implies iterations in which each word is tested for a better class and consequently moved there. While implementing the algorithm we came to an alternative formulation of criteria computation refinement.

Let us enumerate all equivalence classes: $g_i \in \mathbf{G}, 1 \leqslant i \leqslant G$, and introduce C_{ij} for successor and C_{ij}^- for predecessor occurrence.

Assuming that a preceding single classification function $G^-(\cdot)$ applied to w has given g_u, i.e. $G^-(w) = g_u$, we are to check a hypothesis of transition w to another class indexed with v, i.e., $G(w) = g_v$.

The first sum in (1), having the most complicated computations, $O(G^2)$, can be expressed as

$$\sum_{i,j} C_{ij} \log C_{ij} = \sum_{\substack{i,j \\ \{i,j\} \cap \{u,v\}=\emptyset}} C_{ij} \log C_{ij} + \sum_{\substack{i=u,v \\ j}} C_{ij} \log C_{ij} + \sum_{\substack{j=u,v \\ i \neq u,v}} C_{ij} \log C_{ij}. \tag{2}$$

Thus, the analyzed sum is decomposed in three components where the most expensive for computations component, still $O(G^2)$, might be expressed as a recursion relatively to the predecessor:

$$\sum_{\substack{i,j \\ \{i,j\} \cap \{u,v\}=\emptyset}} C_{ij} \log C_{ij} = \sum_{\substack{i,j \\ \{i,j\} \cap \{u,v\}=\emptyset}} C_{ij}^- \log C_{ij}^- =$$

$$= \sum_{i,j} C_{ij}^- \log C_{ij}^- - \left(\sum_{\substack{i=u,v \\ j}} C_{ij}^- \log C_{ij}^- + \sum_{\substack{j=u,v \\ i \neq u,v}} C_{ij}^- \log C_{ij}^- \right) \tag{3}$$

arriving to the computation time complexity of $O(G)$. Proceeding from (1)–(3) we have developed an efficient tool for word clustering and assigning a new word, accomplished with bigram counts, to one of existing classes.

The clustering results have been analyzed proceeding from their relevance to linguistic categories. Firstly automatically obtained classes for Ukrainian in general correspond to syntactic, semantic and phonetic features.

Most word classes have an obvious syntactic interpretation, such as nouns in a genitive form or plural adjectives. Table 1 shows several word classes that have been obtained by bigram clustering on the 250 M corpus for 1000 word classes. The words in each word class are listed in descending word unigram count order. We present three classes completely and the first 7 words for the last class.

Table 1. Bigram clustering examples, $G = 1000$

Words of cluster with meaning	Frequency
багато / many, much	134590
чимало / plenty	24482
безліч / a lot of	7696
немало / quite a lot of	2191
якнайбільше / as many	760
багацько / lots of	255
богато (misspelled багато)	123
які / that, which (plural)	590681
котрі / that, which (plural)	24499
яки (misspelled які)	465
де / where	246376
куди / where to	31966
звідки / where from	15373
звідкіль / where from (colloquial)	120
заявив / [he] stated	163547
вважає / [he, she] supposes	99803
повідомив / [he] informed	80043
заявила / [she] stated	32795
заявляє / [he, she] states	31965
розповів / [he] told	30504
говорить / [he, she] speaks	29756

Often there is some semantic meaning like in the last class containing verbs of communication (for the third person in present and past tenses). Two first classes show that misspelled but still frequent words may join to the class containing a correct version of the word.

In Ukrainian, words may have different forms in dependence of phonetic context. For instance, the conjunction *and* has three forms normally used between consonants, between vowels and in other cases. All these forms were automatically assigned to different classes.

4 Data

The basic dictionary is extracted from the electronic lexicography system subset containing 151 962 lemmas, including over 10 thousand names, that totally makes 1.90 million word forms [10]. Due to shared spelling the actual word form vocabulary consists of 1.83 million words that have different either spelling or primary lexical stress position.

The basic text corpus is derived from a hypertext data downloaded from several websites containing samples of news and publicity (60%), literature (8%), encyclopedic articles (24%), and legal and forensic domain (8%). To be noted that the data downloaded from news websites contains numerous user comments and reviews, which we consider as text samples of the spontaneous speech. A text filter, used for text corpus processing, provides conversion of numbers and symbolic characters to relevant letters, removing improper text segments and paragraph repetitions. Hereafter, we refer to the basic corpus as 275 M corpus. In accordance to the corpus summary shown in Table 2, we observe 6.64 word forms per lemma in average, whereas this relation is twice greater, 12.3, within the dictionary [10]. Adding 200 000 most frequent words to the vocabulary we reduce OOV to less than 0.5%.

Table 2. Basic text corpus 275 M summary

Words	Sentences	Vocabulary			OOV	Homographs
		All words	Known words	Known lemmas		
275 288 408	1 752 371	1 996 897	801 040	120 554	2.51%	16 729 476

Words that have 2 or more valid stress positions, referred as homographs, take over 6% of the average text. While estimating acoustic model parameters all stress versions of homographs were used on a realignment stage.

5 Experiments

We evaluated three language model types on two, however, relatively small test sets with different OOV. Considered error rates are based on both words (WER) and characters (CER). Vocabulary size was set to 100 000 words, in average 1.1 pronunciations per word were generated. Word-based 3-gram language model is denoted as w3 and class-based language models, c3 and c4, are built respectively for 3- and 4-grams. Size of 3-gram class-based LM is 9 times less than word-based LM, 4-gram class-based LM occupies somewhat less space than 3-gram word-based model.

According to our experimental research shown in Table 3, class-based LMs have a certain potency due to character error that is close to or even smaller than the word-based LM error rate. Phonetically close words assigned to same class is a source of mistakes, as far the word with much better membership probability may get better chance to win. It could be compensated by stimulating such words to be placed in different classes.

Table 3. Speech recognition summary for different language models

LM	Error type	OOV = 3.4%	OOV = 2.6%
w3	WER	20.9	15.9
	CER	7.8	4.2
c3	WER	28.2	24.3
	CER	6.9	6.0
c4	WER	28.6	24.6
	CER	10.0	6.5

6   Conclusion

The described real-time system for the Ukrainian speech-to-text conversion demonstrates a potential of focusing on language distinctive features, which makes feasible to attain vocabulary size necessary to reduce OOV below 1% and to introduce punctuation and character case dependency.

For dictating purpose, human-machine interaction is crucial. The system has to suggest recognized utterance refinement based on multi-decision recognition response; moreover, accepted refinements must update the recognition response model. Besides assigning a new word to the unknown word category, we intend to implement updating the class language model by mapping new words to classes and recomputing membership probabilities.

A distance to the closest extrinsic classes should give a clue to predicting homographs and consequent semantic word decomposition that may lead to more homogeneous classes.

For text processing, more precise number and symbol to grapheme conversion is topical in order to predict their correct concordance for the observed context.

The development of the presented system is on an early stage. In near future several improvements will be completed, which will increase accuracy and extend the scope of usage.

Acknowledgments. This research was supported by Special Recording Systems Ltd.

References

1. Vintsiuk, T., Sazhok, M.: Multi-Level Multi-Decision Models for ASR. In: Proc. SpeCom 2005, Patras, pp. 69–76 (2005)
2. Gales, M., Young, S.: The Application of Hidden Markov Models in Speech Recognition. Foundations and Trends in Signal Processing 1(3), 195–304 (2007)
3. Robeiko, V., Sazhok, M.: Real-time spontaneous Ukrainian speech recognition system based on word acoustic composite models. In: Proc. UkrObraz 2012, Kyiv, pp. 77–81 (2012)
4. Lee, A., Kawahara, T.: Recent Development of Open-Source Speech Recognition Engine Julius. In: APSIPA ASC, pp. 131–137 (2009)
5. Young, S.J., et al.: The HTK Book Version 3.4. Cambridge University (2006)
6. Pylypenko, V., Robeiko, V., Sazhok, M., Vasylieva, N., Radoutsky, O.: Ukrainian Broadcast Speech Corpus Development. In: Proc. Specom 2011, Kazan, RF, pp. 244–247 (2011)
7. Robeiko, V., Sazhok, M.: Bidirectional Text-To-Pronunciation Conversion with Word Stress Prediction for Ukrainian. In: Proc. UkrObraz 2012, Kyiv, pp. 43–46 (2012)
8. Hsu, B.-J(P.), Glass, J.: Iterative Language Model Estimation: Efficient Data Structure and Algorithms. In: Proc. Interspeech (2008)
9. Martin, S., Liermann, J., Ney, H.: Algorithms for bigram and trigram word clustering. In: Proc. Eurospeech, Madrid, vol. 2, pp. 1253–1256 (1995)
10. http://lcorp.ulif.org.ua/dictua/

Lexicon Size and Language Model Order Optimization for Russian LVCSR

Irina Kipyatkova and Alexey Karpov

SPIIRAS, 39, 14th line, St. Petersburg, Russia
Saint-Petersburg State University, 7-9, Universitetskaya nab., St. Petersburg, Russia
{kipyatkova,karpov}@iias.spb.su
www.spiiras.nw.ru/speech

Abstract. In this paper, the comparison of 2,3,4-gram language models with various lexicon sizes is presented. The text data forming the training corpus has been collected from recent Internet news sites; total size of the corpus is about 350 million words (2.4 GB data). The language models were built using the recognition lexicons of 110K, 150K, 219K, and 303K words. For evaluation of these models such characteristics as perplexity, OOV words rate and n-gram hit rate were computed. Experimental results on continuous Russian speech recognition are also given in the paper.

Keywords: Language models, automatic speech recognition, Russian speech, Russian text corpus.

1 Introduction

The free word order and inflective nature of Russian makes the creation of language model (LM) for Russian difficult. Because of the complicated word-formation mechanism and multiple inflection rules, in practice, the size of the vocabulary increases a lot, what results in large number of out-of-vocabulary (OOV) words. In terms of OOV rates, Russian is comparable to some other morphologically rich European languages, such as Finnish, Hungarian, Lithuanian or Turkish [1,2,3]. But compared to some analytical languages like English, the OOV percentage can be up to 10 times higher. So, language model with large vocabulary is needed for Russian. To dictate and recognize spoken Russian (and especially spontaneous speech) one has to utilize recognition vocabulary of several hundred thousand words (>100K word-forms). Until recently such vocabularies were considered as very large [4]. Detailed comparison of LMs for the English and Russian is presented in [5]. It has been shown that a 430K vocabulary is needed for Russian to achieve the same vocabulary coverage as a 65K vocabulary for English.

Many small vocabulary ASR systems for Russian have been developed for voice command, incoming phone calls routing, and other similar applications [6], however, there are only a few systems for large vocabulary tasks. For example, in [7], a Russian ASR system for broadcast news recognition is described. A text corpus consisting of 129M words for LM training was collected from the Internet. Three frequency vocabularies were created: general frequency vocabulary, frequency vocabulary of proper

M. Železný et al. (Eds.): SPECOM 2013, LNAI 8113, pp. 219–226, 2013.

names, and frequency vocabulary of common names. A vocabulary of 213K words was selected to cover 98% of the training text data, but the coverage of the test data was not reported. Standard statistical n-grams ($n = 1 \div 3$) were used as LMs. The amount of the speech data for the acoustic model training exceeded 200 hours; 3280 speakers took part in the corpus collection. Recognition accuracy was 60-70% depending on the sound files quality.

Another large vocabulary Russian speech recognition system is presented in [8]. In this work, a model based on separating words into stems and endings is used. The resulting vocabulary consists of 85K stems and 4K endings that cover 1300K word-forms; however, the morpheme-based LM and lexicon did not bring any reduction of the WER.

In [9], a two-pass algorithm for Extra Large Vocabulary Continuous Speech recognition based on Information Retrieval (ELVIRCOS) was studied for Ukrainian and Russian. This algorithm decomposes the recognition process into two passes, where the first pass builds a word subset for the second pass recognition.

Most recently, a large vocabulary continuous speech recognizer that uses syllable-based LM was described in [10]. A method for concatenation of the recognized syllables and error correction is proposed. The syllable lexicon has about 12K entries. The final sentence is constructed from the recognized syllables by the designed co-evolutionary asymptotic probabilistic genetic algorithm (CAPGA).

Another recent work [11] studies the transcription task for Russian conversational telephone speech. For the system training about 8 hours of conversational Russian speech were used, and about 1 hour was used for development. The pronunciation lexicon was created using grapheme-to-phoneme conversion rules. Texts for the LM training were taken from the Web, and transcriptions of broadcast and conversational telephone speech data. The total size of the training text corpus was 297M words. Vocabulary of the system contained up to 500K words and the WER was 50-60% (for real conversational speech data) depending on the used acoustic models and the type of LM training corpus. Another collaborative work [12] of the same authors summarizes the experimental results on speech transcription for 9 European languages (including Russian). Those results were obtained by ASR systems used for the Quaero 2010 and 2011 evaluations campaigns (test data contained various broadcast data including news and conversations). The WER of Russian ASR was 19.2% in 2010 and 18.3% in Quaero 2011 (among 9 European languages only Portuguese ASR system had higher WER).

Finally, for automatic voice search in the Internet, Google Inc. has developed the on-line Voice Search service [13], which uses speech recognition technology. This service allows users to find necessary information in the Internet pronouncing a word or a phrase. For the LM creation, written queries to Google search engine were used. This technology is also applied to other Google services, for example, Google maps, where it is possible to do voice request for searching a place on the map. For short and common sentences it works pretty well, but it fails for conversational Russian speech.

In the paper, we present the process of creation of Russian language model for very large vocabulary speech recognition task. We compare 2,3,4-gram language model with different lexicon size. In the rest of the paper, the process of collection and preliminary processing of the text corpus for creation of a statistical Russian language model is described, as well as the results of a statistical analysis of the corpus are given.

2   Text Corpus for Language Model Creation

At present, there are several large commercial text corpora of Russian, for instance, the Russian National Corpus (www.ruscorpora.ru) and the Corpus of Standard Written Russian (www.narusco.ru), which mainly contain text material of the end of the 20th century. These corpora include different types of texts: fiction, political essays, scientific, etc. They also contain a few shorthand reports in spoken language.

For the language model creation, we collected and automatically processed a new Russian text corpus of on-line newspapers. This corpus was collected from recent news published in freely available Internet sites of on-line Russian newspapers (www.ng.ru, www.smi.ru, www.lenta.ru, www.gazeta.ru, www.interfax.ru, ria.ru) for the years 2006-2013. The database contains text data that reflect contemporary Russian including some spoken language.

The procedure of preliminary text processing and normalization is described in [14]. At first, texts are divided into sentences, which must begin from an uppercase letter or a digit before which inverted commas may be placed. A sentence ends with the full stop marked with the dot, exclamation, question mark or dots. It takes into account that initials and/or a surname can be placed within the sentence. Formally, it is similar to a boundary between two sentences, therefore, if the dot is after a single uppercase letter, the dot is not considered as the end of the sentence. Sentences containing direct and indirect speech are divided into separate sentences. These sentences can be of the following types: (1) direct speech is placed after indirect speech; (2) direct speech is before indirect speech; (3) indirect speech is within direct speech. Then, a text written in any brackets is deleted, and sentences consisting of less than six words are also deleted. Then punctuation marks are deleted, symbols "N^o" and "#" are replaced by the word "number". All numbers and digits are combined in a single class that is denoted by the symbol "N^o" in the resulting text. A group of digits, which can be divided by point, comma, space or dash sign is denoted as a single number. Also the symbol "N^o" denotes Roman numbers that are a combination of Latin letters I, V, X, L, C, D, M, which can be divided by space or dash. Internet links and E-mails are distinguished in single classes and denoted by the symbols "$<>$" and "$<@>$", respectively. Uppercase letters are replaced by lowercase letters, if a word begins from an uppercase letter. If a whole word is written by the uppercase letters, then such change is made, when the word exists in a vocabulary only.

The volume of the corpus after text normalization and deletion of doubling or short (<5 words) sentences is over 350M words, and it has above 1M unique word-forms.

3   Lexicon Creation and Pronunciation Modeling

One of the important challenges for the development of spoken Russian ASR systems is a grapheme-to-phoneme conversion or orthographic-to-phonemic transcription of a recognition lexicon. There are several issues: grapheme-to-phoneme mapping is not one-to-one, stress position(s) in word-forms is floating, substitution of grapheme 'ё' (always stressed) with 'e' in the most of printed and electronic text data, phoneme reductions and assimilations in continuous and spontaneous speech, many homographs, etc.

According to the SAMPA phonetic alphabet, there are 42 phonemes in the Russian language (for 33 Cyrillic letters): 6 vowels and 36 consonants including plain and palatalized versions of some consonants. Russian consonants are: voiced-unvoiced pairs /p/ (Cyrillic grapheme П) and /b/ (Б), /t/ (Т) and /d/ (Д), /k/ (К) and /g/ (Г), /f/ (Ф) and /v/ (В), /s/ (С) and /z/ (З) (they have palatalized versions as well), /S/ (Ш) and /Z/ (Ж); sonorants /l/ (Л), /r/ (Р), /m/ (М), /n/ (Н) (these consonants are not paired, but have palatalized versions) and /j/ (Й), plus velar /x/ (and a soft version /x'/, grapheme Х), /ts/ (Ц), /tS'/ (Ч), /S':/ (Щ). However, according to the International Phonetic Alphabet (IPA), there are 17 vowels in Russian with different levels of reduction between stressed and unstressed vowels up to complete disappearance. Recent experiments showed [15], that distinction between models for stressed and unstressed vowels allows decreasing WER at ASR. Thus, six stressed (/a!/, /e!/, /o!/, /u!/, /i!/ and /1!/ in SAMPA format) and four unstressed vowels are used (/o!/ and /e!/ may have only stressed versions in the standard Russian with a few exceptions).

For the grapheme-to-phoneme conversion, we apply an extended morphological database, consisting of more than 2.3M word-forms with the symbol '!' indicating stressed vowels. This database is a fusion of two different morphological databases: AOT (http://www.aot.ru) and Starling (http://starling.rinet.ru). The former one is larger and has more than 2M entries, but the latter one contains information about secondary stress for many compound words, as well as words with grapheme 'ё', which is always stressed, but usually replaced with 'e' in official texts that leads to loosing of required information on the stress position.

For lexicon creation, the list of word-forms from the training corpus was used. At first, we automatically generated transcriptions for these words by applying several phonetic rules to the list of word-forms. The process of transcription generation is described in [16,17]. The words with automatically generated transcriptions are included in speech recognition lexicon. For 651K words from the text corpus we were able to create transcriptions automatically. Obtained lexicon contains many rare words, therefore it is reasonably to reduce the lexicon size by introduction of a threshold. So, the words, which relative frequency was higher than chosen threshold, were added to the lexicon. We created lexicon with different size, and the best speech recognition results were obtained with 150K lexicon (in this case threshold was equal to 52).

4   Statistical Language Models for Russian

We created 2,3,4-gram language models. The models were created with help of the SRI Language Modeling Toolkit (SRILM) [18]. We used the Kneser-Ney discounting method, and did not apply any n-gram cutoff.

Perplexity and n-gram hit rates (summarized in Table 1) were calculated using text data consisting of phrases (33M words in total) from another online newspaper "Фонтанка.ru" (www.fontanka.ru). Perplexity is given with two different normalizations:

counting all input tokens (PPL) and excluding end-of-sentence tags (PPL1). We have tried several lexicon sizes and the best one in terms of performance / OOV trade-off has 150K words; its OOV rate for the given test set is 5.0%. For comparison, characteristics of models with 110K, 219K, and 303K lexicon are also given in Table 1, and their thresholds were equal to 100, 21, and 8 respectively.

Table 1. Characteristics of the LMs

Language model type	Vocabulary size, K words	OOV rate,%	# n-grams, M	PPL	PPL1	n-gram hit,%
2-gram model	110	6.4	28.8	797	1310	83.2
2-gram model	150	5.0	32.3	857	1406	83.4
2-gram model	219	3.7	34.6	928	1521	83.4
2-gram model	303	3.0	36.1	982	1609	83.3
3-gram model	110	6.4	94.4	516	821	44.5
3-gram model	150	5.0	99.5	553	878	44.4
3-gram model	219	3.7	104.1	597	947	44.2
3-gram model	303	3.0	106.6	630	1001	44.1
4-gram model	110	6.4	133.2	543	868	18.4
4-gram model	150	5.0	140.0	580	925	18.4
4-gram model	219	3.7	145.8	625	996	18.3
4-gram model	303	3.0	148.9	660	1052	18.2

These parameters have quite large values for Russian LMs, which is a great challenge for the LVCSR.

5   Acoustic Modeling

Training of acoustic models of speech units is carried out with the use of the Russian speech corpus. Speech databases with records of large number of speakers are needed to provide speaker-independent speech recognition. In our research, we have used own corpus of spoken Russian speech Euronounce-SPIIRAS, created in 2008-2009 in the framework of the Euro-Nounce project [19]. The speech data were collected in clean acoustic conditions, with 44.1 kHz sampling rate, 16-bit audio quality. A signal-to-noise ratio (SNR) at least 35-40 dB was provided. The database consists of 16,350 utterances pronounced by 50 Russian native speakers (25 male and 25 female). Each speaker read 327 phonetically-balanced and meaningful sentences carefully, but fluently one time only. Total duration of speech data is about 21 hours.

Hidden Markov models (HMM) are used for acoustic modeling, and each phoneme (speech sound) is modeled by one continuous density HMM. A phoneme model has three states: the first state describes phoneme's start, the second state present the middle part, and the third state is phoneme's end. HMM of a word is obtained by connection of phoneme's models from corresponding phonemic alphabet. Similarly the models of words are connected with each other, generating the models of phrases. The aim of training of the acoustic models based on HMM is to determine such model's parameters that would lead to maximum value of probability of appearance of this sequence by training sequence of observations [20].

6   Experimental Results

To test the speech recognition system we used a speech corpus containing 100 continuously pronounced phrases consisting of 1068 words (7191 letters). The phrases were taken from the materials of the on-line newspaper "Фонтанка.ru" (www.fontanka.ru). The speech data were recorded with 44.1 KHz sampling rate (for ASR downsampled to 16 KHz), 16 bits per sample, SNR was 35dB at least, by a stereo pair of Oktava MK-012 stationary microphones (close talking ≈20 cm and far-field ≈100 cm microphone setup) connected to PC via Presonus Firepod sound board. We used recordings of three speakers for testing.

As for acoustic features, we used 13-dimentional Mel-Frequency Cepstral Coefficients (MFCC) with the 1st and 2nd order derivatives calculated from the 26-channel filter bank analysis of 20 ms long frames with 10 ms overlap. Cepstral mean subtraction is applied to audio feature vectors. Continuous density HMMs with 16 Gaussians per state model Russian context-dependent phones. The recognition engine was the open-source large vocabulary decoder Julius ver. 4.2 [21].

Table 2 summarizes the speech recognition results in terms of word error rate (WER) and letter (includes all the letters and the white-space between words) error rate (LER) as well as OOV rate and n-gram hit ratios (for 2-grams, 3-grams, and 4-grams). All LMs were built using the same vocabulary of 110K, 150K, 219K, and 303K words. Real Time Factor (RTF) was about 1.65 real-time for the speech decoder installed on a desktop PC with multi-core Intel Core i7-3770K 3.5 GHz processor.

Table 2. Summary of the results on very large vocabulary Russian speech recognition using various LMs

Language model type	Vocabulary size, K words	OOV rate,%	n-gram hit,%	WER,%	LER,%	RTF
2-gram model	110	1.9	92.8	28.71	9.06	1.58
2-gram model	150	1.1	92.8	**27.81**	**8.96**	1.58
2-gram model	219	0.6	93.1	28.34	9.15	1.66
2-gram model	303	0.5	93.0	28.34	9.17	1.69
3-gram model	110	1.9	56.4	24.47	7.90	1.58
3-gram model	150	1.1	56.2	**23.75**	**7.93**	1.64
3-gram model	219	0.6	56.0	24.19	7.83	1.66
3-gram model	303	0.5	56.0	24.66	7.97	1.69
4-gram model	110	1.9	26.8	24.47	8.03	1.60
4-gram model	150	1.1	26.7	**23.50**	**7.69**	1.64
4-gram model	219	0.6	26.6	23.85	7.74	1.68
4-gram model	303	0.5	26.6	24.06	7.71	1.71

The best results were obtained with 150K vocabulary. In this case, relative number of OOV words was equal to 1.1%. The further increase of vocabulary capacity did not lead to significant decrease of the number of OOV words, and recognition results slightly degraded. Application of the 4-gram language model provided the reduction of WER comparing to 2-gram and 3-gram language models. WER decreased from 27.81% to 23.50%.

7 Conclusion

In this paper, comparison of 2,3,4-gram language models with various lexicon sizes was performed. The text data for statistical processing is taken from the Internet sites of on-line newspapers. The best experimental results on continuous Russian speech recognition were obtained when four-gram language model with 150K vocabulary was used. But though this model is very large (11Gb), it did not cover the test data. 4-gram hits for this model is low. So, we can conclude that four-gram model is not efficient for Russian. The reason of this is inflective nature of Russian language and free word order. To solve this problem syntactic analysis of the training corpus should be carried out. Syntax-based language model will allow taking into account long-distance syntactic dependencies between words.

Acknowledgments. This research is supported by Ministry of Education and Science of the Russian Federation (Federal Program "Research and Development", the state contract N° 07.514.11.4139), the grant of the President of Russia (project N^o MK 1880.2012.8), the Russian Foundation for Basic Research (project N° 12-08-01265), the Russian Humanitarian Scientific Foundation (project N° 12-04-12062) and by Saint-Petersburg State University (project N° 31.37.103.2011).

References

1. Ircing, P., Hoidekr, J., Psutka, J.: Exploiting linguistic knowledge in language modeling of Czech spontaneous speech. In: Proceedings of Int. Conf. on Language Resources and Evaluation, LREC 2006, Genoa, Italy, pp. 2600–2603 (2006)
2. Kurimo, M., et al.: Unlimited vocabulary speech recognition for agglutinative languages. In: Proceedings of Human Language Technology Conference of the North American Chapter of the ACL, New York, USA, pp. 487–494 (2006)
3. Vaičiūnas, A.: Statistical Language Models of Lithuanian and Their Application to Very Large Vocabulary Speech Recognition. PhD thesis, Vytautas Magnus University, Kaunas (2006)
4. Whittaker, E.W.D., Woodland, P.C.: Efficient class-based language modelling for very large vocabularies. In: Proceedings of ICASSP 2001, Salt Lake City, USA, pp. 545–548 (2001)
5. Whittaker, E.W.D.: Statistical language modelling for automatic speech recognition of Russian and English. PhD thesis, Cambridge Univ., 140 p. (2000)
6. Vazhenina, D., Kipyatkova, I., Markov, K., Karpov, A.: State-of-the-art Speech Recognition Technologies for Russian Language. In: Proceedings of the Joint International Conference on Human-Centered Computer Environments, HCCE 2012, Aizu-Wakamatsu, Japan, pp. 59–63 (2012)

7. Viktorov, A., Gramnitskiy, S., Gordeev, S., Eskevich, M., Klimina, E.: Universal technique for preparing components for training of a speech recognition system. Speech Technologies 2, 39–55 (2009) (in Rus.)
8. Oparin, I., Talanov, A.: Stem-Based Approach to Pronunciation Vocabulary Construction and Language Modeling for Russian. In: Proceedings of SPECOM 2005, Patras, Greece, pp. 575–578 (2005)
9. Pylypenko, V.: Extra Large Vocabulary Continuous Speech Recognition Algorithm based on Information Retrieval. In: Proceedings of Interspeech 2007, Antwerp, Belgium, pp. 1809–1812 (2007)
10. Zablotskiy, S., Shvets, A., Sidorov, M., Semenkin, E., Minker, W.: Speech and Language Recources for LVCSR of Russia. In: Proceedings of LREC 2012, Istanbul, Turkey, pp. 3374–3377 (2012)
11. Lamel, L., Courcinous, S., Gauvain, J.-L., Josse, Y., Le, V.B.: Transcription of Russian Conversational Speech. In: Proceedings of SLTU 2012, Cape Town, RSA, pp. 156–161 (2012)
12. Lamel, L., et al.: Speech Recognition for Machine Translation in Quaero. In: Proceedings of International Workshop on Spoken Language Translation, IWSLT 2011, San Francisco, USA, pp. 121–128 (2011)
13. Schalkwyk, J., Beeferman, D., Beaufays, F., Byrne, B., Chelba, C., Cohen, M., Kamvar, M., Strope, B.: Google Search by Voice: A Case Study. Advances in Speech Recognition: Mobile Environments, Call Centers and Clinics, 61–90 (2010)
14. Kipyatkova, I., Karpov, A., Verkhodanova, V., Zelezny, M.: Analysis of Long-distance Word Dependencies and Pronunciation Variability at Conversational Russian Speech Recognition. In: Proceedings of Federated Conference on Computer Science and Information Systems, FedCSIS 2012, Wroclaw, Poland, pp. 719–725 (2012)
15. Vazhenina, D., Markov, K.: Phoneme Set Selection for Russian Speech Recognition. In: Proceedings of 7th Int. Conf. on NLP and Knowledge Engineering, NLP-KE 2011, Japan, pp. 475–478 (2011)
16. Karpov, A., Kipyatkova, I., Ronzhin, A.: Speech Recognition for East Slavic Languages: The Case of Russian. In: Proceedings of the 3rd International Workshop on Spoken Languages Technologies for Under-resourced Languages, SLTU 2012, Cape Town, RSA, pp. 84–89 (2012)
17. Karpov, A., Kipyatkova, I., Ronzhin, A.: Very Large Vocabulary ASR for Spoken Russian with Syntactic and Morphemic Analysis. In: Proceedings of Interspeech 2011, Florence, Italy, pp. 3161–3164 (2011)
18. Stolcke, A., Zheng, J., Wang, W., Abrash, V.: SRILM at Sixteen: Update and Outlook. In: Proceedings of IEEE Automatic Speech Recognition and Understanding Workshop, ASRU 2011, Waikoloa, Hawaii, USA (2011)
19. Jokisch, O., Wagner, A., Sabo, R., Jaeckel, R., Cylwik, N., Rusko, M., Ronzhin, A., Hoffmann, R.: Multilingual speech data collection for the assessment of pronunciation and prosody in a language learning system. In: Proceedings of SPECOM 2009, St. Peterburg, Russia, pp. 515–520 (2009)
20. Rabiner, L., Juang, B.-H.: Fundamentals of Speech Recognition, 496 p. Prentice Hall (1995)
21. Lee, A., Kawahara, T.: Recent Development of Open-Source Speech Recognition Engine Julius. In: Proceedings of Asia-Pacific Signal and Information Processing Association Annual Summit and Conference (APSIPA ASC 2009), Sapporo, Japan, pp.131–137 (2009)

Lingua-cognitive Survey of the Semantic Field "Aggression" in Multicultural Communication: Typed Text*

Rodmonga Potapova and Liliya Komalova

Moscow State Linguistic University, Institution for Applied and Mathematical Linguistics, Moscow, Russia
{RKPotapova,GenuinePR}@yandex.ru

Abstract. The article describes first phase of the complex research of lingua-cognitive mechanisms of formation and development of aggression represented in language and speech. It produces results of content-analysis of the texts in Russian, English, Spanish and Tatar languages aimed at designing the semantic field "aggression". It also describes classification of aggression types and lists linguistic markers of verbal aggression.

Keywords: Verbal aggression, lingua-cognitive mechanisms, multicultural communication, semantic field, text/discourse content-analysis.

1 Introduction

The phenomenon of aggression accompanies human beings during all their lives. It exists in individual and collective consciousness of various ethnics as certain behaviour models in particular stereotyped and extra situations. In one case such models of behaviour are defensive (e.g., in case of self-defense against a criminal), in others – unwarrantable, e.g., in case of premeditated crime.

Speaking of aggression we would hold on to the definition given by L. Berkowitz: "**aggression** – is a kind of physical or symbolic behaviour motivated to injure another person" [3]. If making harm is the main purpose, it's called *direct/inimical/hostile aggression*. Display of aggression by soldiers during the battle can be classified as *instrumental aggression* as these military men do this by order and their principal motive is to win not harm other people.

Researchers have elaborates several classifications of aggressive behaviour, e.g., according to A. Buss & A. Dark, aggressive behaviour can be classified as:

- direct physical aggression / direct verbal aggression,
- indirect physical aggression / indirect verbal aggression,
- auto-aggression / hetero-aggression,
- hostile aggression / instrumental aggression,
- active aggression / passive aggression.

---

* The survey is being carried out with the support of the Ministry of Education and Science of the Russian Federation in the framework of the project 6.4411.2011 at Moscow State Linguistic University.

M. Železný et al. (Eds.): SPECOM 2013, LNAI 8113, pp. 227–232, 2013.

The motivation of direct aggressive behaviour is intentional abuse, teasing, swearing, threats (direct verbal aggression) or direct physical/psychological damage to another person, who doesn't want this [12].

Verbal aggression is defined as "an exchange of messages between two people where at least one person in the dyad attacks the self-concept of the other person in order to hurt the other person psychologically" [8, p. 67].

In other words we can fix a variety of forms and types of aggression which display in language and speech as well as in physical reactions. But as researches mention, "verbal abuse is a prevalent form of communication that has been shown to have damaging effects" [4, p. 71]. Moreover verbal aggression often escalates into physical abuse [16,17,18].

The survey of lingua-cognitive mechanisms of formation and development of aggressive behaviour in inter-lingual and cross-cultural communication demands taking in account theoretical knowledge and experimental data of neurophysiology, psychology, psychiatry, sociology, philosophy, forensic phonetics etc. In this regard we should apply interdisciplinary approach, which is fully implemented in fundamental and applied speechology. Moreover methodology of aggressive behaviour research includes implication of considerable number of factors and as a result leads to accurate description of the research subject.

2 Method and Procedure

The goal of the described survey is elaboration of theoretical grounds for realization of applied methods of potential verbal aggression recognition and development of complex recommendations on how to prevent and deter conflict situations taking into account multiculturality and multilinguality.

Linguistic research groups highlight the importance of special lexical, pragmatical and semantic components of auditory and written speech in case of detecting aggressive content [1,9,14,19]. According to R.K. Potapova, for experimental and special purposes the survey of linguistic and speech indicators of aggressive behaviour reflected in written text/discourse should be carried out on a complex method, including three levels of decoding:

1. semantic decoding,
2. cognitive decoding,
3. interpreting decoding [11, p. 401–403].

To find out whether the state of aggression as a cognitive concept is confirmed in the analyzed languages (Russian, English, Spanish and Tatar) we studied lexicographic resources. And as for the written speech norm we analyzed newspaper articles in Russian, English, Spanish and Tatar languages.

To construct semantic center and semantic periphery of the concept "aggression" we selected a sample among 14 explanatory and bilingual dictionaries. The sample consists of *a*) words meaning directly, literally or figuratively aggression in accordance with its explicit or implicit types and forms (first step of semantisation) and *b*) the descriptors of aggression (second step of semantisation).

According to R.K. Potapova, this survey considers the semantic field "aggression" as an open system, which can be amplified and updated in accordance with the dynamics of functioning of the concept "aggression" at the syntagmatic level in Russian, English, Spanish and Tatar languages.

To analyze written newspaper articles including representatives of aggression a complex research procedure elaborated by R.K. Potapova and V.V. Potapov was applied [10,11]. The corpus of multilingual texts was selected from digital versions of official newspapers of Russia, Great Britain, USA, Spain and Republic of Tatarstan dated between 01.01.2011 – 20.10.2012. The sample consists of provoking and critical articles on armed conflicts, political and geopolitical actions, crime, family violence and aggressive economics. Texts of 500 to 15 000 signs without blank were included in the dimension. We analyzed texts in Tatar language given in Cyrillic recording.

Theoretical and experimental data acknowledge the following selection criteria for the texts with the representatives of aggression:

Lexical-semantic indicators [2,5,20]:

– occurrence of negatively marked lexemes attributing to the semantic field of aggression;
– narration and appeal to a reader with slogans of aggressive or provoking content, aggressive attitudes towards the object of discussion;
– occurrence of invectives.

Grammar indicators:

– usage of imperative mood and pseudo-imperatives [1];
– usage of affective verbs *"wonder"* / «*удивляться*», *"astound"* / «*потрясаться*», *"amaze"* / «*изумляться*» and relevant adjectives [7];
– occurrence of suffixes adding pejorative, insulting or indulgent connotation [19].

Syntactical-stylistic indicators [19]:

– text composition based on the contrast principle;
– usage of colloquial phraseological units;
– usage of incomplete, non-contracted sentences.

Pragmatic indicators [15,9,1,14,13]: usage of relevant communicative strategies and tactics, e.g.

– threatening, telling curses, reproaching, assaulting and strongly criticizing, verbal provoking, abusing;
– depreciation, crossing intimate limits in discussion publicly;
– ideologically labeling with subjective bias;
– roughly demanding, refusing, blaming or mocking.

Written texts analysis demands taking into account also *graphic indicators* of aggressive content such as [19]:

- frequent usage of marks of exclamation;
- usage of marks of omission in the end of incomplete sentence, decomposition of the sentence with marks of omission;
- usage of quotation marks or stage instructions as a way to communicate intonation.

Overall amount of texts corpus at present phase of the research is about 340 000 sings without blanks: 110 000 signs in Russian, 98 000 signs in English, 32 000 signs in Spanish and 100 000 signs in Tatar language.

Because of the fact that aggression could be approvable by social norms and situation (in terms of E. Fromm it's the so called "non-malignant destructivity" [6]), the next stage of analysis demands revealing the ration of aggressive content with negative, positive and neutral connotation in each text of the selected corpus. That operation also allows determining the author's attitude toward the described subject.

Further there are represented preliminary results and conclusions of the survey.

3   Conclusions

The study of lexicographical resources provides the following conclusions:

1. The semantic field "aggression" is widely represented in each of analyzed languages that testifies the fact that **aggressive behaviour as a social phenomenon is the integral part of life activity of the examined lingua-cultures.**

2. The semantic field "aggression" is presented by arch-seme «*агрессия*» in Russian, «*aggression*» in English, «*agresión*» in Spanish. In Tatar language along with not frequently used loan word «*агрессия*» exists a proper word «*яулап алу*».

3. Grammar structure of semantic field "aggression" is complete for each of four languages. But in comparison with a wide verbs, nouns and adjectives categories the adverbs category of the semantic field "aggression" in English, Spanish and Tatar languages is less represented then in Russian.

4. The lexemes corpus of the semantic field "aggression" in analyzed languages contains formally free lexemes as well as set phrases and acronyms.

5. Most of the semantic field "aggression" words build derivational nidus with the exception of highly tailored terms and jargonisms.

6. The semantic field "aggression" is based on generic specifications, derivational, synonymous and antonymous relationships.

7. The semantic field "aggression" semes group in accordance with principles of full resemblance of senses, partial resemblance, contrasting and interchanging of defined sense.

8. The semantic field "aggression" lexemes in each of the investigated languages form antonymic oppositions and synonymic series correlated with types of aggression, aggressor – victim dyad, subject – object of aggression dichotomy, instruments and quality of aggressive acts.

9. Syntagmatic relations establishing between the words of the semantic field "aggression" are characterized by high combinatory power.

10. Stylistic nuances of the words corpus in Russian, English, Spanish and Tatar languages cover literary language, special lexicons, colloquial language slang and jargon.

Relying on the preliminary results of newspapers articles content-analysis at present phase of the survey we can make the following conclusions:

1. The examined corpus in Russian, English, Spanish and Tatar languages can be thematically divided in groups **"military operations"**, **"criminal activity"**, **"politics"**, **"family violence"**. Texts about "means of defense" and "aggressive economics" found a small group.

2. The amount of absolute rate of explicitly represented units of K-variable [10,11] «агрессия» / «aggression» / «agresión» / «яулап алу» fluctuates within limits of 10-25% as applied to the texts of official newspapers.

3. The semantic field "aggression" can conditionally be divided in categories:

– "physical aggression" (description of violent actions, call to violent actions);
– "verbal aggression" (swearing, abuse, teasing, verbal threats, telling curses, reproaching, assaulting);
– "negativism" (prevailing negative estimation and uncontrolled criticism);
– "auto-aggression" (description of destructive emotional experience, negative feelings, offence and guilt).

4   Results

Content-analysis showed that written texts with high concentration of lexemes of the semantic field "aggression" could not be automatically determine as aggression modulates. It also revealed the following texts categories provoking aggression in a recipient:

– texts informing about manifestation of different types of aggression (geopolitical conflicts, criminal behaviour, violence in family, aggressive economics) in combination with author's reproach of defensive aggression and approval of inimical aggression;
– texts as an instrument of intensification of negative aim and communicating possible forms of physical or symbolic aggression towards the object of the text in combination with author's reproach of inimical aggression and approval of defensive aggression (mainly propaganda and ideological texts);
– texts provoking verbal aggression in combination with author's reproach both of defensive and inimical aggression (e.g., extremely critical messages, especially towards unpopular public figures condemning them and distorting facts of present reality).

Communicatory structure of written texts with high concentration of lexemes of the semantic field "aggression" consists of the following basic components:

– presence of image of enemy in the person of public figures;
– presence of implicit/explicit image of a good party contrast to the opponent/absence of opponent;
– context of permissiveness and irresponsibility;
– extremely harsh and unilateral conformations of ruinous consequences of the enemy influence on lives of recipients.

5   Prospects of Investigation

The objective of the next stage of the survey is the assessment of the impact of texts modulating aggression in different audiences of recipients according to the following criterion: 1) theme, 2) concentration of lexemes of the semantic field "aggression", 3) high approval–reproach index.

Availability of the applied approach lies in possibility of automation of the procedure with subsequent expert processing.

References

1. Apresyan, V.Y.: Implitsitnaya agressiya v yazyke. In: Kompyuternaya Lingvistika I Intellektualnye Tekhnologii: Trudy Mezhdunarod. Konf., "Dialog 2003", Nauka, Moscow, pp. 32–35 (2003)
2. Basovskaya, E.N.: Tvortsy cherno-beloj realnosti: o verbalnoj agressii v sredstvah massovoj informatsii. In: Kritika I Semiotika, vol. 7, pp. 257–263. RGGU, Moscow (2004)
3. Berkowitz, L.: Causes and consequences of feelings. Cambridge University Press (2000)
4. Brandt, D.C., Pierce, K.J.: When is verbal abuse serious? The impact of relationship variables on perceptions of severity, pp. 71–78, http://murphylibrary.uwlax.edu/digital/jur/2000/brandt-pierce.pdf
5. Dasko, A.A.: Agressiya: shtrikhi k yazykovoj kartine mira. In: Agressia v Yazyke i Rechi, pp. 194–201. RGGU, Moscow (2004)
6. Fromm, E.: The anatomy of human destructiveness. AST, Moscow (2004)
7. Glebov, V.V., Rodionova, O.M.: Osobennosti rechevoj agressii (2008), http://www.rost-prof.ru/union/partners/rudn/articles/agr.html
8. Infante, D.A., Wigley, C.J.: Verbal aggressiveness: An interpersonal model and measure. Communication Monographs 53(III), 61–69 (1986)
9. Lyubitskaya, E.V.: Rechevoj akt ugrozy v slenge sovremennoj molodezhi (2002), http://conf.stavsu.ru/YOUTH_SCI/SEC7/lubitskaya.htm
10. Potapova, R.K., Potapov, V.V.: Semanticheskoe pole "narkotiki": Diskurs kak obekt prikladnoj lingvistiki. URSS, Moscow (2004)
11. Potapova, R.K., Potapov, V.V.: Yazyk, rech, lichnost. Yazyki slavyanskoj kultury, Moscow (2006)
12. Reitman, D., Villa, M.: Verbal aggression: Coping strategies for children. National Association of School Psychologists, Bethesda (2004), http://blogs.canby.k12.or.us/uploads/ziehla/verbaggression_rk.pdf
13. Scherbinina, Y.V.: Rechevaya agressiya: territoriya vrazhdy. Forum, Moscow (2012)
14. Scherbinina, Y.V.: Verbalnayz agressiaya: territoriya vrazhdy. Editorial URSS, Moscow (2006)
15. Sheigal, E.I.: Verbalnaya agressiya v politicheskom diskurse. In: Voprosy stilistiki. Antropotsentricheskie Issledovaniya, vol. 28, pp. 204–222. Izd. Sarat. un-ta, Saratov (1999)
16. Stets, J.: Verbal and physical aggression in marriage. Journal of Marriage and Family 52, 501–514 (1990)
17. Straus, M.A.: Leveling, civility, and violence in family. Journal of Marriage and Family 36, 13–29 (1974)
18. Walker, L.: The battered women. Harper and Row, New York (1979)
19. Yakimova, N.S.: Sredstva vyrazheniya verbalnoj agressii v kontekste eksperimentalnogo izucheniya lingvokultur: diss. kand. filol. nauk. Kemer. gos. un-t Kemerovo (2012)
20. Zhilves, V.I.: Invektiva. In: Antologiya Rechevykh Zhanrov: Povsednevnaya Kommunikatsiya, Labirint, Moscow, pp. 187–192 (2007)

Method for Pornography Filtering in the WEB Based on Automatic Classification and Natural Language Processing

Roman Suvorov, Ilya Sochenkov, and Ilya Tikhomirov

Institute for Systems Analysis of Russian Academy of Sciences
117312, Moscow, pr. 60-letiya Oktyabrya, 9
{rsuvorov,sochenkov,tih}@isa.ru
www.isa.ru

Abstract. The paper presents a method for pornography detection in the web pages based on natural language processing. The described classification method uses feature set of single words and groups of words. Syntax analysis is performed to extract collocations. A modification of TF-IDF is used to weight terms. An evaluation and comparison of quality and performance of classification are given.

Keywords: text classification, dynamic web content filtering, pornography detection, natural language processing, thematic importance characteristic.

1 Introduction

According to [1] there are 4.2 million pornographic websites (that is 12% of total websites) in the Web. Approximately 34% of users complain on receiving unwanted pornographic exposure. One can easily find pornographic sites using global web search engines. No doubt it's necessary to protect children from adult content.

There is a number of general approaches for web content filtering: URL-based filtering, keyword matching, intelligent analysis of content. URL-based filtering and keyword matching are not capable of effective content filtering under the modern conditions. Most articles on this topic contain a broad survey of major approaches to the web content filtering [2] so we avoid doubling it. A number of articles [2–7] present methods for dynamic content filtering that use textual, structural, visual features and some combinations of them. In this paper we focus on methods for web pages filtering based on automatic classification that take into account textual features only.

There are some surveys that contain comparison of industrial-level products in the area of web content filtering and parental control [6, 8]. Accuracy of existing methods varies from 80% to 99%. There are no articles that provide computational performance measurement or comparison of various methods. Additionally there is no research on Russian language.

Summing up, the challenge of dynamic content filtering cannot be considered to be solved. In this paper we present a method for filtering web content that is based on natural language processing. The quality and performance of the proposed method is

M. Železný et al. (Eds.): SPECOM 2013, LNAI 8113, pp. 233–240, 2013.

evaluated. Additionally, we compare our method and some well known classification algorithms.

The rest of the paper is organized as follows: in Chapter 2 we review methods for text-based filtering; in Chapter 3 we describe the proposed method; Chapter 4 contain description of the used testing technique and the results of the experiment; Chapter 5 summarizes the work and considers some possible directions of the future research.

2   Related Work

In this chapter we review methods for dynamic text-based content filtering that were proposed in various articles.

Chen-Huei Chou et al [9] proposed a text mining approach to detecting Web-based Internet abuse. A two-factor experimental evaluation was provided. Factors defined were a method for term weighting (Information Gain based on both TF or TF-IDF) and a classification method (Naive Bayes, Multimonial Naive Bayes, Neural network, SVM, k-nearest neighbor, C4.5 decision tree). Number of attributes (unique terms used in classification) did not exceed 500. The best results were shown by C4.5 (99.46%), KNN (99.0%), SVM (98.39%). 10000 pages (5000 abuse and 5000 non-abuse) were collected from news Web sites and sites on software engineering.

SU Gui-yang et al [10] proposed an improvement of classical keyword matching method. The key idea was to launch KNN classifier only when some keywords were found on a page. The dataset used for validation contained pornographic and scientific texts in Chinese. Precision of 97% was achieved.

Wai H. Ho and Paul A. Watters [4] compared pornographic pages and non-pornographic pages using statistical and structural analysis. They evaluated frequency distribution of such characteristics as a number of images on a page, a number of links on a page, a number of links to images, a number of words. Additionally they compared lexicon (unigram) used in pornographic and non-pornographic pages. A modified Naive Bayes classifier was used. Accuracy of 99.1% was achieved.

N. Churcharoenkrung et al [11] proposed usage of Multiple Classification Ripple-Down Rules to increase manual maintainability of web content filters. The condition of a rule was defined as a set of keywords. The conclusion of a rule was a decision whether to block a page. The dataset used consisted of 283 web pages divided info two categories: gambling and non-gambling. Accuracy of about 80% was achieved.

Rongbo Du et al [12] proposed to use cosine similarity measure between a page and a class for making a decision of blocking the page. Term Frequency (TF) was used to assign weights to terms. The threshold was selected as an average of distances between N the most similar docs from the training set. An accuracy of 95% was achieved.

Some articles [2, 3, 7] propose using both textual and visual features. We consider only textual techniques. Jantima Polpinij et al [2, 3] reports about achieving 100% accuracy on English pornographic texts. SVM with feature set consisted of bigrams was used as a classification method. Weiming Hu et al [7] used a cellular neural network to classify continuous text found on a page. Accuracy of 97.6% was achieved.

Mohamed Hammami et al [6] achieved a 90% accuracy in the task of binary classification of pornographic web pages using SIPINA decision trees. Feature set consisted of eight values like "whether a URL contains pornographic terms" or "amount of images on a page".

P.Y. Lee et al [5] proposed to use a feature set of 55 terms (without morphology) and modern neural networks (KSON, fuzzy ART). The evaluation was performed using 200 documents. Accuracy of 95% was achieved.

Summing up, evaluation was performed using different (and stingily described) data sets and thus results are hardly comparable. There is no research on Russian language. Nobody has provided performance measurement and comparison. Additionally, no one proposed using advanced techniques of natural language processing. Textual features are usually extracted using stemmer or without any preprocessing (wordform as it appears in a text). Naive Bayes, SVM and KNN are the most frequently used classifiers. Accuracy and over-blocking rate are the most frequently used metrics.

3   A Method for Dynamic Web Content Filtering

In this chapter we present a novel method for dynamic filtering of web pages based on natural language processing techniques.

Let's consider a two-class classification problem: we have a dictionary of n terms, a "white" collection CW that contains $N(CW)$ documents on various topics and a "black" collection CB that contains $N(CB)$ documents on undesired topic (say, pornography). We also refer to "black" and "white" collections as "thematic" and "global". By a term we mean a single word in its normal form or a noun phrase that consists of two words.

Let $N(c)$ be the amount of documents in a collection c; let $L(d)$ be the set of terms that a document d contains; let $O(t, d)$ be the list of occurrences of a term t in a document d; let $O(d)$ be the list of all occurrences present in a document d; let $m(o, d)$ be the weight of an occurrence o of a term in a document d; let $u(t, c)$ be the amount of documents that use term t.

Importance of a term t in a document d at the background of a collection c is determined using the modified TF-IDF formula:

$$lTF(t, d) = \log_{\left(1 + \sum\limits_{o \in O(d)} m(o,d)\right)} \left(1 + \sum\limits_{o \in O(t,d)} m(o, d)\right)$$

$$IDF(t, c) = \log_{N(c)} \left(\frac{N(c)}{u(t, c) + 1}\right)$$

$$lTFIDF(t, d, c) = lTF(t, d)IDF(t, c)$$

lTF is less sensitive to variation of lengths of documents in the training set compared to the traditional TF. Additionally, the markup of an HTML document is taken in account when calculating lTF: $m(o, d_j)$ depends on the HTML tag that contains the occurrence o. $IDF(t, c)$ can be considered as an information entropy associated with the term t at the background of collection c.

Thus we can define a quantity of information associated with a document d at the background of a collection c:

$$I(d, c) = \sum_{t \in L(d)} lTFIDF(t, d, c)$$

Given two collections c_b and c_w the following inequality is true for c_b-specific terms: $IDF(t, c_b) < IDF(t, c_w)$. Thus we can define a change in informativeness of a term t providing that a document d containing the term is classified to the category c_b.

$$\Delta I(t, c_b, c_w) = IDF(t, c_w) - IDF(t, c_b)$$

Having the Heaviside step function $H(\cdot)$ we can introduce non-negative version of $\Delta I(t, c_b, c_w)$:

$$\Delta I^+(t, c_b, c_w) = \Delta I(t, c_b, c_w) H(\Delta I(t, c_b, c_w))$$

Finally we can provide a formula to calculate importance of a term t in a document d at the background of a topical collection c_b and a global collection c_w:

$$lTFtIDF(t, d, c_b, c_w) = lTF(t, d)\Delta I^+(t, c_b, c_w)$$

We call $lTFtIDF(t, d, c_b, c_w)$ a Thematic Importance Characteristic (TIC) of a term t. TIC is a normalized value: $0 \leq lTFtIDF(t, d, c_b, c_w) \leq 1$.

Finally a definition of the TIC of a document can be provided.

$$TIC(d, c_b, c_w) = \sum_{t \in L(d)} lTFtIDF(t, d, c_b, c_w)$$

$$nTIC(d, c_b, c_w) = \frac{TIC(d, c_b, c_w)}{I(d, c_w)}$$

$nTIC(d, c_b, c_w)$ is a normalized form of TIC: $0 \leq nTIC(d, c_b, c_w) \leq 1$. The greater TIC of a document, the closer the topic of a document d and the topic of a collection c_b to each other. The converse is also true: the lesser TIC, the lesser similarity of the topics. This allows usage of TIC to solve a classification problem: a document d belongs to category c_b if $nTIC(d, c_b, c_w) > Threshold(c_b, c_w)$. $Threshold(c_b, c_w)$ is determined at the learning stage so that error rate on the training set is minimal. $nTIC$ does not depend on ratio of training set sizes. A multinomial classification problem also can be solved using the proposed method (with techniques like "winner takes all" etc).

The method was already described earlier in [13] (in Russian). The latter paper contain comparison of TIC with Naive Bayes, SVM and other well-known classification methods in application to classification of advertisements.

4   Experiment

The main goal of the experiment is to evaluate quality of the proposed classifier. The problem used for testing is binary classification of pornographic web pages in Russian and English. We have crawled about 9000 pornographic pages in English and about the same amount of pornographic pages in Russian. As a white collection we use a subset of Wikipedia pages (about 50000 of documents for each language).

The experiment has three factors: language, classification method and feature set. We compared three classifiers: nTIC, SVM and Naive Bayes. As a SVM classifier we used C-SVM with linear kernel provided by libsvm because it performed best on our data (C-SVM and nu-SVM with linear, polynomial, RBF and sigmoid kernels were tested). The Naive Bayes was implemented as described in [14].

We used three types of feature sets: stems, lemmas of words (single words) and a union of lemmas and two-word noun groups. These feature sets will be referred to as *Stemming*, *Unigram* and *Bigram* for brevity. *Stemming* features were extracted using a snowball stemmer provided by libstemming from the Snowball project. *Unigram* and *Bigram* features were extracted using morphological analysis (with homonymy resolution) and full syntax analysis. Features from the *Stemming* set were weighted using traditional TF formula. *Unigram* and *Bigram* features were weighted using the proposed $lTFIDF$ formula.

The linguistic processor used is based on FreeLing [15] (for English) and AOT [16] (for Russian).

Sizes of feature sets are listed in Table 1.

Table 1. Sizes of feature sets

	Stemming	Unigram	Unigram+Bigram
English	829114	1329122	1780795
Russian	1236469	856973	1597297

Let's make basic definitions regarding quality of classification: let $Right(s)$ be the subset of a set s containing correctly classified documents; let $Wrong(s)$ be the subset of a set s containing wrongly classified documents; let $Train(s)$ be the subset of a set s containing documents that were used to train the classifier; let $Test(s)$ be the subset of a set s containing documents that were used to evaluate quality of the classifier.

In order to evaluate quality of classification for each set of factor values we calculate the following metrics:

- overall accuracy of classification $A = \frac{|Right(Test(CW))|+|Right(Test(CB))|}{|Test(CW)|+|Test(CB)|}$;
- false positives rate (over-blocking) $E_1 = \frac{|Wrong(Test(CW))|}{|Test(CW)|}$;
- false negatives rate (under-blocking) $E_2 = \frac{|Wrong(Test(CB))|}{|Test(CB)|}$;
- precision $Prec = \frac{|Right(Test(CB))|}{|Right(Test(CB))|+|Wrong(Test(CW))|}$;
- recall $Rec = \frac{|Right(Test(CB))|}{|Test(CB)|}$;
- F-measure $F = 2\frac{Prec \cdot Rec}{Prec+Recall}$

$Train(s)$ and $Test(s)$ are generated according to tenfold cross-validation technique. To estimate resulting values we use macroaveraging: independently calculate metrics for each set of factor values and then estimate the average. Results of the experiment are presented in Table 2.

Table 2. Quality measurement results (%)

Classifier	Features	Language	A	E_1	E_2	$Prec$	Rec	F
Naive Bayes	Stemming	English	91.98	36.77	0	90.7	100	95.12
Naive Bayes	Stemming	Russian	98.57	10.01	0	98.36	100	99.17
Naive Bayes	Unigram	English	92.87	55.24	0.03	92.46	99.96	96.07
Naive Bayes	Unigram	Russian	97.44	17.92	0	97.11	99.99	98.53
Naive Bayes	Bigram	English	93.86	47.55	0.03	93.44	99.96	96.59
Naive Bayes	Bigram	Russian	99.12	6.11	0	98.99	99.99	99.49
SVM	Stemming	English	99.74	00.56	00.16	99.84	99.83	99.83
SVM	Stemming	Russian	**99.99**	**0**	**0**	**99.99**	**99.99**	**99.99**
SVM	Unigram	English	99.89	00.13	00.10	99.98	99.89	99.94
SVM	Unigram	Russian	99.97	0	0.01	1	99.99	99.99
SVM	Bigram	English	99.9	00.09	00.10	99.98	99.90	99.94
SVM	Bigram	Russian	99.97	0	0.01	1	99.99	99.99
nTIC	Unigram	English	99.44	0.42	1.40	97.14	98.59	97.86
nTIC	Unigram	Russian	99.99	0	0	99.99	99.99	99.99
nTIC	Bigram	English	99.67	0.24	0.86	98.33	99.13	98.73
nTIC	Bigram	Russian	**99.99**	**0**	**0**	**99.99**	**99.99**	**99.99**

General classification algorithm contains two steps: extract features and apply classifier. Corresponding timings are present in Table 3 and Table 4 respectively.

Table 3. Average time to extract features from a document (in seconds)

	Stemming	Unigram	Bigram
Russian	0.35	0.42	1.1
English	0.27	0.35	0.81

Table 4. Average time to classify a document (in seconds)

	Naive Bayes	SVM	nTIC
Average time	0.008	0.013	0.009

5   Conclusion

Quality of classification when varying a feature extraction method depends mostly on the language, the topic and the function of the classified document. Using complicated feature extraction methods for pornographic web pages detection does not worth performance penalties. $Bigram$ and $Unigram$ feature sets can be more useful in multiclass cases, e.g. when a content filter must deny access to content of all known categories for a part of users and only a few of categories for others. The $Bigram$ feature set performs best on a dataset of pornographic pages in Russian. Also $Bigram$ usually performs better than $Unigram$.

Quality of nTIC approximately equals to quality of SVM when classifying pornographic web pages. One advantage of nTIC over SVM is that it learns faster.
The future directions of the work should cover:

- search for datasets that are difficult to classify using only textual features (e.g. social networks and other multi-thematic web sites);
- quality evaluation of multiclass categorization using the proposed method;
- validation of the method on other types of content;
- improving computational performance of the classifier without significant loss of quality;
- development of comprehensive web content classifier that takes into account not only textual features but linkage of hypertext pages, the visual representation of a page, images and embedded video.

Acknowledgments. The project is supported by Russian Foundation for Basic Research grant 12-07-33012. The described method was developed within the Exactus project [17] and is used in the TSA WebFilter software.

References

1. TopTenReviews: Internet pornography statistics (March 2013), http://internet-filter-review.toptenreviews.com/internet-pornography-statistics.html
2. Polpinij, J., Chotthanom, A., Sibunruang, C., Chamchong, R., Puangpronpitag, S.: Content-based text classifiers for pornographic web filtering. In: IEEE International Conference on Systems, Man and Cybernetics, SMC 2006, vol. 2, pp. 1481–1485 (2006)
3. Polpinij, J., Sibunruang, C., Paungpronpitag, S., Chamchong, R., Chotthanom, A.: A web pornography patrol system by content-based analysis: In particular text and image. In: IEEE International Conference on Systems, Man and Cybernetics, SMC 2008, pp. 500–505 (2008)
4. Ho, W., Watters, P.: Statistical and structural approaches to filtering internet pornography. In: 2004 IEEE International Conference on Systems, Man and Cybernetics, vol. 5, pp. 4792–4798 (2004)
5. Lee, P., Hui, S., Fong, A.: A structural and content-based analysis for web filtering. Internet Research 13(1), 27–37 (2003)
6. Hammami, M., Chahir, Y., Chen, L.: Webguard: Web based adult content detection and filtering system. In: Proceedings of the IEEE/WIC International Conference on Web Intelligence, WI 2003, pp. 574–578 (2003)
7. Hu, W., Wu, O., Chen, Z., Fu, Z., Maybank, S.: Recognition of pornographic web pages by classifying texts and images. IEEE Transactions on Pattern Analysis and Machine Intelligence 29(6), 1019–1034 (2007)
8. eTesting Labs: U.S. department of justice: Updated web content filtering software comparison. Technical report, eTesting Labs (2001)
9. Chou, C.-H., Sinha, A.P., Zhao, H.: A text mining approach to internet abuse detection. Information Systems and e-Business Management (2008)
10. Su, G.Y., Li, J.H., Ma, Y.H., Li, S.H.: Improving the precision of the keyword-matching pornographic text filtering method using a hybrid model. Journal of Zhejiang University Science 5(9), 1106–1113 (2004)

11. Churcharoenkrung, N., Kim, Y.S., Kang, B.H.: Dynamic web content filtering based on user's knowledge. In: Proceedings of the International Conference on Information Technology: Coding and Computing (ITCC 2005), vol. I, pp. 184–188. IEEE Computer Society, Washington, DC (2005)
12. Du, R., Safavi-Naini, R., Susilo, W.: Web filtering using text classification. In: The 11th IEEE International Conference on Networks, ICON 2003, pp. 325–330 (2003)
13. Mbaykodzhi, A., Dral, A.A., Sochenkov, I.V.: Short text messages classification method. Information Technologies and Computational Systems (3), 93–102 (2012)
14. Manning, C., Raghavan, P., Shutze, H.: Introduction to Information Retrieval. Cambridge University Press (2008)
15. FreeLing: An open source suite of language analyzers, http://nlp.lsi.upc.edu/freeling/
16. AOT: Automatic text processing, http://aot.ru/
17. Osipov, G., Smirnov, I., Tikhomirov, I., Shelmanov, A.: Relational-situational method for intelligent search and analysis of scientific publications. In: Proceedings of the Integrating IR Technologies for Professional Search Workshop, pp. 57–64 (2013)

Noise and Channel Normalized Cepstral Features for Far-speech Recognition

Michal Borsky, Petr Mizera, and Petr Pollak

Czech Technical University in Prague, Faculty of Electrical Engineering
K13131 CTU FEE, Technická 2, 166 27 Prague 6, Czech Republic
{borskmic,mizerpet,pollak}@fel.cvut.cz

Abstract. The paper analyses suitable features for distorted speech recognition. The aim is to explore the application of command ASR system when the speech is recorded with far-distance microphones with a possible strong additive and convolutory noise. The paper analyses feasible contribution of basic spectral subtraction coupled with cepstral mean normalization in minimizing of the influence of present distortion in such far-talk channel. The results are compared with reference close-talk speech recognition system. The results show the improvement in WER for channels with low or medium SNR. Using the combination of these basic techniques WERR of 55.6% was obtained for medium distance channel and WERR of 22.5% for far distance channel.

Keywords: distorted speech, far-speech recognition, cepstral features, spectral subtraction, cepstral mean normalization.

1 Introduction

The automatic speech recognition (ASR) systems have become a widely used assisting tools in the last decade [1]. The most frequent applications include online personal dictation systems [2], automatic broadcast transcription (subtitling) [3], [4], offline transcription of audio archive, key word spotting or finally systems for voice control of particular devices. The simplicity and convenience of voice interaction with the machines is a strong driving force for the research of deployment of its in office, household, car, or industry devices or machines. There are a lot of applications focused on replacing the current human-to-machine interfaces such as keyboard, mouse or touchpad.

Nowadays, very popular applications of voice driven interface is for a control of various devices or functionalities in so called smart-home [5]. The deployment of ASR system for voice command control in such applications requires a special tailoring at the levels of feature extraction and acoustic modelling as natural performance conditions of these systems are frequently rather adverse and they need to be to compensated because the requirement of speech input naturalness in smart-home environment leads to the usage of middle or far distance microphones, which are usually embedded in devices itself or in the walls or ceiling of the house and which disables the usage of directional microphones. When a microphone with omnidirectional characteristics is used, especially with far distance placement typically, it leads to the inevitable presence of various kinds of noise of rather high levels. Also an attenuation of speech collected

M. Železný et al. (Eds.): SPECOM 2013, LNAI 8113, pp. 241–248, 2013.

by a far microphone is rather high, so consequently, the resulting degradation of speech is really very high, and the accuracy of speech recognition falls down rapidly because standard features as MFCC or PLP are generally susceptible to strong noise [6] presence or to signal degradation.

Within this paper we would like to analyse a contribution and limitations of basic speech enhancement techniques and a possible impact on one-channel far-microphone speech recognition.

2   Far Channel Feature Extraction

As it is written above, middle- and far-speech recognition represent typically task with speech input extremely degraded by convolutory noise given mainly by reverberations, moreover, it may be strongly influenced by additive background noise. Consequently, some noise suppression techniques same as elimination of convolution distortion must be applied in such case.

There are various solutions of robust feature extraction working with signals of various level of degradation. Authors in [7] used the cepstral mean subtraction (CMS) to compensate for possible channel change in telephone band, when a sliding window of 400 frames was employed. It meant an averaging within approx. 4 seconds for their feature extraction setup of 25ms frame with 10ms shift. A similar approach to feature enhancement was implemented in [8] for three different kinds of noise (car, street noise, AWGN). A significant word error rate reduction (WERR) of 25.5% was reached for CAR noise.

Both the CMS and spectral subtraction (SS) were tested for robust speech recognition in [9]. The authors used the SS technique coupled with VAD to estimate noise power spectra obtained by averaging within speech pauses. The CMS algorithm was implemented by computing the long-time average of cepstral coefficient off-line and subtracted from all 13 coefficient but the zeroth. The pre-recorded noises were added to clean telephone signals at four various SNR levels. The results showed that SS could decrease the performance of the ASR system due to the introduction of non-linearities but testing database resulted in the WERR = 22.6 %. The mean word error rate reduction on the whole used database using only the CMS method was rather small, but the combination of SS and CMS yielded the WERR = 28.5 %.

Noise cancellation in feature extraction

There are various approaches for noise cancellation applied in ASR including sometimes quite sophisticated solutions using multichannel input [10]. But these techniques require much complex hardware same as higher computational cost. Due to these facts, they are usually not applied to increase the robustness of speech recognition but simple one-channel techniques are very popular and frequently used for these tasks.

Within our work we use SS technique described [6], [11] for the elimination of additive background noise. This technique was chosen because it works without need of voice activity detector. Within mentioned papers was also proved that it contributes reasonably to speech recognition in very noisy environments. It suppresses non-stationary noise when its spectral characteristics change slowly then speech ones. We can suppose near the same conditions in our approach in smart-home application.

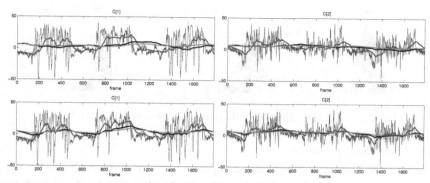

Fig. 1. CMS with cepstral mean estimation as EA/MA and smoothing time 1 s (red), 5 s (black), 10 s (green)

Convolution distortion normalization

Cepstral mean subtraction is the technique known already for several decades [12] or [13] and it is also used in world-wide spread tools for ASR such as HTK Toolkit [14]. General principle is clear and simple, however, the practical implementation differs, e.g. within HTK Toolkit the average cepstrum is computed only over whole utterance. It yields to various number of samples over which the average is estimated. Another drawback is the possibility to apply some approaches of CMS only in off-line mode.

We analyse two approaches of CMS, available now in [15], which can be easily implemented in on-line system. Firstly, it is standard computation of moving average (MA) over the long-time window of given length. The second approach is computation on the basis recursive exponential averaging (EA).

The key question is about a length of long-time window above which an average is compute. Particular authors work with various lengths of this window from 1 s up to values above 10 s. Fig. 1 illustrates averaging results for both solutions and it is clear that this window should be longer than 1 s, on the other hand from a value around 5 s the results starts being near the same.

3 Experiments

As mentioned above, the purpose of this study is to analyse the contribution and possible limitations of this basic techniques in the task of one-channel far-speech recognition. As a model of this situation data from Czech SPEECON database were used. Same utterance were here recorded simultaneously by several microphones located in different positions [16]. Recording conditions of these channels can be described by estimated values of SNR. This information for all channels CS0-CS3 is available in this database in particular annotation files. Statistics and distributions of speech SNR within this database are summarized illustratively in Fig. 2. More than 20 dB difference in SNRs between close and far distance speech proves that far channel data has significantly worse quality and that they well represent far distance input in smart-home application.

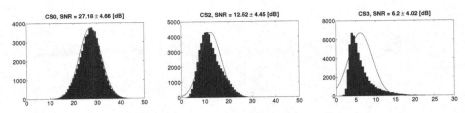

Fig. 2. SNR [dB] distribution in channels with estimated Gaussian fitting

Robust feature implementation

Above described robust features were computed using the tool CtuCopy [17] which offers many various strategies of parametrization in combination with additive noise suppression techniques, also SS technique chosen by us. Also both above described methods of convolution distortion normalization on the basis of CMS was additionally implemented into this tool. CtuCopy enables batch processing of more files (similarly as known HCopy tool [14]), however, the average was carried over signal boundaries. The last version of CtuCopy containing already described approaches of CMS computation is available for public usage.

Finally, we worked with MFCC were computed using the Ctucopy tool [17] with the following setup:

- 12 cepstral coefficients with c[0],
- 25 ms frame length with 15 ms step,
- 30 filters in full band 0 ÷ 8000,
- static, dynamic, and acceleration features used.

Noise cancellation based on spectral subtraction was implemented with the following parameters:

- method extended spectral subtraction,
- spectra of the noise estimated in each frame with no crossover,
- integration constant p = 0.95,
- realized in magnitude domain,
- SS used before the application of the filter bank.

Cepstral mean subtraction was applied using both approaches, i.e. block and exponential averaging. Equivalent time constants for both methods were set to 1, 5, and 10 s. Commonly with SS, 14 different feature extraction setups which are summarized in the Tab. 1 were analysed.

Table 1. Parametrizations summary

Param.	SS	T [s]		
mfcc	no	-		
mfcc_ss	yes	-		
mfcc_b/mfcc_exp	no	1	5	10
mfcc_ss_b/mfcc_ss_cms	yes	1	5	10

Recognition task setup

As the recognition task, small vocabulary recognition of 468 different commands with impossible repetition was chosen in our experiments. The utterances had a single word or multiple words structure and they also contained possibly used commands for household appliances. The testing part consists from 19 speakers with an overall length of about 15 minutes.

Speaker independent *acoustic models* for analysed channels were trained with the same amount of data which was about 51 hours of speech from 190 speakers. Final acoustic models had the following parameters: 43 different monophones including silence and short-pause expanded into tied-state cross-word triphones, 14 mixtures, static, dynamic, and acceleration features in 1 stream.

Results

Since all of the signals were recorded simultaneously using different microphones, channel distortion could be quantified basically by Euclidean cepstral distance computed between the reference CS0 signal and CS2/CS3 signal computed either from complete cepstral vector with coefficient c_0 (*CD0*) or just from the coefficients $c_1 \div c_L$ (*CD1*).

Tab. 2 shows results estimated from subset of approx. 2000 utterances from office part of SPEECON database. The trend observed for both CMS methods was the decrease in the (*CD0*) and (*CD1*) as the averaging time windowed increased in length. The (*CD1*) distance was consistently lower for independent CMS system than for the combined system, regardless of the channel. The differences were however very small.

The first experiments compares the results of a system without any noise suppression and a system with either SS or CMS for all channels. The application of standalone SS increased the robustness only in the case of CS3 channel. In both the CS0 and CS2 channels, the additive noise from the background in rather small, $SNR_{CS0} = 27.18$ dB and $SNR_{CS2} = 12.52$ dB. The induction of non-linearities and musical tones degraded the speech quality, which resulted in the increase of WER.

In the second experiment the accuracy was tested for a system with standalone CMS. In this case a clear improvement was reached for all setups on the CS2 channel, while

Table 2. Cepstral Euclidean distance for various parametrizations

	CS2		CS3	
	CD0	CD1	CD0	CD1
CS0 × CS_x	$\mu \pm \sigma$	$\mu \pm \sigma$	$\mu \pm \sigma$	$\mu \pm \sigma$
mfcc × mfcc	42.57±11.11	37.57±11.30	54.91±16.33	49.11±18.87
mfcc × mfcc_SS	41.99±11.32	38.79±11.52	54.69±17.04	50.36±18.70
mfcc × mfcc_exp1	48.23±14.02	43.44±15.46	54.25±16.80	48.26±19.57
mfcc × mfcc_exp5	45.82±12.45	41.06±13.14	52.93±15.74	46.93±18.29
mfcc × mfcc_exp10	45.27±12.14	40.48±12.71	52.60±15.55	46.57±18.07
mfcc × mfcc_b1	49.25±14.26	44.59±15.62	55.02±17.01	49.15±19.71
mfcc × mfcc_b5	46.07±12.39	41.41±12.84	53.10±15.52	47.18±17.92
mfcc × mfcc_b10	45.51±12.15	40.77±12.67	52.77±15.55	46.78±18.03

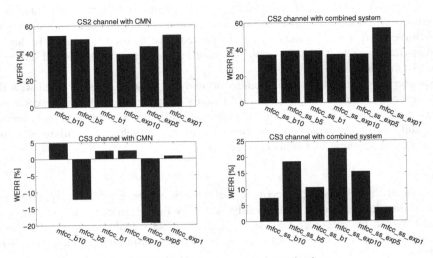

Fig. 3. WERR [%] for various parametrizations

Table 3. Reference and standalone CMS

	CS0		CS2		CS3	
Param	WER [%]	WERR [%]	WER [%]	WERR [%]	WER [%]	WERR [%]
mfcc	1.89	*0*	9.73	*0*	33.51	*0*
mfcc_b10	2.43	*-28.57*	4.59	*52.86*	31.89	*4.83*
mfcc_b5	2.43	*-28.57*	4.86	*50.05*	37.57	*-12.11*
mfcc_b1	2.16	*-14.28*	5.41	*44.39*	32.7	*2.41*
mfcc_exp10	2.97	*-57.14*	5.95	*38.84*	32.7	*2.41*
mfcc_exp5	2.16	*-14.28*	5.41	*44.39*	40	*-19.36*
mfcc_exp1	2.16	*-14.28*	4.59	*52.82*	33.24	*0.8*

Table 4. SS and combined system

	CS0		CS2		CS3	
Param	WER [%]	WERR [%]	WER [%]	WERR [%]	WER [%]	WERR [%]
mfcc_ss	2.43	*-28.57*	12.7	*-30.52*	29.46	*12.08*
mfcc_ss_b10	2.43	*-28.57*	6.22	*36.07*	31.08	*7.25*
mfcc_ss_b5	2.16	*-14.28*	5.95	*38.84*	27.3	*18.53*
mfcc_ss_b1	2.43	*-28.57*	5.95	*38.84*	30	*10.47*
mfcc_ss_exp10	3.24	*-71.42*	6.22	*36.07*	25.95	*22.56*
mfcc_ss_exp5	1.62	*14.28*	6.22	*36.07*	28.38	*15.3*
mfcc_ss_exp1	1.89	*0*	4.32	*55.60*	32.16	*4.02*

the CS0 showed the degradation in accuracy. The results for CS3 channel were mixed. The time constant of 5 seconds for both averaging methods proved to be unfit. The EA/MA methods with time constant 1/10 seconds performed better and increased the accuracy when compared to standard feature extraction.

In the last experiment the combination of both methods was tested. The combined system proved to be the most effective when for both noisy channel an improvement was reached for any setup and even a slight decrease of 0.27% in WER for CS0 channel was observed.

4 Conclusions

The analysis of basic cepstral features applicable into far-talk speech recognition has been realized within this paper. Various setups of cepstral mean subtraction completed by extended spectral subtraction have been tested on the middle- to far-distance microphone recordings and compared to reference headset microphone recordings. The contribution of CMS was overall positive for CS2 channel, while for the the CS3 channel the time constant of 5 seconds proved to worse the accuracy for both block and exponential averaging. The WERR for *mfcc_exp1/10* and *mfcc_block1/10* was up to 5%. In each case the usage of CMS for far-talk channel is necessary. For more noisy far-talk channel (CS3), the contribution of SS was also evident due to significantly lower SNR in this channel. This combination of SS and CMS achieved the best results WER decreased for all CMS setups. Exactly, for CS2 channel the highest WERR = 55.6% was obtained for *mfcc_ss_exp1*, for CS3 channel the highest WERR = 22.5% was obtained for *mfcc_ss_exp10*.

Acknowledgements. Research in this paper was supported by grant SGS12/143/OHK3/2T/13 "Algorithms and Hardware Realizations of Digital Signal Processing".

References

1. Ircing, P., Krbec, P., Hajic, J., Psutka, J., Khudanpur, S., Jelinek, F., Byrne, W.: On large vocabulary continuous speech recognition of highly inflectional language - Czech. In: INTERSPEECH, pp. 487–490 (2001)
2. Newton Media: Newton Dictate Home page (2013), http://www.diktovani.cz
3. Nouza, J., Žďánský, J., David, P.: Fully Automated Approach to Broadcast News Transcription in Czech Language. In: Sojka, P., Kopeček, I., Pala, K. (eds.) TSD 2004. LNCS (LNAI), vol. 3206, pp. 401–408. Springer, Heidelberg (2004)
4. Vaněk, J., Psutka, J.V.: Gender-dependent acoustic models fusion developed for automatic subtitling of parliament meetings broadcasted by the czech TV. In: Sojka, P., Horák, A., Kopeček, I., Pala, K. (eds.) TSD 2010. LNCS, vol. 6231, pp. 431–438. Springer, Heidelberg (2010)
5. Chaloupka, J., Nouza, J., Zdansky, J., Cerva, P., Silovsky, J., Kroul, M.: Voice Technology Applied for Building a Prototype Smart Room. In: Esposito, A., Hussain, A., Marinaro, M., Martone, R. (eds.) Multimodal Signals. LNCS (LNAI), vol. 5398, pp. 104–111. Springer, Heidelberg (2009)

6. Rajnoha, J., Pollák, P.: ASR systems in noisy environment: Analysis and solutions for increasing noise robustness. Radioengineering 20(1), 74–84 (2011)
7. Nouza, J., Silovsky, J.: Fast keyword spotting in telephone speech. Radioengineering 18(4), 665–670 (2009)
8. Schuller, B., Wöllmer, M., Moosmayr, T., Rigoll, G.: Speech recognition in noisy environments using a switching linear dynamic model for feature enhancement. In: INTERSPEECH 2008, pp. 1789–1792 (2008)
9. Kermorvant, C.: A comparison of noise reduction techniques for robust speech recognition. Idiap-RR Idiap-RR-10-1999, IDIAP, IDIAP-RR 99-10 (1999)
10. Wang, L., Odani, K., Kai, A.: Evaluation of hands-free large vocabulary continuous speech recognition by blind dereverberation based on spectral subtraction by multi-channel LMS algorithm. In: Habernal, I., Matoušek, V. (eds.) TSD 2011. LNCS, vol. 6836, pp. 131–138. Springer, Heidelberg (2011)
11. Sovka, P., Pollak, P., Kybic, J.: Extended spectral subtraction. In: EUSIPCO 1996, Trieste (September 1996)
12. Junqua, J.C., Haton, J.P.: Asr of noisy, stressed, and channel distorted speech. In: Robustness in Automatic Speech Recognition. The Kluwer International Series in Engineering and Computer Science, vol. 341, pp. 273–323. Springer, US (1996)
13. Droppo, J., Acero, A.: Environmental robustness. In: Springer Handbook of Speech Processing, pp. 653–680. Springer (2008)
14. Young, S., et al.: The HTK Book, Version 3.4.1, Cambridge (2009)
15. Fousek, P., Mizera, P., Pollak, P.: CtuCopy feature extraction tool (2013), http://noel.feld.cvut.cz/speechlab/start.php?page=download&lang=en
16. Pollák, P., Černocký, J.: Czech SPEECON adult database. Technical report (November 2003), http://www.speechdat.org/speecon
17. Boril, H., Fousek, P., Pollak, P.: Data-driven design of front-end filter bank for Lombard speech recognition. In: Proc. of Interspeech 2006, Pittsburgh (September 2006)

Parametric Speech Synthesis and User Interface for Speech Modification

Alexander Shipilo*, Andrey Barabanov, and Mikhail Lipkovich

Saint Petersburg State University,
Saint Petersburg, Universitetskij pr., 28, Russia
{alexandershipilo,andrey.barabanov,lipkovich.mikhail}@gmail.com

Abstract. A new parametric allophone-to-speech synthesis system of the Russian language is described. It is assumed that a sequence of allophones with prosodic information is given and it is required to compute the corresponding speech signal. Allophones are stored in the database by model parameter sets only. The model of a voiced signal is purely polyharmonic. Modification of pitch, energy and duration can be effectively made to a large extent without loss of quality. The system is based on precise estimation of harmonic parameters at the stage of database parameterization, on the cluster description of allophone merging in the Russian language and on the effective synthesis algorithm with opportunity to arbitrarily change any prosodic parameter through the graphic user interface.

Keywords: parametric synthesis, speech analysis, parametric models, pitch estimation.

1 Introduction

The widely spread concatenative synthesis approach is based on the method of compilation of required speech signal from prepared units stored in a database. These units can be allophones, diphones, syllables, words etc [1,2]. Prosodic characteristics modification is an important problem as, for example, pitch modification can lead to loss of naturalness and also to phase jumps that are usually perceived as clicks. To avoid prosodic characteristics modification, unit selection method is usually used in modern speech synthesis systems. Although it is unit selection method that produces the most natural speech signal, a big speech corpus is required for this method[3] that makes it almost inapplicable for the use on portable devices [2].

The parametric synthesis approach can be considered as a type of the concatenative synthesis. The main difference lies in the units stored in database and in signal restoration procedure. In the parametric synthesis approach a database unit is represented by the set of parameters of a part of the signal (frame) according to a fixed mathematical model. The speech signal generation algorithm decodes signal for each frame by the model with its parameter set, and then the successive frames are merged.

The main advantage of the parametric approach is the fact that a concatenation unit is represented by the set of independent parameters for each frame in the database. Pitch,

---

* The work was supported by Saint Petersburg State University, grant 0.37.92.2011.

M. Železný et al. (Eds.): SPECOM 2013, LNAI 8113, pp. 249–256, 2013.

energy and duration of any database unit can be changed easily with full preservation
of the allophone formant structure. For a voiced allophone all the harmonic phases can
be tuned individually to facilitate frame merging by prevention of phase jumps at the
border. The main disadvantage of the parametric approach is difficulty in mathematical
simulation of a high quality speech signal. In this paper, problems of mathematical
simulation are studied, precise solutions are described and the speech synthesis system
is presented.

2 The Main Models

Each allophone from the database is divided into a sequence of short frames. Normally,
the length of the voiced frame is close to one pitch period. For unvoiced frames the
frame length can be arbitrary but it is constant in the current system. The mathematical
model of a voiced frame is purely polyharmonic, the mathematical model of a voiceless
frame is a stationary random process.

Consider a voiced speech frame of the length of N samples. The model of a speech
signal in the currently developed speech synthesis system is the function

$$s_t = \sum_{k=-M}^{M} A_k e^{\frac{2\pi i}{P} kt}, \qquad -N/2 \leq t \leq N/2-1,$$

where M is the number of harmonics in the model, P is the pitch period in samples,
A_k is the complex amplitude for the k–th harmonic. In detail, A_0 is the constant term,
$A_k = |A_k|e^{i\phi_k}$ for $1 \leq k \leq M$ where $|A_k|$ is the harmonic amplitude, ϕ_k is the
phase of the harmonic at the center of the frame with $t = 0$. Finally, $A_{-k} = |A_k|e^{-i\phi_k}$
for $k = 1, \ldots, M$. The value of M is close to $P/2$, so that the frequency of the last
harmonic is close to the Nyquist frequency.

The parameter set of the voiced speech model consists of the value of P and the
complex vector $A = (A_k)_{k=0}^{M}$. At the stage of signal analysis these parameters are to
be estimated to the high accuracy. At the stage of synthesis the speech signal is decoded
according to the polyharmonic formula.

A voiceless frame is modeled by stationary random process. The model is completely
determined by its spectral density. The spectral density is approximated by the spectral
envelope of the speech signal in the frame. The spectral envelope is estimated by LPC
and signal energy. The parameter set of the voiceless speech model consists of a vector
of LPC and a real value of energy.

The introduced models of voiced and voiceless speech signals differ from the Harmonic plus Noise Model (HNM) proposed by Stylianou [4]. The HNM of any signal
contains both harmonic and noise parts with a regular voiced part in the low frequency
band from 0 to the cut frequency f_c and the noise part in the band from f_c to the Nyquist
frequency. Indeed, the high frequency spectrum of consonants contains important formants that look continuous, without sequence of equidistanced peaks.

Our recent investigation has shown that the reasons of the continuous high frequency
spectrum lie in weak nonstationarity of a sound. Small deviations in amplitudes and
phases and especially in pitch influence mainly the high order harmonics, and the peaks

are blurred covering frequency intervals between them. It is a mathematical problem of precise trend estimation that gives tools for harmonic plus trend description of the high frequency continuous spectrum of consonants. This problem was solved by methods similar to [5] but it is not the subject of this paper. The speech synthesis system under consideration contains purely harmonic or purely noise speech signal frames. The high frequency harmonic trend is simulated by the merging procedure for any two neighbouring frames.

3 Prosodic Modification

Any allophone is stored in the database as the sequence of frames with parameter sets according to voiced or unvoiced model. For any voiced frame of the length N the signal is restored in accordance to the polyharmonic formula

$$s_t = A_0 + 2 \sum_{k=1}^{M} A_k^0 \cos \left(\frac{2\pi}{P} kt + \phi_k \right), \qquad -N/2 \le t \le N/2 - 1,$$

where $A_k = A_k^0 e^{i\phi_k}$. All parameters in this formula can be changed independently.

The restored signal can be modified to a large extent with respect to the signal in database.

3.1 Change of the Spectral Envelope

The spectrum value of $A_k^0 = |A_k|$ corresponds to the frequency $f_k = kF_s/P$ Hz where F_s is the sample rate. Taking all pairs (f_k, A_k^0) as input interpolation data the spectral envelope can be easily obtained by splines. If an another spectral envelope is given by the function $B^0(f)$ then a sound with this spectral envelope is obtained by replacement of A_k^0 by $B^0(f_k)$. All other parameters including phases remain the same.

3.2 Change of Pitch

Assume the pitch P is to be changed by the pitch Q. First, replace P by Q in the formula. The sequence of multiple harmonics $f_k = kF_s/P$ is also changed to $g_k = kF_s/Q$. Since the spectral envelope must be preserved after the intonation change the previous modification of the spectral envelope is to be applied. The spectral envelope is approximated by interpolation points (f_k, A_k^0), $1 \le k \le M$, and the result is applied to the new frequencies g_k. If the duration of the frame is changed proportionally, $T_Q = T_P \cdot Q/P$ then all harmonics hold the same phase differences between the left and the right frame edges. This condition preserves smooth merging of the neighbouring frames.

This technique is illustrated in Fig. 1. The transition from the allophone /a/ to the allophone /n/ was taken from the natural speech signal at 8 kHz. The Fundamental frequency was 152 Hz. The signal was modified with interpolation of the spectral envelope. In Fig. 1 the initial signal is on the left plot and the synthesized signal on the right plot. Their spectra are shown in Fig. 2.

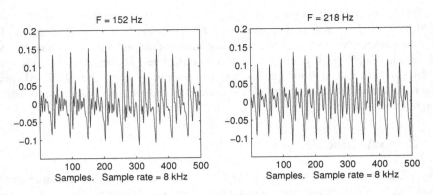

Fig. 1. The source signal (left) with F=152 Hz and the modified signal (right) with F=218 Hz

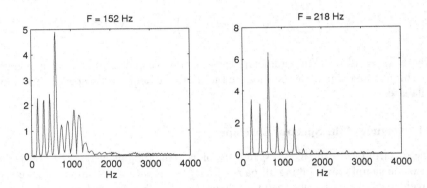

Fig. 2. The spectra of the signals from Fig. 1

3.3 Energy Modification

The function s_t can be multiplied by any gain E_t to change energy while all other prosodic features preserved.

3.4 Duration Modification

Durations of voiced and unvoiced allophones are modified by separate rules. Duration modification of unvoiced signal does not cause a big problem. It suffice to duplicate or to omit the overlapped frames obtained by a random generator with modulation of the spectra by the envelopes calculated from LPC.

Duration modification for the voiced signal is performed in two steps. First, Pitches of all frames for each allophone are replaced according to the prosodic information. Simultaneously, the amplitudes are interpolated to preserve the formant structure. This transformation leads to the length change for each allophone. Then, the durations are corrected and adjusted with the prosodic information by duplication or shifting full pitch periods at the stationary part of the sound. Precise estimation of the Pitches prevents jumps of phases between frames after Pitch and length modification.

For each group of allophone additional rules of Russian language were implemented to indicate which parts of the allophone records in the database must be preserved and where additional periods can be inserted or omitted.

3.5   Change of Phases

In general, the phases can be changed arbitrarily. But the only reason for the change appears at the borders for smooth merging of successive frames and especially for smooth merging of different allophones.

4   The Allophone Database of the Russian language

Perceptual and acoustic characteristics of allophones depend on the contexts they occur in. As shown in [6] the Russian allophones can be grouped into clusters. Any allophone from a cluster influences its neighbour in the same way. Totally 22 left clusters and 14 right clusters are distiguished for vowels in the Russian language. For Russian consonants 3 left clusters and 5 right clusters are distiguished [6].

The vowel allophones depend also on their positions. Any vowel phoneme from any cluster is represented in the database separately by allophones which occur in pre-stressed, stressed and post-stressed syllables. In addidtion , the phoneme /a/ is also represented in the database by the allophone that occurs in the second pre-stressed syllable.

The material for the database consists of separate words and utterances. The material is read by professional male speaker and is recorded with a high quality microphone at the 22.05 kHz sample rate. The collected database contains 2500 vowel allophones and 555 consonant allophones. Also, the database contains 25 inseparable groups of allophones that are produced as one articulation unit. As a rule, such a group contains bi-phoneme combinations of vowels in the word endings or bi-phoneme combinations of consonants that usually occur at the morpheme joint.

Each allophone record of the database is manually marked [7] with following annotation levels:

1. Phoneme transcription.
2. Allophone transcription.
3. V/UV label.
4. Duration modification area.
5. Orthographic transcription.

Each record of an allophone from the source material was encoded and transformed to the sequence of parameter sets. Each parameter set corresponds to a frame. It contains parameters for signal restoration according to the models of voiced and voiceless signals. The frame length of the voiced allophone record is equal to the estimated pitch period. The frame length of the voiceless allophone record is fixed.

5   The Synthesis Algorithm

Assume a sequence of phonemes and their prosodic characteristics are given. It is required to compute the speech signal. Speech synthesis is divided into the following stages:

1. Extraction of the desired sequence of allophones from the database according to clusters of neighbouring phonemes. Extraction of parameter sets for all frames of all extracted allophones.
2. Pitch modification for all extracted frames. This changes the duration and needs interpolation of the spectral envelope.
3. Adjustment of duration of each allophone. An iteration with the previous stage may be needed if intonation changes essentially after the duration adjustment.
4. Computation of the signal in all frames according to the basic models of voiced and voiceless signals.
5. Merging of frames inside each allophone.
6. Merging of frames between allophones.

The last stage may need additional phase adjustment or small deviation of the input prosodic information to prevent big jumps at the borders.

Small trends of all prosodic characteristics between centers of successive frames are simulated by interpolation of phases, amplitudes and pitches between centers of the frames. For a voiced pair of frames all harmonics are divided in pairs by their frequency values. Frequency, phase and amplitude are smoothly interpolated from the previous harmonic to the next harmonic in the pair.

Merging of a voiceless frame with any other frame is easily made by the overlapping technique.

Finally, the MOS test was conducted with 35 native speakers of Russian language. The score 4.4-4.5 for the synthesized speech signal comparing with 4.8-4.9 for the original speech signal looks promising.

6   The Graphic User Interface

A graphic user interface was developed for speech synthesis by the database with manual change of the prosodic features. A user can obtain and listen synthesized speech signal with pitch, duration and energy taken from the curves that can be modified online arbitrarily. The sequence of allophones from the database is the input data for the interface. Duration of the voiced signal can be changed by insertion or omission of a full current period at any place.

Assume a sequence of allophones is fixed. The program loads all parameter sets from the database sequentially for all allophones. The curves of the fundamental frequency and energy are also taken from the initial input data.

A user can create a new plot by introducing new points in the figure window that are shown in red, see Fig. 3. A new point is added by simple clicking at the desired cursor position. The new points are interpolated by spline. Any new point can be easily moved or deleted. The spline function becomes a new curve for intonation in the upper plot or for energy in the lower plot.

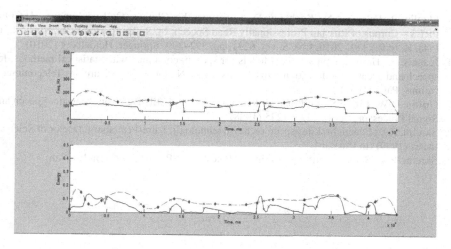

Fig. 3. New points are depicted by red. The new curve is a spline depicted by dash.

Allophone duration is regulated by insertion or deletion of full frames. Length of a voiced frame is equal to the pitch period. The length of voiceless frame is constant. Aditional frames can be inserted or deleted by pushing a special key while the cursor is located at a desired position. The parameters of an inserted frame between two voiced frames are obtained by direct averaging of the corresponding parameters of these two frames. By right clicking at any point of figure the signal calculation procedure is started and the synthesized speech signal is restored.

The main result of the interface program is the synthesized speech signal with the chosen melody curve, energy curve and allophone durations. The auxiliary text files with interpolation data for the curves are also saved.

7   Conclusion

The speech synthesis system is described including the graphic user interface for manipulation with pitch, energy curve and allophone durations. The input data for speech synthesis consists of a sequence of allophones with the desired prosodic features. Allophone units are taken from the database and then modified.

The system is parametric and the database does not contain speech signals but parameter sets for the polyharmonic model or for the stationary random model. Analysis for the database parameterization and synthesis algorithm are based on precise estimation of pitch and all harmonic parameters in small frames. Results of the MOS test look promising.

References

1. Zena, H., Tokudaa, K., Black, A.W.: Statistical Parametric Speech Synthesis. Speech Communication (2009)
2. Lobanov, B.M., Tsirulnik, L.I.: Kompjuternij sintez i klonirovanije rechi, Minsk (2008) (in Russian)

3. Skrelin, P., Volskaya, N., Kocharov, D., Evgrafova, K., Glotova, O., Evdokimova, V.: COR-PRES – Corpus of Russian Professionally Read Speech. In: Sojka, P., Horák, A., Kopeček, I., Pala, K. (eds.) TSD 2010. LNCS, vol. 6231, pp. 392–399. Springer, Heidelberg (2010)
4. Ioannis, S.: Harmonic plus Noise Models for speech, combined with statistical methods, for speech and speaker modification. PhD Thesis. Ecole Nationale Superieure des Telecommunications, Paris (1996)
5. Griffin, D.W., Lim, J.S.: Multiband Excitation Vocoder. IEEE Trans. on Acoustic, Speech and Signal Processing 36(8), 1223–1235 (1988)
6. Skrelin, P.A.: Foneticheskije aspecti rechevih tehnologij, Saint-Petersburg, Doctor of Sciences thesis (1999) (in Russian)
7. Skrelin, P.A.: Segmentacija I transcripcija, Petesburg, SPBGU (1999) (in Russian)

Phrase-Final Segment Lengthening in Russian: Preliminary Results of a Corpus-Based Study

Tatiana Kachkovskaia and Nina Volskaya

Department of Phonetics, Saint Petersburg State University, Russia*
tania.kachkovskaya@gmail.com, volni@phonetics.pu.ru
www.spbu.ru

Abstract. The paper presents preliminary results of a corpus-based study of phrase-final segment lengthening in Russian. The Corpus of Russian Professionally Read Speech (CORPRES) was used to investigate the degree of lengthening for segments immediately preceding phrase boundaries as a function of segment class and boundary type. According to our data, there is a general tendency for shorter segments to show more lengthening than longer segments (in pairs like /f/–/s/, /t/–/tʲ/ etc.). However, this seems to work the opposite way in pairs of fricatives vs. stops. We have also found that boundary depth (sentence-final vs. non-sentence-final) and the presence or absence of a pause have an effect on phrase-final segment lengthening.

Keywords: final lengthening, pre-boundary lengthening, segment duration.

1 Introduction

The phrase-final lengthening effect is traditionally defined as the lengthening of a rhyme (nucleus and coda) occurring before the boundary between prosodic constituents. According to multiple studies on the subject, in many languages this phenomenon is influenced by a number of segmental and prosodic factors [10]. It has been proved that boundary depth has a significant effect on the degree of final lengthening [1] [5] [6], and so does the type of the segment used [3] [5]. However, for Russian there are very few publications on the subject [7] [11] [12].

In this paper we present the results of a corpus-based experiment, in which we analyzed the lengthening of segments immediately preceding prosodic boundaries. In order to obtain reliable results, we have limited our choice to those segment types that frequently occur in phrase-final position. In the end our set included /s/, /t/, /ʃ/, /f/, post-stressed /a/ and post-stressed /i/. For /s/ and /t/ we also included their soft, or palatalized, counterparts, /sʲ/ and /tʲ/.

When analyzing the effects of boundary depth on the duration of segments, we distinguish between two types of intonational units containing nuclear accent: a non-sentence-final unit (prosodic phrase, or p-phrase) and a sentence-final unit (intonational phrase, or i-phrase). Thus, an intonational phrase may consist of more than one prosodic phrase, but not vice versa.

---

* The authors acknowledge Saint Petersburg State University for a research grant (31.37.106.2011).

M. Železný et al. (Eds.): SPECOM 2013, LNAI 8113, pp. 257–263, 2013.

CORPRES [8] developed at the Department of Phonetics, Saint Petersburg State University, is a fully-annotated corpus of Russian speech which contains texts of different speaking styles recorded from 4 male and 4 female speakers. The annotation covers segmental (phonetic and phonemic) transcription as well as prosodic information including the type of pitch movement, the type of boundary, and various degrees of prominence. The results reported in this paper are based on the data obtained from a part of this corpus, which is described as "an action-oriented fiction narrative resembling conversational speech" [8].

2 Experiment Design

2.1 Material

For this experiment we have chosen one of the CORPRES texts recorded from 2 male (A and M) and 2 female (C and K) speakers. From the annotated sound files we obtained duration values for the phrase-final segments of the following types: /s/, /sʲ/, /t/, /tʲ/, /ʃ/, /f/, post-stressed /a/ and post-stressed /i/. The total amount of the analysed phrase-final segments is as follows: /s/ — 198, /sʲ/ — 374, /t/ — 1156, /tʲ/ — 611, /ʃ/ — 263, /f/ — 158, post-stressed /a/ — 2813, post-stressed /i/ — 1647. Examples of the observed segments (speaker C) are given in Figure 1.

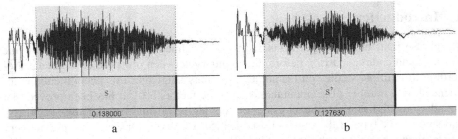

Fig. 1. /s/, 138 ms, taken from the word /ˈtenʲis/ (tennis) at the end of p-phrase before a pause (*a*); /sʲ/, 128 ms, taken from the word /ˈnravʲilʲisʲ/ (liked) at the end of p-phrase before a pause (*b*)

The choice of this set of phonemes was motivated by several factors. In our material some segment types are not very frequent in p-final position, e. g. stressed vowels, /u/, soft /f/, hard and soft /p/. In Russian voiced consonants appear in phrase-final position only when immediately followed by voiced consonants, which means they are impossible before a pause and very rare at boundaries where no pause is present. Post-stressed /e/ and /o/ are also extremely rare since in unstressed syllables they are usually substituted by /i/ and /a/ respectively. It is worth noting here that post-stressed /i/ and /a/ are reduced, both in quality and quantity, compared to their stressed counterparts.

For convenience of comparison we decided to observe pairs or triplets of phonemes differing in only one distinctive feature.

2.2 Method

Using prosodic information obtained from the CORPRES annotation files, we automatically found the segments immediately preceding p- and i-phrase boundaries. Then we calculated the segment duration values using the information presented in the "phonetic transcription" tier which reflects the real pronunciation of segments by a given speaker.

For the purposes of our study, we measured segment duration values relative to the mean duration for this segment type, calculated over the whole corpus, i.e. across all positions within a word or a phrase. (It should be noted here that in our case a relative duration value below 1 does not imply final shortening.) The mean duration values for all segments observed here are presented in Table 1.

Table 1. Mean segment duration values for 4 speakers (ms)

	Speaker A	Speaker C	Speaker K	Speaker M	Mean
/s/	100	88	84	101	93
/sʲ/	107	100	101	116	106
/t/	81	81	84	78	81
/tʲ/	102	100	95	92	96
/ʃ/	105	98	99	113	104
/f/	76	75	62	74	72
post-stressed /a/	72	66	61	56	64
post-stressed /i/	67	52	51	51	55

Since we assume boundary type as one of the factors influencing final lengthening, we analyzed the degree of segment lengthening separately in three groups: before a p-phrase boundary with no pause, before a p-phrase boundary with a pause, and before an i-phrase boundary with a pause (i-phrase boundaries with no pause are extremely rare in this corpus). To decrease the influence of other prosodic factors, we analyzed only those segments taken from words under nuclear stress.

According to our segmentation criteria, a vowel before a pause was judged to last until either the continuous formant structure or voicing ended. Thus, we did not include voiceless or creaky ending.

All the data were subjected to statistical analysis using ANOVA. For pairwise comparison we used two-tailed Welch's t-test.

3 Results

3.1 Segment Type

In Russian soft, or palatalised, consonants are involved in phonological contrasts, which enables us to treat them as individual phonemes. These consonants are on average longer than their hard, or non-palatalised, counterparts [9], which is also confirmed by our data (see Table 1). However, phrase-final lengthening seems to work the opposite way. Figure 2 shows the degree of lengthening (relative to the mean duration calculated for this type of allophone over the whole corpus) for the pairs /s/–/sʲ/ and /t/–/tʲ/, across different boundary types. These values are averaged across all 4 speakers, although each speaker shows the same general tendencies. Here we can see that for each boundary type the degree of lengthening is higher for hard consonants compared to their soft counterparts.

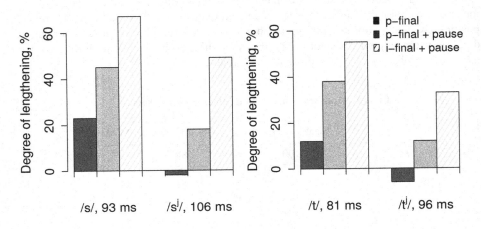

Fig. 2. Degree of phrase-final lengthening for pairs /s/–/sʲ/ and /t/–/tʲ/ averaged across 4 speakers, for three boundary types. For each segment type its mean duration value is provided.

The tendency for shorter segments to show more phrase-final lengthening can also be observed if we compare voiceless fricatives of different types. Figure 3 shows the degree of lengthening for the segments /f/, /s/ and /ʃ/ averaged across 4 speakers. Of these three consonant types, /f/ is on average the shortest (see Table 1), while /ʃ/ is the longest. However, the degree of phrase-final lengthening is the lowest for /ʃ/ and the highest for /f/.

Similar results for /f/ and /s/ can be found in [3] for the English language. Although the authors measure lengthening effect relative to the segment's duration in non-sentence-final position, the data provided in [3] are sufficient to estimate the mean duration values for /f/ and /s/ and then calculate the lengthening effect relative to them. This method enables us to reveal higher lengthening effect for /f/ compared to /s/, which is consistent with our results for the Russian language.

Our data show the same tendency for post-stressed vowels /a/ and /i/ (see Fig. 4): vowel /i/, which is on average shorter, is lengthened more than /a/ in all positions.

However, the tendency for shorter segments to show more phrase-final lengthening than longer segments does not seem to be true for stop vs. fricative voiceless dental consonants (see Fig. 2): according to our data, consonant /s/, despite its higher average duration, shows a greater lengthening effect than /t/ (and the same is observed for their palatalized counterparts, /sʲ/–/tʲ/). These findings are supported by the data provided in [5] for Dutch. Thus, we might suppose that fricatives tend to demonstrate

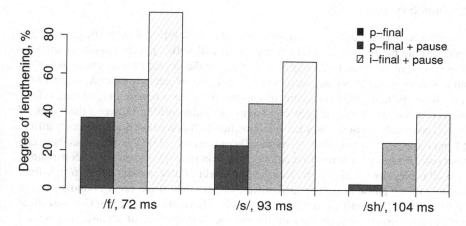

Fig. 3. Degree of phrase-final lengthening for pairs /f/, /s/ and /ʃ/ averaged across 4 speakers, for three boundary types. For each segment type its mean duration value is provided.

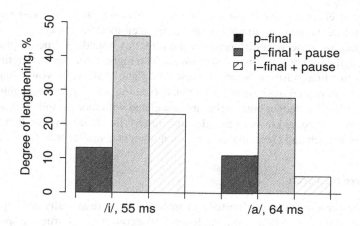

Fig. 4. Degree of phrase-final lengthening for post-stressed /i/ and post-stressed /a/ averaged across 4 speakers, for three boundary types. For each segment type its mean duration value is provided.

more phrase-final lengthening than stops, but this claim needs further investigation with other types of stops and fricatives (e. g. /k/ vs. /x/) involved.

We left other types of segments beyond the scope of the present study since most of them are very rare in phrase-final position and therefore require a much larger corpus. However, it is of great interest whether the tendency described above is true for these rare segment types, and whether it is true for other languages as well.

3.2 Boundary Type

As mentioned above, here we distinguish between three types of prosodic boundaries: p-final with no pause, p-final with a pause and i-final with a pause. Statistical analysis shows that boundary type has a significant effect on the degree of segment lengthening in all cases across speakers and segment types but one, which is speaker A, segment /f/.

For the consonants pairwise comparisons do not always reveal a significant effect. However, some speakers are very consistent in distinguishing between the types of prosodic boundaries. For speaker K i-final position before a pause is significantly different from the other two boundary types for all consonants, while the difference between p-final position and p-final position before a pause in non-significant for all consonants. In a similar way, for speaker C the lengthening effect of all consonants but /f/ in p-final position with no pause is significantly different from that of the other boundary types, which do not differ significantly from each other. Therefore, for speaker C phrase-final lengthening seems to depend only on the presence or absence of a pause, but not on boundary depth. These results seem to confirm the idea that the effect of boundary type on final lengthening is speaker specific. Similar tendencies were observed in Dutch in [2], where the influence of boundary type on word lengthening was found to be speaker specific.

For the vowels pairwise comparisons show a significant effect in a vast majority of cases. Therefore our results did not reveal any speaker-specific traits.

In our data we observe a difference in the effect of boundary type on phrase-final segment lengthening on consonants vs. vowels. The highest consonant lengthening effect occurs in i-final position before a pause (see Figs. 2–3), while vowel lengthening is the highest in p-final position before a pause (see Fig. 4). Thus, consonants seem to confirm the idea that deeper boundaries are associated with more lengthening [5]. Vowels, which are unstressed in our case, do not support the idea; however, there is some evidence for French and German that words lengthen in a similar way [4].

3.3 Future Research

Since in the present study we limited our material to professionally read speech, the next step is to find out whether the tendencies observed here are true for spontaneous speech as well. Another focus area is to include those types of segments which were not observed due to contextual restrictions. Thus we hope to be able to analyse more pairs of consonants in the groups of hard vs. soft and frivatives vs. stops.

4   Conclusions

According to our data, in Russian

- there is a tendency for shorter segments to demonstrate more phrase-final lengthening than longer segments. This is true for the following groups of segments:
    - soft vs. hard voiceless dental consonants: /s/–/sʲ/, /t/–/tʲ/;
    - hard voiceless fricatives: /f/–/s/–/ʃ/;

- post-stressed /a/ vs. post-stressed /i/; (other segment types were not observed in the present study)
- within the group of voiceless dental consonants (/s/–/t/, /sʲ/–/tʲ/) fricatives demonstrate a greater lengthening effect than stops;
- the effect of boundary type on phrase-final segment lengthening is significant for all speakers and all the observed segment types excluding one (speaker A, segment /f/);
- for the consonants, the way boundary type influences phrase-final segment lengthening is probably speaker-specific;
- the boundary type that shows the highest lengthening effect is different for consonants vs. vowels: for the consonants it is i-final position before a pause, while for vowels — p-final position before a pause.

References

1. Byrd, D.: Articulatory Vowel Lengthening and Coordination at Phrasal Junctures. Phonetica 57, 3–16 (2000)
2. Cambier-Langeveld, T.: Temporal marking of accents and boundaries. Dissertation, University of Amsterdam (2000)
3. Cooper, W.E., Danly, M.: Segmental and temporal aspects of utterance-final lengthening. Phonetica 38 (1981)
4. Fery, C., Hoernig, R., Pahaut, S.: Correlates of phrasing in French and German from an experiment with semi-spontaneous speech. In: Gabriel, C., Lleo, C. (eds.) Intonational Phrasing at the Interfaces: Cross-Linguistic and Bilingual Studies in Romance and Germanic, pp. 11–41 (2011)
5. Hofhuis, E., Gussenhoven, C., Rietveld, A.: Final lengthening at prosodic boundaries in Dutch. ICPhS 13, Stockholm: KTH and Dept Linguistics, University of Stockholm, pp. 154–157 (1995)
6. Horne, M., Strangert, E., Heldner, M.: Prosodic boundary strength in Swedish: final lengthening and silent interval duration. In: Proc. XIIIth ICPhS (1995)
7. Krivnova, O.F.: Pre-pausal lengthening of vowels in connected speech. In: ARSO-16, pp. 153–154 (1991) (in Russian)
8. Skrelin, P., Volskaya, N., Kocharov, D., Evgrafova, K., Glotova, O., Evdokimova, V.: A fully annotated corpus of Russian speech. In: Proc. of the 7th Conference on International Language Resources and Evaluation, pp. 109–112 (2010)
9. Tananaiko, S., Vasilieva, L.: Consonant features in spontaneous and read-aloud Russian. In: de Silva, V., Ullakonoja, R. (eds.) Phonetics of Russian and Finnish, pp. 115–132 (2009)
10. Vaissière, J.: Language-Independent Prosodic Features. In: Cutler, A., Ladd, R. (eds.) Prosody: Models and Measurements, vol. 14, pp. 53–66 (1983)
11. Volskaya, N., Stepanova, S.: On the temporal component of intonational phrasing. In: Proc. of SPECOM (2004)
12. Volskaya, N., Stepanova, S.: Pre-pausal lengthening in Russian. In: Experimental Phonetical Analysis of Speech: Issues and Methods, St. Petersburg, vol. 5, pp. 48–55 (2004) (in Russian)

Pseudo Real-Time Spoken Term Detection Using Pre-retrieval Results

Yoshiaki Itoh[1], Hiroyuki Saito[1], Kazuyo Tanaka[2], and Shi-wook Lee[3]

[1] Iwate Prefectural University, Sugo, Takizawa, Iwate, Japan
y-itoh@iwate-pu.ac.jp, g231j018@s.iwate-pu.ac.jp
[2] University of Tsukuba, Kasuga, Tsukuba, Ibaraki, Japan
ktanaka@slis.tsukuba.ac.jp
[3] AIST, Umezono, Tsukuba, Ibaraki, Japan
s.lee@voiser.co.jp

Abstract. Spoken term detection (STD) is one of key technologies for spoken document processing. This paper describes a method to realize pseudo real-time spoken term detection using pre-retrieval results. Pre-retrieval results for all combination of syllable bigrams are prepared beforehand. The retrieval time depends on the number of candidate sections of the pre-retrieval results. Therefore, the paper proposes the method to control the retrieval time by the number. A few top candidates are obtained in almost real-time by limiting the small number of candidate sections. While a user is confirming the candidate sections, the system can conduct the rest of retrieval by increasing the number of candidate sections gradually. The paper demonstrate the proposed method enables pseudo real-time spoken term detection by evaluation experiments using actual presentation speech corpus; Corpus of Spontaneous Japanese (CSJ).

Keywords: Spoken term detection, real-time, pre-retrieval results, syllable bigram.

1 Introduction

Spoken term detection (STD) is one of key technologies for spoken document processing. The function fo STD is demanded to search for scenes of interest in a section of large scale multimedia data. Many STD researches have been conducted recently at the Text Retrieval Conference (TREC) and the 9th and 10th Workshop of the National Institute of Informatics Test Collection for Information Retrieval Systems (NTCIR-9,10) [1,2,3]. The recognition results of an automatic speech recognizer are usually utilized if the query word is found in the recognizer's dictionary. However, the selected query word is often a special term that is not included in such dictionaries. Such a word is so-called OOV (Out Of Vocabulary), and STD systems must deal with such an OOV word as a query word. Therefore, subword units such as monophones and triphones are used to deal with unknown words. Reduction of retrieval time is one of important problems in STD systems based on subword units because considerable time is needed to match all subword recognition results in spoken documents with a subword sequence of a query word.

M. Železný et al. (Eds.): SPECOM 2013, LNAI 8113, pp. 264–270, 2013.

This paper proposes a method to realize pseudo real-time spoken term detection using pre-retrieval results. Pre-retrieval results for all combination of syllable bigrams are prepared beforehand. The method was proposed in [4]. The method enables a reduction of the matching process by referring to the pre-retrieval results generated from the spoken documents in the first step. Given a query in Japanese, the syllable sequence of the query is automatically obtained because Japanese words are inherently composed of syllable sequences. In the second step of the method, the syllable sequence is divided into multiple bigrams. In this step, the candidate sections are filtered by using the scores of the query's syllable bigrams. This process reduces the number of candidates sections. In the third step, detailed matching is performed against these reduced candidate sections and the candidate sections are re-scored.

Let the number of syllable to be N and the number of candidate sections for each syllable bigram to be K. The number of all candidate sections for pre-retrieval results becomes $N \times N \times K$. The retrieval time depends on the number of candidate sections of the pre-retrieval results. For example, there are four syllable bigrams if a query term includes five syllables. The above mentioned system performs detail matching against $4 \times K$ candidate sections at maximum. Therefore, the paper proposes the method to control the retrieval time by the number of candidate sections K. A few top candidates are obtained in almost real-time by limiting K to the small number of candidate sections. A user who performs STD has to confirm whether the candidate sections are correct or not by listening them. While the user is confirming them, the system can conduct the rest of retrieval by increasing K gradually without deteriorating the retrieval performance.

Though many studies have been conducted on subword-based STD systems and methods to increase their retrieval speeds [5]-[10], the majority of these methods have used an inverted index or a suffix array to construct an index of subword recognition results. Performing a robust approximate search on such an index is difficult considering the deletion and insertion errors. As the results, the relation between the retrieval performance and the retrieval time becomes trade-off. In contrast, the proposed method enables approximate searching by retrieving syllable bigrams in advance, and candidate sections can be selected without removing sections that contain errors since these are accounted for in the detailed matching. The paper demonstrates the proposed method enables pseudo real-time spoken term detection without deteriorating the retrieval performance. by evaluation experiments using actual presentation speech corpus; Corpus of Spontaneous Japanese (CSJ).

2 Proposed Method

2.1 Outline of STD System

Figure 1 shows a process chart outlining the STD system in [4]. First, syllable recognition is performed for all of the spoken documents using subword acoustic models and their associated language models, and syllable recognition results of spoken documents are all prepared a priori (1). It can be assumed without loss of generality that any statement that includes a query word also includes all syllable bigrams that make up the query. The target sections can be limited by using the retrieval results of such bigrams of the query. Therefore, pre-retrieval results are prepared a priori by retrieving all combinations of syllable bigrams. When a query is given by a user, the syllable sequence of the query is divided into plural syllable bigrams. By conducting detail matching by Continuous Dynamic Programming (CDP) for only those sections included in the pre-retrieval results of the query's bigrams, fast retrieval is realized. The process of the method is composed of the following five procedures.

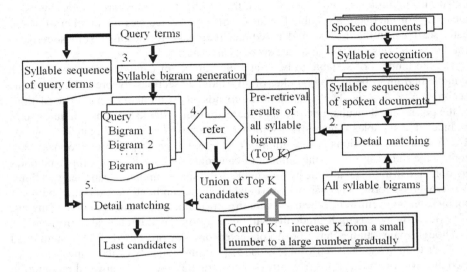

Fig. 1. Outline of STD system using pre-retrieval results of syllable bigrams

1. Syllable recognition using syllables, triphones, and so on is performed for all spoken documents such that they are converted to syllable sequences.
2. Pre-retrieval is conducted by using all combinations of syllable bigrams as queries, and highly ranked candidate sections are retained for each bigram sequence. Here, let K denote the number of candidate sections.
3. When a text query is given by a user, the query is automatically converted into a syllable sequence, which is then divided into syllable bigrams by shifting a syllable bigram window. When the length of a query is L, the number of syllable bigrams is $L - 1$.
4. Pre-retrieval results are referred to for each syllable bigram in the query, and all pre-retrieval results for the syllable bigrams are merged. These candidate sections are called the "first candidate sections".
5. Detailed matching by CDP is performed only for the first candidate sections, which are rescored and submitted to the user as "last candidate sections" according to their ranked order.

When a user inputs a text query, it is automatically converted into a syllable sequence according to a set of conversion rules (2). The phonic sequence of a user-input query term to be pronounced is automatically obtained from the term's syllables. By using Continuous Dynamic Programming (CDP) algorithms, the system then retrieves the target section by comparing a query syllable sequence with all syllable sequences found in the spoken documents (3). We use the acoustic distance as a local distance measure, where the acoustic local distance represents the dissimilarity between two triphones and indicates the statistical distance between any two HMM triphone models. The system outputs multiple candidate sections that have a high degree of similarity to the query word. Each candidate section thus has a distance and a section number of spoken documents.

2.2 Pseudo Real-Time Retrieval

The second procedure in the previous section states that candidate sections within the K candidates are retained, and the fourth procedure states that the number of candidate sections processed for the detailed matching in the fifth procedure is the sum of the $L-1$ bigrams of query terms. Therefore, the number amounts to $K \times (L - 1)$ at maximum. If let K to be 25, 000 to avoid the performance deterioration, the retrieval time required 2.9 seconds for 600 hours spoken documents in [4]. The computation is mainly the fifth procedure to perform CDP against $25, 000 \times (L - 1)$ candidate sections.

The retrieval time depends on the number of candidate sections. Therefore, the paper propose the method to control the retrieval time by the number of candidate sections K. The basic idea of the method is that the top candidate section of query terms is included in the top candidate sections of bigrams included in the query terms. Therefore, even by limiting K to the small number of candidate sections as shown in Figure 1, a few top candidates are not dropped, and the retrieval time can be reduced to almost real-time level. A user who performs STD has to confirm whether the candidate sections are correct or not by listening them. While the user is confirming the top candidate section, the system can conduct the rest of retrieval by increasing K gradually without deteriorating the retrieval performance. The proposed method can make a user feel no-waiting time.

3   Evaluation Experiments

3.1   Experimental Conditions

We used the open test collections of the NTCIR-9 workshop in 2011 [2]. The test collections, which were dry run sets in NTCIR-9, include 50 queries and 177 and 2702 presentation speech data or spoken documents that are the so called "CORE" and gALLh, respectively, using the Corpus of Spontaneous Japanese (CSJ) database. About 2,500 presentation speech data other than the CORE in the CSJ database are used for training acoustic models and language models for a CORE task. The all CSJ data is divided into two data sets by the odd and even presentation numbers for open recognition of an ALL task. The feature extraction conditions used here for acoustic models are listed in Table 1. Julius version 4.1.5 was used as the syllable recognition decoder in experiments.

We used three states and right-to-left Hidden Markov Models (HMM) as acoustic models of each triphone, and syllable bigrams and trigrams as language models.

Table 1. Feature extraction conditions for acoustic models

Sampling	16 kHz 16 bit
Feature Parameter	12-dim. MFCC
	12-dim. MFCC + energy
	12-dim. MFCC + energy
Window Length	25 ms
Frame Shift	10 ms
Acoustic Model	triphone HMM

These models were trained by using the half of CSJ (odd or even ID) mentioned above and were used for recognition of the rest of the half of CSJ. 261 Japanese syllables were used in the experiments. We prepared syllable bigram pre-retrieval results by retrieving all syllables bigram combinations (2612) in the spoken documents a priori. Candidate sections were then stored in hash memory.

We evaluate the method using MAP (mean average precision), precision rate within top candidate sections and its retrieval time. MAP was employed in NTCIR-9. Average precision (AP) for a query is obtained by averaging the precisions at every correct occurrence, and MAP is then the averaged AP of all queries. The processing time was obtained when using a personal computer with an Intel Core i7 2600 processor, 8 GB of memory, and a Linux operating system.

3.2   Results for Pre-retrieval Results of Syllable Bigrams

Table 2 shows the baseline results; the retrieval performance (MAP (%)) and retrieval time (s) for a query according to the number of candidates sections (K) about 600 hours presentation speech data for spoken document. "all" in the table denotes the case of conducting CDP for all speech datasets, and upper limit of the retrieval performance.

Table 2 shows MAP at $K = 25,000$ did not declined compared with that at "all", and the retrieval time was reduced from 16.375 to 2.867 s. Although the method could reduce retrieval time the retrieval time required still more than 2 seconds when sustaining retrieval performance. MAP denotes the total performance of an STD system from

Table 2. Baseline results: Retrieval performance (MAP (%)) and retrieval time (s) for a query according to the number of candidates sections (K)

	All	K	25,000	15,000	7,500	5,000	1,000
MAP(%)	66.37		66.37	66.12	65.86	64.35	54.16
Time(s)	16.375		2.867	1.883	0.964	0.649	0.156

a low precision rate to a high precision rate. When K is small such as 1,000, MAP was low because high recall was not able to be obtained. The results indicates the computation time is required for obtaining high recall rate by processing many candidate sections.

Table 3. Precision rate and retrieval time obtaining top candidates shown to a user according to K

K	The number of top candidates shown to a user				Time(s)
	1	3	5	10	
1,000	94.0	84.7	82.4	69.4	0.156
3,000	96.0	90.0	88.0	74.4	0.398
7,500	96.0	90.0	90.0	78.2	0.964
all	94.0	90.0	90.0	77.8	16.135

Table 3 shows the precision rates and the retrieval time to obtain top candidates that are shown to a user according to K, comparing with those of "all". At $K = 1,000$, the same precision rate for top candidate was obtained as that of "all" within 0.156 second. In the same way, the same precision rate for three candidates was obtained as that of "all" within 0.398 second at $K = 3,000$, and the same precision rates for five and ten candidates were obtained as those of "all" within 1 second at $K = 7,500$. The results indicate the system can offer a user the top candidate within 0.156 second without deteriorating the retrieval performance. The waiting time is short and it is thought that a user can obtain the STD results without feeling the waiting time. Because additional text information is not usually attached to the STD results, a user has to confirm the top candidate. Ten candidates are obtained within 1 second, and all candidates are obtained while the user is listening and confirming the top candidate. The propose method realizes pseudo real-time system for a user.

4 Conclusions

This paper proposed a method to realize pseudo real-time spoken term detection using pre-retrieval results. Pre-retrieval results for all combination of syllable bigrams are prepared beforehand. We controlled the number of candidate sections of pre-retrieval results for detailed matching because the retrieval time depends on the number of candidate sections. The experimental results demonstrated the top candidate shown to a user was obtained within 0.156 second without deteriorating the retrieval performance by limiting the small number of candidate sections for detailed matching. While a user is confirming the candidate sections, the system can conduct the rest of retrieval. Ten candidates are obtained within 1 second, and all candidates are obtained during the user's confirming time. The results showed the proposed method enabled pseudo real-time STD system for a user.

Acknowledgments. This research is supported by Grand-in-Aid for Scientific Research (C) Project No. 24500124, KAKENHI of Japan Society for Promotion of Science.

References

1. Auzanne, C., Garofolo, J.S., Fiscus, J.G., Fisher, W.M.: Automatic Language Model Adaptation for Spoken Document Retrieval, B1, 2000TREC-9 SDR Track (2000)
2. Akiba, T., Nishizaki, H., Aikawa, K., Kawahara, T., Matsui, T.: Overview of the IR for Spoken Documents Task in NTCIR-9 Workshop. In: Proceedings of the 9th NTCIR Workshop Meeting on Evaluation of Information Access Technologies: Information Retrieval, Question Answering and Cross-lingual Information Access, pp. 223–235 (2011)
3. http://research.nii.ac.jp/ntcir/ntcir-10/index.html
4. Saito, Y., et al.: Fast Spoken Term Detection Using Pre-retrieval Results of Syllable Bigrams. In: Asia-Pacific Signal and Information Processing Association, APSIPA, 4 pages (2012)
5. Kaneko, T., Akiba, T.: Metric Subspace Indexing for Fast Spoken Term Detection. In: INTERSPEECH 2010 (2010)
6. Pinto, J., Szoke, I., Prasanna, S.R.M., Hermansky, H.: Fast Approximate Spoken Term Detection from Sequence of Phonemes. IDIPA RESEARCH REPORT 2008 (2008)
7. Miller, D.R.H., Kleber, M., Kao, C.-L., Kimball, O., Colthurst, T., Lowe, S.A., Schwartz, R.M., Gish, H.: Rapid and Accurate Spoken Term Detection. In: INTERSPEECH 2007 (2007)
8. Katsurada, K., Sawada, S., Teshima, S., Iribe, Y., Nitta, T.: Evaluation of Fast Spoken Term Detection Using a Suffix Array. In: INTERSPEECH 2011, pp. 909–912 (2011)
9. Itoh, Y., Otake, T., Iwata, K., Kojima, K., Ishigame, M., Tanaka, K., Lee, S.-W.: Two-stage Vocabulary-free Spoken Document Retrieval - Subword Identification and Re-recognition of the Identified Sections. In: ICSLP, pp. 1161–1164 (2006)
10. Iwami, K., Fujii, Y., Yamamoto, K., Nakagawa, S.: Out-of-vocabulary term detection by n-gram array with distance from continuous syllable recognition results. In: SLT, pp. 200–205 (2010)

Results for Variable Speaker and Recording Conditions on Spoken IR in Finnish

Ville T. Turunen, Mikko Kurimo, and Sami Keronen

Department of Signal Processing and Acoustics, Aalto University,
P.O. Box 13000, FI-00076 Aalto, Finland
{ville.t.turunen,mikko.kurimo,sami.keronen}@aalto.fi

Abstract. The performance of current spoken information retrieval (IR) systems depend on the success of automatic speech recognition (ASR) to provide transcripts of the material for indexing. In addition to the ASR system design, ASR performance is strongly affected by the recording conditions, speakers, speaking style and speech content. However, the average word error rate in ASR is not a relevant measure for spoken IR, where only the extracted index terms or keywords matter. In this paper, we measure the spoken IR performance in variable material ranging from controlled single speaker news reading to real-world broadcasts with variable conditions, speakers, and background noise. The effect of using multicondition acoustic models and online adaptation is also studied, as well as controlled addition of background babble noise. The experiments are performed in Finnish, which is an agglutinative and highly inflected language, using morph-based language modelling.

1 Introduction

Typical applications of speech retrieval include indexing and retrieval from very large audiovisual archives. The archives may cover tens of years of radio or television broadcasts over different channels or even larger collections such as YouTube where millions of users have uploaded recordings. For example, in March 2012, 60 hours of video was being uploaded to YouTube per minute. The research of methods for improving the speech retrieval requires annotated evaluation databases where the performance of the systems can be measured and compared to each other. However, these collections have until recently been much smaller and the annotated documents more homogeneous in style and quality than the archives people now use in their every day lives. The consequence of this mismatch is that best performing automatic speech recognition (ASR) and retrieval systems may not meet the requirements of most users.

The simplest way to evaluate speech retrieval performance for rich large vocabulary speech content, such as news, is to record reading of topically annotated news texts [1]. Difficulty of the task can be increased by using a large number of non-professional readers and allowing natural background noises. Real broadcasts and speech recordings can be used as well, but the more colloquial the speech is, the harder the speech is to transcribe and annotate. Thus, for most languages the preparation of large evaluation databases with heterogeneous and difficult speech data is too expensive given the available resources.

M. Železný et al. (Eds.): SPECOM 2013, LNAI 8113, pp. 271–277, 2013.

In this paper, an experimental study is presented to show how the speech retrieval performance may deteriorate when the speech material becomes more difficult for the real-time speech recognizer. For this material, the effect of the most effective and general online noise compensation methods, multicondition acoustic models and rapid speaker adaptation, is measured also for speech retrieval. The impact of various levels of background noise is evaluated by a controlled addition of babble noise to the speech recordings.

The speech data in the experiments are in Finnish, which is an agglutinative and highly inflectional language. Thus, the large-vocabulary ASR and IR are based on combining words with sub-word language modelling using statistical morphs as the lexical and indexing terms [2,3]. Although the morph-based ASR and IR require some special solutions, it is likely that the current study of the impact of acoustic variability and its compensation methods is indicative also for other languages.

2 Methods

2.1 Morph-Based Speech Retrieval

For speech retrieval performance, two evaluation methods are applied: Spoken Document Retrieval (SDR) and Ranked Utterance Retrieval (RUR) [4].

In SDR, the recognized speech is divided into documents that are indexed based on occurrence of automatically selected index terms. In morph-based ASR and IR [3], the ASR output consists of morphs with word break boundaries marked, and a full text index covers both the recognized morphs and base form words obtained using a morphological analyzer [5]. Automatically generated stop lists, that include the most common words and morphs in the corpus, are used. Other studies where various subword units have been used in speech retrieval include, for example, indexing subword lattices [6] and phonetic transcripts [7].

For ranking the documents, the words in the queries are split into morphs and transformed to base form words by the morphological analyzer. In this work, the ranking is based on the OKAPI BM25 ranking function using Lemur-toolkit [8]. As shown in the earlier work (e.g. [3]) for agglutinative words, SDR also works well using the morphs only, thus avoiding the steps of first building the words and then baseforming them. However, a combined index of both morphs and base forms gives the most accurate results.

In RUR, the task is to rank the utterances by the estimated likelihood that they contain the query term. Standard information retrieval metrics for ranked lists, such as Mean Average Precision (MAP), can be used for evaluation. The utterances that actually contain the query word are the ones considered relevant. For Finnish, a modification to the task was considered appropriate: the query word was always given in its base form, and the task was to find the utterances that contained the word in any inflected form. The documents are ranked in the same way as in SDR by finding the morphs and base forms of the query words, and using OKAPI BM25 ranking function.

The SDR evaluation is somewhat different if the locations in the audio where the topic shifts are not known. The task is then to find and rank the locations where the portion, that is relevant to the user's query, starts. The corpus is first segmented to stories automatically, and OKAPI BM25 is used to rank the discovered documents. The start points of the ranked documents are compared to the list of known relevant replay points using Generalized Average Precision (GAP) [9]. Full score is given to replay points that match the reference point exactly. The score decays linearly until 30 seconds in either direction from the reference point, after which replay points are considered non-relevant.

2.2 Morph-Based ASR

ASR was performed using the Finnish morph-based large-vocabulary ASR system developed at Aalto University [10]. The acoustic models are fairly standard context-dependent triphone HMMs with GMM emission probabilities using MFCC, delta and delta-delta features. The baseline models were trained by selecting the quiet office environment data recorded by close-talking microphones from 310 speakers of the Finnish Speecon corpus. In addition, we constructed acoustic models using a multicondition training set consisting of half noiseless speech and half noisy recordings from the Speecon public place and car environments at three microphone distances. Both training sets had about 19.5 hours of speech.

To study the compensation performance of fast speaker adaptation to speaker, recording environment, and background noise level variability, maximum likelihood linear regression (MLLR) was applied. The constrained MLLR (cMLLR), in which a single transformation matrix is used for for both the Gaussian means and variances, was used to reduce the amount of adaptation parameters and adaptation data requirements.

The language models training corpus consisted of 158M words of newspaper text, books and newswire stories. The corpus was split into morphs before training, and variable order n-grams were trained using VariKN-toolkit [11]. The morph lexicon consisted of 19k morphs, whereas the unsplit corpus had 4.1M unique word forms.

3   Materials and Experiments

To examine the effect of variable acoustic conditions, three different Finnish speech retrieval corpora were used for testing: Newsreader, Classroom, and Broadcast. For studying the impact of various background noise levels, the Newsreader and Classroom speech data sets were mixed with voice babble noise from NOISEX-92 database [12] at signal-to-noise ratios (SNRs) 6 and 9 dB to simulate slightly higher noise levels than usually assumed in speech collections.

The first corpus ("Newsreader") was used for SDR experiments. The corpus has been used previously in e.g. [1,2]. The corpus consists of 288 Finnish news stories read by a single female speaker in a quiet environment. Each news story corresponds to exactly one of 17 different topics. The topic descriptions were used as queries.

The second corpus ("Classroom") is presented here for the first time. It contains recordings of sentences extracted from newspaper texts. The utterances were recorded in a computer classroom using a headset microphone. The recording conditions were not silent: e.g. sounds of keyboards and speech from other people can be heard in the background. The speakers were not professionals: disfluencies such as false starts and fillers commonly occur. A total of 1515 utterances from 94 speakers were collected (3.5 hours of speech).

The Classroom utterances were used for RUR experiments. For generating the queries, base forms of the words in the reference transcripts were found using a morphological analyzer [5]. Compound words were not split, and names of people were considered as a single item. The frequencies of base forms and names were counted and all items that occurred more than 8 times in the corpus were used as queries. Common stop words were manually excluded. There was a total of 171 queries, 8 of which were names of people. Queries include items such as "maakaasu" (*natural gas*), "Keski-Suomi" (*central Finland*), "IAEA", and "Saddam Hussein".

A third corpus ("Broadcast") was used for SDR in an unknown boundary condition. It consists of 136 hours of broadcast radio programs collected as mp3-podcasts. The programs cover multiple topics each and have variable type of material from planned news readings to live telephone and on-location interviews. There are 25 TREC-like topic descriptions with a total of 451 relevant replay points. The topic descriptions were used to prepare two versions of queries: *T-query* for only the short topic field and *TD-query* for both the topic field and the long description field. The material was segmented to stories using a TextTiling-like [13] algorithm on the ASR text [3].

4   Results

Table 1 shows results for the ASR error rate measurements. Only the Newsreader and Classroom corpora have reference transcriptions available. Word Error Rate (WER) is not very descriptive for Finnish ASR, because a concept that takes multiple words in English can be expressed as a single word in Finnish. Small error in e.g. the inflection of the word, will cause the whole word to be counted as wrong. Therefore, Letter Error Rate (LER), was also used.

Results for the speech retrieval experiments are presented in Table 2. The results in the three different corpora are not directly comparable to each other, because the tasks and evaluation metrics vary. However, it is interesting to check the relative effect of speaker adaptation and multicondition acoustic models to the retrieval methods and additive noise.

In Newsreader corpus, where the queries are long and the speaker and recording conditions constant, MAP is not much affected by the ASR. However, in Classroom corpus,

Table 1. Word Error Rates (WER) and Letter Error Rates (LER) for the Classroom and Newsreader corpora. Noise was added the corpora with different signal-to-noise ratios (SNR). Baseline (BL) acoustic models were trained using clean speech and Multicondition (MC) models using data with variable noise. Speaker adaptation by cMLLR was added to both models.

corpus	SNR	BL		BL+cMLLR		MC		MC+cMLLR	
		WER	LER	WER	LER	WER	LER	WER	LER
Classroom		28.9	13.4	25.7	11.8	30.1	14.1	27.0	12.5
Classroom	9dB	61.5	41.9	49.9	31.0	47.7	27.8	41.0	22.3
Classroom	6dB	79.8	62.6	72.8	55.0	59.2	38.2	51.8	31.8
Newsreader		16.7	4.3	15.0	3.6	19.0	5.1	16.5	4.2
Newsreader	9dB	47.3	29.0	26.1	10.6	20.7	6.3	17.7	4.9
Newsreader	6dB	73.0	57.0	55.5	38.7	27.6	10.9	22.0	7.3

Table 2. Mean Average Precisions (MAP) for the Classroom and Newsreader corpora, and Generalized Average Precisions (GAP) for the Broadcast corpus. Noise was added to the Classroom and Newsreader corpora with different signal-to-noise ratios (SNR). Broadcast corpus had long (TD) and short (T) versions of the queries. Indexing was performed using morphs, base forms (bf) or both morphs and base forms (combined). Baseline (BL) acoustic models were trained using clean speech and Multicondition (MC) models using data with variable noise. Speaker adaptation by cMLLR was added to both models.

corpus	SNR	index	query	BL	BL+cMLLR	MC	MC+cMLLR
Classroom		morph		0.5033	0.5132	0.4917	0.5039
Classroom		bf		0.6458	0.6584	0.6277	0.6420
Classroom		combined		0.6975	0.7097	0.6835	0.6988
Classroom	9dB	morph		0.3039	0.3795	0.3989	0.4397
Classroom	9dB	bf		0.3790	0.4705	0.4931	0.5483
Classroom	9dB	combined		0.4133	0.5143	0.5419	0.5953
Classroom	6dB	morph		0.1652	0.2315	0.3193	0.3625
Classroom	6dB	bf		0.2203	0.2868	0.4032	0.4642
Classroom	6dB	combined		0.2367	0.3142	0.4411	0.4952
Newsreader		morph		0.8361	0.8348	0.8279	0.8245
Newsreader		bf		0.8083	0.8131	0.7962	0.8028
Newsreader		combined		0.8544	0.8548	0.8461	0.8487
Newsreader	9dB	morph		0.7361	0.8128	0.8168	0.8264
Newsreader	9dB	bf		0.7003	0.7830	0.7903	0.7952
Newsreader	9dB	combined		0.7671	0.8272	0.8358	0.8449
Newsreader	6dB	morph		0.4637	0.6421	0.8009	0.8164
Newsreader	6dB	bf		0.4804	0.6533	0.7639	0.7906
Newsreader	6dB	combined		0.5256	0.7075	0.8142	0.8362
Broadcast		morph	TD	0.4772	-	0.4746	-
Broadcast		morph	T	0.3491	-	0.3445	-
Broadcast		bf	TD	0.4648	-	0.4665	-
Broadcast		bf	T	0.3722	-	0.3787	-
Broadcast		combined	TD	0.4909	-	0.4871	-
Broadcast		combined	T	0.4063	-	0.4125	-

which has single word queries and variable speakers and conditions, the recognition errors increase substantially and the improvement obtained by adaptation is visible also in MAP. The multicondition trained acoustic models are not helpful on the original recordings, not even on the Broadcast data, but when noise is artificially added to the speech, the models improve MAP significantly. The higher the noise level, the bigger the relative improvements.

The combined indexing of both morphs and base forms seems to perform well also when the data becomes more challenging. While the higher noise levels or shorter queries seem to disturb the morph index more than the base form index, the combined index stays most robust. The combined index also benefits the most from speaker adaptation and multicondition models and is able to recover the performance near the level of the original data. The combined indexing is also clearly better than either morphs or base forms for the Broadcast data.

5   Discussion and Conclusion

In this work, an experimental study was made to show the impact of variable and challenging acoustic conditions to speech retrieval. The effect of compensating speaker variability and noise by adaptation and by using multicondition trained acoustic models is presented as well. Since Finnish is an agglutinative language, the data is indexed by combining both morphs and base forms, which is also shown to be a robust approach for variable acoustic conditions and retrieval tasks.

The results indicate that cMLLR speaker adaptation gives only small speech retrieval improvements in fairly noise free conditions, but larger improvements when the noise level is increased. In added noise, the multicondition models are also particularly helpful, but clearly the best results in noisy conditions are obtained when speaker adaptation is performed with multicondition models.

The effect of more challenging ASR conditions seems to depend on the type of the speech retrieval task. When indexing longer documents, the ASR errors have less effect and longer queries (in Newsreader corpus) are less likely to have as direct relationship to ASR errors as the single word ones (in Classroom corpus).

In previous work [3,1], morphs and base forms were found to perform at about equal level for Finnish SDR, and combining the two lead to best performance. This holds for the SDR experiments in this work also, but not for the RUR experiments, where morphs performed worse. This is explained by the different nature of the tasks. In SDR, the query sentence contains many words, often in different inflected forms. In RUR, the chances of matching the morphs in the document to the morphs in the query are smaller than in SDR. However, combining the morphs with base forms offered again improvements over base form index, showing that morphs provide additional useful information for indexing.

Acknowledgements. This work was supported by the Academy of Finland in projects 251170, 255745 and Tekes in projects NextMedia and Mobster, and Langnet graduate school.

References

1. Kurimo, M., Turunen, V., Ekman, I.: Speech transcription and spoken document retrieval in Finnish. In: Bengio, S., Bourlard, H. (eds.) MLMI 2004. LNCS, vol. 3361, pp. 253–262. Springer, Heidelberg (2005)
2. Turunen, V.T.: Reducing the effect of OOV query words by using morph-based spoken document retrieval. In: Proc. Interspeech, pp. 2158–2161 (September 2008)
3. Turunen, V.T., Kurimo, M.: Speech retrieval from unsegmented Finnish audio using statistical morpheme-like units for segmentation, recognition, and retrieval. ACM Trans. Speech Lang. Process. 8(1), 1:1–1:25 (2011)
4. Olsson, J.S., Oard, D.W.: Phrase-based query degradation modeling for vocabulary-independent ranked utterance retrieval. In: Proc. HLT-NAACL, pp. 182–190. ACL, Stroudsburg (2009)
5. Lingsoft, Inc.: FINTWOL: Finnish morphological analyser [computer software] (2007), http://www.lingsoft.fi/

6. Saraçlar, M., Sproat, R.: Lattice-based search for spoken utterance retrieval. In: Proceedings of the Human Language Technology Conference of the North American Chapter of the Association for Computational Linguistics (HTL-NAACL), pp. 129–136 (2004)
7. Mamou, J., Ramabhadran, B., Siohan, O.: Vocabulary independent spoken term detection. In: Proceedings of the 30th Annual International ACM SIGIR Conference on Research and Development in Information Retrieval, pp. 615–622. ACM, New York (2007)
8. Ogilvie, P., Callan, J.: Experiments using the Lemur toolkit. In: Proc. TREC, pp. 103–108. NIST, Gaithersburg (2001)
9. Liu, B., Oard, D.W.: One-sided measures for evaluating ranked retrieval effectiveness with spontaneous conversational speech. In: Proc. SIGIR, pp. 673–674. ACM, New York (2006)
10. Hirsimäki, T., Pylkkönen, J., Kurimo, M.: Importance of high-order n-gram models in morph-based speech recognition. IEEE Trans. Audio, Speech and Language Processing 17(4), 724–732 (2009)
11. Siivola, V., Pellom, B.: Growing an n-gram model. In: Proc. Interspeech, pp. 183–188 (September 2005)
12. Varga, A., Herman, S.: Assessment for automatic speech recognition: II. NOISEX-92: A database and an experiment to study the effect of additive noise on speech recognition systems. Speech Comm. 12(3), 247–251 (1993)
13. Hearst, M.A.: TextTiling: segmenting text into multi-paragraph subtopic passages. Comput. Linguist. 23(1), 33–64 (1997)

SVID Speaker Recognition System for NIST SRE 2012

Alexander Kozlov[1], Oleg Kudashev[1], Yuri Matveev[1,2], Timur Pekhovsky[1],
Konstantin Simonchik[1,2], and Andrei Shulipa[1]

[1] Speech Technolodgy Center Ltd., St. Petersburg, Russia
{kozlov-a,kudashev,matveev,tim,simonchik,shulipa}@speechpro.com
www.speechpro.com
[2] University ITMO, St. Petersburg, Russia
{matveev,simonchik}@mail.ifmo.ru

Abstract. A description of the SVID speaker recognition system is presented.
This system was developed for submission to the NIST SRE 2012.

Keywords: speaker recognition, GMM, PLDA, JFA, NIST SRE.

1 Introduction

Speaker recognition systems are biometric systems with very wide fields of application,
for example:

- Automatic remote client verification over the telephone
- Forensic investigations
- Working with speech databases

In this paper we describe a text-independent Speaker Verification and Identification
System (SVID), developed for submitting to the NIST (National Institute of Standards
and Technology) Speaker Recognition Evaluation (SRE) 2012 [1]. The main aim of the
SRE series is to evaluate the level of existing speaker recognition technologies and to
define future directions in the industry. Leading companies, universities and laboratories
from all over the world regularly participate in SRE.

The criteria given for the NIST SRE 2012 competition [1] differed from those of
recent years [2], [3] in two ways; (1) several recording sessions involving the same
speakers were provided for building a reference model, and (2) there was an added
artificial noise in the test recordings. The number of recordings provided for building a
speaker reference model was up to several tens. Some recordings were from telephone
channels, and some were from microphone channels (interviews). We used recordings
with known channel types and speaker genders to design the SVID system.

A different solution to the problem of acoustic overlapped speech is presented by the
methods of multichannel spectral subtraction [1], crosstalk cancellation, speech separation [2], beamforming [3]. However, signal filtering leads to speech distortions, which
can decrease speech recognition efficiency (it is necessary to retrain the recognition
system).

M. Železný et al. (Eds.): SPECOM 2013, LNAI 8113, pp. 278–285, 2013.

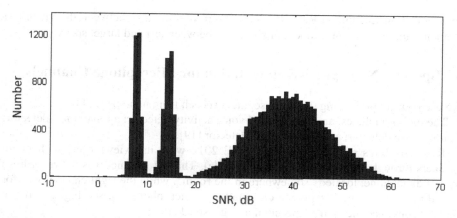

Fig. 1. Histogram of SNR distribution of a test telephone subset of the NIST SRE 2012 data

Fig. 1 shows a histogram of signal-to-noise (SNR) distribution for telephone recordings. The modes of the histogram correspond to different levels of added artificial noise in the test records: with No Added Noise (right mode), with Added Noise of $SNR = 15dB$ (middle mode) and with Added Noise of $SNR = 6dB$ (left mode).

An error detecting cost function (DCF) [1] of the NIST SRE 2012 is a half-sum of error detecting cost functions of the NIST SRE 2008 [2] and NIST SRE 2010 [3]:

$$DCF = 0,5 \cdot DCF_{2008} + 0,5 \cdot DCF_{2010}$$

where $DCF_{2008} = FRR + 99 \cdot FAR$, $DCF_{2010} = FRR + 999 \cdot FAR$, FRR - false rejection error rate, FAR - false acceptance error rate.

2   Stages of Speaker Recognition

Speaker recognition systems perform several operations [4]:

1. Segment speech from non-speech in speech recordings;
2. Extract speech features in speech segments;
3. Build speaker models for reference and test segments;
4. Compare speaker models.

With the comparison operation above, we can define how close the voice of an unknown speaker in a test segment is to the voice of a target speaker and, therefore, can determine whether segments of speech belong to a single person or to different persons. Performance is judged according to how accurately the test segment is classi-fied as containing (or not containing) speech from the target speaker. This is expressed by a score such as the log-likelihood ratio (LLR). The higher the score, the more similar the test segment is to the target speaker.

For each target speaker, we built a set of models using different methods. Results of comparisons for all methods were fused to get a so-called "total decision" which is an overall Log Likelihood Ratio (LLR) measure of similarity between the given test utterance and the reference model of similarity between test and target speakers.

3   Speech / Non-speech Segmentation for Microphone Channels

We used our preprocessing toolkit to segment speech from non-speech [18].

The toolkit includes: an energy based voice activity detector; a tonal noise detector; a pulse noise detector; a signal overload detector [19].

Test recordings provided for NIST SRE 2012 were interviews done with target speakers through microphones (in stereo mode). The left channel was for recordings from a dictaphone, located "somewhere in the room", while the right channel was for recordings from a "head mounted close-talking" microphone [1], see Fig. 2. No one channel contained the "pure" speech of a target speaker.

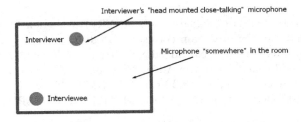

Fig. 2. Recording scheme for microphone channels

To detect speech in these interview recordings, we used a stereo noise cancellation toolkit [5]. The stereo noise cancellation scheme is given in Figure 3.

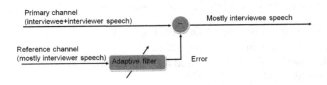

Fig. 3. Stereo noise cancellation scheme

As the filtered signal contained mainly the speech of the target speaker, it was used as input for the speech detection module. The marks of speech segments were used further for the left channel of the original signal, and we build the target speak-ers voice model on these segments of the target speakers speech.

Test telephone recordings were input directly into the speech feature extraction module. The test telephone recordings recorded in stereo format, where in each chan-nel is the speech of only one speaker.

4   Speech Feature Extraction

We used two types of features: MFCC 13 augmented by their delta and double delta coefficients, making 39 dimensional feature vectors; LFCC 13 augmented by their delta and double delta coefficients, making 39 dimensional feature vectors.

The analysis window in both cases has a length of 23 ms with a shift of 11.5 ms. For each vector we used a mean cepstral subtraction (CMS) procedure [6]. We used linear-frequency cepstral coefficients (LFCC) to enhance speaker recognition perfor-mance in telephone recordings.

5   Building and Comparison of Voice Models

At present the most common approaches to the text-independent identification task use Gaussian mixture models (GMM) [4], [6]. To build GMM-models, we used the Joint Factor Analysis (JFA) method [7]-[10] (among other methods). An equal error rate (EER) value of acceptance of a non-target speaker and rejection of a target speaker for the JFA-based method depends on the length of the compared utterances and can reach a value of 1-2%.

In addition to the standard method of factor analysis, a number of methods consider only one, low-dimensional space. This is the so-called "total variability" space, which explains both inter-speaker and inter-channel variability [11]. Thus, when building a speaker GMM-model, we can observe only the combined effect of factors and cant to perform, for instance, the compensation of channel effects (with factor analysis, this can be done). To consider the compensation of channel effects, we had to perform an additional operation based on Probabilistic Linear Discriminative Analysis (PLDA) [11], [17]. Despite the fact that PLDA, like JFA, is a generative method that lets us assess inter-speaker and inter-channel variability, it has some specific features.

First, PLDA represents each utterance in the form of a low-dimensional vector in space with the basis presented by a matrix of total variability. This representation favorably distinguishes the PLDA method from JFA, where Baume-Welch high-order statistics must be calculated for each speaker sentence. Second, to describe the prior distribution of variability factors for both test utter-ances and utterances from the training database, PLDA applies a t-distribution with "heavy tails" (heavy tailed priors). This allows stable estimates of model parameters to be obtained with respect to bursts [16]. Third, a hypothesis choice at a stage of decision-making when comparing test and reference utterances is based on the symmetry of PLDA estimates with respect to these utterances.

EER values for PLDA are comparable with JFA and could be down to 1–2% on recordings with duration 60-90 s or more. However, PLDA as compared to JFA is, as a rule, more robust to channel type and noise level.

6   The Structure of the SVID

SVID is a fusion of 36 different gender and channel dependent subsystems. The subsystems were trained with adaptation to following types of channels: telephone, microphone and mixed (telephone – microphone).

Within each of the three channel types, we trained two gender-dependent subsystems (male and female). For training we used the NIST SRE 1998-2010 speech databases, 60,000 records in total. Overall, we trained 6 subsystems with different channel types and/or speaker genders: 1. Telephone, male; 2. Telephone, female; 3. Microphone, male; 4. Microphone, female; 5. Mixed, male; 6. Mixed, female.

We used 3 different approaches in SVID: PLDA with both diagonal covariance matrix and full-covariance matrix for UBMs, and JFA with diagonal covariance matrix for UBM. For PLDA systems, we used normalization as proposed by Garcia-Romero in [13] and for JFA systems, we used zt-normalization [14] based on 300 sessions of different speakers from the NIST SRE 2008 database. A multisession model of templates was built as follows: for PLDA, the i-vector of the template was calculated as an average of i-vectors of all sentences; for JFA, we calculated total Baum-Welch statistics over all sessions of the template. This template was later used to build a multisession model. Each subsystem therefore had 6 modifications. For example, a telephone subsystem is a mix of the following 6 systems trained for a specific gender:

- PLDA (full-covariance UBM), trained on telephone data with MFCC as features.
- PLDA (diagonal UBM), trained on telephone data with MFCC as features.
- JFA (diagonal UBM), trained on telephone data with MFCC as features.
- PLDA (full-covariance UBM), trained on telephone data with LFCC as features.
- PLDA (diagonal UBM), trained on telephone data with LFCC as features.
- JFA (diagonal UBM), trained on telephone data with LFCC as features.

Each of the interview and telephone systems is also the combination of 6 systems trained on microphone and mixed data, respectively. The total number of UBMs used is 24. The dimension of a diagonal UBM is 2048, and that of a full-covariance UBM is 1024. We used 50 iterations of the EM algorithm. No variance flooring was used.

7 Generation of a Fusion Decision

To increase the performance of a speaker recognition system, we use score-level fusion. Depending on the channel type and speaker gender in the test record, we used one of four trained systems: telephone male, telephone female, microphone male or microphone female. The decision made by each subsystem is expressed as a logarithm of likelihood ratio (LLR) that the speaker in the test recording is the same as the speaker in the template. To calculate the LLR for a fusion decision, we used the BOZARIS [15] program.

We used NIST SRE speech databases from 2006 to 2010 to train the weight of each system in the fusion decision. To enhance the fusion process for noisy recordings, the same databases were artificially "noised" to the SNR levels of 15 dB and 6 dB. The fusion decision was trained for both original ("clean") records and records with added SNR. Thus, depending on the SNR level in the test segment, we used one of the three configurations:

1. $SNR > 20dB$: training the fusion decision on a database without added noise
2. $10 < SNR \leq 20dB$: training the fusion decision on a database with $SNR = 15dB$
3. $SNR \leq 10dB$: training the fusion decision on a database with $SNR = 6dB$

8 Results

The results in the NIST SRE 2012 were evaluated for five conditions depending on the channel type of the test records (in all cases, a multisession reference model was used):

- Interview (microphone)
- Telephone
- Interview with added noise
- Telephone with added noise
- Telephone in a noisy environment

For each condition, we plotted a DET-curve and evaluated two types of errors: minimum detection cost function (minDCF), i.e. the value of the detection cost for the optimal threshold and actual DCF (actDCF), i.e. the value of the detection cost for a

Table 1. SVID Errors (minDCF and actDCF) in Different Channels

Channel	minDCF	actDCF
1. Interview	0.354	0.444
2. Telephone	0.291	0.541
3. Interview with added noise	0.305	0.317
4. Telephone with added noise	0.376	0.504
5. Telephone in a noisy environment	0.285	0.588

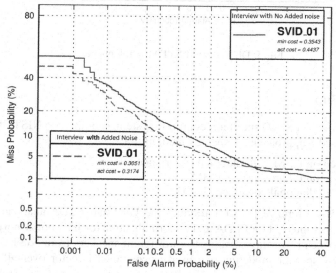

Fig. 4. DET-curves of SVID for Telephone and Interview with Added Noise

threshold defined by developers. Table 1 presents minDCF and actDCF values for tests across the five channel types:

Figure 4 shows DET-curves for "Telephone" and "Interview" channels with added noise. Despite the added noise, minDCF and actDCF for the "Interview" channel are lower. This is a result of both the difference between test speech corpuses and of using the speech extraction schema described earlier. The EER value for "Interview" is 4-5%. The EER value for "Telephone", as shown in Figure 5, is 2.5-3.0%.

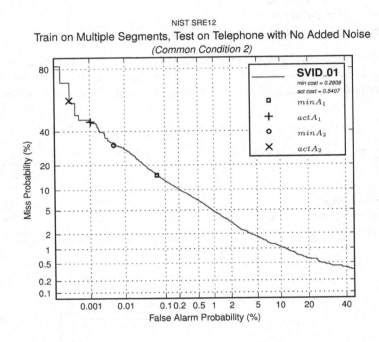

Fig. 5. DET-curve of SVID for Telephone

9   Conclusion

We have described our SVID speaker recognition system, submitted to NIST SRE 2012. In SVID, we used 3 approaches to speaker recognition:

- PLDA based on UBM with diagonal covariance matrix
- PLDA based on full covariance UBM
- JFA based on diagonal covariance UBM

We used VBA-inference [16] for training the Gaussian PLDA-analyzer, Garcia-Romero normalization [13] for PLDA and zt-normalization for JFA. For zt-normalization, we used 300 speech recording sessions from different speakers from NIST SRE 2008 data. For PLDA speaker modeling, we used an averaged i-vector over all i-vectors extracted from every speaker session. For JFA modeling, we used 0,1,2-order Baum-Welch statistics calculated over all speaker sessions.

References

1. The NIST Year 2012 Speaker Recognition Evaluation Plan, `http://www.nist.gov/itl/iad/mig/upload/NIST_SRE12_evalplan-v17-r1.pdf`
2. The NIST Year 2008 Speaker Recognition Evaluation Plan, `http://www.itl.nist.gov/iad/mig/tests/sre/2008/sre08_evalplan_release4.pdf`
3. The NIST Year 2010 Speaker Recognition Evaluation Plan, `http://www.nist.gov/itl/iad/mig/upload/NIST_SRE10_evalplan-r6.pdf`
4. Bimbot, F., et al.: A Tutorial on Text-Independent Speaker Verification. EURASIP Journal on Applied Signal Processing (4), 430–451 (2004)
5. Ignatov, P., Stolbov, M., Aleynik, S.: Semi-Automated Technique for Noisy Recording Enhancement Using an Independent Reference Recording. In: 46th International Conference of the Audio Engineering Society, Denver, CO, USA, pp. 2–3 (2012)
6. Reynolds, D.A.: Experimental evaluation of features for robust speaker identification. IEEE Transactions on Speech and Audio Processing 2(4), 639–643 (1994)
7. Burget, L., et al.: Analysis of feature extraction and channel compensation in GMM speaker recognition system. IEEE Trans. on Audio, Speech and Language Processing 15(7), 1979–1986 (2007)
8. Kenny, P., et al.: A Study of Inter-Speaker Variability in Speaker Verification. IEEE Transactions on Audio, Speech and Language Processing 16(5), 980–988 (2008)
9. Kenny, P., et al.: Joint factor analysis versus eigenchannels in speaker recognition. IEEE Transactions on Audio, Speech and Language Processing 15(4), 1435–1447 (2007)
10. Dehak, N., et al.: Front-end factor analysis for speaker verification. IEEE Transactions on Audio, Speech, and Language Processing 99 (2010)
11. Matejka, P., et al.: Full Covariance UBM and Heavy-Tailed PLDA in i-vector Speaker Verification. In: ICASSP, Prague, Czech Republic, pp. 4828–4831 (2011)
12. Reynolds, D.A., Quatieri, T.F., Dunn, R.B.: Speaker Verification Using Adapted Gaussian Mixture Models. Digital Signal Processing (10), 19–41 (2000)
13. Garcia-Romero, D., Espy-Wilson, C.Y.: Analysis of I-vector Length Normalization in Speaker Recognition Systems. In: Interspeech, Florence, Italy, pp. 249–252 (2011)
14. Vogt, R., Sridharan, S.: Explicit Modelling of Session Variability for Speaker Verification. Computer Speech & Language 22(1), 17–38 (2008)
15. BOSARIS Toolkit, `https://sites.google.com/site/bosaristoolkit/`
16. Kenny, P.: Bayesian speaker verification with heavy tailed priors. In: Odyssey Speaker and Language Recognition Workshop, Brno, Czech Republic, pp. 1–41 (2010)
17. Simonchik, K., Pekhovsky, T., Shulipa, A., Afanasyev, A.: Supervized Mixture of PLDA Models for Cross-Channel Speaker Verification. In: 13th Annual Conference of the International Speech Communication Association, Interspeech 2012, Portland, Oregon, USA (2012)
18. Belykh, I.N., Kapustin, I.N., Kozlov, A.V., Lohanova, A.V., Matveev, Y.N., Pekhovsky, Y.N., Simonchik, K.K., Shulipa, K.: Speaker identification system for the NIST SRE 2010. Inform. Primen. 6(1), 91–98 (2012)
19. Aleinik, S., Matveev, Y., Raev, A.: Method of evaluation of speech signal clipping level. Scientific and Technical Journal of Information Technologies, Mechanics and Optics 79(3), 79–83 (2012)

Segmentation of Telephone Speech Based on Speech and Non-speech Models

Michael Heck, Christian Mohr, Sebastian Stüker, Markus Müller, Kevin Kilgour, Jonas Gehring, Quoc Bao Nguyen, Van Huy Nguyen, and Alex Waibel

Institute for Anthropomatics, Karlsruhe Institute of Technology, Germany
{heck,christian.mohr,sebastian.stueker,m.mueller,kevin.kilgour, jonas.gehring,quoc.nguyen,van.nguyen,waibel}@kit.edu

Abstract. In this paper we investigate the automatic segmentation of recorded telephone conversations based on models for speech and non-speech to find sentence-like chunks for use in speech recognition systems. Presented are two different approaches, based on Gaussian Mixture Models (GMMs) and Support Vector Machines (SVMs), respectively. The proposed methods provide segmentations that allow for competitive speech recognition performance in terms of word error rate (WER) compared to manual segmentation.

Keywords: support vector machines, segmentation, speech activity detection.

1 Introduction

Speech recognition in telephone calls is still one of the most challenging speech recognition tasks to-date. Besides the special acoustic conditions that degrade input features for acoustic modelling, the speaking style in telephone conversations is highly spontaneous and informal. Each channel of a conversation contains large parts with no speech activity. Assuming equal participation of both speakers in the conversation, at least 50% per channel can therefore be omitted for recognition. Omitting non-speech segments on one hand improves recognition speed and on the other hand can improve the recognition accuracy since insertions due to falsely classified noises in the non-speech segments can be avoided, which is especially promising in the variable background noise conditions of telephone and mobile phone conversations.

We investigate two methods of automatic segmentation to determine sentence like chunks of speech and filter out non-speech segments for speech recognition. As a baseline we regard the segmentation on the output of a regular speech recognizer. Our experimental setups make use of a GMM based decoder method and an SVM based method.

Evaluation is done according to speech recognition performance since references for speech segments are not very accurate. The evaluation took place on corpora of four distinct languages, that were recently released as the IARPA Babel Program [1] language collections. babel106b-v0.2f and the subset babel106b-v0.2g-sub-train cover *Tagalog* and are used in two training data conditions, *unlimited* and *limited*, respectively. In the *unlimited* scenario, a full data set covering approximately 100 hours of transcribed audio material was available for training, whereas for the *limited* case only a subset of the

M. Železný et al. (Eds.): SPECOM 2013, LNAI 8113, pp. 286–293, 2013.

available data was approved for training, comprising approximately 10 hours each. The additional three languages collections used for the *limited* case are babel101-v0.4c for *Cantonese*, babel104b-v0.4bY for *Pashto* and babel105b-v0.4 for *Turkish*.

The outline of the paper is structured as follows. Sections 2, 3 and 4 describe the segmentation methods we used. In Section 5 the handling of the training data for the speech/non-speech based methods is described. Evaluation is shown in Section 6 and Section 7 concludes and points out future work.

2 Baseline

For the baseline automatic segmentation a fast decoding pass with a regular speech recognition system on the unsegmented input data is done to determine speech and non-speech regions as in [2]. Segmentation is performed by consecutively splitting segments at the longest non-speech region with a minimal duration of at least 0.3 seconds.

Like all HMM based systems addressed in this paper the speech recognition system used for decoding was trained and tested using the JANUS Recognition Toolkit that features the IBIS single pass decoder [3]. The system employs left-to-right HMMs, modelling phoneme sequences with 3 HMM states per phoneme.

3 GMM Based Decoder Method

Since for segmentation the classification problem only consists of two classes, namely speech and non-speech, in the GMM-based method we use the same Viterbi decoder as in the baseline method and use GMM models for speech and non-speech. We found that splitting the non-speech model into a general non-speech model and a silence model increased performance. Our HMM segmentation framework is based on the one in [4] which is used to detect and reject music segments. This approach was also used in [5] for acoustic event classification. Similar approaches for the pre-segmentation of very long audio parts for speech recognition systems were used in [6] where GMM models were trained for speech, speech + background music, non-speech noise, music and pause. Alternatively a phoneme decoder using regular phoneme models and a phoneme bi-gram model is investigated. HMM based segmentation of telephone speech was also presented in [7].

We use MFCCs with 13 coefficients and its delta and double delta as input features. Window size is 16 milliseconds with a window shift of 10 milliseconds. We tested additional features such as a zero crossing rate, but it did not improve performance. We also tried to stack the MFCC plus delta and double delta features of both audio files for each call to take into account that – neglecting parts of cross-talk – if a segment contains speech in one channel, the other channel does not. However, audio files of both the training and test data set were not synchronised channel-wise, so that the dual channel models decreased performance.

A-priori probabilities are modelled as 2-grams but we assume equal probability for all segments and 2-grams since we handle each telephone call as two channels, one for each speaker, and assume both speakers have the same contingent in the conversation so at least half of each file contains non-speech segments.

All types of segments are modelled as single HMM states, with the minimal segment durations being modelled directly by the HMM topology. For speech segments the minimal duration is 250 milliseconds, for non-speech segments 150 milliseconds. Each GMM consists of 128 Gaussians with 39 dimensions. Models are trained in a maximum likelihood way on the training samples as described in Section 5. The Gaussian mixtures are grown incrementally over several iterations.

Since the GMM based decoder classifies speech segments on a per frame basis and only uses a one frame context from the delta and double delta features, speech segments are cut off very tightly. The speech recognition system can handle non-speech frames that were misclassified as speech, but false negative frames can not be recovered. Expanding the speech segments on both sides by 0.4 seconds improved the segmenter's performance.

4   SVM Based Method

SVMs have already been applied to the closely related voice activity detection (VAD) problem in the past by [8]. Since then, several works such as [9] extended these ideas. The latter work, among many others defines the speech/non-speech discrimination problem as two-class discrimination problem. With works like [10] there also exist studies that extend this task to a multi-class problem by splitting speech/non-speech detection into sub-tasks. Similar to [11], our main objective is to maximize the improved intelligibility of speech under noisy channel conditions.

As SVMs naturally model two-class decision cases, it is straightforward to train a model on reference samples mapped to two distinct classes for speech and non-speech. The mapping is performed as described in Section 5. However, no exact phoneme-to-audio alignments that could serve as references were accessible for our experiments, thus it has been decided to perform training on previously computed labels that have been generated by our baseline system. Consequently, the references for training are not exempt from errors, albeit the quality of references still being high enough to enable an effective training.

4.1   SVM Training

The classifier is trained on the $(train_{svm})$ set, using the LIBSVM library [12]. We decided to use the C-Support Vector Classification (C-SVC) formulation, as it is the original SVM formulation [13], and fits our requirements. The SVM will find a hyperplane a high-dimensional space, which separates the the classes in a linear fashion and with a maximal margin between them. With a soft margin parameter $C > 0$, a penalty parameter of the error term can be used for adjustment [12]. The decision function we use for classification is:

$$\text{sgn}\left(\sum_{i=1}^{l} \boldsymbol{y}_i \alpha_i K(\boldsymbol{x}_i, \boldsymbol{x}) + b\right) \quad \text{with } K(\boldsymbol{x}_i, \boldsymbol{x}_j) = e^{-\gamma||\boldsymbol{x}_i - \boldsymbol{x}_j||^2} \tag{1}$$

where $K(x_i, x_j)$ is the RBF kernel function [12]. The values for (C, γ) are determined automatically during classifier training via a steepest ascent hill climbing algorithm by optimizing the frame based classification accuracy on (dev_{svm}). The C and γ are exponentially growing, following the recommendation of [14]. In order to avoid numerical problems, vector scaling is applied during training and testing [14].

Feature Selection. Initial experiments aimed at the identification of the most useful front-end for automatic segmentation. Similar to [15], a major focus was on testing standard feature vectors such as MFCCs, as they are commonly used for solving other automatic speech processing tasks. Loosely related to [16], we also utilize linear discriminant analysis (LDA) for preferably low-loss dimensional reduction.

The following front-ends have been evaluated: *a*) standard logMel feature vectors comprising 30 parameters *b*) standard 13 dimensional MFCC feature vectors *c*) 15 adjacent MFCC vectors stacked and LDA-transformed.

Our experimental evaluations on dev_{svm} show that it is always of advantage to integrate temporal information. In all cases, the SVMs trained on stacked variants of feature vectors outperformed the non-stacked variants. Moreover, stacking 15 adjacent frames outperformed the computation of Δ and $\Delta\Delta$. Ultimately, the systems using LDA-transformed feature vectors outperformed all other alternatives.

Further improvements were obtained by adding various features such as frame based peak distance or zero crossing rate. The enhancements were tested with all front-ends but the LDA based vectors. Where stacking or Δ computation was applied, the feature vectors were extended before the respective operation.

In order to minimize the dimensionality for reduced training complexity, we experimented with feature selection via the *f-score* measure. Except for logMel feature vectors, the discriminative capabilities of the original features are higher for low dimensions and gradually decrease for higher dimensions. None of the solutions with lower dimensionality was able to outperform the original systems. Contrary to expectations the discriminative abilities of the resulting models decreased, thus rendering dimensional reduction inefficient.

4.2   Post-processing

The output of SVM classification is a string of 1's and 0's, hypothesizing whether a frame belongs to a speech or non-speech region. However, operating on frame-level is too fine-grained and makes post-processing necessary to obtain a useful segmentation of the audio. For smoothing the raw SVM classification data we follow a 2-phase approach. First, smoothing is performed on frame-level to remove false positives and false negatives. Then, merging on segment level is performed to acquire more natural segments of reasonable length.

Smoothing on Frame-Level. The smoothing technique we apply is derived from the well-known *opening* strategy of morphological noise removal in computer vision. An *erosion* step on sequences of frames hypothesized as speech is followed by a *dilation* step. A major difference to the classic operation is that our algorithm is extensive, i.e, the resulting segment is larger than the original. This is achieved by differing factors for erosion and dilation, where $f_{erode} < f_{dilate}$. As a result, the idempotence property of the opening algorithm is also lost.

Our intention is to remove very short segments classified as speech by setting $f_{erode} = 3$, under the assumption that these are likely to be noise or artifacts arising from channel characteristics. A factor of 3 leads to a cut-off of 36 milliseconds of audio on each side of the respective hypothesized speech segment, and the deletion of isolated segments with a duration below 72 milliseconds. These values roughly approximate the estimates for minimal and average phoneme lengths [17]. By a stronger dilation, short gaps of predicted non-speech between parts of speech shall be removed. This has several justifications: For one, the dilation has to compensate for the erosion operation. Then, we follow the assumption that it is likely to reduce falsely rejected speech parts by closing comparatively short gaps. Furthermore, lost data by erroneous segmentation is more harmful than the inclusion of potentially noisy parts for decoding. To avoid too strict segment borders, the dilation step further serves as *padding* operator, extending the segment borders to a certain degree.

Segmentation Generation. Commonly, automatic segmentation maintains a minimal distance seg_{dist} between individual segments, e.g., for establishing sentence-like structures. Our goal was to exclude especially large parts of silence from decoding, and to minimize the occurrence of artifacts, without loss of relevant information. Both phenomenons directly arise from the nature of the recorded telephone conversations. A minimal distance between speech segments was defined by setting $seg_{dist} = 0.5$ milliseconds. Segments with a lower gap in between are merged. Moreover, isolated parts in the signal hypothesized as speech, but having a very short duration are pruned away.

5   Data Selection

To get the training samples for the speech and non-speech models we used forced alignments of the training data with the provided references. For alignment we used the same system than for the decoding experiments, or at least one of similar performance.

For the two-class case of speech/non-speech classification, a phoneme mapping was defined that maps phonemes modelling linguistic sound units to a speech category, and models that represent phenomenons that are considered noise and filler entities to a non-speech category. In the GMM-framework, additionally, non-speech samples classified as silence are mapped to a silence category.

We developed our systems for the Tagalog *unlimited* training data condition, that means around 100 hours of transcribed audio training data was available.

For the GMM based decoder method computational resources were no critical issue for the model training, so all data was used for training.

For the SVM based approach, the vast amount of training samples renders a training on the full data set entirely infeasible. Thus, a sample subset of approx. 200.000 samples was selected as training set ($train_{svm}$), and approx. 100.000 samples were used as development test set (dev_{svm}). Data extraction was conducted equally distributed among the target classes. Therefore, sample vectors were extracted phone-wise. From each utterance, an equal amount of samples was extracted to cover all data. Further, the extraction considers the shares of phonemes in the data. Every sample is belonging to either speech or non-speech, according to the pre-defined mapping. This way, both classes see an equal amount of data, equally distributed over the full data set and representing each original phoneme class according to their respective proportion.

6 Experiments

As ground truth for our experimental evaluation we used the manually generated transcriptions that came along with the development data. It is to distinct between two conditions: First, we performed the experimental evaluation on a test set of the same language the development data belongs to. In addition to this test series, four more automatic segmentation systems were trained for each proposed approach, each in another distinct language, where three of the languages are new and previously unseen during development. Thus, the optimized training pipelines are straightforwardly applied to the new conditions, allowing for evaluation of the generalization capabilities of our setups.

Table 1. Results for the Tagalog unlimited training data condition

	WER	Subst.	Del.	Ins.	#Seg.	dur.	avg.	max.
manual	63.1%	39.3%	16.9%	6.9%	11353	10.7h	3.4s	35.5s
baseline	62.6%	39.5%	15.6%	7.5%	12986	11.1h	3.1s	30.0s
GMM-based	61.9%	37.6%	18.5%	5.9%	15188	9.7h	2.3s	29.3s
SVM-based	62.4%	38.8%	16.5%	7.2%	15293	8.8h	2.0s	36.4s

Table 1 shows that both automatic segmentation approaches can outperform the manual segmentation for *Tagalog*. Our segmentations are further compared to the baseline for automatic segmentation (see 2). The segmentations of both approaches lead to a decrease in WER, if compared to the baseline.

Further analysis reveals considerable differences in the nature of the individual segmentations. By reference to Table 1 it can be seen that the amount of automatically determined segmentations is considerably higher, with at the same time notably shorter average segment length. The higher degree of fragmentation of the audio data leads to a lower accumulated duration. At the same time, recognition accuracy is not only maintained, yet even increased.

Table 2 lists the evaluation results for the *limited* case on all four languages. A direct comparison between both training data conditions of Tagalog reveals that the GMM-based segmentation proves to be superior when applied on the full training set, but it is the SVM-based segmentation that wins over the alternative, when having only a limited amount of training data at hand. For the other languages, none of the automatically generated segmentations can outweigh the manual partition. In the cases of *Cantonese* and *Turkish*, however, the difference to the performance on manual segmentations is

Table 2. Results in WER for the limited training data conditions on all four languages

Segmentation	Tagalog	Cantonese	Pashto	Turkish
manual	78.5%	76.7%	77.5%	74.0%
GMM-based	77.5%	76.8%	78.5%	74.5%
SVM-based	76.9%	76.9%	78.4%	74.3%

0.67% relative at the most. For *Pashto*, both automatic approaches are not able to reach the accuracy of the manual generated data, with 1.2% relative difference to the latter.

7   Conclusion and Future Work

This paper compares model based segmentation methods for unsegmented telephone conversations. Two methods based on the use of general speech and non-speech models (one GMM based and one SVM based method) are compared to a standard method that uses a general speech recognition system. We showed that our speech/non-speech modelling based segmentation methods achieve comparable results to those of manual segmentation. For larger amounts of training data, the GMM based method performed best, while the SVM based method is preferable if the amount is limited.

The languages we worked on are low resourced and not as well investigated as other languages and the corresponding systems we used achieve high WERs. Since the purity of the training data for the models for segmentation depends on the quality of the alignment and therefore on the speech recognition system, the methods have to be evaluated on well researched languages. Moreover, the dependency on the amount of training data could be investigated.

For the GMM based method there are several parameters that have to be optimized. The use of bottle-neck features improves speech recognition significantly (e.g. [18]) so the application on the segmentation seems to be promising. Increasing the front-end's window size should be investigated in general.

LIBSVM provides probabilistic classification, which might be topic of further experiments on SVM-based segmentation. Besides LDA, other transformations could be utilized for reduction of dimensionality. Within the scope of this research, the effect of additional features before LDA transformation remained open.

Acknowledgements. Supported by the Intelligence Advanced Research Projects Activity (IARPA) via Department of Defense U.S. Army Research Laboratory (DoD / ARL) contract number W911NF-12-C-0015. The U.S. Government is authorized to reproduce and distribute reprints for Governmental purposes notwithstanding any copyright annotation thereon. Disclaimer: The views and conclusions contained herein are those of the authors and should not be interpreted as necessarily representing the official policies or endorsements, either expressed or implied, of IARPA, DoD/ARL, or the U.S. Government.

References

1. IARPA: IARPA, Office for Incisive Analysis, Babel Program, http://www.iarpa.gov/Programs/ia/Babel/babel.html (retrieved March 06, 2013)
2. Stüker, S., Fügen, C., Kraft, F., Wölfel, M.: The ISL 2007 English Speech Transcription System for European Parliament Speeches. In: Proceedings of the 10th European Conference on Speech Communication and Technology (INTERSPEECH 2007), Antwerp, Belgium, pp. 2609–2612 (August 2007)
3. Soltau, H., Metze, F., Fügen, C., Waibel, A.: A One-pass Decoder Based on Polymorphic Linguistic Context Assignment. In: ASRU (2001)
4. Yu, H., Tam, Y.C., Schaaf, T., Stüker, S., Jin, Q., Noamany, M., Schultz, T.: The ISL RT04 Mandarin Broadcast News Evaluation System. In: EARS Rich Transcription Workshop (2004)
5. Kraft, F., Malkin, R., Schaaf, T., Waibel, A.: Temporal ICA for Classification of Acoustic Events in a Kitchen Environment. In: INTERSPEECH, Lisbon, Portugal (2005)
6. Beyerlein, P., Aubert, X., Haeb-Umbach, R., Harris, M., Klakow, D., Wendemuth, A., Molau, S., Ney, H., Pitz, M., Sixtus, A.: Large Vocabulary Continuous Speech Recognition of Broadcast News - The Philips/RWTH Approach. Speech Communication 37(12), 109–131 (2002)
7. Matsoukas, S., Gauvain, J., Adda, G., Colthurst, T., Kao, C.L., Kimball, O., Lamel, L., Lefevre, F., Ma, J., Makhoul, J., Nguyen, L., Prasad, R., Schwartz, R., Schwenk, H., Xiang, B.: Advances in Transcription of Broadcast News and Conversational Telephone Speech Within the Combined EARS BBN/LIMSI System. IEEE Transactions on Audio, Speech, and Language Processing 14(5), 1541–1556 (2006)
8. Enqing, D., Guizhong, L., Yatong, Z., Xiaodi, Z.: Applying Support Vector Machines to Voice Activity Detection. In: 2002 6th International Conference on Signal Processing, vol. 2, pp. 1124–1127 (2002)
9. Ramirez, J., Yelamos, P., Gorriz, J., Segura, J.: SVM-based Speech Endpoint Detection Using Contextual Speech Features. Electronics Letters 42(7), 426–428 (2006)
10. Lopes, C., Perdigao, F.: Speech Event Detection Using SVM and NMD. In: 9th International Symposium on Signal Processing and Its Applications, ISSPA 2007, pp. 1–4 (2007)
11. Han, K., Wang, D.: An SVM Based Classification Approach to Speech Separation. In: 2011 IEEE International Conference on Acoustics, Speech and Signal Processing (ICASSP), pp. 4632–4635 (2011)
12. Chang, C.C., Lin, C.J.: LIBSVM: A Library for Support Vector Machines. ACM Transactions on Intelligent Systems and Technology 2, 27:1–27:27 (2011)
13. Cortes, C., Vapnik, V.: Support-Vector Networks. Machine Learning 20, 273–297 (1995)
14. Hsu, C.W., Chang, C.C., Lin, C.J.: A Practical Guide to Support Vector Classification (2010)
15. Kinnunen, T., Chernenko, E., Tuononen, M., Fränti, P., Li, H.: Voice Activity Detection Using MFCC Features and Support Vector Machine (2007)
16. Temko, A., Macho, D., Nadeu, C.: Enhanced SVM Training for Robust Speech Activity Detection. In: IEEE International Conference on Acoustics, Speech and Signal Processing, ICASSP 2007, vol. 4, pp. IV–1025–IV–1028 (2007)
17. Rogina, I.: Sprachliche Mensch-Maschine-Kommunikation (2005)
18. Kilgour, K., Saam, C., Mohr, C., Stüker, S., Waibel, A.: The 2011 KIT Quaero Speech-to-text System for Spanish. In: IWSLT 2011, pp. 199–205 (2011)

Software for Assessing Voice Quality in Rehabilitation of Patients after Surgical Treatment of Cancer of Oral Cavity, Oropharynx and Upper Jaw

Lidiya N. Balatskaya[1], Evgeny L. Choinzonov[1], Svetlana Yu. Chizevskaya[1],
Eugeny U. Kostyuchenko, and Roman V. Meshcheryakov[2]

[1] Tomsk Cancer Research Institute of the Russian Academy of Medical Science 5 Kooperativny
Street, 634050, Tomsk, Russia
[2] TUSUR, 40, Lenina pr., Tomsk, Russia
`{key,mrv}@keva.tusur.ru, balatskaya@oncology.tomsk.ru`

Abstract. Restoration of speech functions after operations on the organs of
speech (production) requires the development of procedures and support programs for rehabilitation. Available means to restore the original voice function
for the patient and for speech therapy. Software tool feature of is the use of a
combination of speech sounds, which are the most common in speech and which
affect the naturalness and intelligibility of speech. It shows the effectiveness of
procedures and programs.

Keywords: Speech rehabilitation, cancer, software, logaoedics, voice, speech
formation path.

1 Introduction

Malignant neoplasms of the head and neck are one of their complex medical and social
problems in modern oncology. Among the malignant tumors of oropharyngeal tumors
occupy the most part of the tongue and the oral cavity (70-80%) in 8-10% of patients
with localized tumor on his or her cheek, yet at least - on the mucous membrane of the
alveolar process (6%), soft palate (4%) [1].

Surgical interventions for cancer of the oral cavity, oropharynx and upper jaw are
different in size and are accompanied with damage to acts of swallowing, chewing,
breathing, articulation and enforcement, as a consequence, a violated pronounce and
phonation. As a result, a significant amount of the operations a marked deformation
of the peripheral speech apparatus. The defects of the maxillofacial area after radical
treatment, the presence of the stump tongue defects palatal arches, no fragment of the
lower jaw, the change of oral cavity lead to the development of polymorphic dyslalia
and changes acoustic sonorous voice, with not only suffers pronounce, but the pace,
expressiveness, smoothness, modulation, voice and breath [2].

The visual localization, traumatic operations dysfunction after surgical treatment determine the complexity of the subsequent speech rehabilitation and social adaptation.
Speech rehabilitation of patients in this category is a very complex and difficult task,
requiring a strictly individual approach.

M. Železný et al. (Eds.): SPECOM 2013, LNAI 8113, pp. 294–301, 2013.

Inability to fully verbal communication deprive the patient's opportunity to work, as a result they receive a disability. According to the literature for more than 40% of patients given location are the most active age from 40 to 60 years. Therefore, medical and social rehabilitation of cancer patients is an important issue. This, in turn, dictates the need for a comprehensive, multidisciplinary approach in the treatment of post-operative recovery and damage [3].

Methods of remedial work is based on the use of intact stereotypes of speech production in the early postoperative period, given the fact that a violation of the anatomy of tongue occurred during the period of the established speech, therefore, the correct focal installations are available and can be used for the development of active muscle movements preserved through the remainder of the compensatory possibilities authority. For speech disorders characterized by their persistent presence having arisen they do not disappear without remedial work and, as a rule, considerably complicate the process of communication. Therefore, an important component of the recovery of the lost tongue functions is to evaluate the quality and intelligibility of speech for the formation of a parametric description, which in turn will allow setting diagnosis of speech and making formal description of speech disorders, allowing objectively evaluate changes in speech quality in the rehabilitation process [4].

2   Software

Formation is a problem of quality assessment of the patient's speech during the speech rehabilitation of patients after operations on the tract speech [6]. In most cases, the evaluation on the exhibiting speech quality after training therapist session. This software offers to use to evaluate the quality of speech quality evaluation methods of transmission channels of voice data. Methods taken from standard GOST 50840-95 "Voice over paths of communication" [7]. Methods for assessing the quality, legibility and recognition reoriented to evaluate the performance of speech formation tract.

This standard provides methods for assessing the intelligibility of phrase, syllable intelligibility, intelligibility on a selective grounds for pairwise comparison of communication channels, enabling applied to patients to assess the quality of speech production compared with the healthy person, and track changes in the speech of one patient over time.

The software product "Speech" is designed to automate the process of assessing the quality of speech as applied to problems in speech quality assessment of patients in the process of speech rehabilitation after surgery on the organs of speech formation tract.

The interface provides the user (speech therapist) with the ability to specify user's personal data (name, surname, first name, age), specify the amount of surgery, the diagnosis of which was held by the intervention, as well as logaoedic diagnosis in which classes are conducted with a speech therapist in voice rehabilitation.

For each of the evaluation sessions speech shows the date of the session and the type of methodology used estimates of speech intelligibility (syllable, phrase intelligibility, voice quality assessment on grounds of selective and evaluation method of paired comparisons). Also specify the data describing the source of information for the utterance. The rest of the field corresponding to the estimated speech quality is filled automatically after the evaluation session.

The appearance of the program window with the results of quality assessment on various criteria of the intelligibility is shown in Figure 1.

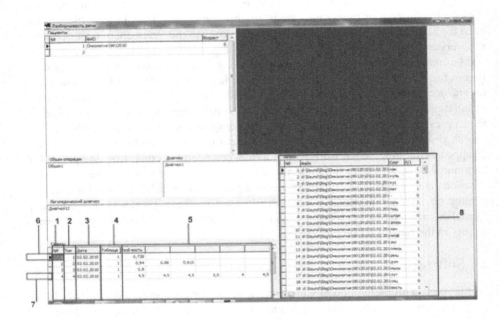

Fig. 1. The session window. 1 - number of session 2 - session type, 3 - the date of the session, 4 - number of the first table to be read from the GOST 50840-95, 5 - results of intelligibility, 6 - the current record, 7 - the last record, 8 - edit box records.

Upon receipt of syllabic assessment of speech intelligibility patient pronounces the syllables of special tables to evaluate speech intelligibility on the screen. A speech therapist is gaining heard a syllable. After the session assesses the correctness recognition heard a syllable and the calculation of the proportion of correctly recognized syllables. This is estimate of the voice quality share through syllable intelligibility. The patient or logopedist can listen to any previous recording session.

Evaluation mode of phrase designed to evaluate the intelligibility of speech quality on offer. The patient says sentences from the respective table GOST 50840-95 [7], appearing on the screen. The speech therapist evaluates the quality of the phrase uttered by a binary system of assessment and records in a table. After the assessment for the average rate of spoken sentences can be evaluated for the accelerated pace of utterance. It is possible the estimation of phrase intelligibility and reduction of intelligibility score with increasing tempo after the session.

In assessing the speech quality by pairwise comparisons of assessment is carried out by comparing the patient uttered phrases and standard phrases, which may be the healthy person phrase a or a previously recorded phrase of the same patient, which allows you to track the dynamics of change in the quality of speech in the course of employment with a speech therapist.

When voice quality assessment on grounds of selective speech therapist assesses whether patients in a speech characteristic defects.

The developed program allows you to automate evaluation process of speech quality made by speech therapist in voice-patient rehabilitation. Speech therapists have the opportunity to see the results of previous sessions, and listen to recordings that were made earlier, that allows to evaluate the dynamics of change in the patient's speech in the rehabilitation process.

3   Experiment

The system allows control to maintain patient records and allows tracking of changes in the dynamics of intelligibility. In addition, all entries, obtained when working with patients, remain, and can be listened to if necessary in the future evaluation of speech dynamics. Furthermore, the data base of speech signals accumulated during the operation of the complex may be used to analyze the speech parameters in determining the objective. These parameters are considered during the estimation of the voice quality. An example of this is the use of speech analytics in the rehabilitation of patients after surgery on his or her tongue [5].

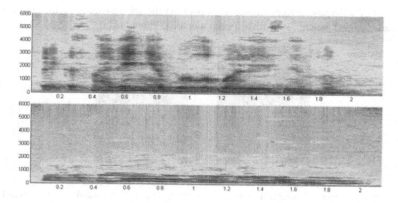

Fig. 2. Windows research complex signal spectrum illustrating the healthy human (top) and the patient "A" after surgery before rehabilitation speech (bottom)

Figure 2 shows a fragment of a research complex window, showing the signal spectrum of healthy human (top) and after the operation, the patient immediately before the start of classes with a speech therapist (bottom). The phrase "touch was painful". Recordings were made using the same equipment under the same initial conditions. Attention is drawn to the upper section of the frequency spectrum at 1-1.5 kHz. This feature is presented in all records Patient A made before classes begin with a speech therapist. After the sessions with a speech therapist spectrum is corrected. The spectrum of the speech signal after rehabilitation is shown in Figure 3. It is seen a significant rise of higher frequency spectrum.

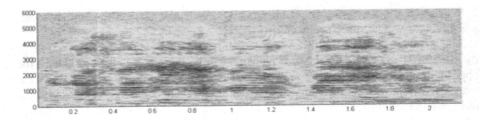

Fig. 3. Detail of windows research complex, illustrating the spectrum of the signal after patient "A" with a speech therapist

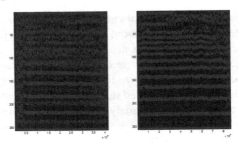

Fig. 4. Detail of windows research complex, illustrating the spectral mask of the signal before (left) and after (right) patient "B" with a speech therapist. Phoneme [a].

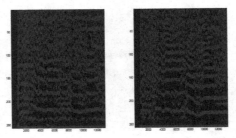

Fig. 5. Detail of windows research complex, illustrating the spectral mask of the signal before (left) and after (right) patient "B" with a speech therapist. Word [sto dvadcat' odin].

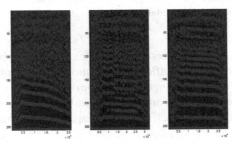

Fig. 6. Detail of windows research complex, illustrating the spectral mask of the signal before (left), in process (center) and after (right) patient "C" with a speech therapist. Phoneme [i].

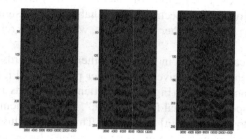

Fig. 7. Detail of windows research complex, illustrating the spectrum of the signal before (left), in process (center) and after (right) patient "C" with a speech therapist. Phoneme [i].

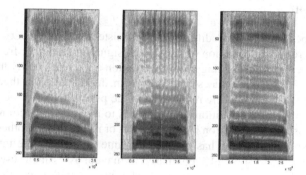

Fig. 8. Detail of windows research complex, illustrating the spectral mask of the signal before (left), in process (center) and after (right) patient "C" with a speech therapist. Word [sto dvadcat' odin].

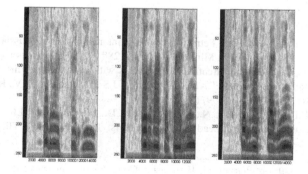

Fig. 9. Detail of windows research complex, illustrating the spectrum of the signal before (left, in process (center)) and after (right) patient "C" with a speech therapist. Word [sto dvadcat' odin].

Figure 4 shows a results of frequency mask for patient before and after classes with therapist for single phoneme [i], patient 'B'. Axis X is time in discrete. Frequency of sample is 12000 Hz. Axis Y is number of channel, 0 (top) is 4000 Hz, 255 (bottom) is 50 Hz. Informant structure of spectrum after rehabilitation is significant higher, harmonic structure can be seen to higher frequencies, where before rehabilitation noise is presented.

Same dependence can be found in Figure 5 (other signal, words [sto dvdcat' odin], patient 'B'. This dependence is universal for other phonemes (Figure 6 - patient 'C', single phoneme [i]) and patients (Figure 7 - patient 'C', words [sto dvdcat' odin]). Figure 8 and 9 show spectrum signal for patient 'C', single phoneme [i] (Figure 8) and patient 'C', words [sto dvdcat' odin] (Figure 9). This figures illustrate the process of spectrum correction in dynamic of trainings with therapist. Increasing of top informant frequency is distinctly presented.

4 Conclusion

Speech signal spectrum (with modification) is consistent with the theory of the speech production, whereby the formation of the speech signal in the upper frequency signal appearing at upper portions passing speech formation tract, particularly the mouth [8].

Resection first fragment reduces obstructions in the signal path, thereby reducing the width of the spectrum. During rehabilitation the patient receives the speech signal formation skill in the new conditions, which leads to a partial correction of spectrum. Currently, there is an accumulation base to support or refute this hypothesis.

Application software system has reduced the time to evaluate the intelligibility of the speech, the method [7] by 74% compared to manual assessment used in the early stages, and provided means for storing and further processing of speech signals in the studies conducted by the Tomsk Cancer Research Institute of the Russian Academy of Medical Science.

References

1. Chissov, V.A., Starinskiy, V.V., Petrov, G.: Malignant neoplasms in Russia in 2011. FSE "MNIOI im. P.A Herzen" Health Ministry of Russia, 288 p. (2012) (in Rus.)
2. Epidemiologiya, diagnosis and treatment of patients with cancer of the mouth, tongue and throat: Sat Articles. Edited akad.RAMN, Sidorenko, J.S., Svetitskogo, P.V., Rostov-on-Don, publishing voRGMU, 202 p. (1999) (in Rus.)
3. Choinzonov, E.L., Balatskaya, L.N., Kitsmanyuk, Z.D., Muhamedov, M.R., Dubskiy, S.V.: Rehabilitation of patients with head and neck tumors. Tomsk: Izd.vo YTL 2-3, 296 p. (in Rus.)
4. Balatskaya, L.N., Choinzonov, E.L., Kostjuchenko, E.: Acoustic analysis of the speech function in patients with oropharyngeal. II Eurasian Congress of Cancers of the head and neck. Book of abstracts. Almaty. Kazakhstan, p. 163 (2011)
5. Kipyatkova, I., Karpov, A., Verkhodanova, V., Zelezny, M.: Analysis of Long-distance Word Dependencies and Pronunciation Variability at Conversational Russian Speech Recognition. In: Proceedings of Federated Conference on Computer Science and Information Systems, Fed-CSIS 2012, Wroclaw, Poland, pp. 719–725 (2012)

6. Meshcheryakov, R.V., Bondarenko, V.P., Konev, A.A.: Biologic feedback formation by vocal rehabilitation. In: Proceedings of the International Workshop SPEECH and Computer (SPECOM 2006), St. Petersburg, Russia, June 25-29, pp. 251–257 (2006)
7. Standard GOST 50840-95 Voice over paths of communication. Methods for assessing the quality, legibility and recognition January 01, 1997, 234 p. Publishing Standards, Moscow (1995)
8. Sapozhkov, M.A. (ed.): Acoustics: A Handbook, 2nd edn., Rev. and add. Radio and communication, 336 p. (1989)

Speaker Turn Detection Based on Multimodal Situation Analysis

Andrey Ronzhin[1,2] and Victor Budkov[1]

[1] SPIIRAS, 39, 14th line, St. Petersburg, Russia
[2] Saint-Petersburg State University, 7-9, Universitetskaya nab., St. Petersburg, Russia
{ronzhin,budkov}@iias.spb.su
www.spiiras.nw.ru/speech

Abstract. The main stage of speaker diarization is a detection of time labels, where speakers are changed. The most of the approaches to the decision of the speaker turn detection problem is focused on processing of audio signal captured in one channel and applied for archive records. Recently the problem of speaker diarization became to be considered from multimodal point of view. In this paper we outline modern methods of audio and video signal processing and personification data analysis for multimodal speaker diarization. The proposed PARAD-R software for Russian speech analysis implemented for audio speaker diarization and will be enhanced based on advances of multimodal situation analysis in a meeting room.

Keywords: Speaker diarization, multimodal analysis, face tracking, sound source localization, speech recognition.

1 Introduction

The main goal of the development of systems of formal logging activities is to automate the whole process of transcription of the participant speech. However, the automatic recognition of conversational speech remains today one of the major unsolved problems in the field of speech technology. The automatic speech recognition is the conversion of an acoustic speech signal received from the microphone into a sequence of words, which can be used for analysis and interpretation of the meaning of the speech utterance. One of the possible ways to improve the accuracy of speech recognition is to configure the speaker dependent system parameters for automatic speech processing. Therefore it is not less important to the processing of audio records of speech is the speaker diarization stage providing segmentation of cues of each speaker in the single-channel audio signal and the subsequent grouping of utterances relating to a particular speaker.

In task of speaker diarization, unlike authentication tasks, the number of speakers participating in the discussion is unknown beforehand, and therefore, the respective speaker models are automatically created and trained during the records analysis that greatly complicates the processing of the speech signal. Another factor reducing the performance of the diarization systems is the presence in an audio signal of the following phenomena: the "overlapping" speech when several people talking at the same

M. Železný et al. (Eds.): SPECOM 2013, LNAI 8113, pp. 302–309, 2013.
© Springer International Publishing Switzerland 2013

time, speech artifacts (smack, clatter language), non-verbal pauses (cough, laugh), and short remarks. One approach to improve the accuracy of determining the boundaries of a speaker voice is attracting other sources of information other than the audio signal. Further, the methods for parametric representation of signals in multi-modal and multi-channel systems of speaker diarization, as well as their contribution in determining of speaker turn are discussed.

2   Methods of Data Recording and Feature Extraction

To improve the accuracy of speakers authentication and diarization besides of the audio signal processing it is appropriate to involve other methods of analyzing the situation in the room where the meeting is held. Figure 1 shows the classification of methods of recording speaker data depending on: the number of channels that receive signals of the same type; the type of sensors involved in the monitoring of the discussion; as well as the number of types of used sensors. The use of contact diarization ways, for example by switching microphones by hand, is the most effective to date, but it requires a complicated complex of equipment and staff involvement at the time of the meeting. A more promising approach to solving the diarization problem is a multi-channel processing of multiple natural modalities [1]. But in some cases, such as phone calls using video analysis tools will be unavailable owing to the absence of appropriate sensors in the devices involved in the dialogue.

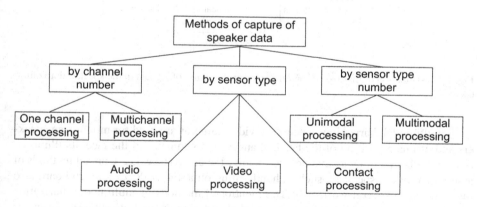

Fig. 1. Classification of methods of recording data in the speaker diarization task

Now let us to consider the classification of methods of parametric representation of signals that can be used in the problems of authentication and diarization of speakers (Figure 2). Well-established methods of temporal and spectral analysis, as well as their combination in a single vector of features are used for parametric representation of the audio signal. The most commonly used features are parameters calculated on the basis of MFCC (mel-frequency cepstral coefficients), in some cases together with the first and/or second derivative [2].

Also other types of characteristics: short-term energy of the signal, the number of zero-crossings, fundamental frequency, the spectrum energy of speech segment, the distribution of the energy spectrum bands, coefficients of linear prediction, as well as prosodic features such as duration of phonemes and pauses, rate of speech are used during the speaker diarization [1].

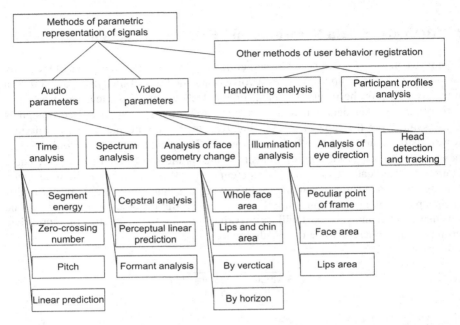

Fig. 2. Classification of methods of parametric representation of signals in the speaker diarization task

In multimodal diarization systems the video cameras are used for monitoring speakers and estimate position of the head, changing the geometry of the face, its illumination, and other parameters that help to identify the current speaker. Contact methods of assessment of the speakers, such as handwriting on a Tablet PC or a touch board also investigated in several works [3]. The mentioned methods of multimodal diarization based on a joint analysis of the data recorded audio, video and other types of sensors will be considered in the next section.

3   Multimodal Speaker Diarization Methods

The number of papers, in which the analysis of visual cues (such as facial movement, line of sight) is involved and is used with a combination of audio parameters for solving the problem diarization speakers, is increasing every year [1,4,5,6]. In the first studies the correlation of facial movement and the sound component of the speech was analyzed, then it was suggested that evaluation of synchronous audio and video component of speech for the speakers localization based on the calculation of the mutual information of acoustic energy level and variability of speaker face illumination [7]. Evaluation of mutual information can be computed for the entire frame, and certain facial zone, for example, corresponding speaker's lips. In [8] the classical correlation analysis was adapted for the problem of estimating the synchrony of audiovisual speech components. In these studies the experiment was performed on the small material, which mainly took into account the non-overlapping speech, and speaker face was directed to the video camera. In [4] the method of evaluation of mutual information and correlation analysis is compared with the method of assessing the synchronicity of audio and video component of speech. Applying the assessment of synchronicity audio and video component as the mutual information for static meetings the error diarization was 13%, and 29% for the dynamic meetings [7].

Analysis of head movement and its direction may also be useful in identifying the speaker. In particular, it is known from psychology that [9]: (1) audience tends to look in the direction of the speaker, (2) before starting to speak, a new speaker founds eye contact with the current speaker, (3) finally, before we begin to speak, audience transfers to us their views. Determining the direction of the head is a certain approximation to the gaze direction and is used more often, as it can be implemented with more simple equipment. Another way to determine the voice activity is video analysis, which is based on the analysis of illumination changes of the corresponding points in adjacent frames. To improve the processing accuracy of the area of analysis is preliminary limited by determining the part corresponding to the color of the skin, the contour of the face, lips, or lip area together with the chin [4,6].

The methods of head detection and tracking are successfully applied in the problem of speaker diarization [7]. The method of Lucas-Kanade and its modifications are aimed at determining the direction of displacement of object points vertically and horizontally, and serve as parameters to determine the speaker. In [10], correlation analysis is applied to the evaluation of synchronous lip movements and audio stream, where visual signs are described by the contour of the lips and their movement through a set of parameters calculated on the basis of the two-dimensional discrete Fourier transform and Lucas-Kanade analysis of the key points of the lips.

4   Multi-channel Audio Speakers Diarization Methods

Now another class of diarization methods based on the use of multi-channel audio processing will be considered. Usage of two or more microphones is implemented in speech signal processing to assess the spatial acoustic environment [11]. Besides the direct function of sound recording, microphone array is used for spatial localization of sound sources and filtration of the desired signal by controlling the directivity of the microphone array. This system analyzes and perceives the sound coming from the limited region of the working space and suppresses sounds arriving from all other directions.

Problems of speech recording and recognition using microphone array at different distances from the user is studied by a wide range of researchers [1,11]. Nevertheless, the problem of speech signal localization is not completely solved yet. First of all, this is owing to the fact that the mentioned methods were initially focused on the localization of narrow-band signals, and at the speech processing, which varies in the range of 20-20000 Hz, it is required to change them.

When designing systems analyzing the signals propagating through space, primarily problem is interference of various signals. If the desired signal and interferences have the same frequency-time characteristics, the timing signal filtering is not effective. However, the sources of useful signal and noise are often located in different points of the space, in this case possible to use the spatial filter to attenuate the noise level.

The problem of sound source localization in most of the approaches is solved by spectral methods of audio signal processing as well as statistical methods [1]. Spectral methods are quite attractive from the practical point of view, so they are used more often. Now the priority issue of research deals with the stability of the system to noise interference and reverberation.

Another class of multichannel diarization systems based on the use of personal microphones and estimating the presence of voice activity in each channel. A preliminary segmentation of the signal on frames containing silence or speech, allows the system to reduce considerably the level of speech recognition errors and to raise speed of processing. Unfortunately, the methods for voice activity detection based on an estimation of the level of energy of the signal or its spectrum, well proved at the single channel speech recognition, give poor results at the processing of multi-channel audio records with several speakers [12]. The matter is that personal microphones capture not only speech of the speaker, but also speech of the neighbors with high level of energy, because usually participants sit close to each other on the meeting table. An opposite situation, when speech of the same speaker can appear in several channels simultaneously that leads to system's decision on activity of several speakers, is likely as well. For solution of this problem the methods based on a normalization of energy of the multi-channel signal, an estimation of channel cross-correlation, or Hidden Markov Models, are used [1,11,13]. The accomplished survey was used at the development of the speech analysis software for Russian. The software is used to create multimedia reports of distributed meetings that helps to reduce labor costs in the preparation of text materials and allows participants to monitor meeting statistics and get a quick search to multimedia archives [14,15,16,17].

5   PARAD-R: The Speech Analysis Software for Russian

In this section the software of automatic analysis, recognition and diarization of Russian speech (PARAD-R) will be outlined. Figure 3 shows the architecture of PARAD-R software, built on the basis of a three level processing (client, server, program-mathematical core). The client and server can be located either on the same computer or on different computers and communicate over a computer network. The exchange of information between client and server is implemented using protocols MRCPv2 (Media Resource Control Protocol) and RTSP (Real-Time Streaming Protocol).

The server consists of the following software modules: a server application - MRCP server, the modules of vocabulary editor, language model generator and quality estimator. Each of these modules, except the last, is implemented as an executable file running OS MS Windows XP/Vista/7. In addition to these software modules, the server is also

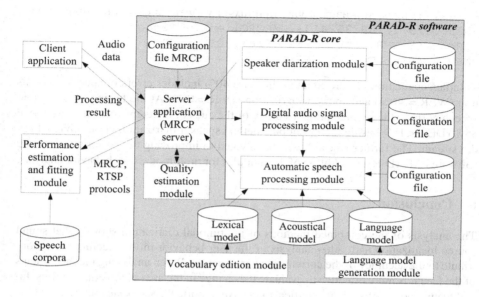

Fig. 3. The architecture of the PARAD-R software

linked to the core of mathematical software, which includes: digital audio processing, speaker diarization, automatic speech recognition [18,19]. Each of these modules is implemented as a static library to be connected to the server application.

Experimental verification of the software system was carried out using the speech corpora with the following parameters [20]: 1) 50 speakers - native Russian speakers (25 women and 25 men), 2) the age of speakers from 16 to 60 years, 3) the signal / noise ratio greater than 20 dB; 4) the text contains 327 phonetically balanced sensible sentences in Russian. The software supports the processing of audio files with WAV-format, sampling rate of 8000 Hz and 16000, 8 bits and 16 bits, the coding type A-law, -law, or PCM. Assessment of the quality of the developed complex operation was carried out by methods that take into account the metric WER (Word Error Rate), LER (Letter Error Rate), SWER (Speaker Attributed Word Error Rate) and DER (Diarization Error Rate). The result of processing the input data is transferred to the client and is written in a local text file by the server application for further analysis of the software performance. Example of the file fragment is shown below:

```
2013.3.29 16:39:35:400:  MRCPClient - Recognizing
- File Name: D:PARAD_test\sp009\Mic1\009_1_0a1_004.wav
2013.3.29 16:39:35:400:  MRCPClient - Recognizing
- Received from ASR: своей жизни уже принимал участие
судебных процессов
2013.3.29 16:39:35:400:  MRCPClient - Recognizing
- Received from diarization: своей(4) жизни(4) уже(4)
принимал(4) участие(4) судебных(4) процессов(4)
2013.3.29 16:39:35:400:  MRCPClient - Recognizing
```

```
- Real : в своей жизни я уже принимал участие в судебных процессах
2013.3.29 16:39:35:413:  MRCPClient - Recognizing
- Result: WER = 40%; LER = 16%; DER = 0%;
SWER = 40%; RT = 1; SNR = 17
```

Complex evaluation SWER equal in this case 40% includes errors of speech recognition (WER = 40%) and speaker diarization (DER = 0%). At the testing of the whole speech corpora the segmentation accuracy of the cues of different speakers was above 85% (DER <15%) using the developed method speaker diarization in one channel audio stream. The further research will be devoted to improving the performance of the software PARAD-R and addition of the modules for multimodal user behavior analysis.

6   Conclusion

The analysis of the combined methods of multimodal diarization showed that sound source localization and video analysis of the user behavior in the meeting room contribute to the accuracy of the current speaker selection. When analyzing the movements of the face it is more effective to evaluate the change in the area of the image of lips, facial feature points offset in the vertical plane. An important issue is the integration of the parameters obtained from the analysis of video and audio data. Problems synchronizing audio and video segments, forming a single weighted feature vector in the majority of approaches are resolved during the preliminary fitting the diarization system. In addition, evaluation of natural asynchrony of audio (oral speech) and video (lip movements and other elements of the face) is used in some studies as an additional parameter to determine the current speaker. Also statistical analysis of participant profiles including the frequency of their appearances at meetings and monitoring the overall situation in the room for speaker selection based on the analysis of the direction of gaze (head) of all the other participants are used for speaker diarization task.

Acknowledgments. This research is supported by Ministry of Education and Science of the Russian Federation (Federal Program "Research and Development", the state contract N° 07.514.11.4139), RFBR (grants 12-08-31520-mol_a and 13-08-0741) and Saint-Petersburg State University (project # 31.37.103.2011).

References

1. Noulas, A., Englebienne, G., Kröse, B.J.A.: Multimodal Speaker Diarization. IEEE Transactions on Pattern Analysis and Machine Intelligence 34(1), 79–93 (2012)
2. Sinha, R., Tranter, S.E., Gales, M.J.F., Woodland, P.C.: The Cambridge March 2005 University speaker diarisation system. In: Proceedings of the European Conference on Speech Communication and Technology, pp. 2437–2440 (2005)
3. Tsiaras, V., Panagiotakis, C., Stylianou, Y.: Video and audio based detection of filled hesitation pauses in classroom lectures. In: Proceedings of the 17th European Signal Processing Conference (EUSIPCO 2009), Glasgow, Scotland, pp. 834–838 (2009)

4. Garau, G., Dielmann, A., Bourlard, H.: Audio and Visual Synchronisation for Speaker Diarisation. In: Proceedings of International Conference on Speech and Language Processing, Interspeech, Makuhari, Japan, pp. 2654–2657 (2010)
5. Friedland, G., Hung, H., Yeo, C.: Multi-Modal Speaker Diarization of Real-World Meetings using Compressed Domain Video Features. In: Proceedings ICASSP, pp. 4069–4072 (2009)
6. Dai, P., Tao, L., Xu, G.: Audio-Visual Fused Online Context Analysis Toward Smart Meeting Room. In: Indulska, J., Ma, J., Yang, L.T., Ungerer, T., Cao, J. (eds.) UIC 2007. LNCS, vol. 4611, pp. 868–877. Springer, Heidelberg (2007)
7. Hershey, J., Movellan, J.: Audio-Vision: Using Audio-Visual Synchrony to Locate Sound. In: Proceedings NIPS, pp. 813–819 (1999)
8. Slaney, M., Covell, M.: FaceSync: a linear operator for measuring synchronization of visual facial images and audio tracks. In: Proceedings NIPS, pp. 814–820 (2000)
9. Padilha, E., Carletta, J.: Nonverbal Behaviours Improving a Simulation of Small Group Discussion. In: Proceedings of the 1st Nordic Symposium on Multimodal Communications, pp. 93–105 (2003)
10. Eveno, N., Caplier, A., Coulon, P.-Y.: Accurate and Quasi-Automatic Lip Tracking. IEEE Trans. on Circuits and Systems for Video Technology 14(5), 706–715 (2004)
11. Omologo, M., Svaizer, P., Brutti, A., Cristoforetti, L.: Speaker Localization in CHIL Lectures: Evaluation Criteria and Results. In: Renals, S., Bengio, S. (eds.) MLMI 2005. LNCS, vol. 3869, pp. 476–487. Springer, Heidelberg (2006)
12. Pfau, T., Ellis, D., Stolcke, D.: Multispeaker Speech Activity Detection for the ICSI Meeting Recorder. In: IEEE ASRU Workshop, pp. 107–110 (2001)
13. Ronzhin, A.L., Prischepa, M., Karpov, A.: A Video Monitoring Model with a Distributed Camera System for the Smart Space. In: Balandin, S., Dunaytsev, R., Koucheryavy, Y. (eds.) ruSMART/NEW2AN 2010. LNCS, vol. 6294, pp. 102–110. Springer, Heidelberg (2010)
14. Yusupov, R.M., Ronzhin, A.L.: From Smart Devices to Smart Space. Herald of the Russian Academy of Sciences, MAIK Nauka 80(1), 63–68 (2010)
15. Ronzhin, A.L., Budkov, V.Y.: Multimodal Interaction with Intelligent Meeting Room Facilities from Inside and Outside. In: Balandin, S., Moltchanov, D., Koucheryavy, Y. (eds.) NEW2AN/ruSMART 2009. LNCS, vol. 5764, pp. 77–88. Springer, Heidelberg (2009)
16. Budkov, V.Y., Ronzhin, A.L., Glazkov, S.V., Ronzhin, A.L.: Event-Driven Content Management System for Smart Meeting Room. In: Balandin, S., Koucheryavy, Y., Hu, H. (eds.) NEW2AN/ruSMART 2011. LNCS, vol. 6869, pp. 550–560. Springer, Heidelberg (2011)
17. Karpov, A., Kipyatkova, I., Ronzhin, A.: Very Large Vocabulary ASR for Spoken Russian with Syntactic and Morphemic Analysis. In: Proceedings INTERSPEECH 2011 International Conference, ISCA Association, Florence, Italy, pp. 3161–3164 (2011)
18. Karpov, A., Kipyatkova, I., Ronzhin, A.: Speech Recognition for East Slavic Languages: The Case of Russian. In: Proceedings of the 3rd International Workshop on Spoken Languages Technologies for Under-resourced Languages, SLTU 2012, Cape Town, RSA, pp. 84–89 (2012)
19. Kipyatkova, I., Karpov, A., Verkhodanova, V., Zelezny, M.: Analysis of Long-distance Word Dependencies and Pronunciation Variability at Conversational Russian Speech Recognition. In: Proceedings Federated Conference on Computer Science and Information Systems FedCSIS 2012, Wroclaw, Poland, pp. 719–725 (2012)
20. Jokisch, O., Wagner, A., Sabo, R., Jaeckel, R., Cylwik, N., Rusko, M., Ronzhin, A., Hoffmann, R.: Multilingual Speech Data Collection for the Assessment of Pronunciation and Prosody in a Language Learning System. In: Proceedings 13th International Conference SPECOM 2009, St. Petersburg, pp. 515–520 (2009)

Speech and Crosstalk Detection for Robust Speech Recognition Using a Dual Microphone System

Mikhail Stolbov and Marina Tatarnikova

Speech Technology Center Limited, St. Petersburg, Russia
{stolbov,tatmar}@speechpro.com
www.speechpro.com

Abstract. This paper proposes a practical speech detection technique for robust automatic speech recognition, suitable for use under various interference conditions. This technique consists of a dual microphone system and an algorithm for processing their signals. The microphone module is placed in the workplace of the target speaker. The module consists of two symmetrical supercardioid microphones directed in opposite directions. The algorithm of target speaker detection is proposed for this scheme. This algorithm makes it possible to implement spatial filtering of speakers. Experiments with real recordings demonstrate a significant reduction of speech recognition errors for the target speaker due to suppression of acoustic crosstalk. The main advantage of the proposed technique is simplicity of its use in a wide range of practical situations.

Keywords: speech activity detection, multi-channel audio, crosstalk.

1 Introduction

In many areas (public transport, control points, call centers, etc) observing speech regulations (SR) is important. To control SR observance, it is possible to use speech recognition systems that analyse the operators signal received from the microphone at his or her workplace. The problem is that operators usually work in areas where other operators are present. So other operators speech is also recorded by the target speakers microphone, which leads to a significant deterioration of recognition system results. An additional source of errors can be the speech of a customer located close to the operator.

A traditional solution to the problem of acoustic crosstalk detection is using adequate microphones: individual headset microphones, lapel microphones. However, in some cases work regulations are such that headsets or microphones on clothes cannot be used.

A different solution to the problem of acoustic overlapped speech is presented by the methods of multichannel spectral subtraction [1], crosstalk cancellation, speech separation [2], beamforming [3]. However, signal filtering leads to speech distortions, which can decrease speech recognition efficiency (it is necessary to retrain the recognition system).

More suitable are methods of crosstalk detection, which can detect the fragments of original undistorted operator speech in the signal. Different solutions to the task of crosstalk detection have been proposed for different micro-phone position schemes

M. Železný et al. (Eds.): SPECOM 2013, LNAI 8113, pp. 310–318, 2013.

[4]. Such crosstalk detection systems use different cross-channel features that use the signals of the microphones of the target speaker and non-target speakers [1], [5]-[9]. In this case, each non-target speaker has to have their own micorphone, whose signal is compared to the operator signal, which makes it difficult to use such systems in unprepared areas.

The idea in our approach is to use an independent microphone module for separating the operators speech from the environment sounds. This paper proposes a flexible scheme with two combined symmetrical microphones that are located autonomously on each workplace. This system allows to simplify the voice detection algorithm and to make it robust to environment variations. For this scheme we developed an algorithm for target speaker detection which is based on a simple energy criterion. The paper describes a classification algorithm with four states: background, target speaker, interfering speakers, overlap of the target speaker and the interfering speakers. Results of experiments on location are reported.

2   Proposed Dual Microphone System

Acoustic environment is characterized by the following features:

- An office with many employees (operators) whose speech reaches the workplace of the target speaker.
- Location of the interfering operators, whose positions are not known beforehand and can change.
- A speaker (customer) can be located near the operator.
- The target speaker (operator) is located in his or her workplace and can insignificantly change position and turn his or her head relative to the microphone.

The main idea was to use a second microphone to gather sounds from the environment.

We propose using two combined supercardioid microphones in each workplace, pointed in the opposite directions: one towards the operator, the other towards the customer and the surrounding environment. Each microphone records the operators speech and the sounds of the acoustic environment.

The two microphone system is shown in Figure 1.

Fig. 1. The symmetrical two microphone system

3   The Model of Sounds Separation by Using Two Microphones

The supercardioid microphones point in the opposite directions: the first (the main microphone) is directed towards the target speaker, the second (the reference microphone) is directed towards the customer and the environment. Diagrams of the directivity of the microphones are shown in Figure 2. The polar pattern of the two microphone system is shown in Figure 2.

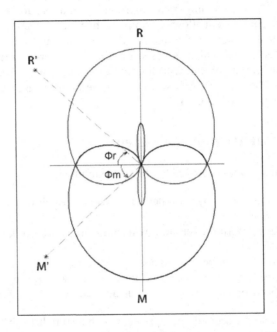

Fig. 2. Polar pattern of the two microphone system

Let Φ is the angle from the direction perpendicular to the microphone axis: positive towards the main speaker and negative towards the interfering speakers.

The microphone has the main directivity petal with the characteristic $D(\Phi)$ in the $\Phi > 0$ space and the reverse directivity petal with the characteristic $B(\Phi)$ in the $\Phi < 0$ space. Since the polar patterns of the main and the reference microphones are symmetrical so we have the following relations: $Dr(-\Phi) = D_m(\Phi) = D(\Phi)$, $Br(\Phi) = B_m(-\Phi) = B(\Phi)$.

Because the characteristics of each microphone are symmetrical with respect to the microphone axis so we have the following relations: $D(\Phi) = D(\pi - \Phi)$, $B(\Phi) = B(\pi - \Phi)$.

For the supercardioid microphones in the $\Phi > 0$ space:

$$A(\Phi) = D_m(\Phi)/B_r(\Phi) > 1$$

Let us examine the main variants of the acoustic environment.

The following four hypotheses are made for each frame of the signal:

H_0 : No speech activity (environment noise).

H_1 : The first main speaker is active.

H_2 : Another (not the first) speaker is active.

H_3 : Local channel operator overlapping with one or more speakers.

Let the target speaker be located in the direction $\Phi_m > 0$, his or her speech with the intensity L_m reaches the microphones of the main and reference channels, the non-local speaker is situated in the direction Φ_r, and the sound of his or her speech with the intensity L_r reaches the microphones of the main and reference channels. Then the power of the signals of the main and reference microphones can be represented as follows:

$$P_m = L_m D(\Phi_m) + L_r B(\Phi_r) + P_0$$
$$P_m = L_m B(\Phi_m) + L_r D(\Phi_r) + P_0$$

Where P_0 is the power created by the environment noise.

We use the ratio of the signal powers for the main and reference microphones as the criteria for detecting the speech of the main speaker and the interfering speaker:

$$R_m = P_m/P_r = 1/R_r$$

3.1 H_0 : No Speech

During pauses, both microphones record the background environment noise in equal proportions. For this reason, $R_m \approx 1$, $R_r \approx 1$.

3.2 H_1 : Speech of Target Speaker

$$R_r(\Phi_m) = A(\Phi_m)C(\Phi_m),$$

where $C(\Phi_m) < 1$

$$C(\Phi_m) = [(1 + 1/SDR(\Phi_m))/(1 + 1/SBR(\Phi_m))].$$

Signal-to-Direct Ratio and Signal-to- Backward Ratio are the follows:

$$SDR(\Phi_m) = L_m D(\Phi_m)/P_0 \; SBR(\Phi_m) = L_r D(\Phi_m)/P_0$$

The decision about speech activity of the target speaker is taken according to the condition:

$$R_r(\Phi_m) = A(\Phi_m)C(\Phi_m) > T_0.$$

This relation will hold in a certain interval of angles $\Phi_m \geq \Phi_{\min} > 0$, depending on polar patterns, the threshold value, the noise level and the intensity of the target speakers speech. Environment noise imposes restrictions on the minimal intensity and the sector of angles in which the target speakers speech will be detected.

3.3 H_2 : Concurrent Speaker

The decision of the speech activity of the non-local speaker is taken in the same way according to the value R_r exceeding the threshold T_r in the $\Phi_r < 0$ space.

$$R_r(\Phi_r) = A(\Phi_r)C(\Phi_r) > T_r > 1.$$

This condition will also hold in a certain interval of angles $\Phi_r \leq \Phi_{\min} < 0$.

3.4 H_3 : Targed Speaker Is Overlapping with One or More Speakers

The doubletalk state is characterized by changing states, depending on which speakers speech is louder.

If $L_m >> L_r$ we have $R_m >> 1$, $R_r << 1$.

If $L_r >> L_m$ we have $R_m << 1$, $R_r >> 1$.

Therefore, in case of doubletalk of the target and the interfering speaker, the states $R_m >> 1$, $R_r << 1$ and $R_m << 1$, $R_r >> 1$ are interchanging.

It follows from the analysis that the ratios R_m, R_r can be used as indicators for the speech activity of the target and interfering speaker.

To sum up, the paired symmetric microphone system makes it possible to separate the speech of the target speaker from both far-field and near-field sound sources.

4   The Algorithm

The observed signals of microphones and the source signals are described by

$$M(k,n) = S_m(k,n) + B_m(k)S_r(k,n)$$
$$R(k,n) = S_r(k,n) + B_r(k)S_m(k,n)$$

where k, n are the frequency and frame indices, respectively, S_m, S_r - are the signals from the main speaker and the interfering sound.

In order for separate speaker phrases to be detected as a whole, without pauses between sounds, we smooth in time the spectra of the main and reference channels computed on overlapped frames:

$$P_m(k,n) = (1-\mu)P_m(k,n-1) + \mu|M(k,n)|^2$$
$$P_r(k,n) = (1-\mu)P_r(k,n-1) + \mu|R(k,n)|^2$$

where μ is the smoothing factor.

Using smoothed spectra, for each frame we compute the powers and power ratios: Main-to-Reference Ratio R_m, Reference-to-Main Ratio R_r:

$$P_m(n) = \sum_{k=KL}^{KH} P_m(k,n)$$
$$P_r(n) = \sum_{k=KL}^{KH} P_r(k,n)$$
$$R_m(n) = P_m(n)/P_r(n)$$
$$R_r(n) = 1/P_m(n)$$

Where $[KL, KH]$ is the frequency range $[200, 4000]$ Hz.

4.1 Local Speech Detector

In the course of the experiment we examined the behavior of the parameters R_m, R_r on an operator speech fragment ($+90°$ angle), two interfering speaker fragments ($45°$ and $90°$ angles) and a fragment of overlapping operator speech (operator angle $+90°$, interfering speaker angle $45°$). Figure 3 shows the diagrams of $R_m(t)$ and $R_r(t)$ and classification process.

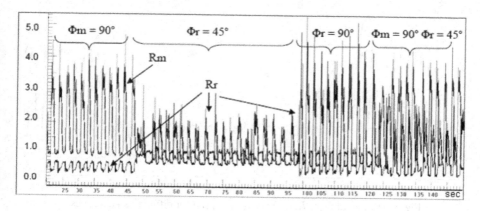

Fig. 3. The diagrams of $R_m(t)$ and $R_r(t)$ for different signal states

Therefore, by estimating $R_m(t)$, $R_r(t)$ and choosing a threshold value T_0 , the signal frames can be labeled according to the following rule:

$$H_0 : R_m < T_0, P_r < T_0$$
$$H_1 : R_m > T_0, P_r < T_0$$
$$H_2 : R_m < T_0, P_r > T_0$$
$$H_3 : R_m > T_0, P_r > T_0$$

4.2 Non-local Event Segmentation

For identifying signal fragments (states) we propose to use the envelopes E_m, E_r of the ratios $R_m(n)$ and $R_r(n)$:

$$E_m(n) = (1 - \beta)E_m(n - 1) + \beta R_m(n) \text{ if } R_m(n) > E_m(n - 1) \text{ else}$$
$$E_m(n) = (1 - \alpha)E_m(n - 1) + \alpha R_m(n)$$

$$E_r(n) = (1 - \beta)E_r(n - 1) + \beta R_r(n) \text{ if } R_r(n) > E_r(n - 1) \text{ else}$$
$$E_r(n) = (1 - \alpha)E_r(n - 1) + \alpha R_r(n)$$

where α is the release coefficient, β is the attack coefficient.

Hypotheses are accepted based on the following rule:

$$H_0 : E_m(n) < T_e, E_r(n) < T_e$$
$$H_1 : E_m(n) > T_e, E_r(n) < T_e$$

$$H_2 : E_m(n) < T_e, E_r(n) > T_e$$
$$H_3 : E_m(n) > T_e, E_r(n) > T_e$$

where T_e is the threshold of decision state.

Figure 4 shows the diagrams of $E_m(n)$, $E_r(n)$ for $\alpha = 0.002$, $\beta = 1$.

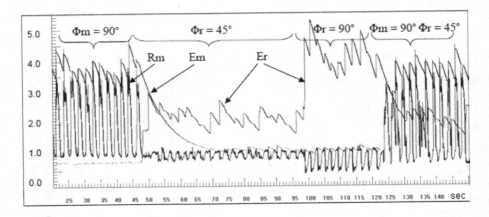

Fig. 4. The diagrams of $R_m(n)$, $E_m(n)$, $E_r(n)$ for different signal states

The Figure 4 is demonstrated on the classification process. Hypotheses based on the $E_m(n)$ and $E_r(n)$ are accepted with a delay due to the low value of release coefficient.

4.3   Details of the Algorithm

The main goal of the algorithm is to extract the fragments that contain the operators speech from the recording. The recordings were processed in the following way.

The short-time energy is computed over a Hann window of 20-30 ms with 50% overlapping. The smoothing factor $\mu = 0.2$. Since the operator detection algorithm works with a certain delay, in our algorithm the results of the segmentation were applied to earlier data, moved backward by 40ms.

The fragments of the recording where the operators speech was detected were left in the output signal without changes, on the remaining fragments the input signal was suppressed by 40dB.

To sum up, the proposed algorithm makes it possible to detect operator speech frames, as well as to detect the fragments of overlapping speech of the operator and an interfering speaker.

5   Description of Experiment

The algorithm was assessed by results of on-line acoustic keyword spotting. Our phoneme recognizer based on the use of ANN GMM/HMM. The TRAP-like long-term features used for recognition. The acoustic models are trained on 100h of telephone conversations.

The vocabulary consisted of 33 words. For the purposes of the experiment, the interfering speaker pronounced the same words. The microphone was located on the desk at the distance of 0.5-1m from the operator.

We show the recognition results of our experiments in Table 1.

Table 1. Recognition results

Conditions	Before processing		After processing	
	FR	FA	FR	FA
Target speaker only	1/33	0	1/33	0
Interfering speaker only	1/33	25/33	1/33	0
Both speakers speaking simultaneously	7/33	9/33	3/33	0

The results demonstrate that these features provide a marked improvement (18% relative) over a baseline system using single-channel features. The algorithm leads to a reduction in both FR and FA.

The analysis of the recordings shows that it is possible to achieve an acceptable recognition quality given a high-quality target speaker recording with a sufficient loudness level.

6   Conclusions

We addressed the task of automatically recognizing separate words of an operator using an automatic speech recog-nition system for different working conditions. The aim of our work was to develop a technique for detecting the operators speech.

The technique for operator speech detection proposed in this paper combines a microphone module and an algorithm for processing the signals of the microphones. Using the information obtained from the microphone module it is possible to perform spatial segmentation between the operators speech and the interfering speakers using the criteria of their location in space and the intensity of their speech signals. For this module, we proposed a robust algo-rithm which allows us to segment the signal of the main channel microphone into four states: pause fragments, oper-ators speech, interfering speakers speech, overlapping speech of the operator and interfering speakers. Since the microphones are identical and their position is symmetrical, we can significantly simplify the algorithms compared to other similar algorithms.

Experimental evaluation of the proposed scheme demonstrated the efficiency of operator speech detecting when speech from other speakers is present. Experimental results verify that these goals are reached.

Applying the operator speech detection algorithm in real-life conditions yielded a reduction in both FR and FA errors with the same recognition level.

Using the proposed technique provides a possibility to organize operator speech detection systems for various working conditions.

The main result of our research has been the creation of a novel technique fulfilling the criteria of applicability in different conditions.

References

1. Nasu, Y., Shinoda, K., Furui, S.: Cross-Channel Spectral Subtraction for meeting speech recognition. In: Proceedings of the IEEE International Conference on Acoustics, Speech, and Signal Processing, ICASSP 2011, Prague Congress Center, Prague, Czech Republic, May 22-27, pp. 4812–4815. IEEE (2011)
2. Cao, Y., Sridman, S., Moody, M.: Multichannel Speech Separation by Eigendecomposition and Its Application to Co-Talker Interference Removal. IEEE Trans. on SAP 5(3) (1997)
3. Morgan, P., George, E., Lee, T., Kay, M.: Co-Channel Speaker Separation. In: ICASSP, Part 1, May 9-12, vol. 1, pp. 828–831 (1995)
4. Wrigley, S.N., Brown, G.J., Wan, V., Renals, S.: Speech and Crosstalk Detection in Multi-channel Audio. IEEE Trans. on SAP 13(1) (2005)
5. Chakraborty, R., Nadeu, C., Butko, T.: Detection and positioning of overlapped sounds in a room environment. In: Proc. Interspeech 2012 (2012)
6. Boakye, K., Stolcke, A.: Improved Speech Activity Detection Using Cross-Channel Features for Recognition of Multi-party Meetings. In: Proc. Interspeech 2006 (2006)
7. Yakoyama, R., et al.: Overlapped Speech Detection in Meeting Using Cross-Channel Spectral Subtraction and Spectrum Similarity. In: Proc. Interspeech 2012 (2012)
8. Yen, K.-C., Zhao, Y.: Robust Automatic Speech Recognition using a multi-channel signal separation front-end. In: Proc. ICLSP 1996 (1996)
9. Laskowski, K., Schulttz, T.: A geometric interpretation of non-target-normalized maximum cross-channel correlation for vocal activity detection in meetings. In: Proc. of NAACL HLT 2007, pp. 89–92 (2007)

Speech and Language Resources within Speech Recognition and Synthesis Systems for Serbian and Kindred South Slavic Languages

Vlado Delić[1], Milan Sečujski[1], Nikša Jakovljević[1], Darko Pekar[2], Dragiša Mišković[2], Branislav Popović[1], Stevan Ostrogonac[2], Milana Bojanić[1], and Dragan Knežević[2]

[1] University of Novi Sad, Faculty of Technical Sciences, Novi Sad, Serbia
vdelic@uns.ac.rs
[2] "AlfaNum - Speech Technologies", Novi Sad, Serbia
darko.pekar@alfanum.co.rs

Abstract. Unlike other new technologies, most speech technologies are heavily language dependent and have to be developed separately for each language. The paper gives a detailed description of speech and language resources for Serbian and kindred South Slavic languages developed during the last decade within joint projects of the Faculty of Technical Sciences, Novi Sad, Serbia and the company "AlfaNum". It points out the advantages of simultaneous development of speech synthesis and recognition as complementary speech technologies, and discusses the possibility of reuse of speech and language resources across kindred languages.

Keywords: speech technologies, speech and language resources, South Slavic languages.

1 Introduction

Automatic speech recognition (ASR) and text-to-speech synthesis (TTS) enable two-way human-machine speech communication and, as such, have the potential to revolutionize human-machine interaction in many areas of industry and everyday life. However, both ASR and TTS are heavily language dependent, and for each language most of the modules they use have to be developed independently. Even though scientific and technological development over the last decades is evident, quality ASR and TTS systems have emerged only in languages well covered by speech and language resources [1].

A number of valuable speech and language resources for Serbian and other kindred South Slavic languages have been created within several joint projects of the Faculty of Technical Sciences and the company "AlfaNum". Apart from these resources, a number of expert systems, machine learning systems as well as mathematical models have been developed and deployed in the first speech enabled products in the western Balkans, the region where South Slavic languages are predominantly spoken. In the rest of the paper the speech recognition and synthesis technologies developed within this cooperation will be jointly referred to as "AlfaNum" speech technologies.

M. Železný et al. (Eds.): SPECOM 2013, LNAI 8113, pp. 319–326, 2013.

The paper is organised as follows. The speech and language resources are described in the context of text-to-speech and speech-to-text systems, presented in Section 2. The language resources, including morphological dictionaries and POS-tagged text corpora are presented in Section 3. The speech resources, including phonemically labelled speech corpora are described in Section 4. The modules using these resources are described in Section 5, including a text preprocessor, a POS-tagger, and a rule-based predictor of prosodic elements from given text. The abovementioned resources also enabled a number of machine learning systems to be developed, including sets of transformation rules for POS tagging (used in TTS, but also in the creation of some ASR resources) as well as a regression-tree-based system for the generation of acoustic representation of prosodic features of speech, all of these also described in Section 5. The language modelling technique used within the ASR system, suited to highly inflective languages such as Serbian, is presented in Section 6.

2   ASR and TTS Modules Related to Speech and Language Resources

A TTS system consists of natural language processing (high-level synthesis) and signal synthesis (low-level synthesis) modules, while an ASR system is based on speech modelling and speech signal processing modules. The relations among all principal modules of "AlfaNum" ASR and TTS systems and the corresponding speech and language resources are shown in Fig. 1. The figure corresponds to the systems for Serbian, Croatian or any other standardized register for Serbo-Croatian, as well as Macedonian to a significant extent (with some modifications that will be explained in further text). The most relevant resources are listed in Table 1, and will be explained in more details in the remainder of the paper. It should be noted that a number of other speech and language resources have been developed, which are, however, not used by the latest versions of "AlfaNum" speech recognition and synthesis systems.

3   Textual Resources

Within TTS, textual resources enable tasks such as morphological analysis, grapheme to phoneme conversion in NLP as well as recovery of prosodic information from text. As to ASR, pronunciation and language models are also based on some textual resources, while the phonetic tagging of ASR corpus is also supported by NLP resources as regards stress types and positions.

3.1   Morphological Dictionaries

Morphological dictionaries of Serbian and Croatian (covering also other standardized registers of Serbo-Croatian to an extent) are among the most important NLP resources for both ASR and TTS. Each of them contains about 100.000 lemmas and about 4 million inflected word forms. The entries in these dictionaries also contain data related to accentuation, as well as morphological information structured in positional part-of-speech (POS) tags. Besides these dictionaries, there is also a corresponding dictionary

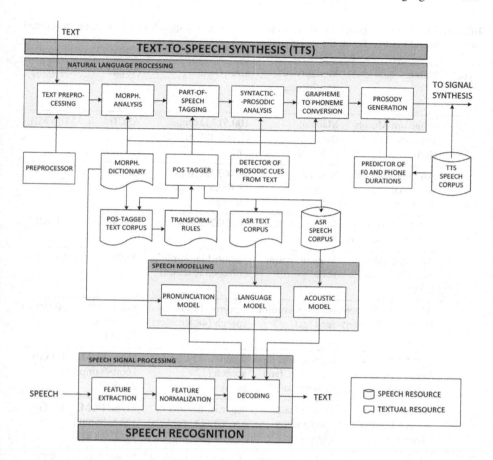

Fig. 1. Speech and language resources in text-to-speech and speech-to-text systems developed for Serbian and kindred South Slavic languages

of Macedonian, however, due to highly predictable accentuation rules and significantly simpler morphology of Macedonian, this dictionary lists only exceptions (mostly words of foreign origin as well as proper nouns) in the form of tokens rather than entries with full morphological specification. This dictionary contains about 40.000 tokens and provides a satisfactory coverage of arbitrary text in Macedonian. It is primarily used for Macedonian TTS, while the ASR for Macedonian is realized only for medium-sized dictionaries, using resources for Serbian where possible (as there is a significant match between phonetic inventories of these two languages).

3.2 POS-Tagged Text Corpus for TTS

The POS-tagged text corpus of Serbian has been created with the intention of improving the accuracy of the existing part-of-speech tagger, which will be described in

Table 1. Speech and language resources in text-to-speech and speech-to-text systems developed for Serbian and kindred South Slavic languages

Type	Name	Modality of acquisition, source	Size	Format	Memory
text	AlfaNum Morph. Dictionary of Serbian	Manual; dictionaries, online texts	100,517 lexemes (3,888,407 inflected forms)	ASCII	106 MB
	AlfaNum Morph. Dictionary of Croatian	Manual; dictionaries, online texts	98,603 lexemes (3,760,538 inflected forms)	ASCII	97 MB
	AlfaNum Text Corpus of Serbian	Manual; online texts	200,027 words	ASCII	13 MB
	AlfaNum ASR Text Corpus of Serbian	Manual; online texts	16,066,138 words (178,865 lexemes)	ASCII	138 MB
speech	AN_Books Speech Database (Serbian)	Studio recording; read text	Approx. 190 hours of speech (48 speakers)	Mono PCM; 16bits/samp., 22/44 kHz	36 GB
	S70W100s120 Speech Database (Serbian)	Reel-to-reel tape recording, later convert. to PCM	Approx. 10 hours of speech (120 speakers)	Mono PCM; 16bits/samp., 22050Hz	1.7 GB
	AN_Broadcast Speech Database (Serbian)	Online material; spontaneous speech	Approx. 6 hours of speech (44 speakers)	Mono PCM; 16bits/samp., 11/22/48 kHz	1.1 GB
	AlfaNum SpeechDatII(E) (Serbian)	PSTN recording; read text	Approx. 12 hours of speech (800 speakers)	Mono A-law; 8bits/samp., 8000Hz	1.9 GB
	TTSlsSnezana (Serbian)	Studio recording; various texts	Approx. 12 hours of speech (1 speaker), whereof 4 hours fully annotated	Mono PCM; 16bits/samp., 44100Hz	7 GB
	TTSlsMarica (Croatian)	Studio recording; various texts	Approx. 1.5 hours of speech (1 speaker)	Mono PCM; 16bits/samp., 22050Hz	310 MB

Section 5.2, by detection and application of transformation-based rules [2] or some other machine learning technique such as hidden Markov models (HMM) [3]. The corpus of 11.000 phrases (200.000 words) contains mostly newspaper articles, and it was assigned the same tags as in the morphological dictionaries (with some exceptions such as numbers expanded into words or words changing their accentuation due to

phonological context). The initial tagging was performed automatically, while the remaining errors were removed manually. While it was established that machine learning techniques do not achieve the same tagging accuracy as the expert system (with error rates of 10.4% for transformation rules and 10.3% for HMM, as opposed to 6.7% achieved by the expert system on a set of 748 POS tags), it was discovered that a set of less than 20 most appropriate transformation rules reduced the error rate of the previous version of part-of-speech tagger by 0.9%. These transformation rules were consequently introduced into the expert system (with certain modifications).

3.3   POS-Tagged Text Corpus for ASR

Another POS-tagged text corpus for Serbian used within the described systems is the one intended for large vocabulary continuous automatic speech recognition (LVCASR). This corpus of texts belonging to various functional styles of the Serbian language is of much greater size, containing approximately 16 million words, whereof 12 million belong to the journalistic style, 3 million to the literary style, 700 thousand to the scientific style and the remaining 300 thousand words to the administrative style. Because of its size, the corpus was POS-tagged only automatically, and then used for the construction of a language model for LVCASR, covering statistics related to occurences of particular tokens (surface forms), lemmas as well as word classes (corresponding to POS tags). Language modelling for speech recognition will be described in more detail in Section 6.

4   Speech Resources

ASR and TTS need different kinds of speech resources, in terms of quantity, quality and the number of speakers. Within the "AlfaNum" speech recognition system, an ASR speech corpus is used for off-line training of the acoustic model, based on HMM modelling of phonemes in context. On the other hand, the "AlfaNum" speech synthesis corpus has multiple uses, which will be discussed in detail in this section.

4.1   Speech Corpora for ASR

The speech corpus for Serbian ASR contains more than 200 hours of utterances from various sources, mostly (approx. 190 hours) studio recordings of audio-books read by 50 speakers. The corpus also contains 10 hours of studio recordings of 120 speakers (a digitalized version of a corpus recorded in 1983, containing command words, digits and phonetically balanced sentences) as well as approximately 6 hours of radio broadcasts (44 speakers, speech only). The entire corpus has been semi-automatically labelled for phonetic boundaries, and marked for stressed syllables as predicted by the POS tagger (see Section 5.2). Semi-automatic labelling was carried out by speech recognition with forced alignment of phonetic boundaries. Starting from a small portion of the database previously manually labelled, larger portions of the database were labelled automatically and then corrected manually using AlfaNum SpeechLabel software [4], while the most part of the database remains automatically labelled. For the lack of appropriate resources and owing to phonological similarity of different registers of Serbo-Croatian, the same corpus is used for Croatian ASR. For proof of concept tests, a smaller manually labelled corpus is used (approx. 12 hours). It contains utterances from 800 native speakers (400 male and 400 female), recorded via public telephone network according to the SpeechDatII(E) standard.

4.2 Speech Corpora for TTS

The Serbian TTS corpus contains 4875 sentences (approximately 4 hours of speech) uttered by a single female speaker. General intonation in the corpus ranged from neutral to moderately expressive. The corpus was recorded in a sound-proof studio, sampled at 44 kHz, and annotated with both phonological and phonetic markers (phonemic identity and information related to the manner of articulation) as well as markers related to prosody (lexical pitch accents, prosodic phrase boundaries and prominence). Phonemic/phonetic annotation was carried out semi-automatically (ASR was used for time-alignment of phone labels, and the errors have been corrected manually), while prosodic annotation was entirely manual. In both cases manual annotation was carried out using AlfaNum SpeechLabel. A similar but significantly smaller corpus of Croatian (about 1.5 hours of speech) was prepared along the same lines.

The TTS corpora are used for high-level synthesis, enabling accurate prediction of acoustic realization of prosodic features (primarily f_0 and phone durations), as will be described in Section 5.4. They can also be used in signal synthesis either off-line, for training an HMM-based synthesiser [5], or on-line, for the selection of phonetic segments for concatenative synthesis [6].

5 ASR and TTS Modules

There are several language dependent modules developed for Serbian and kindred South Slavic languages and used within "AlfaNum" ASR and TTS systems. Some of them are realized as expert systems while others rely on machine learning techniques.

5.1 Text Preprocessor

The first step in a TTS system is text preprocessing. "AlfaNum" text preprocessor for Serbian and Croatian (the differences are minor and related primarily to lexis), is an expert system charged with segmentation of text into sentences, as well as context-dependent expansion of elements such as numbers, Roman numerals and abbreviations into their canonical orthographic forms. This system is also used for the detection and interpretation of multi-token expressions such as dates, web or e-mail addresses, as well as decimal numbers with various types of separators.

5.2 POS Tagger

The module on which most natural language processing within "AlfaNum" ASR and TTS is based is the POS-tagger for Serbian and Croatian [7]. As was the case with the preprocessor, regardless of minor differences related to lexis, for the sake of brevity they will be referred to as a single module for both languages. The POS tagger is an expert system based on a beam search through a trellis of partially decoded sentences. In the measurements of its accuracy for Serbian [8], on a dictionary with 3.8 million entries (its volume at that moment) its accuracy on a previously unseen text of 10,000 words has been established at 93,3% for a tagset containing 748 tags. Having in mind that the primary purpose of POS tagging is accentuation within TTS, its accuracy in accentuation was also measured at the same corpus, and was established at 98.7%.

5.3 Detector of Prosodic Cues from Text

Syntactic-prosodic analysis of text is based on the expert system for detection of prosodic cues from given text. This system operates on POS-tagged text, using a number of rule templates with various prosodic events at their outputs. These prosodic events include indicators of prosodic boundaries of various levels, as well as indicators of predicted prosodic prominence or deaccentuation related to each word. Because of a certain degree of freedom in the choice of positions of both prosodic boundaries and prominence/deaccentuation, no objective assessment of the accuracy of this module is possible, but its positive impact on the naturalness of synthesized speech has been confirmed through subjective evaluation (see Section 5.4) [9].

5.4 Predictor of Pitch and Phone Durations for TTS

The module for prediction of acoustic realization of prosodic features (f_0 and phone durations) is based on a machine learning system containing a set of independent regression trees [9]. The TTS speech corpus of 4 hours (in case of Serbian) provides approximately 517,000 phoneme instances for training, using a standard set of features (in case of Croatian this number is smaller). In the absence of a specific acoustic model of intonation, f_0 targets are predicted directly. The prediction of phone durations is based on an independent regression tree operating on a similar set of features. As to objective measures of TTS quality, an RMSE of 18.2 Hz was achieved for f_0 and 15.85 ms for durations, and an MAE of 16.33 Hz was achieved for f_0 and 12.02 ms for durations. The listening tests showed that the naturalness of speech generated with thus set prosodic features was estimated at 3.94 according to the MOS scale.

6 Language Modelling

Due to high inflection of Serbian and Croatian, the language model was realized as a combination of 3 N-gram models, the first based on tokens (surface forms), the second one based on lemmas and the third one based on class N-grams, where word classes roughly correspond to POS tags as described in Section 5.2 [10]. The most recent version of the framework proposed for combining these 3 independent language models also allows for the use of N-grams where each of the elements can belong to either of the classes: tokens, lemmas or POS tag. This is an interesting detail, having in mind a wide range of collocations that such an arrangement covers (e.g. in the syntagm *"predsednik*

Srbije"/"the president of Serbia", the first word is declinable while the second one remains in the genitive case, suggesting that this is a collocation of (1) a lemma and (2) a POS tag or a token).

7 Conclusion

Through the descriptions of speech and language resources used within ASR and TTS systems for Serbian and some other kindred South Slavic languages, it has been shown that there is a significant overlap in the resources that these two complementary technologies rely on as well as in the modules that they use. It was also shown that, notwithstanding the fact that speech and language resources are heavily language dependent and that most of the modules have to be developed from scratch for each language, in case of greater or lesser similarity between two languages (or standardized registers of a single language), some of the developed resources can indeed be reused within speech technology systems, usually with some necessary modifications.

Acknowledgments. The results presented in this paper were supported in part by the Ministry for Education, Science and Technological Development of the Republic of Serbia, within the project "Development of Dialogue Systems for Serbian and Other South Slavic Languages".

References

1. Vitas, D., Popović, L., Krstev, C., Obradović, I., Pavlović-Lažetić, G., Stanojević, M.: The Serbian language in the digital age. White paper series. Springer (2012)
2. Brill, E.: Transformation-based error-driven learning and natural language processing: A case study in part-of-speech tagging. Comput. Linguist. 21(4), 543–566 (1995)
3. Merialdo, B.: Tagging English text with a probabilistic model. Comput. Linguist. 20, 155–172 (1994)
4. Obradović, R., Pekar, D.: C++ library for signal processing – SLIB. In: Digital Signal and Image Processing Conference DOGS, Novi Sad, Serbia (2000)
5. Pakoci, E., Mak, R.: HMM-based speech synthesis for the Serbian language. In: 56th ETRAN, Zlatibor, Serbia, vol. TE4, pp. 1–4 (2012)
6. Sečujski, M., Obradović, R., Pekar, D., Jovanov, L., Delić, V.: AlfaNum system for speech synthesis in Serbian language. In: Sojka, P., Kopeček, I., Pala, K. (eds.) TSD 2002. LNCS (LNAI), vol. 2448, pp. 237–244. Springer, Heidelberg (2002)
7. Sečujski, M.: Obtaining prosodic information from text in Serbian language. In: EUROCON, Belgrade, Serbia, pp. 1654–1657 (2005)
8. Sečujski, M.: Automatic part-of-speech tagging in Serbian. PhD thesis, University of Novi Sad, Serbia (2009)
9. Sečujski, M., Jakovljević, N., Pekar, D.: Automatic prosody generation for Serbo-Croatian speech synthesis based on regression trees. In: Interspeech 2011, Florence, Italy, pp. 3157–3160 (2011)
10. Ostrogonac, S., Popović, B., Sečujski, M., Mak, R., Pekar, D.: Language model reduction for practical implementation in LVCSR systems. In: Infoteh, Jahorina, Bosnia and Herzegovina (accepted for publication, 2013)

Statistical Language Aspects of Intonation and Gender Features Based on the Lithuanian Language

Michael Khitrov, Ludmila Beldiman, and Andrey Vasiliev

Speech Technology Center, Krasutskogo st., 4, 196084, St. Petersburg, Russia
{khitrov,beldiman,vasilyev-a}@speechpro.com
www.speechpro.com

Abstract. The article deals with one of modern speech technology trends –
defining of language aspects applicable in various tasks. It is proposed a method
that is based on typical statistical performance for pitch pattern of chosen language. Obtained typical ranges of parameter variation are compared for languages
of different language families: Lithuanian on one side and Uzbek and Azerbaijani
on the other side. It is also presented a gender analysis of intonation patterns for
Lithuanian speech.

Keywords: speech technologies, statistical aspects of intonation, the Lithuanian
language.

1   Introduction

The problem of speaker native language aspects is one of the challenging problems
of modern speech technologies. One of the methods suitable for solving this problem
consists in analysis of speaker pitch statistical performance and definition of typical for
chosen language statistical parameter ranges of different speech segments [1], [2]. It
is important to note that borders of such ranges and frequency of certain speech segments appearance significantly depend on speaker's gender. This article is dedicated to
statistical performance analysis of pitch patterns in language aspects defining problem
and gender specifics of performance and speech segments based on the Lithuanian language. The work was financially supported by the Ministry of Education and Science
of Russian Federation.

2   Research Basis

The research was performed on the basis of 78 phonograms of Lithuanian speakers, 55
of them contained the speech of 15 men and 23 – the speech of 7 women. The phonograms included both Lithuanian and Russian phrases. Data processing consisted of pitch
files obtaining, minimal correction and preparation of tables containing parameter nu-
meric values of typical Lithuanian speech intonation units and speech periods (phrase
sequences of 10-20 sec duration). The typical intonation units were represented by syntagmas and their structural elements (nuclear tone, nucleus + tail, head, prehead) [3],

M. Železný et al. (Eds.): SPECOM 2013, LNAI 8113, pp. 327–332, 2013.

[4], [5]. Speech sections chosen for analysis contained positive statements of complete/incomplete intonation and identical emotional coloration.

The following characteristics were taken as parameters of considered speech periods and local segments: segment minimal, maximal and average frequencies measured in Hz, segment frequency interval measured in Hz and semitones, pitch change speed measured in semitones per second, segment irregularity coefficient [1], [2]. One should note that these characteristics are frequency-domain so they are dealt with logarithmic methods.

3   Statistical Performance Analysis

Each parameter values for all considered speech periods of all speakers of one gender are carried on diagrams. Specially developed software allows defining main statistical performance for the obtained distributions, including expectation, root-mean-square deviation and, as a final result, range of typical values with confidence coefficient of 95% (tabl. 1, 2, 3, 4).

Two examples of such parameter distributions are shown below. They describe frequency interval parameter measured in semitones for Lithuanian female speakers (fig. 1) and Lithuanian male speakers (fig. 2). Fixed confidence interval borders marking the ranges of typical parameter values of the Lithuanian language are clearly seen on figures.

Parameter distribution analysis has shown that irregularity coefficient, maximum value and pitch change speed demonstrate performance close to normal distribution both in male and female parameter sets. Interval parameters and minimum and average values tend towards regular distribution within the confidence interval and fast decay outside its borders. It is important to note that there are several irregular peaks both within and outside the confidence interval in distributions of female interval values and male average frequency values, and also some values of male statistical parameters that are significantly outside the confidence interval (e. g. fig. 2). These irregularities can be explained by defects of few recorded phonograms, the estimated percentage is within permitted statistical error.

Defined range values apparently demonstrate gender difference, female speech segments tend towards higher frequencies, male – towards lower frequencies. Also female speech segments represent wider frequency intervals. The remaining statistical performance generally matches for genders, the specifics are revealed when comparing with other languages.

For the purpose of comparative evaluation of Lithuanian typical parameter values are used averaged typical parameter values of Uzbek and Azerbaijani (both Turkic) languages. Ranges of typical values for these languages were obtained by analysis and processing of wide set of long speech periods. The data contained the speech of 59 Azerbaijanian language speakers (13 female, 46 male) and 84 Uzbek language speakers (49 female, 35 male). The comparison was performed for men and women separately.

It has been shown as a result that the Lithuanian male minimal pitch frequencies vary in wider range than the Turkic ones, the maximal pitch frequencies are also more variative but their range tends towards lower frequencies. Frequency intervals of speech

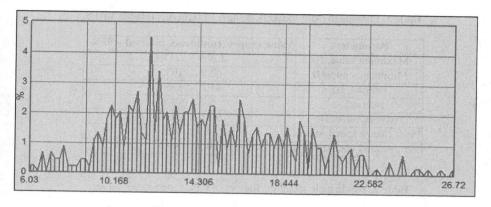

Fig. 1. Lithuanian female speakers. Parameter distribution for interval measured in semitones.

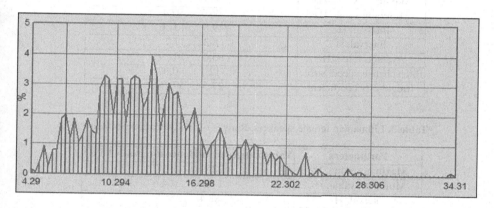

Fig. 2. Lithuanian male speakers. Parameter distribution for interval measured in semitones.

periods measured in Hz and semitones are wider for the Lithuanian language than for Uzbek and Azerbaijani. The irregularity coefficient is lower for Lithuanian speech samples than for Turkic ones. It indicates the use of more smooth intonation in Lithuanian phrases.

Maximum pitch frequencies of female Lithuanian speech vary in wider range comparing with Turkic female speech but minimal pitch frequencies lie in area of lower frequencies and vary in more narrow borders comparing with Uzbek and Azerbaijanian women. The values of average frequency parameter demonstrate that Lithuanian female voices are deeper than Turkic ones. Pitch change speed values are higher in Lithuanian case; the irregularity coefficient also varies in wider range comparing to Turkic languages.

The Lithuanian parameters comparison was performed not only on one certain language family – Turkic – but also on a general averaged parameter base across wide set of different languages and language families. The obtained results allow to determinate following specifics. Maximum frequency values that are typical for the Lithuanian

Table 1. Lithuanian male speakers. Ranges of typical parameter values.

Parameters	Value ranges (confidence interval – 95%)
Maximum value, Hz	129.9 ... 217.4
Minimum value, Hz	63.9 ... 103.6
Interval, Hz	41.7 ... 136.8
Interval, st	6.7 ... 18.8
Average value, Hz	90.1 ... 143.7
Pitch change speed, st/sec	-9.1 ... 1.3
Irregularity coefficient	24.3 ... 49.3

Table 2. Turkic male speakers. Ranges of typical parameter values.

Parameters	Value ranges (confidence interval – 95%)
Maximum value, Hz	133.6 ... 218.8
Minimum value, Hz	66.3 ... 97.4
Interval, Hz	49.8 ... 131.6
Interval, st	8.3 ... 17.7
Average value, Hz	95.0 ... 141.9
Pitch change speed, st/sec	-12.1 ... -0.07
Irregularity coefficient	27.5 ... 50.25

Table 3. Lithuanian female speakers. Ranges of typical parameter values.

Parameters	Value ranges (confidence interval – 95%)
Maximum value, Hz	225.8 ... 395.7
Minimum value, Hz	102.9 ... 164.6
Interval, Hz	88.4 ... 254.5
Interval, st	8.7 ... 19.6
Average value, Hz	156.3 ... 242.0
Pitch change speed, st/sec	-7.3 ... 1.5
Irregularity coefficient	26.6 ... 46.4

Table 4. Turkic female speakers. Ranges of typical parameter values.

Parameters	Value ranges (confidence interval – 95%)
Maximum value, Hz	255.1 ... 383.4
Minimum value, Hz	124.4 ... 196.4
Interval, Hz	96.3 ... 221.7
Interval, st	8.2 ... 16.3
Average value, Hz	177.7 ... 251.8
Pitch change speed, st/sec	-9.3 ... 0.52
Irregularity coefficient	28.3 ... 45.2

language are lower than the corresponding averaged values across the database; the difference is more significant in male case. This feature together with common matching of minimal frequency values gives more narrow frequency interval (it is approximately quarter less for male speakers). Average pitch change speed for the Lithuanian language tends to be a small value; it's half less for male speakers. The irregularity of typical Lithuanian speech segments attests to more smooth pitch frequency changes comparing with averaged values. In general the Lithuanian language tends towards smooth speech in narrow frequency interval. For the male speakers are common more significant deviations from averaged parameters, female speakers demonstrate in common more coinciding statistical performance. As far as language base contains typical data of different language families it's hard to make conclusions on correlation of the Lithuanian language and other Baltic languages.

4 Speech Segment Analysis

The intonational structures set analysis has shown that an outstanding feature of female speech consists in significantly more frequent using of rising intonational pattern comparing to men (tabl. 5). In speech of Lithuanian male speakers syntagmas with rising and falling termination appear with equal frequency regardless of language (Lithuanian or Russian) while in speech of Lithuanian female speakers syntagmas with rising termination drastically prevail (363 realizations against 189 consequently).

Table 5. Lithuanian speakers. Realization frequency of different intonational structure types.

Type	Subtype	males	females	males	females
		number of speech segments		number of speakers	
Syntagma	rising termination	598	189	15	7
	falling termination	598	**363**	15	7
Nuclear tail + segment	falling tone	**475**	142	15	7
	rising tone	415	**195**	15	7
	falling-rising tone	83	**101**	12	7
	rising-falling tone	58	18	13	6

The same performance is presented in realization of nucleus plus tail segments belonging to syntagmas of Lithuanian speaker speech. The male speakers use the falling tone in nucleus plus tail segments more frequently than the rising tone. The falling-rising and the rising-falling structures appear in rear cases. Female speakers tend to use frequently the rising tone in nucleus plus tail segments; the falling tone isnt comparable in this case. Also falling-rising tone is typical for womens speech as contrasted with the mens speech.

5 Conclusion

On the results of this paper several conclusions can be made. Lithuanian according to its speech performance tends towards low frequencies and that fact can be explicitly demonstrated on the male speech. Also the narrow frequency interval and smoothness of pitch frequency change are typical for this language. Male and female speech differ not only in explicit fixation of male voices on low frequencies and female on high ones but also in facts that male parameters are more distinct from the averaged values across the most common language families than female parameters and that women demonstrate tendency towards incomplete intonation in positive statements. Delivered conclusions are hold for identical emotional coloration.

This paper presents the primary demonstration of possibilities that are given by method of intonation pattern statistical analysis in language aspects defining problem. The following work assumes more systematic approach. The reasonable continuation consists in significant language families data gathering and its analysis because it might increase the results accuracy and serve as the first step in developing language analysis software tools. Moreover, analysis and identification might be taken on two different levels with different precision borders: for language within its language family/branch and for various language families and branches. Another direction which introduces systematic approach consists in segments analysis of speech with distinct emotional coloration. The results of this paper are applicable to various problems such as speaker and language identification.

References

1. Koval, S.L., Labutin, P.V., Pekhovskiy, T.S., Proshchina, E.A., Smirnova, N.S., Talanov, A.O.: Method of speaker voice and speech identification based on phonogram complex analysis. In: Dialog 2007 (2007), http://www.dialog-21.ru/digests/dialog2007/materials/html/39.htm (retrieved June 7, 2013)
2. Smirnova, N.S.: Speaker Identification based on the comparison of utterance pitch contour parameters. In: Dialog 2007 (2007), http://www.dialog-21.ru/digests/dialog2007/materials/pdf/77.pdf (retrieved June 7, 2013)
3. O'Connor, J., Arnold, G.: Intonation of colloquial English. Longman, London (1973)
4. Bryzgunova, E.A.: Intonation. In: Russian Grammar, Moscow, vol. 1, pp. 96–123 (1980)
5. Svetozarova, N.D.: Prosodic System of the Russian language. Leningrad University Press, Leningrad (1982)

Text Understanding as Interpretation of Predicative Structure Strings of Main Text's Sentences as Result of Pragmatic Analysis (Combination of Linguistic and Statistic Approaches)

Alexander A. Kharlamov[1], Tatyana V. Yermolenko[2], and Andrey A. Zhonin[3]

[1] Institute of Higher Nervous Activity and
Neurophysiology, Russian Academy of Science, Moscow, Russia
Moscow State Linguistic University, Moscow, Russia
kharlamov@analyst.ru
[2] Institute of Artificial Intelligence Problems, Donetsk, Ukraine
naturewild71@gmail.com
[3] State Institute of Information Technologies and Telecommunications "Informika",
Moscow, Russia
neurofish@yandex.ru

Abstract. This paper reports on an approach to presentation of a text in its minimized form in metalanguage that allows restoring a text similar to the origin. Here such text representation is a string of extended predicative structures of the text sentences, isolated by ranging and further removal of sentences insignificant according to the semantic net of the text. The extended predicative structures are a result of a comprehensive linguistic analysis of text sentences. Analysis of the semantics of the whole text is made by statistical methods.

Keywords: comprehensive linguistic sentence analysis, statistical semantic text analysis, pragmatic analysis, predicative structures.

1   Introduction

Automatic sense analysis of a natural text is usually conducted by using either linguistic methods or statistical methods. In the first case a sense structure of an isolated sentence is revealed as an extended predicative structure with a subject, direct and indirect objects included [1,4]. A sense analysis of the whole text is carried out using statistical approaches. Here one builds the semantic net of the whole text, which contains correlation of the key text notions (words and word combinations), and their weight characteristics [3].

Text understanding is usually perceived as an interpretation of text content in some metalanguage that allows restoring a text if necessary, in another form but with the sense kept [5].

The aim of this work is the presentation of a text in its minimized form in a metalanguage that allows restoring a text similar to the origin. Such text representation is a string of extended predicative structures of the text sentences, isolated by ranging and further removal of sentences insignificant according to the semantic net of the text.

M. Železný et al. (Eds.): SPECOM 2013, LNAI 8113, pp. 333–339, 2013.

The division of semantic analysis into two stages (semantic and pragmatic analysis) enables to build some text representation that on the one hand keeps important semantic details of the original text, and on the other hand allows restoring the text from this representation in a form similar to the original one. Semantic analysis of the whole text is here understood as revealing key notions of the text in their correlations and their weight characteristics. Pragmatic analysis is here understood as drawing out of the text some sentences that describe the content of the text. During semantic analysis one can range key text notions by weighting them and thus retrieve from the text the most significant, according to the text structure, sentences. At the stage of pragmatic analysis these sentences are joined into sequences that characterize text pragmatics: these sequences form either description of something or algorithm of implementing something. Strings of extended predicative structures corresponding to the sequence of sentences mentioned above are the metapresentation, that later can be used for restoring the original form of the text.

Methods of a comprehensive linguistic analysis are used for finding extended predicative structures and include text processing at the graphematical, morphological and syntactical levels.

Pragmatic analysis then consists of finding a text frame structure (descriptive or algorithmic sentences) that characterizes the dynamics of development of the situations described in the text.

Text understanding in this paper is seen as revealing significant strings of extended predicative text structures, which describe the content of the text in the metalanguage of predicative structures.

2 Automatic Text Analysis

Automatic text analysis consists of graphematical, morphological, syntactical, semantic and pragmatic levels of processing.

2.1 Graphematical Level of Processing

At graphematical level of text analysis a text is cleaned of nontextual information, and is segmented into words and sentences. The unit of graphematical analysis is a string of symbols, marked out on both sides with blanks. The marked out string of symbols undergoes a step-by-step processing by heuristics: punctuation marks are cut off, presence of vowels, interchange of upper case and lower case in the string are checked.

2.2 Morphological Analysis

Full word forms are analysed at the morphological level. The main aim of this processing is to divide the whole set of word forms into subsets due to belonging to this or that lexeme and as far as it is possible to define unambiguously grammatical characteristics.

As most of words from the text belong to the invariable basis of language and can be described by a vocabulary of about 100,000 words and the other part of lexicon (which is more rare but nonetheless important) is always increasing and does not have distinguished boundaries (especially concerning proper names and word-formative variations of well-known words), methods with both declarative and processing orientation are used for morphological analysis [2].

2.3 Syntactical Analysis

Syntactic analysis of sentences is carried out in several steps: sentence fragmentation, combination of homogeneous fragments, establishment of hierarchy among fragments of different types, combination of fragments into simple sentences, building of simple syntactical groups within fragments.

Then predicative minimum is marked out from every simple sentence, other members of the simple sentence that are objects of detected predicate are singled out and new syntactical groups where object of the predicate becomes subject are built. A set of Russian simple sentences is specified by a list of minimal structural sentence schemes that describe the predicative minimum of a sentence. Then a sequential search of a proper template of a minimal structural sentence scheme is conducted in every segment of a sentence unless it is enclosed or homogenous. According to the found template every leading member of a sentence is given a corresponding value.

Then the problem of obtaining the extended predicative structure of simple sentences and filling predicate valences is the one described in [1]. Other members of a simple sentence (semantically significant objects and attributes) are detected through a step-by-step comparing of words from the sentence with argument structure of a verb, which is done using the verb valency dictionary.

2.4 Semantic Analysis of the Whole Text

Statistical approach allows revealing the semantic structure of the whole text - a global inner structure of the text. Statistical semantic text analysis is based on the technology of processing text information - TextAnalyst [3], it enables to detect key notions in the text automatically only on the basis of information about the structure of the text itself (regardless of the subject area and language - for the European languages). For this purpose a frequency portrait is formed. It contains information about the frequency of text notions, which are represented there as roots of corresponding words and their set-phrases found in the text and also information about their pairwise occurrence in the text fragments (for instance in sentences). The frequency portrait thus contains information about the notion frequency and their pairwise occurrence frequency (in terms of their associative relationships) in a text.

Iterative renormalization procedure allows the move from notion frequency to semantic weight. At that bigger weight is gained by the notions that are connected to the biggest amount of other notions with large weight i.e. the notions that attract the semantic structure of the text to them. Weight of relationship stays unchanged.

Gained semantic weights of the key notions show the significance of these notions in the text. Later on this information is used for detecting sentences of the text that contain the most important (from the structural point of view) information in the text. To do this the semantic weights of sentences are calculated on the basis of semantic weights of notions. Then semantic weights of sentences are ranged and all the sentences whose weight is lower than threshold are deleted from the text.

2.5 Pragmatic Level of the Analysis

Predicate is defined as following: $P = < c_i, r_{ij}, c_j >$, where c_i - subject, r_{ij} - relation, describing the connection of the subject and the main object and other arguments of the predicate, and $c_j, j > 1$ – other objects of the predicate. And $r_{i1} \simeq r_p$, where r_p - predicative relation, c_1 - main object.

In this paper pragmatic analysis is understood as revealing of the frame of the text (text corpora), represented as a string (strings) of extended predicative structures, corresponding to those left after deleting insignificant sentences of the text. The frame describes the dynamics of the development of the situation shown in the text (text corpora). Such string can be either descriptive or algorithmic. In first case frame characterises perception, in the second – action. Pragmatic analysis must be preceded by semantic analysis as it is necessary to form a semantic model of the text before creating text pragmatics. Input text is projected on the key notions of the semantic model.

Thus the pragmatic analysis consists of marking out strings of predicative sentence structures, that after semantic analysis are revealed to be the most weighty in the subject area to which the text belong. Strings of extended predicative structures represented by their subject-object pairs $W_i = (< c_i, r_{ij}, c_j >) = (P_1, P_2, ...)$, correspond to the sequences of sentences containing them as they appear in the text.

2.6 Text Understanding

Understanding of the concrete text is connected to the revealing of the predicative structures $P_i = < c_i, r_{ij}, c_j >$, that characterize the semantics of separate sentences of the text and as well strings of these predicative structures $W_i = (P_1, P_2, ...)$, that pass the sense of sequences of text sentences. Thus any text of this subject area, generating a string of predicative structures, can be treated as a sequence of text sentences that contain them. Text understanding here means the projection of strings of predicative structures of the text on the set of corresponding strings of predicative structures of text corpora that characterise the subject area to which the text belongs and naming these text strings as subthemes of the subject area to which strings of predicative structures of text corpora belong. Meanwhile the strings of the input text are projected on the strings of predicative structures of text corpora. Segmentation on subareas and detection of their main themes is also carried out automatically [3].

3   Example of a Pragmatic Text Analysis

As an example of text understanding described above a Russian text on physics is given [http://www.kodges.ru/ Т.И. Трофимова «Курс физики», Москва, «Высшая школа», 2001].

Here is the text example after all the steps of the linguistic analysis of the sentences of the text, after constructing the semantic net of the text as a result of statistical text

Table 1. Extended predicative structures of the sentences left in the way they appear in the text

No. sent	Pred-icate	Sub-ject	Rela tion	Ob ject	Rela tion	Attribute	Addressee Instrument Locatives	Rela tion	Attribute
1	NULL	дина-мика	R_G	точка	R_A	матери-альный			
			R_G	дви-же-ние	R_A	поступа-тельный			
					R_G		тело	R_A	твердый
2	1. NULL	Закон Нью-тона				R_A	первый		
	2.сох-ра-нять	точка				R_A	всякий		
						R_A	матери-альный		
			R_O	состо-яние			покой		
							движе-ние	R_A	прямо-линей-ный
								R_A	равно-мерный
	3.не за-ста-вить изме-нить	воз-дей-ствие	R_G	сто-рона	R_G		тело	R_A	другой
			R_O				точка		
			R_O				состо-яние	R_A	это
. . .									

Table 2. Marking of relations in the predicative sentence structure

Marking of the relation	Syntactic group
Valencies of the predicate	
R_S	Predicate-Subject
R_O	Predicate- Object
R_I	Predicate-Instrument
R_L	Predicate-Locative
Relations at the attributive level	
R_A	Object-Attribute
R_A_P	Action-Attribute
Syntactic groups of objects of the predicate	
R_G	Genitive attribute in postposition

processing, after calculating all the weights of the sentences and after ranging and deleting insignificant sentences according to the semantic text analysis. Sentences left after everything mentioned above are marked out in bold type (see below).

«Глава 2. Динамика материальной точки и поступательного движения твердого тела. § 5. Первый закон Ньютона. Масса. Сила Динамика является основным разделом механики, в её основе лежат три закона Ньютона, сформулированные им в 1687 г. Законы Ньютона играют исключительную роль в механике и являются (как и все физические законы) обобщением результатов огромного человеческого опыта. Их рассматривают как систему взаимосвязанных законов и опытной проверке подвергают не каждый отдельный закон, а всю систему в целом. Первый закон Ньютона: всякая материальная точка (тело) сохраняет состояние покоя или равномерного прямолинейного движения до тех пор, пока воздействие со стороны других тел не заставит её изменить это состояние. Стремление тела сохранять состояние покоя или равномерного прямолинейного движения называется инертностью. Поэтому первый закон Ньютона называют также законом инерции. Механическое движение относительно, и его характер зависит от системы отсчета. Первый закон Ньютона выполняется не во всякой системе отсчета, а те системы, по отношению к которым он выполняется, называются инерциальными системами отсчета. Инерциальной системой отсчета является такая система отсчета, относительно которой материальная точка, свободная от внешних воздействий, либо покоится, либо движется равномерно и прямолинейно».

Table 1 shows the extended predicative structures of the sentences left in the way they appear in the text.

4 Discussion

The implemented approach is sufficiently labor-consuming as it needs a comprehensive linguistic analysis of the text. Statistic-semantic analysis of the whole text is fulfilled much easier when compared to the pragmatic analysis. Nevertheless the calculating complexity of this approach to the pragmatic analysis of texts is justified. On the one hand it enables representation of the text as compact metadescription – strings of extended predicative structures – that can be unfolded the other way round, as some text presentation, semantically similar to the input text, that is it enables text understanding. On the other hand this metadescription can be interpreted by an expert as a sequence of text sentences (quasiabstract) and such a presentation is user-friendly as usual text in natural language.

5 Conclusion

The paper describes a method of pragmatic text analysis with the use of uniting comprehensive linguistic and statistic-semantic approaches to the text analysis. The method discussed enables to show a text as a minimal set of pragmatic strings – strings of extended predicative sentence structures that hold the main sense of this text. The strings of extended predicative structures are a compact metadescription of the semantics of the text that can be interpreted in sentences of natural language. This description can be used for automatic text comparison and for automatic text classification.

References

1. Bondarenko, E.A., Kaplin, O.A., Kharlamov, A.A.: Predicative Structures in the System of Machine Text Recognition Speech Technologies, vol. 3, pp. 45–57 (2012) (in Russian)
2. Dorohina, G.V., Gnit'ko, D.S.: Automatic Detection of Syntactically Related Words of a Simple Extended Sentence. In: "Modern Informational Ukraine: Informatics, Economics, Philosophy": Conference Reports, May 12-13, Donetsk, vol. 1, pp. 34–38 (2011) (in Ukrainian)
3. Kharlamov, A.A.: A Neural Network Technology of Representation and Processing of Information (Natural Representation of Knowledge). Radiotekhnika, Moscow (2006) (in Russian)
4. Kharlamov, A.A., Yermolenko, T.V., Dorohina, G.V., Gnit'ko, D.S.: Meth003 of Extracting of the Main Sentence Parts as Predicative Structures Speech Technologies, vol. 2, pp. 75–85 (2012) (in Russian)
5. Martynov Universal Semantic Code - Minsk: Science and technology (1977) (in Russian)

The Diarization System for an Unknown Number of Speakers

Oleg Kudashev[1] and Alexander Kozlov[2]

[1] National Research University of Information Technologies, Mechanics and Optics,
St. Petesburg, Russia
kudashev@speechpro.com
[2] STC-innovations Ltd., St. Petersburg, Russia
kozlov-a@speechpro.com
speechpro.com

Abstract. This paper presents a system for speaker diarization that can be used if the number of speakers is unknown. The proposed system is based on the agglomerative clustering approach in conjunction with factor analysis, Total Variability approach and linear discriminant analysis. We present the results of the proposed diarization system. The results demonstrate that our system can be used both if an answering machine or handset transfer is present in telephone recordings and in the case of a summed channel in telephone or meeting recordings.

Keywords: diarization, speaker segmentation, speaker recognition, clustering.

1 Introduction

The speaker diarization task consists of detecting speech segments and clustering the segments belonging to one speaker. This task is an important part of automatic speech processing systems. These systems include automatic speaker recognition.

Speaker diarization tasks can be divided into two types depending on the presence of a priori information about the number of speakers. The task is greatly simplified if this information is available. In practice, this information does not always exist. For example, even in a single channel telephone recording, an answering machine and handset transfer can be present. Consequently, up to 4-5 speakers can be present in a summed channel of a telephone conversation. The goal of our work is to develop a diarization system for the case in which the number of speakers is unknown.

We propose a solution to the speaker diarization task based on the state of the art achievements in the task of text-independent speaker recognition. These achievements include factor analysis with the Total Variability approach for creating generative speaker models, as well as linear discriminant analysis (LDA) for intra-speaker and channel variability compensation [1]. The proposed speaker diarization system is based on the well-known agglomerative clustering approach [2], which allows us to determine the number of speakers.

M. Železný et al. (Eds.): SPECOM 2013, LNAI 8113, pp. 340–344, 2013.

2 Speaker Modeling

The methods used in most baseline diarization systems determine the parameters of speaker models by means of local audio recording data [3], [4]. As shown by [5], the use of a priori information significantly improves the quality of speaker diarization and speaker recognition systems. The universal background model (UBM) and Total Variability approach provide such information. A generative model of a speaker is a Gaussian mixture model obtained by MAP-adaptation of UBM through changing of mean vectors:

$$s = \mu + Tw,$$

where s is speaker- and session-dependent stacked mean vector (supervector) from a GMM; μ is UBM supervector; T is a rectangular matrix of low rank that defines the Total Variability subspace; w is a low dimensional vector of hidden parameters (factors), w has a standard normal distribution.

This approach allows us not only to select the most informative characteristics of speakers, but also to significantly reduce the amount of data needed to training the speaker model.

3 Comparison of Models

A lot of metrics are used for comparing speaker models. These metrics include: Bayesian Information Criterion (BIC), Cross Likelihood Ratio (CLR), cosine distance, KL-divergence. One of the main requirements for a chosen metric is its robustness. The main causes of threshold instability are intra-speaker variability, channel variability and different amounts of data used for training the speaker model.

To compare models, we decided to use the LDA approach, which is well-established in text-independent speaker recognition, together with support vector machine (SVM) for score normalization. As the main metric we take the distance from the w-vector of one speaker to the SVM-hyperplane separating the w-vector of another speaker and the set of imposters. Thus, the cosine serves both as a distance and as an SVM kernel.

This approach provides fast model comparison and a robust decision threshold.

4 Description of the System

The UBM and T-matrix of the system were trained using data derived from the following speech databases: NIST SRE 1998, NIST SRE 1999, NIST SRE 2002, NIST SRE 2003, NIST SRE 2004, NIST SRE 2005, NIST SRE 2006. We used 512 Gaussians for the UBM. A T-matrix of 400 dimensions was trained. Dimensions are reduced to 200 during the training of the LDA system. The acoustic features consist of 13 mel-cepstral coefficients (MFCC) with deltas, double-deltas and mean normalization. The imposters were 1300 gender-balanced speaker models taken from the training data.

The diarization algorithm includes voice activity detection (VAD), feature extraction, speaker models building for short-time sliding windows with fixed length, speaker changes detection, agglomerative clustering and Viterbi re-segmentation.

4.1   Speaker Modeling and Pairwise Comparison

We used an energy VAD algorithm during the training and testing of the system. The features were extracted according to the parameters listed above. The non-speech features were excluded.

The speaker models were built for every window with a 1 second length and with 0.5 seconds shifting. All models were compared with each other. Thus, the similarity matrix was obtained. For example, the similarity matrix of a recording containing two speaker change points is presented in figure 1.

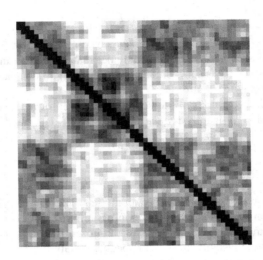

Fig. 1. The similarity matrix of a recording containing two speaker change points

The light areas of the figure correspond to the comparisons between different speaker models. Thus, it is clear that there are two speakers in this example. The beginning and the end of the recording belong to the first speaker and the middle of the recording belongs to the second speaker.

4.2   Speaker Change Points Detection and Clustering

The local minima of the comparisons between the models that follow one another (subdiagonal elements of the similarity matrix) not exceeding the threshold λ_{SCP} determine the speaker change point.

The speaker models situated between two consecutive change points are merged in one model. The merged model is obtained by averaging the w-vectors and rebuilding the SVM hyperplane. These merged models form an initial clustering.

Next, the sequential agglomerative clustering is performed. This clustering involves pairwise comparison of speaker models and merging the pair of models with the minimal comparison result not exceeding the threshold λ_{AC}. This procedure is repeated until the merging can be performed.

Finally, the speaker segmentation obtained by clustering is used for training speakers GMM and Viterbi re-segmentation of the speakers segments. In addition, the second agglomerative clustering with the threshold AC2 can be performed after resegmentation.

5   Results

We formed several test sets depending on different cases. These cases include the presence of an answering machine (ANSWER-MACHINE test set), the presence of handset transfer (CHANGE-SPEAKER test set), a summed channel of telephone conversation from NIST SRE 2008 [6] (NIST2008 test set), a summed channel of telephone conversation with the presence of a tube transfer or answering machine (SUMMED test set), meeting recordings (AMI test set [7]). In additional, we used a test set with recordings of only one speaker (MONOLOG test set). The description of the selected test sets can be found in Table 1.

Table 1. Description of the test sets

Test set name	Summed channel, yes/no	Channel type, tel/mic	Speaker number	Number of files	Average duration of recording, sec
ANSWER-MACHINE	no	tel	2	50	350
CHANGE-SPEAKER	no	tel	2	17	150
NIST2008	yes	tel	2	100	300
SUMMED	yes	tel	3	100	400
AMI	yes	mic	4	55	1800

The main metric for diarization systems rating is Diarization Error Rate (DER) proposed by NIST [8]. We used the diarization evaluation tool from NIST RTE 2006 [9] for calculating DER with the collar of 0.25 seconds. Since we are not interested in the quality of VAD we will present only speaker error rate.

Table 2. Diarization results

#	System	Speaker error rate, %					
		ANSWER-MACHINE	CHANGE-SPEAKER	NIST2008	SUMMED	AMI	MONOLOG
1	SPD + clustering	3.85	1.59	13.72	9.8	14.8	1.11
2	SPD + clustering + Viterbi	3.75	1.46	8.52	7.5	6.48	1.28
3	SPD + clustering + Viterbi + 2nd clustering	3.74	1.64	5.96	4.76	10.16	0.82
4	IB clustering + Viterbi	4.67	2.85	15.05	5.34	7.83	10.83

We examined the diarization system based on Information Bottleneck (IB) [10] for the comparison of the results. We used the same VAD, features extractor and Viterbi re-segmentation algorithm, so the only difference between our system and the IB-system is the clustering procedure. The testing results of both the proposed diarization systems (#1-3) and the IB diarization system (#4) are presented in Table 2. All results reported for one system were obtained under the same parameters.

6 Conclusion

As shown in Table 2. our final system (#3) performs better on all test sets except the AMI test set. This fact can be explained by the insufficient number of microphone recordings in the training data.

The low value of speaker error in the MONOLOG test set indicates that the developed diarization system can determine the correct number of speakers if there is only one speaker. It is an important characteristic of the system because the most one-channel telephone recordings do not include an answering machine or handset transfer. For this reason, this implementation is helpful for separating answering machines and detecting handset transfer.

In addition, it should be noted that the proposed system can also be applied in case of summed channel of telephone conversation and meeting recordings, but these results do not look so impressive. It can be explained by the fact that these cases include frequent changes of speakers and overlapping speech segments of different speakers.

The work was financially supported by the Ministry of Education and Science of Russian Federation.

References

1. Dehak, N., Kenny, P., Dehak, R., Dumouchel, P., Ouellet, P.: Front-End Factor Analysis for Speaker Verification. IEEE Transactions on Audio, Speech, and Language Processing 19(4), 788–798 (2011)
2. Jin, Q., Laskowski, K., Schultz, T., Waibel, A.: Speaker segmentation and clustering in meetings. In: Proceedings of the 8th International Conference on Spoken Language Processing, Jeju Island, Korea (2004)
3. Reynolds, D., Kenny, P., Castaldo, F.: A Study of New Approaches to Speaker Diarization. In: Proc. Interspeech, pp. 1047–1050 (2009)
4. Tranter, S., Reynolds, D.: An Overview of Automatic Speaker Diarisation Systems. IEEE Transactions on Audio, Speech, and Language Processing 14(5), 1557–1565 (2006)
5. Kenny, P.: Bayesian Analysis of Speaker Diarization with Eigenvoice Priors. Technical report. Centre de recherche informatique de Montreal (CRIM), Montreal, Canada (2008)
6. 2008 NIST Speaker Recognition Evaluation Test Set, http://www.ldc.upenn.edu/Catalog/catalogEntry.jsp?catalogId=LDC2011S08
7. AMI Meeting Corpus, http://corpus.amiproject.org/
8. Rich Transcription Evaluation Project, http://www.itl.nist.gov/iad/mig//tests/rt/
9. Rich Transcription Spring 2006 Evaluation, http://www.itl.nist.gov/iad/mig/tests/rt/2006-spring/
10. Vijayasenan, D., Valente, F., Bourlard, H.: An Information Theoretic Approach to Speaker Diarization of Meeting Data. IEEE Transactions on Audio, Speech, and Language Processing 17(7), 1382–1393 (2009)

The Problem of Voice Template Aging in Speaker Recognition Systems

Yuri Matveev[1,2]

[1] Speech Technology Center Ltd., St. Petersburg, Russia
matveev@speechpro.com
www.speechpro.com
[2] University ITMO, St. Petersburg, Russia
matveev@mail.ifmo.ru
en.ifmo.ru

Abstract. It is well known that device, language and environmental mismatch adversely affect speaker recognition performance. Much less attention is paid to effect of age-related voice changes on speaker recognition performance. In this paper we attempted to answer if speaker recognition algorithms have the re-sistance to age-related changes, and how often we have to update the voice bi-ometric templates. We have investigated such effects basing on the speech da-tabase collected during the period 2006-2010 and have found a clear trend of degradation of the performance of automatic speaker recognition systems in a time interval of up to 4 years.

Keywords: template aging, template update rate, speaker recognition.

1   Introduction

One challenge with a biometric template is that it acts as a snapshot of certain bio-metric characteristics taken at a particular point in time. For biometrics such as voice, a dependence exists between the performance of speaker recognition (verification, iden-tification) methods and the time lapse between the recording of reference samples and test speech signals. This dependence is widely known in the speaker recognition re-search community, and has been described in many studies (see, for example, [1], [2] and [3]).

Some authors have analyzed this challenge in terms of such factors as physiological changes [4] and emotional changes. The combinations of such changes are not very well understood and are sometimes bundled into one category collectively called time-lapse effects [2]. Among these changes, some get worse over time. Rather than focusing on these time-lapse effects, we are concerned with what the literature calls aging, deals with much longer effects lasting beyond the range of these shorter term studies. Aging effects deal with more of the physiological changes affecting speakers over substantial lengths of time.

The concept of biometric template aging refers to the way in which individual bi-ometric data deviate from enrollment and therefore must be updated. One way of

M. Železný et al. (Eds.): SPECOM 2013, LNAI 8113, pp. 345–353, 2013.

addressing the template aging problem is to renew the template with a certain periodicity. However, this can be an unnecessary step, especially if the biometrics have not changed, and can be costly, time consuming and resource intensive for large organizations such as governments or defense departments. On the other hand, if the template is not updated, an individual (genuine speaker) may not be recognized. An even greater risk is that an imposter may be recognized as a genuine speaker due to changes in his or her own physical traits over time.

The template update rate can vary from a relatively short period of time to once every few years. In this paper, we present the results of assessing the rate of update of voice templates versus the accuracy of a speaker recognition system over an extended period of time.

2   Background

It is noted in [5] that while current biometric systems enroll human beings by captur-ing biometric traits over a very short span of time (minutes or hours), the databases used for testing are collected over a time period of a few weeks to months. Biometric features such as voice change gradually with time. This may occur due to aging, illness or other environmental factors. Field biometric systems do not consider this aspect during enrollment and it is not common practice to take samples over the period of a few months or years. The authors of [5] have proposed that the complete feature set be re-enrolled after a certain amount of time.

The periodicity of biometric template change is not easily determined. Although the concept has been defined, no known research has investigated what happens to comparisons between original enrollment templates and future comparisons of verification templates as individuals age over time. There are studies that show aging effects on the human face, fingers, body, voice and gait (see, e.g., an overview in [6]). These studies only show the effects against algorithms, they do not incorporate the ways in which the effects result in the authentication of applications or do not show matching scores over time.

Recent studies ([7], [8], [9] and [10]) have focused on inferring chronological age from utterance-level and frame-based acoustic features. As noted in [11], it might be more useful to predict the need for specific adaptations directly with no detour through age recognition. We can estimate a speakers age from vocal cues because age-related changes in anatomy and physiology affect the vocal folds and the vocal tract. In particular, F0-related measures such as jitter, shimmer and overall F0 statistics have been shown to correlate with ageing [4]. Long-term average spectra also change [4]. State-of-the-art algorithms for age recognition exploit MFCCs and other features commonly used in speaker recognition [8].

In our models, we only use features that are easy to extract from the speech waveform: pitch-related features, formants frequency features, mel-frequency cepstral coefficients (MFCCs).

2.1   Lack of Ample Databases

To study the performance of speaker recognition methods in relation to the time interval between the recording of reference samples and test speech signals, one needs a representative speech database of the same speakers for a long time.

Currently there are no such databases for reasons provided in [3]:

– Biometrics is a relatively young field;
– Technological problems: equipment and measurement protocols must be maintained over long periods of time;
– Problems with availability of volunteers for sample collection;
– Sociological resistance (e.g. creating and using childrens biometric tem-plates).

As noted in [7], aging effects on voice recognition cannot therefore be clearly or easily distinguished, partly due to limited data.

The Linguistic Data Consortium LDC (`http://www.ldc.upenn.edu/`) is one resource that may offer some potential in this area; its speech databases have been collected over 15 years. These databases provide the foundation for large-scale tests of speaker recognition systems systematically conducted by the National Institute of Standards and Technology (NIST) [12]. However, these databases have been collected by different companies and there is no guarantee that intersection of speakers at a time in-terval of more than 2-3 years takes place. As noted in [13], only 14 speakers participating in NIST collections have templates that are over ten years old, and most of the participating speakers have templates that are less than three years old. In the most recent investigation [14], a new speaker aging database was collected, but it contains speech from only 18 speakers over a 30-60 year time span.

2.2   Typical Solutions to the Biometric Template Aging Problem

The biometric template aging problem is typically addressed in the following ways [3]:

– frequent (and forced) template updates;
– use of age invariant biometric features;
– simulation of aging effects;
– age progression compensation methods.

Due to the lack of adequate databases, it is very difficult to develop such solutions. In this paper, we report the results of our research on assessing the rate of updating voice templates versus the accuracy of these updates over an extended period of time.

2.3   Effect of Voice Aging on the Performance of Automatic Speaker Recognition Systems

In [15], the authors hypothesize that voice aging affects the performance of automatic speaker recognition systems. Fig. 1 (from NIST SRE 2005 [12]) shows the impact of elapsed time between the record of enrollment speech and the record of test speech samples.

It was noted that for a given, realistic threshold, the miss-probability error increases by a factor of two when the duration between enrollment and test recordings exceeds one month. However, other factors were unfortunately also correlated with elapsed time, such as corpus collection bias (e.g. there were different proportions of non-English speakers). The hypothesis that factors other than voice aging are implied in Figure 1 results is also supported by the fact that this very large aging loss was not found in SRE 2006 [15].

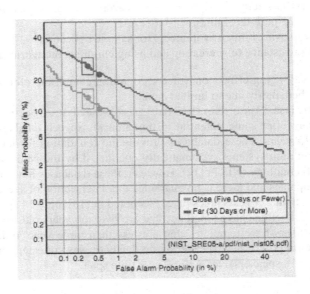

Fig. 1. Effect of time between enrollment and test recordings, NIST SRE 2005

3   Material

3.1   Data Collection

To study the effect of voice template aging on the accuracy of a speaker recognition system, a speech dataset [16] was used (hereafter, referred to as Speech DB). The Speech DB only included speakers who participated in database collection between 2006 and 2010.

The Speech DB consists of Russian conversational microphone speech used as training data and test data, along with metadata.

A histogram showing speaker age and collection periods is depicted in Fig. 2

The Speech DB is divided into three groups:

A: recordings collected in 2006 and 2007;

B: recordings collected in 2008 and 2009;

C: recordings collected in 2010.

The main characteristics of the Speech DB are provided in Table 1 (the sign refers to the intersection of groups of speakers).

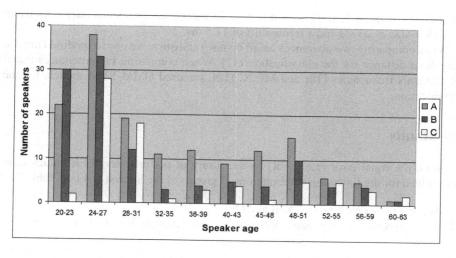

Fig. 2. Histogram of speaker age in the Speech DB

Speech was recorded over microphone channels. This type of channel was selected as offering the least variation in order to neutralize the effects of channel mismatch that is always present in speech databases collected in different years. In addition, the methods developed for automatic speaker identification have been trained on independent large training sets (NIST speech database) collected over several types of channels. Since these methods compensate for channel effects, they are useful in researching the template aging problem.

Table 1. Main characteristics of the Speech DB

Group	Years of collection	Number of files	Number of speakers M F	Total	Number of sessions
A	2006-2007	602	99 51	150	1-5
B	2008-2009	486	60 51	111	1-8
C	2010	188	46 26	72	1-3
A ⊗ B	2006-2007/2008-2009	300	17 18	35	5-10
A ⊗ C	2006-2007/2010	300	17 18	35	5-10
B ⊗ C	2008-2009/2010	291	24 17	41	6-11

3.2 Features and Methods

As primary features, we used statistics for an utterance pitch and instant formants frequencies (for frames, where formants exist).

In addition to these acoustic features, we used Mel Frequency Cepstral Coefficients (MFCC). We computed 13 MFCC, augmented with their delta and double delta coefficients (making 39 dimensional feature vectors) from the speech utterances using a window size of 23 ms and a frame shift of 11.5 ms.

When comparing two utterances based on pitch statistics, we used a modified nearest neighbour distance for the classification [17]. When comparing two utterances based on formants frequencies [18] and MFCC [19], we used GMM-SVM models for the classification.

4   Results

We used the equal error rate (EER) as a measure of performance. EER values were determined for the following combinations of groups of the Speech DB (see Table 2):

1. Separately for each group, A, B and C;
2. For different pairs of groups: A or B (reference records), B or C (test records).

Table 2. Combinations of groups within the Speech DB

Time lapse	Combinations of groups		
Less than 1 year (weeks-months)	A	B	C
1 - 2 years	$A \otimes B$	$B \otimes C$	
3 - 4 years	$A \otimes C$		

The results of the experiments are presented in Tables 3-5.

Table 3. EER (%) in dependence of time interval between recording the enrollment speech and the test speech (based on the pitch statistics method)

Time lapse	A	B	C	$A \otimes B$	$B \otimes C$	$A \otimes C$
Less than 1 year (weeks-months)	11,5	15,3	11,9	-	-	-
1 - 2 years	-	-	-	16,3	15,8	-
3 - 4 years	-	-	-	-	-	16,7

Intergroup differences in EER over the time interval of 1-2 years for the pitch statistics method is within the margin of error. Therefore, we can conclude that changes in speaker pitch in this time interval does not affect the performance of speaker identification. However, a change in speaker pitch in a 3-4 year time interval deteriorates the performance of speaker identification by 40%.

As we can see from Table 4, the performance of speaker identification based on formants frequencies degrades by approximately 20% every 1-2 years.

As we can see from Table 5, the performance of speaker identification, based on the MFCC-GMM-SVM method, also degrades by approximately 20% every 1-2 years.

Table 4. EER (%) in dependence of time interval between recording the enrollment speech and the test speech (based on the formants frequencies method)

Time lapse	A	B	C	A⊗B	B⊗C	A⊗C
Less than 1 year (weeks-months)	8,9	8,3	8,2	-	-	-
1 2 years	-	-	-	10,1	9,1	-
3 4 years	-	-	-	-	-	13,9

Thus, we have performance degradation on 3.2% in a time interval of 4 years. This correlates with the results in [20] where was found the verification accuracy degradation on 0.5% in a time interval of 10 months and on 3.7% in a time interval of 5 years, i.e. on the same 3.2% in a time interval of 4 years.

Table 5. EER (%) in dependence of time interval between recording the enrollment speech and the test speech (based on the MFCC-GMM-SVM method)

Time lapse	A	B	C	A⊗B	B⊗C	A⊗C
Less than 1 year (weeks-months)	2,6	2,6	4,6	-	-	-
1 2 years	-	-	-	3,2	4,0	-
3 4 years	-	-	-	-	-	5,8

5 Discussion

In the paper we found that there is a clear trend towards deteriorating performance of automatic speaker recognition systems in time intervals of up to 4 years (where this interval is the time between the recording of enrollment speech and test speech).

We can comment this conclusion by the following arguments.

First of all, to compensate the differences in the environment, in a type of channel, in an emotional state, the Speech DB was recorded in the same environmental conditions (office) with comparable signal-to-noise ratio and reverberation time, over the same channel (microphone), in the same emotional state (neutral). All recordings are in the same language (Russian) and have a minimal length of 1 min of pure speech. So the trend cannot be explained by the mismatch in environmental conditions, type of the channel and length of utterances, or by emotional and linguistic noises.

Secondly, we have used the speech database Speech DB that at least more than several times larger, than the known speech databases that was previously used to estimate voice template aging. Thus, we have more robust statistical results than in the previously known experiments.

Finally, the dynamic of the performance degradation provides an unambiguous interpretation of the observed effect as one of speaker aging, that is, a change in the speakers vocal tract over time, his motility of speech formation, etc.

6 Conclusions

We have presented the results of assessing the degradation rate of the accuracy of a speaker recognition system over the extended period of time (months-years).

As mentioned in our Discussion section, we have found a clear trend towards the degradation of the performance of automatic speaker recognition systems where there are intervals of up to 4 years between the recording of enrollment speech and test speech.

We have only touched upon the issue of template aging and plan to do further research in this area to make speaker recognition more robust in the fact of such effects. Our study is presently being expanded to include more speakers and to experiment with more re-enrollments (re-recordings) to observe how template aging effects follow the trends seen here.

References

1. Schötz, S., Müller, C.: A Study of Acoustic Correlates of Speaker Age. In: Müller, C. (ed.) Speaker Classifcation II. LNCS (LNAI), vol. 4441, pp. 1–9. Springer, Heidelberg (2007)
2. Beigi, H.: Effects of time lapse on speaker recognition results. In: Proc. 16th Int. Conf. on Digital Signal Processing (DSP 2009), pp. 1260–1265. IEEE Press, Piscataway (2009)
3. Czajka, A.: Call for cooperation: biometric template ageing. In: Proc. of IBPC 2010, NIST (2010)
4. Linville, S.E.: Vocal Aging. Singular Publishing Group, San Diego (2001)
5. Mishra, A.: Multimodal Biometrics it is: Need for Future Systems. International Journal of Computer Applications 3(4), 28–33 (2010)
6. Carls, J.W.: A framework for analyzing biometric template aging and renewal prediction. Ph.D. Thesis, Air Force Institute of Technology (2009)
7. Ajmera, J., Burkhardt, F.: Age and gender classification using modulation cepstrum. In: Proc. Speaker Odyssey (2008)
8. Metze, F., Ajmera, J., Englert, R., Bub, U., Burkhardt, F., Stegmann, J., Müller, C., Huber, R., Andrassy, B., Bauer, J., Littel, B.: Comparison of four approaches to age and gender recognition for telephone applications. In: Proc. ICASSP, vol. 4, pp. 1089–1092 (2007)
9. Muller, C., Burkhardt, F.: Combining short-term cepstral and long-term prosodic features for automatic recognition of speaker age. In: Proc. of Interspeech (2007)
10. Simonchik, K.: Identification system of the speaker's age group by spontaneous record. Scientific and Technical Journal of Information Technologies, Mechanics and Optics 82(6), 89–93 (2012)
11. Wolters, M., Vipperla, R., Renals, S.: Age Recognition for Spoken Dialogue Systems: Do We Need It? In: Proc. of Interspeech, pp. 1435–1438 (2009)
12. Przybocki, M.A., Martin, A.F., Le, A.N.: NIST speaker recognition evaluations utilizing the mixer corpora - 2004, 2005, 2006. IEEE Trans. Audio Speech Lang. Process. 15(7), 1951–1959 (2007)
13. Kohler, T.: The 2010 NIST Speaker Recognition Evaluation. IEEE Speech and Language Processing Technical Committee's Newsletter, SLTC Newsletter (2010)
14. Kelly, F., Drygajlo, A., Harte, N.: Speaker Verification with Long-Term Ageing Data. In: International Biometric Conference (2012)
15. Campbell, J.P., Shen, W., Campbell, W.M., Schwartz, R., Bonastre, J.-F., Matrouf, D.: Forensic speaker recognition. IEEE Signal Processing Magazine 26(2), 95–103 (2009)
16. STC Ltd., The database for speaker identification RUASTEN, registration certificate – 2010620533, RU (2010)

17. Labutin, P., Koval, S., Raev, A.: Speaker identification based on the statistical analysis of f0. In: Proc. IAFPA, Plymouth, UK (2007)
18. Labutin, P., Koval, S., Raev, A., Smirnova, N., Stolbov, M., Tampel, I., Khitrov, M.: Speaker recognition system for standard telephone network. In: Proc. SPECOM 2005, Patras, Greece, pp. 563–566 (2005)
19. Matveev, Y.N., Simonchik, K.K.: The speaker identification system for the NIST SRE 2010. In: GraphiCon 2010, St. Petersburg, Russia, pp. 315–319 (2010)
20. Furui, S.: Comparison of speaker recognition methods using statistical features and dynamic features. IEEE Transactions on Acoustics, Speech and Signal Processing 29(3), 342–350 (1981)

The Use of Several Language Models and Its Impact on Word Insertion Penalty in LVCSR

Gregor Donaj and Zdravko Kačič

Faculty of Electrical Engineering and Computer Science,
Smetanova ul. 17, 2000 Maribor, Slovenia
{gregor.donaj,zdravko.kacic}@um.si
http://www.feri.um.si

Abstract. This paper investigates the influence of hypothesis length in N-best list rescoring. It is theoretically explained why language models prefer shorter hypotheses. This bias impacts on the word insertion penalty used in continuous speech recognition. The theoretical findings are confirmed by experiments. Parameter optimization performed on the Slovene Broadcast News database showed why optimal word insertion penalties tend be greater when two language models are used in speech recognition. This paper also presents a two-pass speech recognition algorithm. Two types of language models were used, a standard trigram word-based language model and a trigram model of morpho-syntactic description tags. A relative decrease of 2.02 % in word error rate was achieved after parameter optimization. Statistical tests were performed to confirm the significance of the word error rate decrease.

Keywords: large vocabulary continuous speech recognition, morpho-syntactic description tags, word insertion penalty.

1   Introduction

The task of a decoding algorithm [2] for large vocabulary continuous speech recognition (LVCSR) is to generate several hypotheses for a spoken utterance, to score them, and to return either the 1-best hypothesis or a list of N-best hypotheses. The scoring is based on acoustic and language models. The acoustic model is used to estimate an acoustic probability that the hypothesis presents the spoken utterance.

The language model estimates the probability that a hypothesis could occur as a sentence in a given language. The most widely used language model is the standard n-gram word-based language model. It models the probability of a word conditional on the previous $n-1$ words. This kind of language model tends to prefer shorter hypotheses as every additional word decreases the score.

Decoding algorithms tend to prefer shorter words to longer words [9]. The word insertion penalty (WIP) is a heuristic used to counter-effect this phenomena by adding a constant negative value for every word to the final score.

In Slovene [12] and other morphologically rich languages, additional knowledge sources are often used to increase the recognition accuracy in LVCSR. One possible source is linguistic information in terms of morpho-syntactic description (MSD) tags

M. Železný et al. (Eds.): SPECOM 2013, LNAI 8113, pp. 354–361, 2013.

that have proven to be useful in reducing word error rate [6]. If we were to use n-gram models of MSD tags, we would already have two language models preferring shorter hypotheses.

It is the aim of this paper to investigate the impact of hypothesis length on the estimated language model probability and its possible effect on the accuracy in LVCSR. A theoretical view is first presented and then supported by experiments, in which a change in the optimal value of WIP is observed, when an addition language models is included in the rescoring algorithm. The experimental system was a two-pass recognition algorithm that makes use of two different language models. The first is a standard trigram word-based model and the second is a trigram model of MSD tags. The system improved the LVCSR accuracy on the Slovene Broadcast News database (BNSI) [14].

The impact of hypotheses' lengths on language scores was recognized quite early in [10]. However, little attention has been given in the past to theoretical views on WIP. Most papers reported only optimization procedures, e.g. [9]. To the authors' knowledge, there is no research available on how the optimal values of WIP are influenced by the use of several language models.

In LVCSR, statistical tests like bootstrap resampling [4] are used to confirm the significances of improvements. We decided to use the approximate randomization (AR) test [11], which is more conservative when showing significance. Statistical tests give their results in form of a p-value. To call a difference statistically significant, this value must be below a chosen threshold α, called the significance level. The significance of our improvements was confirmed at $\alpha = 0.01$, during our experiments.

Section 2 describes the basic scoring principle in LVCSR. Section 3 describes the impact of different hypotheses lengths on language model scores. Section 4 describes the used language resources and the proposed experimental system. The experimental results for recognition accuracy and statistical significance are given in Section 5. The conclusion is provided in Section 6.

2 Language Models in Speech Recognition

The task of the speech decoding algorithm is to find the word sequence W with the best probability, given a time sequence of observation vectors O [2]. These scores are often implemented as log-probabilities. The total score of a hypothesis W can be expressed as

$$\log P(W|O) = \alpha \log P_A(O|W) + \beta \log P_L(W), \qquad (1)$$

where P is the total score, P_A the acoustic score, and P_L the language score. The language model estimates the probability $P_L(W)$, that the word sequence W could appear in the language. The term $\log P(O)$ is ommited since it is constant over all hypotheses. The factors α and β are the weights of the acoustic and language models, respectively. We can fix $\alpha = 1$ and scale β appropriately.

However, an additional term is used in LVCSR – WIP. The above equation becomes

$$\log P(W) = \log P_A(W|O) + \beta \log P_L(W) + I \cdot N, \qquad (2)$$

where I is the word insertion penalty and N is the number of words in W. The weights β and I are determined experimentally on a data set separated from the training and test data. Usually I has a negative value [9].

Let us denote $W = \{w_1, w_2, ..., w_N\}$. Using the chain rule for probabilities we can express the language score as a sum of conditional log-probabilities

$$\log P_L(W) = \sum_{i=1}^{N} \log P_L(w_i | w_1, ..., w_{i-1}). \tag{3}$$

Due to data sparsity we make the Markov assumption that the conditional probabilities of words are conditional on the last $n-1$ words. We define the standard n-gram model with

$$\log P_L(W) = \sum_{i=1}^{N} \log P_L(w_i | w_{i-n+1}, ..., w_{i-1}). \tag{4}$$

3   Impact of Hypothesis Length

3.1   Scoring Different Hypotheses

Let us assume that we have a two-pass recognition algorithm [2]. In the first pass a list of N-best hypotheses was generated using acoustic and language models. The task of a language model used in the second pass is to rescore them. Hypotheses for the same utterance often differ only in one or a few words. Language models will, in these cases, prefer shorter hypotheses. In order to support this statement let us, for example, look at two hypotheses:

$$\begin{aligned} W_1 &= \{<s>, A, B, C, D, </s>\}, \\ W_2 &= \{<s>, A, B, E, C, D, </s>\}, \end{aligned} \tag{5}$$

where $<s>$ and $</s>$ are start-of-sentence and end-of-sentence markers, respectively. The letters $A, B, ...$ represent words. It is easy to mathematically prove that an unigram language model will always assign a higher score to the hypothesis W_1. Since W_2 has one more word in it, the calculated score has one more term in equation 4, while all other terms are the same.

By using a bigram language model, the two scores would be

$$\begin{aligned} \log P_L(W_1) = {} & \log P_L(A|<s>) + \log P_L(B|A) \\ & + \log P_L(C|B) + \log P_L(D|C) \\ & + \log P_L(</s>|D) \end{aligned} \tag{6}$$

and

$$\begin{aligned} \log P_L(W_2) = {} & \log P_L(A|<s>) + \log P_L(B|A) \\ & + \log P_L(E|B) + \log P_L(C|E) \\ & + \log P_L(D|C) + \log P_L(</s>|D). \end{aligned} \tag{7}$$

We omitted the term $\log P_L(<s>)$ since its value is 0 and it has no effect on the score. The two equations are the same in most terms. The difference between both scores is

$$\log P_L(W_2) - \log P_L(W_1) = \log P_L(C|E) + \log P_L(E|B) - \log P_L(C|B). \tag{8}$$

Log-probabilities are always negative numbers. We sum two negative numbers and subtract another one. It is rare that the log-probability of a bigram inside a language model will have a value that is smaller than the sum of two others. Consequently the difference in equation 8 will, in most cases, be negative. Thus, a bigram model is also likely to assign a better score to hypothesis W_1. Equation 8 can be generalized to higher order models.

Let us say that the hypothesis W_2 in the example above is the correct one and W_1 the best hypothesis of the recognizer. This would be an example of an deletion error. A standard n-gram language model used for hypotheses rescoring would likely be unable to correct this error.

3.2 Compensating Hypotheses Length

Let L_N be the set of all possible word sequences of length N. If W has length N, we can write

$$\log P_L(W) = \log P_L(W|L_N) + \log P_L(L_N). \tag{9}$$

This equation can be proved using total probability.

The first term in the above equation is the conditional probability that a word sequence is W, given that its length is N. These probabilities can be compared without considering the effects of their lengths, as described in the previous section.

The second term in the equation is the a-priory probability of a sentence having length N. We want to know how this probability changes if we increase N by 1. First we consider the case of a unigram model. For every N we can write

$$\log P_L(L_N) = N \cdot \log\left(1 - P_L(</s>)\right) + \log P_L(</s>). \tag{10}$$

The first term is the probability of having a word that is not the end-of-sentence marker and the second is the probability of the end-of-sentence marker itself. It follows that the difference in log-probabilities D_1 for different lengths is a constant:

$$D_1 = \log P_L(L_{N+1}) - \log P_L(L_N) = \log\left(1 - P_L(</s>)\right). \tag{11}$$

In continuation, we now consider the case of using a bigram model. It can be deduced that the difference is now

$$D_2 = \log\left(1 - \sum_{v \in V} P_L(</s>|v) \cdot P_L(w_N = v)\right), \tag{12}$$

where v runs over all words in the vocabulary V. Here $P_L(w_N = v)$ is the probability that the Nth word in a word sequence is v given all possible word histories and their respective probabilities. This is no longer a constant as it depends on N. However, we can assume that for every v, if N is high enough, $P(w_N = v)$ converges to a constant. Consequently the value in equation 12 will also converge. Equation 12 can also be generalized for higher order models.

3.3 Relation to the Word Insertion Penalty

If we want to compensate for the different a-priory probabilities $P(L_N)$, we should add the term

$$-\beta D_n \cdot N \tag{13}$$

into equation 1. Being D_n negative, this term is positive. We already have such a term in equation 2. It is the word insertion penalty, but this is usually experimentally determined to be negative.

If we have a two-pass recognition algorithm, we can add more language models to rescore the hypotheses. It this situation we can assume that the optimal value of the word insertion penalty would increase[1]. In order to test this assumption, we prepared an experimental system, as described in the following section of this paper.

4 Experimental System

4.1 Slovene Language Resources

Slovene [12] is an inflectional language and belongs to the group of Slavic languages. It is morphologically rich and allows for relatively free word orders in sentences compared to a non-inflectional language like English. It shares these characteristics with other Slavic languages.

The major part-of-speech words (nouns, adjectives, adverbs and verbs) are inflected by changing word-endings based on the grammatical categories of the words. The most important categories are gender, case, number, and person. Minor part-of-speech words are not inflected (pronouns, prepositions, conjunctions, particles, interjections).

The Slovene Broadcast News (BNSI) database [14] consists of 36 hours of transcribed speech. It is divided into a 30 hour training set, a 3 hour development set, and a 3 hour test set. The training set was used for training the acoustic models used in the first pass of our algorithm. The development set was used to determine the optimal values for the model weights and WIP. The test set was used to evaluate the performances of the recognition systems.

The FidaPLUS [1] corpus is the second largest Slovene language corpus and consist of approximately 620 million words. The corpus was mainly collected from newspapers and journals. Most of the corpus is also considered as proofread. The corpus is also automatically lemmatized and tagged with MSD tags from MULTEXT-East V3 [8].

In the JOS [7] project, a new set of morpho-syntactic specifications for Slovene was developed that is now compatible with MULTEXT-East V4 [8]. The ssj500k [5] corpus contains 500.000 words of text from FidaPLUS. Is it also lemmatized and tagged with MSD tags specified by JOS. The lemmas and tags within the corpus were manually validated by students and professors of linguistics. It is the largest Slovene corpus with hand-validated MSD tags.

---

[1] Word insertion penalties are usually negative. Thus, an increase in value means a smaller decrease of the score for each additional word.

4.2   First-pass Decoding and N-best Lists

In the first pass of the proposed algorithm Viterbi decoding [2] with beam pruning was used to generate a list of 100 hypotheses for each utterance in the test and development sets.

The acoustic features were 12 mel-frequency cepstral coefficients with log-energy and their first and second derivatives. The acoustic models were tied-state cross-word triphone HMMs with 16 Gaussian mixtures. The language models were standard word-based trigram language models trained on the FidaPLUS corpus. Good-Turing smoothing and Katz back-off were applied. 4-gram language models were also build, but they were only used during the second pass of the proposed algorithm.

4.3   Reduced MSD Tagging

We used the Obeliks [5] tagger for taggin the hypotheses from the first pass. The tagging models were trained on the ssj500k corpus.

Tags from the JOS specifications define part-of-speech (POS) and 15 different attributes for different parts-of-speech. We reduced the MSD tags to the more informative attributes: POS, gender, case, number, person.

4.4   Factored Language Model Rescoring

The tagged hypotheses were rescored using the factored language model (FLM) [3] tools of the SRILM [13]. We chose to use these tools and language models' forms due to their generality of word feature representations.

All the hypotheses were rescored using three models: a 4-gram standard word-based language model, a trigram MSD model, and a 4-gram MSD model.

Every utterance now had a set of different scores obtained by several language models as well as the probability from the acoustic model and the number of words. These scores were later weighted and used to re-rank the hypothesis list and obtain a new best hypothesis.

4.5   Parameter Optimization

The language model weights and WIP were optimized using N-best lists from the BNSI development set. Several starting points were used for the simplex amoeba search integrated within the SRILM tool-kit. The obtained values were used to weight scores while rescoring the N-best list of the BNSI test set.

5   Results

The first step after rescoring was to compare scores obtained using language models of different orders. We found that the scores were virtually identical when comparing rescoring using trigram and 4-gram models. Consequently the recognition accuracy results were identical.

Table 1. Recognition results on the first and second recognition passes

	first pass	second pass	absolute Δ	relative Δ [%]
WER [%]	25.67	25.15	−0.52	−2.02
Deletions	1446	1281	−165	−11.4
Substitutions	3991	3981	−10	−0.50
Insertions	401	458	+57	+14.2

The word error rate results are given in Table 1. The results are given for the best hypothesis scores after the first and the second passes, where the MSD model was added to the rescoring and the scoring weights were optimized. The change in word error rate is also presented in absolute and relative values.

We can see a decrease in word error rate after the second pass. The two results were compared using the AR statistical significance test. We chose a significance level of $\alpha = 0.01$. The test results had a p-value of even less than 0.001. We therefore considered the improvement statistically significant at our significance level α.

Table 1 also provides exact numbers of different types of errors on the test set. We can see a decrease in deletion and substitution errors, and an increase in insertion errors.

The scoring weights were optimized for the lowest word error rate in the first and also in second pass of the proposed algorithm. The results are given in Table 2. After the MSD language model was added, we could see a decrease in word-based model weight.

Table 2. Optimal values of models weights and WIP

Weight	first pass	second pass
Acoustic model	1	1
Word-based model	15.0	14.0
MSD-based model	–	2.0
WIP	−6.5	−2.5

We also see an expected large increase of the WIP from -6.5 to -2.5. This supported our theoretical findings that the use of several language models has an impact on the optimal value for WIP.

6   Conclusion

This paper presented the bias of language models for preferring shorter hypotheses and its effect on optimal word insertion penalty values. The problem has been theoretically justified. This phenomena can best be observed with the use of additional language models during N-best list rescoring. Experiments were performed to empirically support these findings.

The experimental system was a two-pass LVSCR system for Slovene. Rescoring was performed by using morpho-syntactic description tags of words inside hypotheses.

The proposed algorithm resulted in an decrease in word error rate that was also confirmed to be statistically significant. It was shown that the use of MSD tags could increase LVCSR performance.

The same approach could be applied when having other types of information available. Due to similarities between languages, this approach could be used for LVCSR of other Slavic languages if adequate language resources are available.

Acknowledgments. This work was partly financially supported by the Slovenian Research Agency ARRS under contract number 1000-10-310131.

References

1. Arhar, Š., Gorjanc, V.: Korpus FidaPLUS: Nova generacija slovenskega referenčnega korpusa. Jezik in slovstvo 52, 95–110 (2007)
2. Aubert, X.L.: An overview of decoding techniques for large vocabulary continuous speech recognition. Computer Speech and Language 16, 89–114 (2002)
3. Bilmes, J.A., Kirchhoff, K.: Factored Language Models and Generalized Parallel Backoff. In: Proceedings of Interspeech 2005 – Eurospeech, Lisbon, pp. 4–6 (2005)
4. Bisani, M., Ney, H.: Bootstrap Estimates for Confidence Intervals in ASR Performance Evaluation. In: Proceedings of ICASSP 2004, Montreal, pp. I:409–I:412 (2004)
5. Grčar, M., Krek, S., Dobrovoljc, K.: Obeliks: statistični oblikoskladenjski označevalnik in lematizator za slovenski jezik. In: Zbornik Osme Konference Jezikovne Tehnologije, Ljubljana, pp. 89–94 (2012)
6. Huet, S., Gravier, G., Sébillot, P.: Morphosyntactic Resources for Automatic Speech Recognition. In: Proceedings of the Sixth International Conference on Language Resources and Evaluation (LREC 2008), Marrakech (2008)
7. JOS Project, http://nl.ijs.si/jos/index-en.html
8. Multext-East Home Page, http://nl.ijs.si/ME/
9. Nejedlová, D.: Comparative Study on Bigram Language Models for Spoken Czech Recognition. In: Sojka, P., Kopeček, I., Pala, K. (eds.) TSD 2002. LNCS (LNAI), vol. 2448, pp. 197–204. Springer, Heidelberg (2002)
10. Ogawa, A., Takeda, K., Itakura, F.: Balancing acoustic and linguistic probabilities. In: IEEE International Conference on Acoustics, Speech and Signal Processing 1998, Nagoya, pp. I:181–I:184 (1998)
11. Riezler, S., Maxwell III, J.T.: On Some Pitfails in Automatic Evaluation and Significance testing for MT. In: Proc. of ACL 2005 Workshop on Intrinsic and Extrinsic Evaluation Measures for MT and/or Summarization, Ann Arbor, Michigan (2005)
12. Sepesy Maučec, M., Rotovnik, T., Zemljak, M.: Modelling Highly Inflective Slovenian Language. International Journal of Speech Technology 6, 245–257 (2003)
13. Stolcke, A., Zheng, J., Wang, W., Abrash, V.: SRILM at Sixteen: Update and Outlook. In: Proceedings IEEE Automatic Speech Recognition and Understanding Workshop, Hawaii (2011)
14. Žgank, A., Verdonik, D., Zögling Markuš, A., Kačič, Z.: BNSI Slovenian Broadcast News Database – speech and text corpus. In: Proceedings of Interspeech 2005 – Eurospeech, Lisbon, pp. 2525–2528 (2005)

The Use of d-gram Language Models for Speech Recognition in Russian

Mikhail Zulkarneev, Pavel Satunovsky, and Nikolay Shamraev

FSSI "Research Institute "Spezvuzautomatika", Rostov-on-Don, Russia
zulkarneev@mail.ru,
p.satunovsky@niisva.com,
ncam1977@yahoo.com

Abstract. This article deals with a description of a method of accounting of syntactic links in language model for hypotheses obtained after the first passage of decoding of speech. Several stages of processing include POS tagging, dependency parsing, and using factored language models for hypotheses rescoring. The use of fast parsing algorithms such as 'shift-reduce' algorithm and rejection of constituency grammar in favor of the dependency grammar allows overcoming the main drawback of the previous approaches, the exponential growth (to the number of lattice nodes) of computations with increase of word lattice size.

Keywords: Speech Recognition, dependency parsing, factored language model, syntactic language model.

1 Introduction

The language model is one of the important components of the automatic speech recognition system. Its role in the recognition is very large, since the use of only acoustic features does not allow to distinguish accurately enough to recognize objects (phonemes, words, etc.) due to their strong overlap in the feature space. Speech perception of human is multi-level, and a listening person uses syntactic, semantic and other information during recognition process. The use of the language model is an attempt to include these types of information into automatic speech recognition. In this paper we consider a method for accounting syntactic links[1].

Previously different approaches were proposed for the task of the speech recognition-accuracy improvement by taking into account syntactic relations in the sentence in the Russian language. The first approach was to use the rules of a context-free grammar, obtained by the analysis of a large corpus of text data by applying Baker algorithm (inside-outside algorithm, [1]). The choice of optimal recognition hypothesis from lattice hypotheses was made by CYK algorithm modification for a lattice of words (running for defined time intervals rather than word indexes)[2]. Application of this method has improved the accuracy of recognition, but slow performance and large memory requirements for the processing of large word lattices have limited its use in practical applications.

---

[1] The work was financially supported by the state contract GK 07.524.11.4023 (Minobrnauka RF).

M. Železný et al. (Eds.): SPECOM 2013, LNAI 8113, pp. 362–366, 2013.

The second approach is a method for constructing the grammar (PCFG) explicitly taking into account the syntactic classes (and morphemes) of words and associations between them [3]. The use of this kind of rules significantly increased the processing speed of the lattice (about 8 times), without loss of accuracy, but not allowed overcoming the main disadvantage of both methods - the exponential growth (to the number of lattice nodes) of computations with increase of word lattice size.

This article discusses the method of accounting for syntactic information using parsing of sentences based on dependency grammars (as opposed to constituency grammar) and factored language models which are a generalization of n-gram models from the point of view of the other possible relationships (factors) that influence the probability of sentence, except for a word order.

The main idea is to extract pairs of syntactically dependent words in a sentence (hypothesis) and use this information in the factored language model. The use of fast algorithms for parsing such as "shift-reduce" algorithm and the rejection of constituency grammar in favor of the dependency grammar allows overcoming the main drawback of the first algorithms, the exponential growth of computations with increase of word lattice size.

2 Dependency Grammars

Sentence parsing based on dependency grammars is an alternative version of the classical methods of parsing methods using constituency grammars.

Dependency grammar defines a set of rules according to which each word in the sentence matches the word on which it depends, and the main word is also determined (usually denoted as 'Root' or 'Start' word). Such partition of the words in pairs uniquely identifies a dependency tree, similar to a tree obtained by parsing the sentence using constituency grammars (for example, using CYK algorithm).

At the present time parsers based on dependency grammars are most widely used for parsing sentences in Russian [4]. This is due to the fact that the algorithms for dependency parsing are generally simpler and work much faster than parsing algorithms based on constituency grammar.

3 Description of the Method

Application of the method using FLM for accounting syntactic links in sentences (hypotheses) can be described by the following steps:

1. Extraction of hypotheses - linear sequences of words from the lattice of words.

2. Determination of parts of speech (POS tagging) for each word in hypothesis. Only the most probable sequence of parts of speech is selected.

3. Determination of syntactic links between words in sentence (hypothesis). We select the most probable dependency structure of words in each sentence.

4. The calculation of the probability of the hypotheses based on established syntactic links with the help of the trained factor language models.

5. Using a probabilities obtained by factor language models in the combined language model score.

The N-best lists of hypotheses are extracted as the experimental data from the word lattices on the first step. They are created with fixed set of optimal values for speech recognition parameters: acoustic probability (likelihood), linguistic likelihood, and word penalty.

4   TreeTagger and Maltparser Programs

For the second step the TreeTagger program [5] was used for determination of the parts of speech in hypotheses (POS tagging). TreeTagger takes list of hypotheses as an input, and then it outputs the most probable sequence of parts of speech for each hypothesis.

For the third step another parser, the Maltparser program [6] is used for retrieving of word dependencies in each sentence. As input Maltparser gets a sequence of tagged words together with additional grammatical characteristics of the word: gender, number, case, animacy (example of a noun). As an output Maltparser determines main word (Root) in hypothesis and set of pairs of dependent words (each word except Root should depend on some other).

MaltParser program is a successful realization of the inductive dependency parsing of words in a sentence. In contrast to the classical approach, where due to given grammar sentences are parsed according with the grammar rules, inductive parsing is a data-driven parsing. Given a treebank in dependency format, MaltParser can be used to induce a parser for the language of the treebank. The program implements its own classifier to new data, i.e. explicit formal grammar is not specified, it is "hidden" inside the classifier.

For the experiments we used text corpus, parsed by linguists. The training data contained about 30,000 parsed sentences in Russian. Based on these data MaltParser classifier determined syntactic dependencies of words in a sentence. Best accuracy in parsing was shown by Nivre-eager algorithm using Libsvm library.

5   Factored Language Models

Factored language model (FLM) is a generalization of n-gram language model, in which the sequence of words is replaced by a sequence of feature vectors (factors).

Thus the word W_t is represented as

$$W_t = \{f_t^1, f_t^2, ..., f_t^K\} \tag{1}$$

Different features can be factors, including morphological classes, stemming, root of the word, and other similar features (for Russian and other inflective languages). Two-factor FLM generalizes the standard class-based language model in which one factor is the class of the word, and the second one is the word itself. FLM is a model of the factors, i.e. probability $p(f_t^{1:K}|f_{t-1:t-n}^{1:K})$ can be expressed as the product of the probabilities of the kind $p(f|f_1, f_2, ..., f_N)$.

While designing a good factor language model it is necessary to solve two problems:
- Choose a suitable number of factors;
- Find the correct statistical model for these factors.

6   The Application of Factored Models (Fourth Stage)

A detailed description of the construction of factored language models is provided in [7]. It describes experimental studies of d-gram language models using the Russian text corpus. As training and testing data we used available sentences from Russian National Corpora - syntactically annotated part (http://www.ruscorpora.ru/corpora-structure.html). It consists from modern Russian prose, non-fiction and news articles from magazines (1980-2004), and texts of news produced by Russian news agencies. Training data contained about 100.000 sentences and testing data 227 sentences (smaller part of corpora used for perplexity evaluation). Testing data for evaluating language model was taken from actual text news. Vocabulary size of language model was approximately 80000 words.

The results of experiments to measure the value of perplexity for n-gram and mixed factor models are presented in Table 1.

Table 1. Experiment results on perplexity value

Model	Perplexity value
3-gram	1419.149
3-gram + H1 factor	1109.85
H0 factor	2903
H1 factor	682.021
2-gram + H1 factor	1476
H1 factor + H2 factor	650.854

Two types of experiments were performed: experiments with basic 3-gram language model and words, and experiments with language models, which included the main words (heads) of dependency in addition to the words (denoted by "H" in the table 1). The figure standing after H indicates the time shift, that is, H0 - is the main word for the current word, H1 is the main word for the previous word, H2 - the main word for the word with a time shift of 2 in past. Language model "H0 factor" takes into account the dependence of the word from its head (main word), language model "H1 factor" takes into account the dependence of the previous word from its head, etc.

7   Experiment Results for N-best List Hypotheses

Reevaluation of the hypotheses in N-best list was performed with the software packages SRILM and HTK. Each model selected one hypothesis from 20 candidates according optimal score for every sentence from test set (80 sentences).

Table 2. Experiment results of the best hypotheses selected by different models

Model	Sentence correctness(SENT:%)	Word Error Rate(WORD:%)
3-gram model	Corr = 47.50	Corr = 91.14, Acc = 90.51
3-gram + H1 factor	Corr = 52.50	Corr = 91.77, Acc = 91.14
3-gram + H0 factor	Corr = 52.50	Corr = 90.32, Acc = 90.51
mixed model w1+H1+H0	Corr = 40.00	Corr = 89.56, Acc = 88.92
H1 factor + H2 factor	Corr = 40.00	Corr = 89.56, Acc = 88.92

8 Conclusion

In the article [7] it is shown, that from the point of view of perplexity the d-gram language model is better than standard n-gram model. Thus, it is possible to expect that use of d-gram models will allow raising accuracy of recognition of speech.

Experiments have shown that only one of mixed models showed slightly better results than the simple 3-gram model. This means that the direct correlation between the perplexity for language models and word recognition accuracy is not observed for this type of models.

This can be explained by the fact that the values of perplexity for language models were obtained on test data, labeled by experts manually. A serious drawback is not so high accuracy of parser programs used for arbitrary sentence in Russian. Also hypotheses, derived from the lattice of words, do not always constitute a completed sentence.

Nevertheless, the approach based on factor models as a way to account syntactic relations looks promising. The main advantage of the proposed method in the article is the speed of processing hypotheses, compared to the previously discussed methods based on the CYK algorithm. Syntactic dependency of the words in pairs was the only factor considered, but it is possible to use different morphological or grammatical factors. The further progress can be achieved by using the Viterbi algorithm type to choose an optimal hypothesis directly from the lattice of words.

References

1. Levenson, S.C.: Mathematical models for speech technology. John Wiley & Sons Ltd., NJ (2005)
2. Zulkarneev, M.Y., Salman, S.H., Shamraev, N.G.: Use of the Syntactic Information to Increase the Accuracy of Speech Recognition. In: Proceedings of the 14th International Conference on Speech and Computer "SPECOM 2011", Kazan, pp. 164–166 (2011)
3. Zulkarneev, M.Y., Shamraev, N.G.: Methods of Rules Generation for Chomsky's Probabilistic Context-free Grammar in the Problem of Speech Recognition. In: Proceedings of the Science Conference "Session of the Scientific Council of Russian Academy of Science on Acoustics and XXIV Session of the Russian Acoustical Society", vol. 3, pp. 21–23. GEOS, Moskow (2012) (in Russian)
4. Toldova, S.J., Sokolova, E.G., Astaf'eva, I., Gareyshina, A., Koroleva, A., Privoznov, D., Sidorova, E., Tupikina, L., Lyashevskaya, O.N.: NLP Evaluation 2011-2012: Russian syntactic parsers. In: International Conference on Computational Linguistics "Dialog", Moscow (2012)
5. Schmid, H.: Probabilistic Part-of-Speech Tagging Using Decision Trees. In: Proceedings of International Conference on New Methods in Language Processing, Manchester, UK (1994)
6. Nivre, J., Hall, J., Nilsson, J., Chanev, A., Eryiğit, G., Kubler, S., Marinov, S., Marsi, E.: Malt-Parser: A language-independent system for data-driven dependency parsing. Natural Language Engineering 13(2), 95–135 (2007)
7. Zulkarneev, M.Y., Shamraev, N.G.: D-gram language model investigation for Russian language modeling. Neirokompiutery: razrabotka, primenenie (Neurocomputers, in Russian). Radiotechnika, Moscow (in press, 2013)

Author Index